The
Old Faith and
the Russian Land

A volume in the series

CULTURE AND SOCIETY AFTER SOCIALISM
edited by Bruce Grant and Nancy Ries

A list of titles in this series is available at www.cornellpress.cornell.edu.

The
Old Faith and
the Russian Land

A HISTORICAL ETHNOGRAPHY
OF ETHICS IN THE URALS

Douglas Rogers

Cornell University Press *Ithaca & London*

Publication of this book was made possible, in part, by a grant from the Office of the Provost, Yale University

First published 2009 by Cornell University Press
First printing, Cornell Paperbacks, 2009

Printed in the United States of America

Library of Congress Cataloging-in-Publication Data

Rogers, Douglas, 1972–
   The old faith and the Russian land : a historical ethnography of ethics in the Urals / Douglas Rogers.
        p. cm. — (Culture and society after socialism)
   Includes bibliographical references and index.
   ISBN 978-0-8014-4797-6 (cloth : alk. paper) —
   ISBN 978-0-8014-7520-7 (pbk. : alk. paper)
   1. Ethics—Russia (Federation)—Sepych (Permskaia oblast')—History.   2. Old Believers—Russia (Federation)—Sepych (Permskaia oblast')—History.   3. Ethnology—Russia (Federation)—Sepych (Permskaia oblast')   4. Sepych (Permskaia oblast', Russia)—Moral conditions.   I. Title. II. Series: Culture and society after socialism.

BJ852.R64   2009
170.947'43—dc22

                                                2009019279

For the people of Sepych,
past and present,
and for my family

Contents

Illustrations

Maps

Figures

Preface

This book is a historical ethnography of ethics, an account of how the inhabitants of a particular place have sought to fashion ethical lives across three centuries of precipitous transformations. The story unfolds largely in Sepych (pronounced SEP-itch), a small town on the western edge of the Russian Perm region. Sepych was settled in the late seventeenth and early eighteenth centuries by religious dissenters fleeing eastward from the joint persecution of tsar and Russian Orthodox Church. Factions of Old Believers, as these dissenters and their descendants came to be known, have sought to follow a narrow, difficult road to Christian salvation ever since. Like other religious groups who challenged the might of the Russian Orthodox Church, the Old Believers of Sepych have demanded of themselves—and of one another—specialized textual knowledge and highly elaborated ritual practice in less than friendly surroundings. But the story of ethics in Sepych is not simply dictated by Old Belief. The residents of Sepych have also been, by turns, serfs on a feudal estate, peasants in a thriving merchant town, exemplary Soviet state farmers, and shareholders in a struggling post-Soviet agricultural enterprise. Each of these organizations of labor, land, and money, and of state power and rural landscape, has generated ethical expectations and aspirations every bit as powerful—if also often in conflict with—the precepts and practices of Old Belief.

Across these historical periods and domains of social and cultural life, I suggest, the residents of Sepych have drawn on an identifiable yet quite malleable set of sensibilities about ethical practice in order to engage and, frequently, to divert an accumulating series of projects intended to fashion them into new kinds of people. Sepych is not a place of enduring tradition or persistent backwardness, of peasant rationality or peasant resistance, of rural isolation or irredeemable drunkenness—all tropes that have long bedeviled the study of rural Russia. It is certainly not the den of moral corruption—part exotic, part deplorable—that so many Western commentators associate with all things Russian. Rather, I view Sepych as one point in an ethical field, a node at which an array of large-scale processes have converged and sedimented to shape three centuries of dilemmas about how to live a life in this world and, perhaps, beyond it.

Although the chapters that follow stay close to Sepych (current population around 1,400) and its many specificities, this book is also crafted with a set of broader ethnographic, historical, and theoretical conversations in mind. Ethical dilemmas and debates of the sorts that saturated the lives of townspeople I came to know were hard to miss for those who took the time to live and listen in the postsocialist world. Accordingly, invocations of morality, moral personhood, and ethics have played a supporting role in many of the pathbreaking ethnographies of the region. Most often, pointing to morality or ethics has allowed anthropologists to underscore the extent to which nearly any element of postsocialist "transition" participates in the reshaping of basic ideas and practices of what it means to be human. These concepts have thus been crucial in anthropologists' collective effort to improve upon the dry and manifestly inadequate theories of transition that have guided the vast majority of social science and policy work on the region for nearly two decades now.

Nevertheless, despite the presence of morality and ethics in so many ethnographic studies of the region, a central premise of this book is that ethics itself has been inadequately theorized. Indeed, I would go further to say that ethics has become the underspecified fulcrum of the recent anthropology of postsocialist Eurasia: everywhere invoked, almost nowhere placed at the center of analysis. As the novelty of challenging decontextualized social scientific theories of transition (or is it now the "return to Russian authoritarianism"?) wears off, the time is ripe to attend far more closely to ethics itself. In so doing, I use the historical ethnography of a single town over three centuries to engage not only recent developments in the historiography of Russia and the Soviet Union but also much broader conversations in the growing body of social and cultural theory dedicated to ethics.

Acknowledgments

This book has been long in the making; it is a pleasure to thank the many institutions and people who helped it—and me—along the way.

My fieldwork in Russia was supported by grants and fellowships from the German Marshall Fund of the United States (Research Support Program 2000); the International Dissertation Research Fellowship of the Social Science Research Council (with funds provided by the Andrew W. Mellon Foundation); the International Research and Exchanges Board (IREX), with funds from the United States Department of State through the Title VIII Program; the Fulbright-Hays Doctoral Dissertation Research Abroad Fellowship, administered by the United States Department of Education; the University of Michigan International Institute; and the Havighurst Center for Russian and Post-Soviet Studies at Miami University of Ohio. Much of the first version of this book was written at the University of Michigan's Institute for the Humanities; much of the final version took shape during a year of concentrated writing supported by the Kennan Institute of the Woodrow Wilson International Center for Scholars and a postdoctoral research fellowship from the Eurasia Program of the Social Science Research Council. Kevin Dwyer, Theda Purdue, and Brooke Larson were the best of writing companions at the Wilson Center that year, and Katherine Pruess was a stellar research assistant, providing not only much of the bibliography but also a running stream of incisive comments on my drafts. I am particularly grateful to the staffs and program officers at these institutions for their frequent encouragements and logistical acumen. None of these organizations bears any responsibility for the views expressed here.

Earlier versions of chapters 5, 6, and 7 appeared as Rogers (2005, 2006b, and 2008). I am grateful to the American Anthropological Association, Cambridge University Press, and the Woodrow Wilson Center Press, respectively, for permission to reprint material here. UMI/Proquest permitted me to reproduce the manuscript images in chapters 1 and 2. Thanks are due, as well, to Peter Wissoker, John Ackerman, and Ange Romeo-Hall at Cornell University Press, the copyeditor Jamie Fuller, Bill Nelson of Bill Nelson Maps, and Kate Mertes of Mertes Editorial Services, all of whom played valuable parts in producing the final book.

Over the years, numerous friends and colleagues have commented on ideas, proposals, and chapter drafts, often in detail and often more than once. I am especially grateful to Marjorie Mandelstam Balzer, Megan Callaghan, Summerson Carr, Liviu Chelcea, Ema Grama, Erica Lehrer, Sonja Luerhmann, Mark Steinberg, Maggie Paxson, Genese Sodikoff, Scott Kenworthy, Irina Papkova, Steve Norris, Venelin Ganev, and Karen Dawisha. Cathy Wanner deserves special thanks for reading the entire manuscript in its penultimate form; so, too, does Melanie Boyd, whose keen interpretive sense has been extremely valuable as I refined everything from turns of phrase to my primary arguments. Bruce Grant and Nancy Ries continue to go above and beyond the call of duty in commenting on manuscripts submitted to the series they edit at Cornell University Press—their careful readings have considerably improved many aspects of this project. Seminars, workshops, and reading groups at Georgetown University, Miami University of Ohio, the University of Michigan, Middlebury College, Moscow State University, the Woodrow Wilson Center, and Yale University have also pushed me to sharpen and refine various sections.

This book originated, it is sobering to recall, as a senior thesis about Old Believers at Middlebury College. It then simmered in the background as I worked on other projects at the Institute for Social and Cultural Anthropology, Oxford University; the imprint of my years there can, to my mind at any rate, still be discerned in the argument below. The book's next incarnation was as a dissertation at the University of Michigan, where it benefited from a general atmosphere sympathetic to experimentation at the intersection of anthropology and history and from the specific promptings of Webb Keane, Valerie Kivelson, and Alaina Lemon. To Katherine Verdery, I am grateful for more than can easily be acknowledged: sheaves of detailed comments, unwavering support for this project (even as it extended backward in time another two or three decades each time we discussed it), and, most of all, her vision of rigorous and generous scholarship.

A great many institutions and individuals in Russia made my research in the Perm region possible, productive, and enjoyable. S. A. Dimukhametova, O. L. Kut'ev, E. S. Lykova, V. A. Gilёva, and especially M. I. Leont'eva—all of them cultural affairs employees—opened countless doors and often accompanied me through them. My indebtedness to colleagues in Russian universities, archives, and museums is best saved for part of the story to come, but suffice it to say for the moment that every step of my field and archival research has been supported by the wide circle of scholars associated with Moscow State University's

Archaeographical Laboratory. These students of old Cyrillic texts and the Russian religious groups who use them (the "arch" in archaeography is for old, the "graphy" for writing) invited me on an expedition to Sepych and the surrounding region in 1994. They have encouraged my research ever since. I. V. Pozdeeva, one of the most courageous, visionary, and productive scholars I am ever likely to know, has been my constant interlocutor and, on occasion, stern critic. I also owe thanks to G. N. Chagin, A. V. Dadykin, V. I. Erofeeva, T. D. Goriacheva, E. V. Issaeva, E. V. Litviak, V. P. Pushkov, I. P. Smirnov, I. V. Boiko, E. B. Smilianskaia, E. M. Smorgunova, and, at the Moscow State University Center for Visual Anthropology, E. V. Aleksandrov and the late L. S. Filimonov. Natalia Litvina, Tat'iana Mordkovich, and Irina Parmuzina have each spent months—years, in Natalia's case—on expeditions in the region around Sepych. Their intellectual company has been a rare treat for an ethnographer trained in the single-fieldworker model of Anglo-American anthropology. Each has contributed to my research, enriched my life, and helped me to navigate the ethical dilemmas of scholarship on Old Belief in numerous ways. In the places in the following chapters where I disagree with the Russian colleagues who have so generously supported my work, I do so explicitly and forthrightly, believing that their scholarship deserves every bit as much attention—and citation—as that of my colleagues in the Western academy. If, in the process, I have reproduced some of what my Russian friends have often sought to convince me are the shortcomings of anthropology and history as I practice them, I can only plead stubbornness; I hope nevertheless to have helped make the impressive work of archaeographers more widely known.

I cannot thank the people of Sepych by name, but I owe them my deepest appreciation for taking a chance on the American who wanted to live for a while in their corner of the Urals. I hope I convey to them some sense of the depth of my gratitude by thanking them in the same sentence as my parents, Carole and Leo Rogers, who have enthusiastically supported this and every one of my endeavors, and Melanie Boyd, Caden Rodems-Boyd, and Ella Rodems-Boyd, who joined me en masse halfway through this project and without whose companionship it, and everything else, has become scarcely imaginable.

Note on Translation, Transliteration, and Names

All translations from Russian and Church Slavonic are my own, although I gratefully acknowledge many colleagues' suggestions on how to render some of the trickier sections of peasant Old Believer manuscripts into English. For transliterations of modern Russian, I use a slightly modified Library of Congress system, with ë representing the Cyrillic ё (pronounced as a stressed *yo* as in "yoke"). For Russian words that appear frequently in the text, I eliminate terminal soft signs (Perm rather than Perm'), shorten most soft endings (Evdokia rather than Evdokiia), and make other idiosyncratic changes to facilitate easier reading for non-Russian speakers. Except where noted explicitly, transliterations of modern spoken Russian do not reflect local dialect. For sources written in Church Slavonic, pre-1918 Russian, or various hybrid forms—for which some of my translations may be more debatable—I provide a full transliteration, retaining, for instance, soft endings and *yers*. Apparent misspellings and scribal errors are not "corrected."

In keeping with standard anthropological practice, I use pseudonyms chosen from the pool of locally popular names in the relevant historical period to identify everyone who appears in this book; the only exception is townspeople who both died before 1950 and are mentioned in publicly available sources. In some cases, I also alter personal and/or family details to further disguise identities and protect privacy. Shifts among Russian naming conventions track with my own relationship to the person in question. Thus, if I was on a first-name basis with someone, I use a first-name pseudonym when writing about that person; if I had a more distant or more formal relationship, I use first name and patronymic. In the case of manuscripts and archives, I follow the text under discussion (for example, initials and surname for Soviet bureaucratic documents such as secret police files).

The
Old Faith and
the Russian Land

Introduction

Ethics, Russia, History

No one could say with much certainty when Sepych's town library first opened its doors. No anniversaries had been marked in the past, at least as far as anyone could recall, and neither the librarians' consultations with elderly townspeople nor their archival inquiries had yielded any conclusive evidence. Nevertheless, state workers in cultural affairs jobs, local dignitaries from in and out of town, and a smattering of interested townspeople gathered in late November 2001 to celebrate what would be, it had been estimated after some discussion, the ninetieth anniversary of the Sepych Rural Library. As it turned out, some of the anniversary events juxtaposed very different perspectives on Sepych's past and present, on the founding of the town and the kinds of people who had walked its roads and plowed its fields over the past three centuries, and on how best to uncover and represent knowledge about both past and people. This book is also about these topics, so I begin on the stage in Sepych's club—once a Soviet House of Culture—in a celebratory atmosphere oriented, however uncertainly and tentatively, toward the town's history.

As at so many similar club gatherings, both Soviet and post-Soviet, gifts and certificates of achievement changed hands, schoolchildren recited poetry, and Sepych's folk ensemble performed. Among the out-of-town dignitaries in attendance that day was Father Vasilii, a priest from the district center of Vereshchagino and a moving force behind the new Old Believer church in the center of Sepych. Invited to say a word or two about the importance of books on the anniversary of Sepych's library, Father Vasilii delivered a nearly twenty-minute extemporaneous address that ranged in some detail over several periods of Russian history, contemporary regional politics, Orthodox theology and doctrine, the alarming decline in Russian birthrates in the 1990s, and the thriving Muslim population of the Perm region. Introduced as the folk ensemble completed its first number, Father Vasilii elected to speak from the floor rather than the stage, his booming voice easily filling the club without a microphone. He began by picking up a local history album the librarians had recently completed, entitled *Chronicle of the Town Sepych:*

> Before I begin to talk about books, I would like to draw serious attention to the relationship of a book to a chronicle, [because a chronicle] can leave an incorrect perception of past events. Today, literally a few minutes ago, I opened this *Chronicle of the Town Sepych,* and immediately ran into a very significant departure from historical truth. So [reading from the first page], "The town arose in 1665." I can't dispute that date, and can't say whether this is the way it was or not, but as to whether the first *Russian* residents of Sepych appeared in that year....It's possible to argue with this assertion. Why? Because the first [Russian] residents of this town were...garrison troops [*strel'tsy*] who fled Moscow as a result of the uprising in 1698. And they didn't immediately flee here, to the town of Sepych, but to the river Kerzhenets. At first to Guslitsa, in the Moscow region, and then from Guslitsa to Kerzhenets in the Nizhnyi Novgorod region, and after Bishop Pitirim of Nizhnyi Novgorod chased them out with a detachment of troops in 1720, only then, maybe in 1721 or 1722, did they appear here in this region, populated by Komi-Permiaks.

Father Vasilii went on to correct other assertions on the first page of the *Chronicle,* backing up his counterclaims with a torrent of dates, statistics, names, and linguistic etymologies. Sorting out and explaining all the *Chronicle*'s errors about precisely which factions of Old Believers had arrived in Sepych, when, and what had happened since then would, he concluded, "take a whole day."

Father Vasilii's remarks went on to link this narrative of historical events in Sepych—and Russia more broadly—to a particular variant of Orthodox Christian morality. He suggested that both proper history and proper morality were attainable through a specific way of apprehending the past, a historical consciousness that departed in important respects from the remainder of the anniversary celebration. Putting down the *Chronicle,* he picked up a thick tome, its aging covers held together by leather and metal clasps, and introduced it as "the main book of Old Believers, by which those who call themselves Old Believers lived and live every day—the *Kormchaia Kniga.*"[1] Father Vasilii spoke first not about the contents of the *Kormchaia Kniga* but about the materiality of the book itself and, more generally, about old religious books as a privileged route into proper conceptions of history and morality. He recounted that this particular *Kormchaia Kniga* had been passed down through many generations in a family of Old Believer clergy, repeatedly underlined,

---

1. The *Kormchaia Kniga* ("Book of the Pilot" or "the Rudder") is a collection of church statues and canon law (a *nomocanon*) inherited from the Byzantine Church and first published in Russia in 1649–50. Father Vasilii was almost certainly holding a *Kormchaia Kniga*—or, more likely, a copy of one—that predated the edition issued by Patriarch Nikon in 1653.

annotated, and inscribed along the way. With a glance over his shoulder toward the stage, he emphasized that the book was actually used—by him, most recently—rather than gathering dust on a shelf as books in a library do. To relate to this book, Father Vasilii suggested, was not just to read it but to understand oneself as connected to a past and a way of being *through* the book's physical characteristics.

Only as his allotted word or two stretched past the fifteen-minute mark did Father Vasilii take up the moral codes and regulations of old Russian Orthodoxy that comprise the *Kormchaia Kniga*:

> This is a book that tells us literally everything. How to marry. How many marriages are permitted. What sort of marriages. How to baptize. How to receive someone from a heresy. What these heresies are. Literally everything is listed. For our society, this book is a distinctive means of revelation. Why? Because, if you open it and start to read, every one of us will start to think, "Look how far I have moved away from God and how hard it will be to return to Him, because I'll have to give up this, that, and the other thing." Some will say, "Why give these things up? Maybe we've gotten so used to all of these things that it's possible to live without these ancient books and without these ancient rules." It turned out that no, without them we can't get by.

Father Vasilii's remarks, which none too subtly challenged rather than praised the work of the library, created a decidedly uncomfortable atmosphere in the club. Townspeople I talked to later were impressed to the point of being overwhelmed by the priest's erudition, his command of history and current events, and his forceful speaking style. Yet they also found his sermon and polemics—not to mention the length of his comments—somewhat out of place at the event. This discomfort was not lost on Father Vasilii himself, who actively cultivated such moments and saw his ability to disrupt and impress at the same time as a potential prelude to winning new converts to his group of Old Believers. Despite his growing congregation in Sepych, however, he and his fellow clergy had stirred only a few to begin reading the *Kormchaia Kniga* or monitoring their lives in the rigorous way he advocated.

As I show in some detail in my discussion of the postsocialist period, Father Vasilii's address at the library's anniversary celebration was but one salvo in a decade-long struggle for religious, political, and economic supremacy in and around post-Soviet Sepych. For the moment, however, I want to emphasize that by forging a historical narrative, a moralizing vision, and a brand of historical consciousness into a combined critique and exhortation, Father Vasilii joined a centuries-long string of powerful outsiders who had come to Sepych with the goal of remaking its people. Indeed, many such visitors had lectured or preached from precisely the spot on which Father Vasilii stood that day. For much of the Soviet period, Sepych's House of Culture was home to Communist Party lectures and socialist holiday celebrations; before the revolution, the same building was a Russian Orthodox mission church built to proselytize Sepych's recalcitrant Old Believers. Still other unfamiliar histories and moralizing discourses have been far less explicitly propounded than the *Kormchaia Kniga* or the *Moral Code of the Builder of Communism*. The capital markets of the late nineteenth and late twentieth centuries and the informal sector of the rural Soviet economy, for instance, were no less transformative for townspeople in Sepych for not always having clearly elaborated guidelines preached from the center of town.

The chapters that follow explore the ways in which residents of Sepych have encountered histories and moralizing discourses that were, like those so forcefully set out by Father Vasilii in the club, unfamiliar to them—at least initially and at least to some degree. These encounters have usually featured multiple, often conflicting, views about the very categories through which everyday interactions can be comprehended, reproduced, and potentially transformed: proper and improper, insider and outsider, past and present. At stake, again and again, have been the kinds of people the residents of Sepych should and could be. What relationships should they have to one another? To themselves? To larger institutions such as markets and states? To inhabitants of another, invisible world? A cacophony of shifting answers to these questions will emerge over the long view I adopt. And yet, cacophony notwithstanding, generations of townspeople in Sepych have oriented themselves with remarkable frequency by elements of what I will suggest is an "ethical repertoire"—a protean set of sensibilities, dispositions, and expectations often overlooked or grasped only fleetingly and obliquely by outsiders.

I certainly came upon this ethical repertoire fleetingly and obliquely myself at first, understanding it more fully only as my time in Sepych passed a year and as, at the encouragement of townspeople and Russian colleagues, I began to read back through archives and manuscripts into three centuries of Sepych's history. In contrast to the articulated, abstracted moralizing codes of the *Kormchaia Kniga* or the one-size-fits-all guides to entrepreneurial success offered by economic reformers, I came to see a fluid and often debated ethics: refracting differently through lenses of gender and generation; encompassing yet dividing activities of work and prayer; moving along material vectors of food, drink, money, and labor; and sunk into the very landscape of Sepych and its environs. Embodied and tacit, this ethics was only rarely articulated in anything approaching an easily explicated quotation or comment. The opening scene at the Sepych Rural Library's ninetieth-anniversary celebration, however, came close.

As the house lights dimmed and the preshow audience buzz faded, one of Sepych's three librarians emerged and took a seat on a chair at stage right. The head scarf and apron she had donned for the scene lent her a grandmotherly air. As she spoke, her hands were busy with knitting needles. Whereas Father Vasilii would soon speak easily and confidently in his preacher's voice, the librarian stumbled and paused tentatively at several points as she opened the celebration:

> How did the soldier serve! Twenty years he served. Twenty years and then another five. He returned, he returned, to his native home. He looked around. [There were] people from elsewhere, unfamiliar people. And he asked, "Where have you come from?" An old man took off his hat and said to him, "We have come from far away, from the river Kerzhenets. We have brought with us the Russian faith, the old faith, and we have also brought chests with wit and reason [*sunduki s umom-razumom*], and the ability to cultivate the Russian land."

With this, she abruptly stopped and called upon Sepych's folk ensemble to perform its first number.

The librarian's opening lines, I suggest, covered grounds quite similar to those in Father Vasilii's sermon but in a very different way. In contrast to Father Vasilii's presentation, based on expert knowledge about the past uncovered through historical research and backed up with intricate detail, the librarian's brief scene presented an imagined historical conversation recounted by an old woman. To know history here was not to study the materiality and contents of old books with the goal of establishing incontrovertible truth (and assertively correcting less accurate, less expert accounts) but to hear the past recounted by the eldest generation of one's own townspeople, perhaps by one's own grandparents. By placing the audience in the position of younger generations listening to a grandmother tell a story about the first residents of Sepych, this opening scene conjured an intimate way of encountering history familiar to everyone in the crowd. It was, in fact, most often in the moments of intergenerational conversation evoked by this scene—moments of dialogue rather than monologue—that I glimpsed the distinctive contours of ethical dilemmas and sensibilities in Sepych.

Delivered within the trappings of a historical consciousness that differed from Father Vasilii's, the librarian's lines also hint at the ethics I trace through the centuries in Sepych. The old man in her story describes the kinds of people who have resided in Sepych by enumerating what the town's early settlers brought with them from far away, including "the Russian faith, the old faith" and "the ability to cultivate the Russian land." Indeed, one of my early lessons in Sepych was that when it comes to questions of history and ethics, the old faith and the cultivation of the land have never been as far apart as might be suggested by the abstract terms "religion" and "rural economy." Thinking of the residents of Sepych exclusively in a religious vein misses the importance of townspeople's shifting relationships to the cultivation of the land as serfs, free peasants, collective and state farmers, and, most recently, shareholders in a post-Soviet commercial farm. Conversely, many who have aggressively preached the worldly tenets of socialism or capitalism have not accounted for the role of the old faith in informing townspeople's expectations about the flow of life and death, gender and generation, or worldly and otherworldly powers.

Focusing too narrowly on external categories like religion or rural economy thus effaces the ways in which the residents of Sepych have so often attempted, sometimes even with a measure of success, to find their place in the world by managing and reconfiguring the ever-shifting relationships between the old faith and the cultivation of the land. The librarian's lines are again instructive: between faith and cultivation, the old man of the grandmother's story lists "chests with wit and reason" among the things that Sepych's early Old Believers brought with them.[2] The placement of the inherently situational exercise of wit and reason *(um-razum) between* the old faith and the cultivation of the land is significant. Again and again, townspeople's attempts to resolve ethical dilemmas have entailed the practice of wit—the Russian *um* conveys a combination of cleverness and intelligence often lost in English—and reason at the points where the old faith, the cultivation of the land, and the unfamiliar yet often seductive projects of powerful outsiders like Father Vasilii have met and clashed. My aim, then, is to follow the practical sensibilities conveyed by the librarian's formulation of wit and reason through the centuries in Sepych and, in the course of doing so, to account for and reflect on their continuities and discontinuities. This, too, was a familiar project to everyone I knew in Sepych.

It is just this issue that confronted the soldier in the librarian's opening story upon his return to Sepych. What does it mean to return to a native place after a quarter century away? What combinations of familiar and unfamiliar does one find? What new people? What new kinds of faith? What new relationships to the land? Is it still the same place? The scene of a soldier coming home to an uncertain welcome is well known across a range of Russian performative genres. Indeed, the first part of the librarian's lines closely mimics the opening phrases of the popular Russian poem/song "Kak Sluzhil Soldat" that is itself about the ways in which the passing of time threatens to upend the most familiar of relationships. In the song, a soldier returns home after twenty-five years of service and mistakes his daughter for his wife, who has died.[3] In the librarian's very composition of a scene in which a soldier returns home to find Old Believers, then, we find an instance of what I argue has been a quite common phenomenon: townspeople in Sepych adopting widely circulating Russian discourses or practices and infusing them with their own sensibilities and modes of historical consciousness.

2. The "chests" part of this line is somewhat puzzling and may be either a reference to the wooden chests in which religious books were often stored or, judging from the librarian's nervous cadence, a misspoken line.

3. I am grateful to Maria Sidorkina Rives for pointing out this similarity to me.

THE earliest Old Believers of Sepych were Christian ascetics of the most resolute sort, intent on isolating themselves—geographically, ritually, economically, and politically—from a world in the clutches of the Antichrist. These early Old Believers' elaborate efforts to attain Christian salvation by shunning a sinful and tempting world influenced the ethical sensibilities of their descendants without fully constraining them or providing incontrovertible guidelines for new sorts of dilemmas. Variants of old dilemmas thus required new deliberations, a process significantly complicated by encounters with new ways of organizing work and prayer. For example, by the mid-nineteenth century, a modified version of the early Old Believers' efforts to flee the world emerged in Sepych. Likely in response to the increased state regulation of the Russian countryside, local Old Believers removed the active practice of the old faith to the oldest generation of townspeople; only late in life would they withdraw into heavily ritualized and nearly monastic seclusion. By contrast, younger and middle generations remained free to cultivate the land "in the world" of serfdom and postemancipation agrarian capitalism without provoking their serf masters or agents of the state hostile to Old Belief. At other times, new resolutions to old dilemmas have been deeply gendered. In the late Soviet period, after decades of engagements with the ideologies and practices of rural socialism, it was almost entirely women who aspired to the austere ideals of Old Believer elders, even as their husbands and children often continued their association with the local Communist Party or State Farm Sepych.

Each of these provisional arrangements of the old faith and the Russian land emerged from and depended upon the ongoing working out of intricate and intimate ethical dilemmas. In both generational and gendered examples, for instance, the partitioned relationships of worldly work and otherworldly prayer often struggled to coexist under the same roof. What happens when elderly parents attempt to withdraw from the world, not even touching worldly food or drink, yet their children continue to live very worldly lives in the same house? What is to be done when a wife summons the elders to pray in the main room while the husband is a devoted member of the party and quite convinced there are no such things as inhabitants of another world toward which to direct prayers? In attending to these kinds of concrete dilemmas at multiple historical junctures, I chart the specific ways in which townspeople have sought to fashion ethical lives even as—precisely as—the very categories informing their conceptions of proper relationships have themselves been so frequently on the move.

The uneasy juxtapositions of the library's anniversary celebration are thus but one particularly illustrative example of townspeople's long-running efforts to bring a set of diffuse, malleable, recombinant, and very local expectations about the proper constitution of people and relationships—an ethical repertoire—into tentative conversation with powerful outsiders who have usually been better at preaching than at listening. In more fully rendering this ethical repertoire in the chapters that follow, I adopt and reorganize some of the conventions of both the priest's sermon and the librarian's lines. As will become abundantly clear in the next section, I, not unlike Father Vasilii, frequently make use of sources, styles of argument, and "expert" language not directly familiar to many in Sepych. In my overall analysis, however, I seek to channel these approaches through the librarian's quite different historical and ethical epistemologies. For this reason, rather than summing up the library's anniversary celebration with a desiccated list of ethical principles guiding life in Sepych, I prefer to let townspeople's ethical repertoire unfold slowly over the course of this book's substantive chapters—in all of its lived indeterminacy, its latent embodiment in people and landscapes, and its shared and disputed sensibilities about what makes a human being. To be gained in this approach, I believe, is a more faithful portrayal of townspeople's historical and present-day experience in their own terms. This kind of understanding is, in turn, a precondition for more fully comprehending the larger, at times global, processes from which Sepych has never been as isolated as some, including many of its own residents, have considered it to be.

Ethics

There was ethical significance, I have suggested, to several of the moments of the library celebration—from the materiality of the priest's manuscript to the generational distinctions enacted by the librarian's dress and lines, from the setting of a former Soviet House of Culture to the relational distinction between the old faith and the ability to work the Russian land. Indeed, I have found that an analytical language centered on ethics affords me the best tools with which to understand the course of three centuries' worth of open conflicts and less overt juxtapositions like the one that so unexpectedly played out on stage at the library's ninetieth anniversary. I grant that "ethics" will not appear an intuitive or transparent choice to some readers, so I devote some time at the outset to a specific account of why and how I use this term and its derivatives.

Ethics and morality are, to begin with, politically charged concepts. "The word 'moral,'" E. P. Thompson once reflected wryly, "...is a signal which brings on a rush of polemical blood to the academic head" (1993, 271). Thompson was responding to critics of his writings on moral economy, the "consistent traditional view of norms and obligations" that, in his view, helped to explain peasant riots in eighteenth-century England (1971). The skirmish between Thompson and opponents who objected to his use of the term "moral" usefully illustrates a persistently complicating dynamic in the study of morality and ethics: when scholars work on these topics, they often tread on territory that is far from theirs alone. Definitions and pronouncements about morality are quintessential elements of modern states' ongoing efforts to establish legitimacy and regulate their populations. States, as Moore (1993) puts it succinctly, moralize; so, too, do their internal and external opponents. Moreover, academic discussions of morality and ethics are often more heavily implicated in high-stakes political fields than some might think. The rise and spread of universities has meant that a substantial portion of moralizing discourse in the political arena draws on, seeks to counter, or otherwise engages expert research generated within the academy. In the case of moral economy, and given Thompson's involvement with the British academic and political Left in the 1960s and 1970s, it should be no surprise that using the word "moral" in connection with peasant uprisings against the market helped to outrage cold war–era champions of Adam Smith. Moral economy became controversial in part because it challenged the ways in which Western states were themselves attempting to define morality and mobilize their populations against the non-market states of the Soviet bloc.[4]

Substantial political freight thus attaches to the mere mention of the words "moral" and "ethical" as they relate to Russia and the Soviet Union. Morality was, after all, very much the coin of the realm in twentieth-century political rhetoric about the Soviet project—whether that rhetoric was directed outward into the international arena or inward toward a particular state's supporters and potential dissenters. As early as 1920, Lenin was responding to a barrage of accusations that the communists had no morality, affirming to the Russian Young Communist League that "of course" there are such things as communist ethics and communist morality. U.S. ambassador George Kennan's famous Long Telegram revived the charge at the dawn of the cold war: "In the name of Marxism," he cabled from Moscow in 1946, "[the Bolsheviks] sacrificed every single ethical value in their methods and tactics." Later still, Ronald Reagan's "evil empire" speech, delivered to the National Association of Evangelicals in 1983, included a lengthy section that carefully unpacked and rebutted Lenin's views on morality and then went on to summon Americans to a new "test of moral will and faith." Morality even attended the last days of the Soviet Union: Mikhail Gorbachev's December 25, 1991, address conceded that cold war militarization had done grave "moral" damage to the Soviet populace, while George Bush's response, delivered just hours later, declared "victory for the moral force of our values."[5] Both in and beyond the academy, brushes with states' and other institutions' attempts to assert control over the domain of the moral can easily distort or divert empirical studies of morality—often by

4. For more on the history of "moral economy" and the political field it entered, see Eley (2005) and Sivaramakrishnan (2005).

5. See also Gal and Kligman's discussion of cold war "morality tales" (2000, 10 and passim). Morality has now even earned a significant spot in grand accounts of the struggles of the twentieth century, including recent appearances in cold war history (Gaddis 2005, 156–95) and retrospectives on the clash of democracy and totalitiarianism (e.g., Todorov 2003).

reducing complexities and contingencies to moral absolutes. How often are we still told, even by scholars who should trade in far more subtle explanations, that the Soviet Union collapsed because it was "morally corrupt"?

My hope is that such absolutist cold war rhetorics have now subsided enough to make a more nuanced historical and ethnographic study of ethics in Russia possible and instructive.[6] Morality and ethics, after all, remain high on the global agenda in the post–cold war era. New technologies, new medicines, new politics, and the vertiginous dislocations of economic globalization have provoked deep dilemmas about how to begin, orchestrate, and end human lives the world over. The evidence is everywhere—from corporate board-rooms to factory sweatshops, from scientific laboratories to megachurches. Apparently settled codes of conduct regulating proper relations among human beings—most recently and stunningly the "personal dignity" clauses of the Third Geneva Convention—are suddenly up for debate. Religion has refused to disappear as so many modernization theorists once predicted it would; instead, it provides ever more prominent models for the organization of lives and societies. Expanding awareness of connections among people on a global scale has led an increasing number to adjust their everyday habits of consumption and exchange in efforts to mitigate gaping inequalities and ecological destruction. From the distance of historical analysis, it is easy to see these phenomena as the ongoing symptoms of yet another age in which what it means to be human is being comprehensively, if divergently, revised. In the intimate spaces of ethnography, however, it is not historical ages that are most evident but rather the abiding uncertainties and clashing certainties of lives lived, and lost, in search of new moorings.

Ethics has also been on the agenda of social and cultural theory of late—often precisely as an analytical tool with which to think across these orders of magnitude. Within the porous borders of anthropology, and especially in the subfields of medical anthropology, the anthropology of religion, and science and technology studies, a theoretical language of ethics and morality has proven useful for linking the concrete projects and predicaments so salient in ethnographic fieldwork to ongoing transformations of human life at the largest scales.[7] At the same time, the "moral economy" proposed by Thompson and

6. I grant, of course, that a range of new moralizing discourses has blanketed the region in the wake of the cold war, especially the grim prediction that "transition" will falter and collapse on the entrenched moral corruption of postsocialist societies (see also Hayden's very instructive discussions of moralizing discourses about community, scholarship, and ethnicity in the former Yugoslavia, 2007a, 2007b). This new spread of moralizing discourses has not, for the most part, reached the point of precluding the kinds of research on which this study rests its claims about practical ethics. By contrast, the entrenched and absolutist moralizing positions of both sides during the cold war made for precious little access to lived ethics on either side of the Iron Curtain.

7. In science and technology studies and in medical anthropology, which are not as close to my interests here, see, for instance, Kleinman (1995), Fischer (2003), and Petryna (2005). See Pandian (2008) on ethics as a productive route into the anthropology of development in colonial and

expanded most influentially by James C. Scott (1976) has recently been extracted from years of stale debate with "political economy" and revived in the service of understanding twenty-first-century peasant populations (Edelman 2005). There is a great deal of productive disagreement in these studies about how best to understand and theorize ethics, as well as about how this anthropology of ethics might relate to other recent conversations and longer-term disciplinary and interdisciplinary trajectories. I do not propose to survey and adjudicate among these many approaches here; I do, however, offer a working definition and some ways to operationalize the concept of ethics.

I understand ethics to indicate a field of socially located and culturally informed practices that are undertaken with at least somewhat conscious orientation toward conceptions of what is good, proper, or virtuous.[8] These practices are historically situated and play out in an often-competitive arena of partially shared, partially discordant sensibilities. They may be directed toward oneself or toward others. They may succeed or fail. Often, they are responses to perceived disjunctures between how a person or a group should or could act and how that person or group is perceived to be acting.[9] As an initial way of clarifying what this definition does and does not include, I describe the relationships between my use of ethics and some other key terms in social and cultural theory: morality, society, culture, and power. In some cases, my choices about terminology are tactical attempts to avoid semantic confusion or terms already overburdened with meanings I wish to avoid. In other cases, some preliminary discussion allows me to indicate more specifically the kinds of questions that will occupy me throughout the chapters that follow.[10]

---

postcolonial contexts. Further afield, see Harpham (1995) on literary theory and Lowe (2006) for a recent example in sociology. I do not treat ongoing debates and controversies over anthropology's own ethics here (e.g., Scheper-Hughes 1995; Castañeda 2006), except to note that they should themselves be understood as participating in global recalibrations of ethics for the post–cold war era (on this point, see esp. Jacob and Riles 2007).

8. I use the concept of "field" as a way to situate variously positioned actors and groups and to chart their interactions across both time and space. Although this usage is inspired by the writings of Pierre Bourdieu (e.g., 1993), I do not adopt the conceptual language usually associated with Bourdieu's field theory (such as capital conversions and hierarchies of prestige).

9. This definition places me broadly with the Aristotelian stream of thinking about ethics (see, above all, Lambek 2000, 2008), a stream that anthropologists have rediscovered by reading backward through Bourdieu's concept of habitus (1977, 1980) and Foucault's writings on ethics (esp. 1976, 1985, 1994). Conversations with scholars of virtue ethics and communitarian philosophy (themselves interested in Aristotle's *Nicomachean Ethics*, 1976) have also proven fruitful (e.g., Lakoff and Collier 2004; Widlock 2004, both of them in conversation with Alasdair MacIntyre 1981). Despite their internal diversity, scholars in this Aristotelian stream would generally agree that the categorical imperatives and universals of Kantian moral philosophy are quite inadequate tools with which to comprehend the everyday practices that are anthropology's lifeblood. On the ethnography of moralities and morality as an "odd-job" concept, see Howell (1997).

10. Although this is not the place for a full accounting, my thinking about ethics has been significantly shaped by many of the studies of the postsocialist world that take up this topic, especially as it relates to law (Borneman 1997), gender and health (Rivkin-Fish 2005), everyday economies (Humphrey 2002b; Humphrey and Mandel 2002; Wanner 2005), religion (Balzer 1999; Wanner

In both everyday speech and scholarly literature—even in moral philosophy itself—the lines between morality and ethics have blurred considerably. Within anthropology, this terminological morass is especially evident in attempts to gain some analytic traction on the relationships between abstract, assertively universal codes of conduct and specific practices and predicaments. For instance, Arthur Kleinman (1998, 2006) has written extensively and persuasively about the "local moral worlds" that shape human experiences of suffering and illness, counterposing them to the globalizing, scientistic discourses of "bioethics" that threaten to obliterate so much local specificity. By contrast, James Laidlaw (2002) counsels adopting distinctions similar to those made by Nietzsche in his *On the Genealogy of Morals* (1999). Morality, in this understanding, refers not to "local worlds" but to abstracted codes and conventions (of Christianity, in Nietzsche's critique), while ethics indicates the full spectrum of possible answers to questions about how to live properly. As far as the realms indicated by moral worlds and ethics go, the differences between Kleinman and Laidlaw are more semantic than substantive. I elect to align my terminology with the second camp while continuing to draw on some of the insights generated by those who, like Kleinman, use "moral" and "morality" to refer to arenas of practice. I reserve "morality" and "moral" to refer to lawlike codes, formal systems, or conventions like Father Vasilii's *Kormchaia Kniga* or the *Moral Code of the Builder of Communism*. (I make exceptions only in cases where it would be awkward to do otherwise, as in the well-established term "moral community," on which more shortly). As I have already suggested with reference to cold war rhetorics, abstracted moralities are often associated with states' and other powerful actors' clashing attempts to regulate and mobilize specific populations.

In thinking about ethics as a field of practice, I find it useful to employ some of the conceptual language associated with theories of society and social structure. Social structural fault lines—divisions of labor, class, gender, and generation—often interact in telling ways with the cleavages along which differential ethical sensibilities fall. By intention or happenstance, large-scale projects aimed at remaking subjects and communities often hook into precisely these kinds of differences, setting parents against children, say, or men against women. Moreover, ethical dilemmas are often most acutely felt as people encounter emerging social distinctions, puzzle through the ensuing practical dilemmas, or reflect on how society should or could be organized. For all their insights, studies of morality and ethics that rely too heavily on diffuse "discursive formulations" or narrow their analytic scope to individual "moral narratives" (as in Faubion 2001a or Zigon 2008) often miss opportunities to

---

2003, 2007; Steinberg and Wanner 2008), ecology (Metzo 2005), narrative (Ries 2002), property (Hann 1998; Verdery 2003), labor (Dunn 2003), journalism and governmentality (Wolfe 2005), consumption (Patico 2008), and social networks (Ledeneva 1998, 2006; Caldwell 2004).

account for the social distinctions that channel discourse or help call narratives into being. I do not, I emphasize, argue for the primacy of "society" in the field of ethics, merely for its role as a continued partner with the much more commonly invoked "discourse."

I write about ethics rather than culture for two reasons. First, as I discuss in more detail below with respect to scholarship on Old Believer traditions, I have found no easy way to speak of culture in its noun form without also invoking a host of associations and echoes that I wish to avoid: timelessness, romanticism, boundedness, and the production of national ideologies. European peasant communities—Sepych among them—have too often served as the ethnographic and historical locations for theories of culture in precisely these registers. I can think of few ways to more effectively flatten out the intricacies and historical transformations of ethical life in Sepych than to bundle them into a culture or to suggest that they stand for or against the chimera of Russian culture. Although I could certainly follow others by addressing these issues through careful definition—and anthropology's culture concept certainly contains room aplenty for the kinds of claims I wish to make—I find a shift in terminology both simpler and, given my broader goals and audiences, more productive.

Second, although I wish to eschew the noun form of culture, I do use the adjective "cultural" to help understand those aspects of ethics concerned with the production and circulation of meaning. In addition to its social elements, then, ethics is also cultural terrain: indigenous meanings and understandings of choice, constraint, change, dislocation, materiality, and much else powerfully mediate what is considered an ethical dilemma, what resolutions are judged to be available, and what counts as successes or failures in attempted resolutions. Indeed, it is useful to see ethics as a subset of cultural activity, one that is concerned with the conscious contemplation and practice of meaning-laden sensibilities about what makes for proper human beings and relationships among them. Ethics is not, however, the same sort of subset that some might suggest art or religion is. It is a *roving* subset of cultural activity. The wheres and whens of ethics are substantially empirical issues, for any and all domains of human meaning-making can become, at particular conjunctures, arenas for reflection and deliberation on whether practices within them are or are not ethical. These conjunctures may range from fleeting moments brought on by small-scale quarrels to long-term, systemic crises associated with social or economic dislocations. They extend, as well, to social, economic, or religious movements intent on spreading new modes of relating to oneself or others. And, of course, having left behind static, timeless notions of culture, we must recognize that meanings themselves are nothing if not dynamic.

This brings us to the issue of power. Ethics is caught up with power in several overlapping ways. Perhaps most obviously, the social cleavages and cultural meanings of ethics are political in that they are often fields of struggle and contestation in which various parties seek to impose their understandings of proper persons and relationships on one another. This we might call simply the politics of ethics. But we can also go further to specify how this politics works. As Joel Robbins has argued with particular clarity, the field of ethics is distinguished in good part by the fact that it hovers between freedom and constraint (2004, 314–15; see also Faubion 2001b; Laidlaw 2002). To seek to act ethically is to be at least partially aware that one has some degree of freedom yet also to be aware that one's choices are directed by expectations and forces not entirely within one's control. The anthropological study of ethics as I conceive of it, then, is a species of practice theory inasmuch as it seeks to split the difference between social theories privileging determining structures and those emphasizing freely choosing individuals (see, for instance, Ortner 1984). But attention to ethics also supplements Pierre Bourdieu's overly economistic theory of practice—or perhaps returns it to its roots in Aristotle—by looking beyond the accumulation and conversion of different kinds of capital to considerations of virtue, goodness, and propriety in human action (Bourdieu 1977, 1980; and see esp. Lambek 2000, 2008).

A final aspect of the relationship between ethics and power reminds us that the units seeking to act ethically, within cultural contexts and from social locations, are never autonomous individuals who exist outside of or prior to power relations. The analytic ambit of ethics extends to inquiry into the ways in which various types of subjects are constituted and exist *within* configurations of power rather than responding to or resisting from a position external to power itself. It is on this score that the approach to ethics I am outlining most clearly parts company with the central weight of Western social science. A liberal subject—autonomous, choosing, individualized—remains the assumed unit of analysis in most social science, particularly in contemporary economics and political science. Liberal assumptions about subjectivity have proven difficult to eradicate even from anthropology and cultural theory, as Mahmood (2005) has so convincingly shown in her work on women's subjectivity and agency in Egypt's Islamic revival. Yet the project of studying ethics must hold open the possibility of different subjectivities shaped through different modalities of power in different times and places.

In recent cultural theory, this approach to ethics, subjectivity, and power is most commonly traced to Foucault's writings and interviews on ethics (esp. 1976, 1985, 1994). Foucault is central here, to be sure, but many anthropological students of ethics have, in the process of embracing Foucault, often passed too swiftly over anthropology's long tradition of attention to what Marcel Mauss (1985) called different "categories of the person." True, Mauss's original essay, published in 1938, is marked by his evolutionism and unfortunate tendency to assume that each society has its own specific concept of the "social person" (*personne morale*). But successive efforts to reinterpret Mauss, particularly in later generations of British social anthropology, remind us to attend to ethics as a domain for making and remaking *others* as much as oneself. They thus provide a useful counterweight to the focus on selfhood and discourse most commonly taken up Foucault's followers (if not in his own works).[11] I suggest, for instance, that manifestly social phenomena such as interpersonal senses of place, differential kinship arrangements, and patterns of exchange have long been key shapers of differential ethical sensibilities in Sepych.

Thus far, I have argued that the study of ethics should be distinguished from the study of morality and has interlocking social, cultural, and political dimensions. Before turning to some of the reasons why I think ethics is a particularly significant and timely topic in post-Soviet Russia, I want to carve up the field of ethics in a second, more operational manner. In order to link the analytic aspects of ethics I have been describing to the complexities of everyday life in Sepych, I find it helpful to think about "moralizing discourses," "materials of ethics," "moral communities," "ethical regimes," and "ethical repertoires." These terms, as I introduce them here, guide my analysis throughout the book.

Moralizing discourse. By moralizing discourse, I mean an explicit set of instructions about how human choices and practices should be organized in a given group, whether that group be a state, a religious community, some other kind of collectivity, or, in many cases, all of humanity. Father Vasilii's *Kormchaia Kniga* and the clashing moral claims of Western and Soviet politicians during the cold war are prime examples of moralizing discourses, as each seeks to shepherd a variety of differences into a homogeneous totality (see also Corrigan and Sayer 1985). What interests me most about moralizing discourses is their fate as they interact with one another and with the indeterminacies and contingencies of practice in specific times and places. By what powers and through what channels do moralizing discourses have their effects? Under what conditions do particular people find one or another moralizing discourse compelling as a way to organize their lives? Do they seek to subvert or transform it to some degree, to adapt it to their own expectations and sensibilities? With what results and implications?

Materials of ethics. Diffuse experiential categories such as ethical sensibilities, expectations, and modes of historical consciousness must somehow become material in order to be efficacious in the practical creation and reworking of ethical selves and relationships. What kinds of objects, substances, rituals, or speech acts populate the contested fields of ethics? By what kinds of material evidence is ethical practice evaluated or judged by others? How, in

---

11. For studies of personhood in this vein, see Fortes (1971), Carrithers, Collins, and Lukes (1985), and Pocock (1986, 1988). Far and away the best ethnographic combination of Maussian and Foucauldian approaches to power and ethics is to be found in Wendy James's wonderful ethnography of the Uduk of Sudan (1988).

short, do material things create ethical human subjects and moral communities (Myers 2001; Miller 2005; Keane 2007)? How are they understood to relate to the immaterial, invisible world of such concern to Christians (Engelke 1997)? In Sepych, it was often in terms of circuits and objects of exchange that people understood ethics to play out, and so I will frequently discuss material objects transacted between people: food, drink, labor, rubles, and, in the post-Soviet period, U.S. dollars.[12] Likewise, the material landscape around Sepych itself—an inhabited geography of villages, fields, houses, roads, and cemeteries—has been an important material in the formation of worldly ethical relationships. So, too, have Old Believer books and manuscripts; recall that Father Vasilii began his discussion of morality at the library's anniversary celebration with a description of the material characteristics of the old book he held aloft.

Moral community. I employ the concept of a moral community because I find it important to account for the ways in which people engage in ethical practice with expectations about how variously positioned others will understand and respond to that practice. Although my distinction between ethics and morality as analytic domains suggests that I should prefer "ethical" over "moral" as a modifier to community, I retain the term "moral community" because it is so well established in existing scholarship in a variety of fields (e.g., Steinberg 1992). Moreover, my usage will make clear that making or breaking communities is *always* a practical matter, however much it is also caught up in moralizing discourses. At the most basic level, there must be a community in which practice can take place—something that townspeople in Sepych have not always had the luxury of taking for granted (in times of heavy outmigration, for instance, or, more monstrously, in Stalin-era purges). For more stable times, thinking about moral communities allows me to capture the ways in which one type of action or material of ethics might be appropriate for a fellow townsperson, another for a fellow townsperson of a lower social status, still another for a visiting state official, and a fourth for an imagined moral community like the "Russian people." All are types of ethical practice, but recognizing the different moral communities in which they are embedded and toward which they are directed helps to clarify the stakes involved as people muddle through different possible resolutions to dilemmas.

I do not use the term "community" naively. As Gerald Creed and his collaborators have powerfully argued (2006), moral communities—indeed, any

12. Labor stands as a somewhat peculiar "object" in this list—it is rarely to be found in studies of "commodity chains," "regimes of value," and materiality that have proliferated in the wake of Arjun Appadurai's *Social Life of Things* (1988). However, taking my cue from townspeople in Sepych—who have long paid attention to what they have received in exchange for their labors—I aim in this book to reintroduce labor, and therefore production, into the many studies of objects that focus on circulation and consumption (see also Rogers 2005, 64–65).

communities—are riven with power relationships, conflicts, and inequalities that threaten to tear them apart (see also Dudley 2000). Claims about community often operate precisely by elevating only one of many possible visions of what a community is and attempting either to impose it on others or to exclude them. Although I am sympathetic to the critical instinct to unravel and expose the power relations at the heart of community, I am also persuaded by Mikael Karlström's (2004) insistence that anthropology's recent romance with theories of power has come at the expense of more careful attention to the ideals and aspirations that can be articulated in the language of moral community.[13] Without neglecting power, Karlström shows that ritual articulations of moral community in Uganda have served as important foundations for collective hopes and the possibilities of community regeneration in the wake of crisis. So it has often been in Sepych, although these kinds of communal aspirations have not always lasted for long, and their potential for realization has often been deferred to life beyond the grave.

Ethical regime. I have emphasized the extent to which I view ethics to be centrally about practice, about people's attempts to create what they understand to be good or even virtuous relationships to themselves and others. When varieties of ethical practice, materials of ethics, and particular kinds of moral communities cohere into a more or less stable pattern extended through time, I speak of an ethical regime. By stable pattern, I do not mean that nothing changes or that people face no ethical dilemmas, although these will likely be of a lesser order or occur less frequently than at times of large-scale transformation. Nor do I mean that the subjectivities characteristic of a particular ethical regime are entirely stable, although they are likely to be unstable in patterned ways. Rather, I intend the concept of an ethical regime to open my analysis to history. I take inspiration here from a number of excellent studies of the ways in which particular arrangements of ethics have given way to others. Foucault's *History of Sexuality* (1976, 1985), which began to trace transformations of the care of the self from the Greco-Roman world into the Christian, is paradigmatic in this regard.[14] So, too, are other, less historically sweeping projects such as Heather Paxson's (2004) fine-grained study of the ways in which mothering in Greece has been transformed from an "ethic of service" to an "ethic of well-being" over the course of the twentieth century. In the organization of my argument below, for example, I speak of the ethical regime of the periods of

13. On the ethnography of aspirations, see also Appadurai (2006).

14. I thus combine some inspiration from Foucault with a range of other approaches that I have found appropriate to my field and archival material; see Collier and Lakoff (2005) for a highly elaborated, more insistently Foucauldian take on ethics and contemporary "regimes of living." Aihwa Ong (2006, 22), also writing in a more fully Foucauldian vein, uses the term "ethical regime" to refer broadly to any configuration of discourses and practices directed at an ethical goal.

serfdom and socialism in Sepych, while I see the especially turbulent decades after emancipation in the 1860s, the Russian Revolution in 1917, and the fall of socialism in 1991 as characterized chiefly by struggles to impose or define emergent ethical regimes.

Ethical repertoire. Finally, I use the term "ethical repertoire" to explore one of the most intriguing aspects of ethics in Sepych: through a long succession of massively different ethical regimes, there have been unmistakable similarities and continuities in the salient ethical dilemmas, relevant moral communities, and key materials of ethics characterizing life in Sepych. These similarities cannot be adequately accounted for by a range of popular but manifestly ahistorical explanations such as the strength of Old Believer traditions, the alleged conservatism of Russian culture, or some sort of enduring peasant mentality. But they also give the lie to fully constructivist positions, in which people are continually remade, and remake themselves, in the image of the age. How can we account for these patterns of reproduction and transformation, and of continuity and discontinuity, over the long term? By using the metaphor of a repertoire, I am working toward a term that will open these layers and intersections to long-term historical analysis without slipping out of history into essentializing narratives of timelessness, boundedness, (under)development, or transition. Repertoires do not unfold over time according to universal or predictable models but as a result of particular choices, contingencies, and contexts that have to do in large part with the special competencies of those involved. They are not stale and rigid—elements of a repertoire can be added, subtracted, or modified. Not everything in a repertoire is performed or on display at the same time or in the same way; many possibilities are often latent and can be brought back into circulation after a period of absence or quiescence. In sum, attending to the fate of a repertoire allows me to track the shifting interrelationships among a wide variety of elements and therefore to avoid reductive or determinist accounts of social, cultural, and historical change.[15]

With respect to ethical repertoires, then, the central question becomes, By what mechanisms—and they are certain to be plural—are materials of ethics, varieties of moral communities, or kinds of ethical subjectivities and relationships transformed, reproduced, preserved, or revived within and across multiple ethical regimes? Some of these mechanisms derive from the characteristics of large-scale systems such as capitalist modes of production and exchange. Holding the agrarian markets of the postemancipation and post-Soviet periods together, for instance, will allow me to evaluate the extent to which the general conditions of market exchange create similar ethical dilemmas for townspeople in Sepych in otherwise vastly different historical situations. But, as should be

---

15. Maurer (2006), following Guyer (2004), makes a similar argument about the importance of attending to repertoires in his review of the recent anthropology of money.

clear by now, these large-scale mechanisms are far from sufficient for the kind of analysis I have in mind; it will be important to look for other mechanisms as well.

Central among these is historical consciousness. If, as I have argued, the field of ethics is characterized in part by conscious choices about what kinds of actions and relationships are good or proper, then it is also important to ask how these senses of propriety come to be inhabited. How are dilemmas in the present informed by and understood in relationship to what came before? How, indeed, is what came before known at all? These questions can reasonably be asked of any period, but times of rapid change make historical consciousness particularly salient, as ever more domains of life present unfamiliar dilemmas that require new kinds of reflection and action. To return for a moment to the Sepych Rural Library's ninetieth anniversary, Father Vasilii's explicit moral codes and academic histories are only a small corner of the ways in which people in Sepych have come to know their past and have used this knowledge to inform practice in the present. More important to townspeople has been the librarian's brand of historical consciousness—one rooted in diffuse expectations about kin, working the land, and the dividing line between this world and the other world. In attending closely to these malleable vocabularies, materialities, and sensibilities of what makes a human being, we are able to trace continuities and discontinuities without relying on ahistorical essences. We are able to trace, in other words, an ethical repertoire.

Ethics in the Field

Sepych, an easy twenty-minute walk from end to end, may appear to some a rather small place from which to address issues of the scale I have introduced thus far. However, size and remote location by themselves do not make events and people in Sepych less relevant, or more of an exception, to processes unfolding elsewhere in Russia or on a global scale. Like most anthropologists, I make no claim that a single research setting is representative of anything in a part-for-whole, random-sampling sense. The utility of this kind of study rests, rather, on the broader connections and theoretical questions that Sepych's rich and varied history permits me to address. I begin by describing some of the more obvious links between Sepych and the wider world as I came to know them.

Near the crossroads at the center of Sepych stand a handful of merchant houses, the slightly decrepit remnants of the prerevolutionary period. Some are abandoned; others have been honeycombed into apartments for young families or dormitories for schoolchildren boarding from distant villages. The large socialist-era central store now competes with a local entrepreneur who has opened three small shops, also near the center. Other two-story brick buildings,

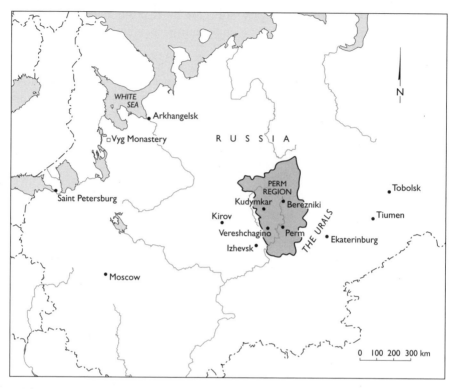

1. The Perm region in the Russian Federation.

emblems of rural socialism, are nearby: offices of the now-privatized state farm
and local administration and a twelve-family apartment house constructed in
1980s. The shell of a Russian Orthodox church sits on slightly higher ground
in one corner of the center. Closed and shorn of its bell tower in the 1920s, the
church building served as grain storage in the early Soviet period and later as a
rural House of Culture. When I lived in Sepych in 2001, it was part House of
Culture, part bar, entirely in need of repairs.

Residential homes, each with its own outbuildings and abutting garden plot,
fan out in all directions from the center of Sepych. The remaining prerevolutionary houses near the center fade gradually into rows of nearly identical state
farm duplexes, built mostly in the 1970s and 1980s by fondly remembered
brigades from Ukraine and the Caucasus. As Sepych grew over the centuries,
it overtook several surrounding villages; these parts of town have their own
noticeably prerevolutionary peasant homesteads. Farther still from the center, on the outskirts of town, lie the construction projects of the 1990s: bigger and privately built houses, some with garages or second floors, more and
more with satellite dishes. New and bigger barns for livestock, testaments to

1. A street in Sepych, with backyard gardens in bloom. Most residents planted additional fields of potatoes on the outskirts of town, often in a corner of their family's pastureland.

townspeople's increasing reliance on domestic production, dot the backyards of houses of all sorts. In the summer, gardens flush green with onions and cucumbers, cabbage and tomatoes, carrots and radishes, and most of all potatoes. In the long winter months, smoke from scores of chimneys flows into hazy eddies over the town.

Beyond the houses lie the fields, a few of them the domain of Sepych's small and struggling handful of private farmers, some designated as communal pastureland, still others the hay fields residents maintain to provide for their livestock. The biggest and best fields remain in the hands of AOZT Sepych, the privatized descendant of the Soviet-era State Farm Sepych. A single main road slices through Sepych's fields, connecting the main towns of the western Vereshchagino district. Depending on the time of year, between two and four milk trucks leave AOZT Sepych's barns each morning, heading east on the one-hour ride to the district center of Vereshchagino or the three-and-a-half hour ride to Perm, the regional center. There is not much to the west. It is around five kilometers to "the Sokolovo side," as townspeople refer to the collection of villages west of Sepych, now gathered into the Sokolovo rural administration. Beyond Sokolovo, over roads that can be traversed only in the summer, and then with some difficulty, lies the border between the Perm region and the Republic of Udmurtia (in Soviet times the Udmurt Autonomous Republic and before that Viatka Province). It is not simply terrain that has made this route largely impassable. In fact, the distribution of religious communities in this region and records of pre-Soviet market days indicate that the links between merchants in Sepych and those across the western border in Viatka Province were at least as strong as those between Sepych and towns to the east. In the Soviet planned economy, however, there was no official drive to develop horizontal links among administrative units, since both plans and goods were intended to flow vertically along the region-district-city-town-village axis. With nowhere to go west of Sokolovo, buses turn around and retrace their route, back through the old merchant villages of Sepych, Dëmino, Krivchana, Putino, Zapol'e, and Elokhi, depositing their passengers at the bus station in Vereshchagino.

Sepych has never been far from the east-west arteries connecting Russia's capitals with the Urals and Siberia: the first documented settlers along the river Sepych were Old Believers following a well-trodden path to Siberia; the "tsar's road" passed directly through Sepych; and Vereshchagino, a city of some twenty thousand, is now a brief stop for nearly all trains on routes between European Russia and Siberia. There had long been dirt roads along the merchant corridor that connected Borodulino, Sepych, and Sokolovo, but Soviet emphasis on industry over agriculture meant that this route was bypassed in the allocation of paving resources. A paved road from Vereshchagino to the northern factory town of Severnyi Kommunar was built decades ago, but asphalt extended through Sepych to Sokolovo only after 2000. These links to Vereshchagino and Perm are now reliable, whereas in recent memory a day or two of solid rain or melting snow could close the road to all but the most powerful of tractors. When I lived in Sepych, heavy rain still turned minor roads into thick, clay-based mud that demanded knee-high rubber boots, doubled walking time, and prompted townspeople to suggest—only half-jokingly—that someone could make a fortune reopening the town's prerevolutionary brick factory.

My original plan was to study the revival of Old Belief in the post-Soviet period. That carefully constructed research program disintegrated rapidly as I learned what townspeople wanted to talk about and found myself partially entangled in the labor exchanges, religious disputes, competitive gardening, and endless gossip of town life in the early twenty-first century. The unraveling of my research plans was not entirely a surprise to me; it is, after all, one of anthropology's most enduring tropes. It was, however, a frequent source of amusement for the former Soviet citizens of Sepych, who knew all about the careful crafting, inevitable inadequacy, and subsequent backdoor improvisation of plans. These ironies provided a humorous backdrop for many of the

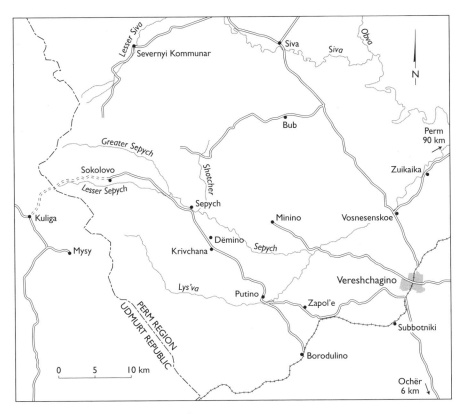

2. Sepych among its neighboring settlements.

hundreds of semiformal interviews, unanticipated interactions, and chance encounters that form the backbone of this work. The arguments about ethics that
I make here have their origins over dinner and moonshine, atop laden tractors
and in overheated furnace rooms, in commercial farm offices and school caf-
eterias. Their fuzzy outlines appeared while I was slaughtering livestock and
visiting cemeteries, standing at the back of religious services long before sunrise, and unloading hay carts long into the night.

   Back in the early 1980s, I was once told, when new duplexes and small
apartment buildings were rising at a healthy clip in State Farm Sepych, a visiting researcher would have been allotted his or her own apartment. But those
days were gone by the time I lived in Sepych. Instead, it was my good fortune
to live with two families in town, for roughly six months with each. Each
household was composed of a middle-aged couple with resident and nonresi-
dent children, the most appropriate environment in which a visiting unmarried male might board for a stretch of several months. In each house, I had to
myself a small room that had been recently vacated by older children studying

or working in cities. Both households had large extended families scattered throughout Sepych and the surrounding villages, which meant that my acquaintances with relatives were often the first stepping-stones to further contacts. I formed many of my first impressions of post-Soviet Sepych in the course of adjusting to domestic life with these two quite different households. I spent much of my fieldwork developing these impressions in conversations—and labors—with members of families whose histories, employment patterns, incomes, and household compositions were different from the ones I knew best.

As I got accustomed to life in Sepych, the tasks of household labor began to take up much of my time. Eventually, they opened the door to many of the arguments I make about ethics, labor, and exchange. Conversations while we worked—the plentiful lower-skill tasks were usually mine—provided natural contexts for talking about the differences between Soviet and post-Soviet configurations of labor, exchange, and accumulation. With little prompting from me, these conversations often turned precisely on the matter of ethics. What did current and past arrangements of labor mean for how people related to one another? How they felt about themselves? How *should* labor and exchange be arranged? Significantly, these conversations unfolded in the course of *doing* things—one reason I insist that there is more to ethics than narrative and discourse. My rapidly expanding ability to chat about the cycle of domestic production also became an entry into the primary topic of town conversation in the months Sepych was not blanketed in snow. Who was planting what and when? How was the harvest? How big were the potatoes? Who had cut their hay already and where did they get that tractor anyway? Whose turn was it to herd the neighborhood cattle to pasture? What price were people getting for meat? Here, too, was ethics. What kinds of people were succeeding or failing and how? At what cost to themselves, their family, or their friends and neighbors? How did these patterns of work and exchange trace the borders of shifting moral communities?

In some cases, my conversations in Sepych actually included words or phrases for "morality" and "ethics" (*nravstvennost', moral'nyi obraz zhizni*) or, more commonly, talk about different kinds or attributes of a "person" (*chelovek*). The crucial Russian concept of *lichnost'*, nowhere better defined than by Michele Rivkin-Fish (2005, 119) as "a fully mature self-in-relation, a person with self-knowledge, self-respect, and the ability to engage in ethical relations with others," occasionally came up. In many cases, however, these terms did not directly enter conversations that I understand to be about ethics. I have taken an expansive view of what constitutes talk about morality and ethics, not limiting myself to those times when townspeople used these terms explicitly. This choice means that my analytic terminology does not precisely mimic local speech in all cases, but it also enables me to track multiple vocabularies for ethics as they shift over the centuries and interact in different contexts. Townspeople no longer trade accusations about fornicators (*bliudoliubtsy*), as they did in the 1880s, and state officials no longer carry on "the battle with licentiousness" (*bor'ba s raspustvom*) in Sepych, as they did in the 1840s. These vocabularies have, however, been replaced by other conventions for talking about ethics in ways that are important to trace through local speech.

These conversations took place not just in the barns and gardens of those families I knew best. I began to help their extended family members on occasion as well, and then more distant friends and other acquaintances, all the while talking to and hearing stories from (and about) still other townspeople. To a lesser extent, my work extended beyond the household sector. On one occasion, I hired myself out to repaint the town hall and wallpaper the office of Sepych's lone police officer. In between trips to the meadow during haying season, I helped a group of culture workers from out of town assemble some of the exhibits in Sepych's new museum of folk culture. By popular demand, I clumsily taught some English for high school students caught between the foreign language requirement for admission to higher education and the Ministry of Education's refusal to allocate a language specialist to Sepych. I declined several suggestions that I take a job in AOZT Sepych on the grounds that, for all the terrific ethnographic material such work would provide, a full-time job would limit my flexibility to track down all the other leads I was pursuing.

All of my running among households and miscellaneous jobs did not go unnoticed; indeed, it made me ripe for teasing. A few younger townspeople joked that I should move to Sepych and set up an independent peasant farming operation, an absolutely thankless task that required round-the-clock work with precious little to show for it. One of the elderly women I knew best, upon hearing that I had helped to plant something like seven large potato gardens in the spring—a total of three or four hectares of potatoes—announced that my nickname would henceforth be "Foma," or Thomas. "Who's he?" I asked. "Foma Pogonii was a rich man!" she replied, chuckling and recalling one of Sepych's wealthy merchant families before collectivization. "He was everywhere, always working," she said. (Thankfully, the nickname didn't catch on in town; it remained a semiprivate joke between us until her death.)

Once a week, I took the early morning bus from Sepych to Vereshchagino, the district center, where I spent the day in libraries, archives, and museums. I also spent a great deal of time having tea and lunch with state officials in the Vereshchagino district administration. Occasionally, I accompanied them on day trips to Perm, chatting about everything from state business to international relations on the nearly three-hour ride. As time went on and I became more familiar with Sepych, I did not always take the bus as far as Vereshchagino, stopping instead for a day in one of the other towns or villages in the district. In exchange for a couple hours of answering schoolchildren's questions about myself and the United States (something I was often invited to do), I looked for significant similarities and differences with Sepych by comparing my provisional understandings of rural life with those of local government officials, schoolteachers, and independent farmers in these villages. These conversations outside Sepych itself were invaluable for my understandings of the broader configurations of power in which townspeople's ethical dilemmas were situated. They also illuminated a whole range of other ethical dilemmas, fields of ethical practice, and moral communities: those of higher-level state officials working hard to accomplish their jobs in circumstances that were often as uncertain and trying as those in Sepych's cattle barns.

Although I became more enmeshed in the daily and seasonal rhythms of agricultural life in Sepych, I did not simply abandon the aspects of my original project that had to do with Old Belief. On the contrary, I began to notice the ways in which townspeople themselves encountered and grappled with questions about the nature of the other world, the efficacy of rituals, and the politics of competition among religious groups. Here, yet again, was ethics. Believing townspeople often wondered whether they were making the correct choices in their attempts to live according to the principles of Old Belief—a situation complicated considerably by the fact that no fewer than three separate, competing factions of Old Believers were represented in town. What kinds of relations in this world and to the other world did each faction envision and attempt to enact? How to choose? What potential consequences for one's relatives and one's own soul did these choices entail? Which was more likely to lay the groundwork for salvation after death? How did the moral communities associated with these religious groups mesh and clash with other moral communities, such as the former state farm?

Only occasionally did I rely on structured interviews to understand the ways in which townspeople wrestled with these kinds of questions. More often, I encountered Old Belief as many in town did: when it simply came up in conversation or when it suddenly confronted otherwise uninterested townspeople—most often on the occasion of a birth or death. I attended as many services and religious occasions as I could, including holidays, baptisms, funerals, trips to the cemetery, three separate services in the course of one very long Easter night, and numerous Old Believer church services in Vereshchagino and Perm. Not an Old Believer myself, I stood for hours ostentatiously not participating at the back of these services. I sat for more hours in kitchens in Sepych, helping younger friends prepare meals for their parents and grandparents praying in the next room. I regularly spoke with the elderly women who were the main participants in Sepych's religious services. On my trips to the cities, I arranged interviews with current and former state officials charged with the regulation of religious affairs and with library and club workers who had long conducted antireligious propaganda. Contrary to some of my original assumptions, Old Belief could not be understood apart from the world of domestic economies or work on the commercial farm. The older women who most often attended religious services could not be viewed apart from skeptical younger men. And none of this could be seen as a bounded community, insulated from connections that stretched to Vereshchagino, Perm, Moscow, and beyond.

In the years since my primary fieldwork, I have corresponded with towns-people by mail and, less frequently, by phone or e-mail. I also returned to Sepych in the summers of 2002, 2004, 2006, and 2008. The inadequacies of short-term fieldwork and the still-changing economic, political, and religious scenes in Sepych have meant that I remain most confident in the materials about everyday life that I accumulated in 2000–2001. However, I have worked hard to keep abreast of more recent transformations and incorporate them as much as possible. These briefer visits—ranging from a few days to a month—also enabled me to discuss my more developed understandings with townspeople, both in an array of informal conversations and in more formal, invited presentations in the town and district libraries.[16] The sometimes spir-ited nature of these discussions has led me to revise many points, although on others I continue to disagree. I do not expect that everyone in Sepych will agree with everything that I write here, but I believe our discussions to date indicate that most townspeople see this book as one among many legitimate contributions—a good number of them now published by local historians and enthusiasts in Sepych itself—to the ongoing conversation about what the town has been, is now, and might become.

Histories, Archives, Ethics

The historical dimensions of this book have their roots in two sets of conversa-tions, each related in its own way to transformations of knowledge production following the end of the Soviet Union. First, many of my colleagues based in Russian universities, only recently able to study religion openly, have insisted from our very first acquaintance in 1994 that my work must include history. Field archaeography, the study of old Cyrillic writings in their present-day contexts, has housed some of the best scholars of Old Belief; it, along with ethnography, is a historical subspecialty in the Russian academy. For both ar-chaeographers and ethnographers, attention to the present without the deep past is virtually inconceivable. Indeed, some of my archaeographer colleagues were surprised that I wanted to do much fieldwork, suggesting instead that they had already collected so much material about Old Belief in and around Sepych that an archival project would be easier and more interesting. I encoun-tered a second set of conversations about history during my time in Sepych. Townspeople, it did not take me long to notice, were themselves engaged in all manner of reflection on the past: writing to state archives for information on repressed relatives; participating in museum surveys or after-school local his-tory circles; staging commemorations like that marking the library's ninetieth

16. See Rogers (2009) for a summary of research findings that was discussed with townspeople in Sepych, shared with Russian colleagues, and subsequently published in Russian.

anniversary; asking elderly relatives questions they had once found uninteresting or dared not broach; and reflecting and commenting on the ways in which the transformations of the post-Soviet period were only the most recent changes to wash over their town.

Ultimately, I heeded the advice of all these interlocutors and, in addition to paying special attention to memories in Sepych, spent nearly eight months working in various archives. What has emerged from these many conversations and sources is neither the kind of history of Old Belief that archaeographers do so well nor the kind that limits itself to the content and structures of townspeople's present-day recollections. Instead, I have taken these many pointers toward the past as an invitation to join a multilateral conversation about the history of the present—in Sepych, in Russia, and in the world. I therefore offer an account of history and ethics based in Sepych that moves between the historical sensibilities of townspeople and the standard conventions of professional ethnography and historiography. I do so, moreover, with an eye toward advancing an engagement between history and anthropology that is attuned less to European colonialisms and postcolonialisms—the *locus classicus* of historical anthropology in its theory-generating mode—than to global trajectories into and out of socialism. The links in this argument run along a chain from the particular kinds of archives in which I worked to, once again, ethics—this time as a way of thinking about patterns and processes of reproduction and transformation, both across scales and over the long term.

The archival holdings of the Archaeographical Laboratory at Moscow State University now stretch from floor to ceiling. Since the 1960s, the primary work of field archaeographers has been to discover, collect, preserve, and study old Cyrillic manuscripts and printed editions.[17] Because Old Believers rejected many liturgical and orthographic reforms in the Russian Orthodox Church, they often held on to the oldest available editions and produced new texts in the oldest possible styles. Far-flung communities of Old Believers, or at least their Soviet-era descendants, were thus ideal candidates for summer expeditions in search of manuscripts that dated as far back as the sixteenth century. Archaeographical expeditions first reached Sepych in 1972 and have continued, nearly every summer, to the present. Over nearly four decades, residents of Sepych and the surrounding area have contributed thousands of items to the archaeographers' collection: service and doctrinal books, hagiographies, collections of spiritual verse, records of local councils, letters to and from other Old Believer communities, and polemical tracts. The archaeographers' archive also includes other material from field expeditions, including thousands of photographs, close to one hundred detailed field journals written by expedition members, an index card file of every house visited and every single one

---

17. I discuss Soviet and post-Soviet field archaeography in more detail in chapters 4 and 7.

of the thousands of manuscripts seen, an audiotape collection of interviews and spiritual verse, scores of letters to the archaeographers, and, since 1994, hundreds upon hundreds of hours of video footage. The manuscripts and old printed books in this archive provide much of the basis for my arguments about the eighteenth and nineteenth centuries in Sepych, while the archaeographers' field material has proven invaluable for the chapters about the Soviet and post-Soviet periods.

For all its richness, the archaeographers' material also posed significant problems for my emerging analysis. Although this archive often provided fascinatingly detailed information about Sepych, it bears all the hallmarks of the circumstances of its creation. Given what I was seeing, hearing, and doing when I lived in Sepych myself, the most notable of these circumstances was an almost exclusive concern with tradition. There was little to be learned in this archive about economic or political configurations, still less (at least on the surface) about anything recognizably Soviet. Similarly, the flow of everyday life so evident in long-term fieldwork is largely invisible to short-term collecting expeditions like those mounted by archaeographers. One of my responses to these limitations has been to balance the kinds of information available in the archaeographers' archive with other material: from the archives of the Stroganov family estates in the years before emancipation in 1861; from various local state and Communist Party organs for the period of collectivization; from the archives of the Soviet Council on Religious Affairs; from the recently declassified files of the NKVD (the *Narodnyi Komissariat Vnutrennykh Del*, or People's Commissariat for Internal Affairs, a forerunner of the KGB) on the arrest and interrogation of sectarian "counterrevolutionaries" in the Stalin period; from the logs and plans of State Farm Sepych and organs of local governance in the late Soviet period; and from Soviet newspaper collections.

Although these additional archival sources helped round out my historical understanding, the information they contained was often quite different from townspeople's memories of earlier periods. My second strategy for coping with the difficulty of reconciling archival and fieldwork material has therefore been simply to embrace it rather than to try to iron such diverse materials into a seamless narrative. My overall goal is to describe and explore the ethical sensibilities of townspeople in Sepych—townspeople who have themselves been forced to understand and wrestle with a wide variety of sources over the centuries. Identifying an easy, unifying narrative in the archives and fieldwork would thus help to eliminate the contradictions and complexities that I aim to bring to the fore. Instead, I have made no single decision about how to arrange material gathered in archives and in the field, preferring instead to make a series of tactical decisions about what works best to illuminate my overall argument about ethics. In some cases, I use combinations of different sorts of evidence to better illuminate a particular event or era—archival manuscripts and recent memories, for instance, fit together in my analysis of the strife that rocked Sepych township in the postemancipation period. At other times, such as in the later Soviet period, it is precisely the tension between the different kinds of historical portraits offered in archives and other sources that illustrates my argument about the ethical regime of the time.

This combination of archival and fieldwork methodologies, along with the general ways in which I understand ethics as an analytic category, has implications for the kinds of secondary literature in Russian and Soviet history with which I have found it most productive to engage. For all of their terrific insights into Sepych and Old Belief, for instance, field archaeographers' master analytic device has long been the preservation of Old Believer traditional culture. Archaeographers usually assume a once strong, systematic, coherent Old Belief and set out to measure the level of traditional culture still remaining in various locales. There is little analytic room in these studies for lived practice, for dilemmas and contradictions, or, in general, for evidence to be understood as pointing to anything other than the laudable preservation of Old Believer tradition or, often simultaneously, to its impending and tragic demise. Although several recent anthropological studies of ethics have persuasively retained tradition as an analytic category, they have done so in part because it is an important indigenous term of reference—such as in self-consciously traditionalizing communities (Herzfeld 2004; Paxson 2004; Mahmood 2005; Hirschkind 2006). In present-day Sepych, as will become apparent, talk about tradition is simply not a very significant element of ethics; townspeople I knew often found it quite amusing that many visiting scholars seemed to think it was. (Self-conscious traditionalists, however, are to be found in abundance in urban Old Believer communities often populated by intellectuals.)

Similarly, I have not found the analytic orientations of much of the Western historiography on Old Belief to be particularly well suited to my approach. Somewhat more skeptical about traditional culture than archaeographers, this literature nevertheless often relies on other kinds of culture: Old Belief as "popular culture" (Crummey 1993a, 1993b) or as a Russian "subculture" (Robson 1995). Although these studies have drawn crucial attention to the importance of symbols, meaning, and interpretive and textual communities among Old Believers—all elements I draw on here—they also tend to have rather flat and homogenized views of how symbols and meanings operate. In these analyses, shared religious meaning functions in attempts to preserve Old Belief inside their communities, while power, modernity, or the state threatens from outside. Although this dynamic is often part of Old Believer rhetoric, including some that I heard in Sepych, stopping at this point leaves the impression of communities more uniform and less fully implicated in wider processes and power relations than was the case in Sepych and, I suspect, elsewhere. Moreover, as a partial consequence of these studies' focus on largely shared meanings within a religious community, they do not have good tools for dealing with power-laden transformations of subjectivity or with the social location of ethical dilemmas.

My claim is that thinking about ethics—and following townspeople in extending the sphere of ethics beyond obviously religious domains of life—provides a more accurate way to understand and situate the social and cultural dimensions of Old Belief in Sepych. As I have already noted, I simply avoid analytic use of the noun "culture" in order to mark my distance from studies of Old Believer "traditional culture," "popular culture," and "subcultures."[18]

Other recent developments in the historiography of Russia and the Soviet Union are absolutely central to the chapters that follow. Many Russian and Soviet historians have themselves turned to the topics of morality, values, virtue, self-fashioning, and subjectivities.[19] Most of these existing studies are based entirely on archival, literary, and other textual kinds of evidence; they thus quite correctly privilege certain modes of self-fashioning such as discursive formulations, narratives, and autobiography. My study suggests that there should be room in our historical imaginations for a great many other materials and practices of ethics as well. Lived practices of labor and exchange, more easily glimpsed in the kinds of fieldwork I carried out than they are in archives, are just as significant as autobiographies for the formation of different kinds of subjectivities.

Scholars of Russia and the Soviet Union have also recently taken up longer stretches of time and topics extending across once firmer temporal boundaries. Although the long view I adopt here means that I cannot hope to match the detail with which narrowly focused period studies can illuminate specific transformations of ethics, longer-term histories and historical ethnographies can raise other useful questions (see also Rogers 2006a). There are, for instance, many resonances between Sepych's long history of transformations and the findings of two other historical ethnographies of Russia. Bruce Grant suggests that the Nivkhi of Sakhalin have lived "a century of perestroikas" (1995), while Nikolai Ssorin-Chaikov argues that, for the Evenki of the Podkamennaia Tunguska basin, and indeed for Russian/Soviet statehood itself, transformation has long been "ontologically prior to [any] given social form" (2003, 5). In these cases, as in Sepych, we find times of instability and emergence to be more rule than exception.[20]

In sum, it is through both fieldwork and archives—and with the aid of analytic frameworks derived from both anthropology and history—that I have encountered townspeople in Sepych in the process of fashioning ethical lives for themselves and for one another. Why, in the end, ethics? If ethics appears

18. See Rogers (2004) for a more detailed review of my differences with this literature.

19. See, for instance, Kotkin (1995), Halfin and Hellbeck (1996), Kharkhordin (1999), Engelstein and Sandler (2000), Hoffmann (2003), Halfin (2003), and Hellbeck (2006).

20. Shevchenko's (2008) exploration of experiences of "crisis" in postsocialist Moscow nicely illustrates both how this sort of instability can be experienced at the level of everyday practice and how it was reproduced over time—as the crisis of socialism morphed into a series of postsocialist crises.

to be everywhere in Sepych's history, it is perhaps because the changes that give rise to ethical dilemmas and debates have come to this town with uncommon frequency and intensity. What remains for the ethnographer and for the historian is to follow the resulting trails of ethical aspiration and to insist that, for our understanding of human social and cultural life, striving matters.

PART I

An Ethical Repertoire

O glorious wilderness,
Accept me into your realm.
As a mother teaches her child,
Teach me all that is good.
O glorious wilderness,
Take me away from all that is vain
And I will run to you—
In you I yearn to live.
I will be a hermit in the wilderness,
In the wild, distant forest.
O my Christ, emperor over all,
I thank you always, Lord.
Abide by me, a sinner.
Save me from eternal torment
And in death grant me joy and happiness
With the saints in heaven.

—Priestless Old Believer spiritual verse, popular in the Upper Kama
  (see ORKiR NB MGU, PV, 641, l. 160)

1 *In Search of Salvation on the Stroganov Estates*

Conventional narratives of Russian history rarely miss the opportunity to tell of the dissent of the Old Believers. In the middle of the seventeenth century, the story commonly runs, Patriarch Nikon, with the support of Tsar Aleksei Mikhailovich, instituted a set of ritual and orthographic reforms in the Russian Orthodox Church. What would appear to some to have been minor adjustments (such as the number of fingers with which one crossed oneself or the spelling of Jesus' name) were not, however, understood as such by a significant portion of the Russian population. For these dissenters—a few learned monks and clerics but mainly masses of ordinary believers—Nikon's reforms represented nothing short of a mortal threat to central tenets of Christianity. These Old Believers, the story continues, clung defiantly to the old rituals and uncorrected service books, sometimes erupting into outright protest against the state and church, sometimes fleeing persecution to remote corners of the empire. The result was a schism in which the Old Believers were expelled from mainstream Russian Orthodoxy. For Old Believers, of course, the schism was understood differently, as the final falling away of the Russian Orthodox Church and, perhaps, as a sign of the end times.

In addition to featuring prominently in popular histories of Russia, this narrative of mass protest against church reform nestled snuggly in the guiding assumptions of more than one school of professional historiography. For scholars working in—or at least needing to publish in—the frameworks of Marxist-Leninist historical materialism, protests from below were a prime place to explore the class conflicts assumed to characterize all modes of production. For many Western historians and observers, the emergence of a schism over minor ritual differences was good evidence for the backwardness, exoticism, and inferiority of Russian Orthodoxy (in implicit contrast to the rational, theological, belief-centered heights of Western Christianity; see Kivelson and Greene 2003, 1–5). More recent scholarship on the late seventeenth and early eighteenth centuries, however, has begun to uncover far more complex inter-sections of religious practice and state power than those captured in the stan-dard narrative of reform, dissent, and schism (on Old Belief, see, above all, Michels 1999). It is, consequently, no longer possible to assume that the label "Old Believer" by itself tells us much of significance about the history or prac-tices of a specific community or what it actually meant, in a particular time or place, to challenge the mainstream Russian Orthodox Church.

In the case of Sepych, fortunately, early manuscripts provide some clues. We know, for instance, that three devout Christians made their way from the monastic redoubts of the Russian north to Sepych—a trek of over 1,200 kilo-meters—in 1731 or 1732. Grigorii Iakovlevich and his two assistants were, as one manuscript account has it, "elected by two thousand of the brethren who lived in the Solovki monastery, all of whom had learned the service accord-ing to the ancient fathers."[1] Solovki (or Solovetskii) Monastery, perched on a White Sea island, was perhaps the most famous of the religious communities arrayed against the joint power of church and state emanating from Moscow in the seventeenth century. In the wake of the monastery's capitulation in 1676 and mounting persecution during the reign of Sophia (see Michels 2001), many of the remaining dissenters in the Russian north gravitated to the desolate val-ley along the Vyg River, just south of the White Sea (see map 1 in the introduc-tion). It was here that the men's and women's monastic communities of Vyg and Leska emerged and grew to become the thriving center of Pomortsy (by the sea) Old Belief (Filipov 1862; Crummey 1970). Traveling parties like Brother Grigorii's came and went from Vyg and the White Sea littoral, ferrying manu-scripts and goods and spreading their version of the old faith among dissenting religious communities across the length and breadth of Russia.

One of these communities was near Sepych, hidden in the thick forests at the western edge of the Stroganov family lands. It was home to a group of around a hundred religious dissenters who had fled Moscow after the uprising of gar-rison troops in 1698.[2] Brother Grigorii's party carried a letter of introduction from Vyg to the fugitives of Sepych:

> Word of your love of God and how much you submit to the holy laws has reached us in the Pomorskii monastic community. We hear that you do not accept the

---

1. ORKiR NB MGU, PV, 1574, l. 1r.

2. This region was not part of Ivan IV's original land grant to the Stroganov family in 1558. The area around Sepych remained part of state holdings in the Solikamsk region of Perm Province until 1700, when Peter I gifted additional land and some eleven thousand peasants in western Perm Province to G. D. Stroganov in gratitude for his support in the Great Northern War (see Pushkov 2005b, 44, and RGADA, f. 1278, op. 2, d. 3309). On the history of the Stroganov landholdings in the Urals, see esp. Dmitriev 1889–92 and Kut'ev 2004. Perm Province was a popular destination

baptism and ordination of heretics and have no dealings with them. We here rejoice...that in such a time a spark of true piety fell in that remote corner....[We]
appoint for you brother Grigorii; do not ignore [him].[3]

That any introduction was needed at all suggests that the small community
in Sepych was not, eighty years after Nikon's reforms, tightly linked to other
groups of dissenters or part of a coherent movement opposed to the Russian
Orthodox Church. Moreover, this letter, with its "word has reached us" and
"we appoint for you" phrasing (not to mention its flattery), supports an alternate view: that the Vyg Monastery was actively working to create a unified
Old Believer movement by seeking out and pulling in diverse communities of
dissenters stretching across Russia. As Michels (1993) has shown, panegyric
collections like Semën Denisov's *Russian Vineyard,* composed at Vyg, accomplished this task textually, by massaging (or simply inventing) biographical
facts from the mid-seventeenth century in order to establish a canon of Old
Believer texts and founding fathers.[4] Traveling preachers like Brother Grigorii
accomplished the same task socially and geographically: they made contact
with and instructed far-flung communities of religious nonconformists, in the
process transforming them from assorted dissenters into self-identifying Old
Believers.

It is not clear whether Brother Grigorii knew in advance of the destruction
he and his two companions would find when they arrived in the Upper Kama
River region (Verkhokam'e), as the area around Sepych was known. A peasant
had reported the cluster of dissenters' monastic settlements near Sepych to the
local military governor, who diverted a detachment of troops to demolish it in
around 1726 (see Pozdeeva 1982, 53).[5] Those monks and nuns who managed
to escape secreted themselves among the sparse but already sympathetic local
population, composed mainly of first- and second-generation settlers from

---

for religious dissenters of all stripes in the seventeenth and eighteenth centuries (Piankov 1863;
Pochinskaia 2000; Shilov 2001); statistics compiled by government officials showed higher num-
bers of Old Believers in Perm than in other provinces and regions into the twentieth century (e.g.,
Ershova 1999, 73–76; Gus'kov 2000, 89–93).

3. ORKiR NB MGU, PV, 803, l. 271r, 272r; see also l. 165r–67v.

4. Paert (2001a) makes a similar argument for versions of the famous *Tale of the Boyarina
Morozova* produced in the early eighteenth century at Vyg. Still other Vyg publications, such as the
Answers of the Pomortsy (Pomorskie Otvety), written by the brothers Andrei and Semën Denisov,
set out theological and doctrinal refutations of the Russian Orthodox Church on which much of
priestless Old Belief came to rest. Engelstein (2003, 24–25) suggests that such "inventions of tradition" (Hobsbawm and Ranger 1983) were perhaps more common than assumed in the standard
historiography of Russian Orthodoxy and its dissidents.

5. There was considerable unrest among the population of religious dissenters in the Urals
and western Siberia in the first half of the 1720s, including the revolt of the entire Tarsk Cossack
garrison and several instances of self-immolation (Pokrovskii 1974, 34–66). Although there is no
evidence of an uprising in Sepych itself, the destruction of the settlements near Sepych was likely
connected to the suppression of this more general disquiet.

farther north and east in Perm Province.[6] If the three travelers from Vyg were not explicitly dispatched to reconstitute a community shattered by state violence, then they unexpectedly found themselves doing precisely that.

At the time of Brother Grigorii's journey in the early eighteenth century—and in part as a result of scores of missions like it—the label "Old Belief" was only beginning to come into widespread use as a term uniting theretofore heterogeneous and largely unconnected strands of religious dissent.[7] The emergence of Old Belief in Sepych, then, was not a simple transplantation of the old rites from Moscow or the Russian north to the Urals, but a process of invention and identity construction in which outsiders played a key role. Rather than finding an authentic pre-Nikonian Orthodoxy in the early decades of Old Belief in Sepych, I see the dawn of a centuries-long series of inventions, modifications, and reinventions of what it meant to be a Christian—and an ethical subject more broadly—in and around Sepych.

This chapter traces the considerable success of Brother Grigorii's project over the next century and a half: the formation and growth of a large peasant Old Believer community on the Stroganov estates of the western Urals. It does so not by means of a chronological event history or a comprehensive engagement with existing historiography but with the primary aim of elaborating key elements of the ethical repertoire that subsequent generations in the Upper Kama would inherit and, from many different perspectives, look back upon. Sepych's early Christians strove to follow and bring others with them along a quite narrow path to salvation, one from which, in their view, most of the rest of the world had already fallen away. Their many writings on aspects of this path to salvation—along with the less plentiful observations of outsiders—allow us to explore the distinctive ethical lives of these Old Believers and to situate them in both the historical contexts of serfdom and Russian Orthodoxy and the

6. On the slow pre-1698 settlement and population of the Upper Kama, see Chagin (1998b), Pushkov (2005b), and Aleksandrov (1989). According to the census report (*revizskaia skazka*) presented to G. D. Stroganov when he received the lands, Sepych had a mere twelve households in 1700 (RGADA, f. 1278, op. 2, d. 3309, l. 125–26). The arrival and later destruction of the community of former garrison troops is recounted in Piankov (1863, 44–45).

7. Michels (1999) usefully suggests using the term *raskol* to refer to varied groups of late seventeenth-century religious dissenters who were not necessarily in agreement or contact with one another. He reserves "Old Belief" for those dissenters who self-identified as Old Believers—a rather small number, he argues, until the eighteenth century. The Russian state refused to employ the term "Old Believers" until much later, preferring "schismatics" (*raskol'niki*). Imposing labels on a shifting situation always does some injustice to local processes; nevertheless, for the sake of simplicity, I use the term "Old Believers" to refer to the Christians of Sepych after the arrival of Brother Grigorii and the advent of sustained contact with Vyg.

analytical frameworks of the anthropology of Christianity, especially its recent theories of material practice and historical consciousness.[8]

One important context for the efforts of Brother Grigorii and his spiritual descendants was that the Old Believers of the Upper Kama had to contend with relatively few proximate or powerful opponents during the eighteenth and first third of the nineteenth centuries. The Fedoseevtsy—Old Believers of a different and opposed concord—were active to the west in Viatka Province beginning in the mid-eighteenth century, but they posed little developed threat to the Upper Kama.[9] The same was true of the "one faith" (*edinoverie*) churches, which were established in the nineteenth century to lure Old Believers back into the Russian Orthodox fold by allowing parishes to use the old rites while submitting to the Russian Orthodox Church hierarchy (Kut'ev 1998). Still later in that century, Old Believers of the Belokrinitsy hierarchy opened several parishes further to the east in Perm Province, near the Stroganov factory town of Ochër (Pozdeeva 1996, 9; see map 2 in the introduction). Except for a brief period in the early twentieth century, these parishes exerted no influence over the Upper Kama until the 1990s. Nor did the Old Believers of the Upper Kama face effective Russian Orthodox proselytism or sustained persecution by organs of the state from around the 1730s to the middle decades of the nineteenth century (see also Smilianskaia and Kobiak 1994, 7). Indeed, the Russian Orthodox missionary Archimandrite Palladii, after a brief visit to Sepych in the 1850s, cautioned in his report that the destruction in 1726 of the monastic settlements built by Sepych's first wave of dissenters had not stopped the spread of religious dissent in the area. He attributed the growth of Old Belief in the Upper Kama throughout the eighteenth and early nineteenth centuries to the absence of a Russian Orthodox parish and the unwillingness of the nearest Russian Orthodox priests to preach in Sepych (Piankov 1863, 44–45).

Even when the Russian Orthodox mission began, its representatives enjoyed mixed results. In 1833–35, not long after the opening of a concerted campaign against Old Belief throughout Perm Province, a Russian Orthodox mission church was at last built in the center of Sepych and a priest assigned to the town.[10] Even by accounts published in the official bulletin of the Perm Diocese,

8. In viewing a central problematic of Christianity to be the discernment of a proper path to salvation in a materially shifting—that is, historically dynamic—world, I follow not only many Old Believers in Sepych but an array of instructive approaches to Christianity within anthropology, especially Parry (1986), Cannell (2006), and Keane (2006, 2007).

9. On Fedoseevtsy Old Believers in the region, see Pochinskaia (2000, 43–84), Semibratov (2001, 2005), and the discussion of marriage polemics, below. There remain a few isolated memories of priestless Old Believers in Sepych who became True Orthodox Christian wanderers (*stranniki*)—locally known as members of the "red faith" (*krasnovertsy*)—in the early twentieth century.

10. The Russian Orthodox mission to Old Believers in Perm Province dates to September 1828, when Bishop Meletii of Perm and Ekaterinburg passed on a decree from the tsar and Holy Synod

however, the church was sparsely attended (Lukanin 1868, 256–57); census takers counted a mere fourteen Russian Orthodox parishioners several decades later (Krasnoperov 1896, 158). Across the border to the west in Viatka Province, at the opposite edge of the Upper Kama region, the Russian Orthodox church in the town of Kuliga was built in 1890. By 1912, the diocese reported only 118 Orthodox parishioners amid a surrounding population of nearly 4,000 Old Believers (Viatka Diocese 1912; see also Lukanin 1868). Far from the centers of both Perm and Viatka provinces and brimming with adroit Old Believer polemicists, the mission parishes of the Upper Kama were hardship assignments for Russian Orthodox clergy (compare Chulos 2003, 24). Nevertheless, the periodic offensives against Old Belief by church and state officials did not entirely pass over Sepych, especially as the Russian state and landholding families intensified their efforts to regulate serfs' everyday lives in the first half of the nineteenth century. As I discuss below, for instance, Nicholas I's campaign against religious dissenters in the 1830s and 1840s manifested itself in Sepych largely through Count Stroganov's keen interest in policing the intersection of sexual practices, Old Belief, and marriage patterns on his lands.

The Old Believers of the Upper Kama, I show in this chapter, sought salvation through the careful elaboration and arrangement of a particular complex of rituals, texts, social structures, and modes of historical consciousness. Moreover, they did so from within the classic Christian dilemma of seeking to transcend a world that they continued to inhabit—a world populated not only by their own families and religious communities but by temptations of the mind and flesh; by other, unfriendly religious groups; by agents of the Russian state; and by the exploitative and sometimes cruel serf owners whose fields they tilled. Such was the universe in which this "spark of true piety," blown east from Moscow in 1698 and kindled anew by Brother Grigorii and his confreres from Vyg in the 1730s, fought extinction. Or, as we might put it in somewhat different terms, such were the conditions for the genesis of an ethical repertoire. By genesis, I have in mind neither creation ex nihilo nor a single creation; we can, however, be quite specific about the times and conditions under which many elements of ethical practice still significant in the Upper Kama today emerged in a recognizable, if already protean, configuration. In other words, the antecedents of the ethical dilemmas and debates so evident in Soviet and post-Soviet Sepych have little to do with such ahistorical abstractions as peasant communalism, authentic Old Belief, or Russian national traditions. They have everything to do with the efforts of particular women and men to carve out ethical lives and shape moral communities at identifiable

---

issued in May of that year. In 1830, Protoierei Georgii Piankov "opened a conversation" with the Old Believers of the Okhansk district, in which Sepych was located. See RGADA, f. 1278, op. 2, d. 1539, l. 95–96. On the broader missionary activities of the Perm Diocese in the Synodal Period, see Piankov (1863) and Nechaev (2003).

intersections of very large-scale fields of cultural meaning, social interaction, and material practice.

"On Pastors"

Brother Grigorii from the north lingered in Sepych for some time and later moved on to Tavatui, another Old Believer outpost in what is now the Sverd-lovsk region, where he died.[11] A much-copied genealogy of spiritual fathers sets out one way to view the legacy he left in the Upper Kama:

> [Brother] Grigorii Iakovlevich blessed Avvakum Mikhailovich, from the Pomortsy settlements [*pomorskii*]; Avvakum blessed Gavrill Evseevich, from the Pomortsy settlements; Gavrilo and Avvakum blessed Ioann Isaevich, the first from here [*pervago zdeshniago*]; Ioann blessed Fedos Timofeevich, the second from here [and?] the third, Nikita Iosifovich...Efim blessed the eighth, Kiril Vasil'evich, Kondratii Vasil'evich, Iosif Vasil'evich. Iosif blessed Evdokim Feodorovich; Evdokim blessed Artemii Epifanovich and Maksim Gregor'evich.[12]

Brother Grigorii from the north appears here as progenitor. His line of spiritual authority stretches back through the Vyg and Solovki monasteries to Christ and his apostles and forward to the spiritual fathers of the late nineteenth cen-tury. The contrast between the first three spiritual fathers "from the Pomortsy settlements"—Avvakum Mikhailovich and Gavrill Evseevich were Grigorii's original traveling companions—and those "from here" marks the indigeniza-tion of Old Belief in the Upper Kama, its entwining in the shifting local land-scapes that it still inhabits today. The genealogy also points to a particular view of Christian history and ethics, one that proceeds through a masculine chain of religious authority passed along an unbroken chain of spiritual fathers—pastors—who serve as guardians and shapers of a moral community in search of salvation.

Questions of ethics are inextricable from questions of who has the power to regulate proper practices and relationships. Are they men or women? Are they young, old, or middle-aged? On what basis do individuals or groups of indi-viduals seek to set the boundaries of a moral community through disciplines such as penance and excommunication? How is this ability transmitted over time? How can it be challenged or terminated and by whom? These questions are structural and normative as well as social and cultural. They have to do

11. ORKiR NB MGU, PV, 803, l. 214r. "On pastors" is a colophon in the top margin of one manuscript copy of an eighteenth-century letter, discussed below, from Vyg to the spiritual fathers of the Upper Kama. See ORKiR NB MGU, PV, 803, l. 254r.

12. ORKiR NB MGU, PV, 1574, l. 1r–v. This genealogy appears in several historical miscella-nies from the Upper Kama, including ORKiR NB MGU, PV, 803, l. 207v, and was a common way of imagining the history of an Old Believer community (compare Pochinskaia 2000, 11–12).

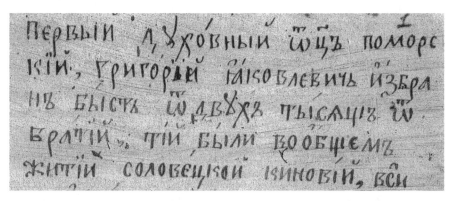

2. The beginning of a local genealogy of Pomortsy spiritual fathers of the Upper Kama, copied in the early twentieth century. ORKiR NB MGU, PV, 1574, 1r. Reproduced courtesy of UMI/ Proquest Microfilms.

with the institutions in place to handle disputes or disagreements and also with cultural expectations about what hierarchy, inequality, discipline, and community should look like. Within them lurk further questions of subjectivity. How does one understand and mold oneself in relationship to power, to others, to oneself? On what modes of exclusion does the formation of subjects and communities rest? Exploring these questions as they relate to the office of spiritual father begins to illuminate the multiple facets of moral community in the Upper Kama—especially its deep implication in relationships of power and authority and its centrality to collective and personal aspirations for salvation from a fallen world. While in many ways particular to the Upper Kama, this mode of pastoral power should also be viewed as one among many social, cultural, and ethical trajectories of Christianity in a distinctively Eastern Orthodox key—a key that has been little appreciated by either classical or contemporary anthropologists of religion and Christianity more broadly (see also Herzfeld 2004, 42–49).

Debates about the proper nature of religious authority in the context of moral community began not long after the arrival of Brother Grigorii. One of the oldest texts discovered near Sepych is a response "from the Pomortsy settlements" to a letter sent by the Old Believers of the Upper Kama. Although the original letter from the Upper Kama is lost, copies of the reply appear in several surviving historical miscellanies.[13] In the mid-eighteenth century, it seems, many had come to think of Brother Grigorii in such glowing terms that

13. ORKiR NB MGU, PV, 803, l. 254r–64v. See also ORKiR NB MGU, PV, 1127, l. 53r–65v, and ORKiR NB MGU, PV, 1983, l. 1r–15r. The Russian Orthodox missionary Lukanin was apparently shown a copy of this letter during his visit to Sepych in the middle of the nineteenth century (see Lukanin 1868, 260).

they placed his judgment on a higher level than that of other spiritual fathers. It is unclear whether their letter was written before or after Grigorii's departure from the Upper Kama, but it appears that local Old Believers either wanted to install him as the ultimate local religious authority or were at a loss as to how to organize themselves without his authoritative word on spiritual matters.

The response from Vyg, emphasizing at nearly every turn its own origin in collective deliberation, reminded the Old Believers of the Upper Kama in firm but gentle terms that "the Lord did not place such burdens, that there would be a single father to whom the whole world listened and from whom the blessing for all things would come."[14] The letter criticized Grigorii for allowing his followers to think this way and chided the Old Believers of the Upper Kama themselves for being so deferential to his authority. In an argument carefully supported with citation to Scripture and fathers of the church, the letter from Vyg urged the Old Believers of the Upper Kama to choose their own pastors, not permitting any one of them to gain power over others. It was all to the good, they reasoned, if a single pastor with more authority than others remained pure and holy. But if a single pastor in a position of authority fell from the path, there would be no one to rein him in. He would lead his whole flock into darkness. The brethren in the north counseled the Old Believers in the Upper Kama to choose worthy pastors from their own midst, pastors who would tend to the spiritual needs of small communities—"a flock of ten or twenty sheep"—and who would be in agreement with one another "in a single church with Christ at its head as pastor."[15] Pastors should not, the letter went on, interfere in the flocks of other pastors and should not accept into their community those who had been expelled by other pastors.

This line of reasoning and idealized model of Christian moral community have not been shared by Old Believers everywhere (far less by Christians in general). In the heterogeneous field of religious dissent that acquired the label "Old Belief," a prominent distinction emerged between "priestly" and "priestless" communities.[16] Priestly Old Believers developed multiple hierarchies of ordained clergy separate from and critical of the mainstream Russian Orthodox Church. By contrast, priestless Old Believers, including those of Vyg and the Upper Kama, were convinced that Patriarch Nikon's reforms had driven sanctity from the world and inaugurated the reign of the Antichrist. Ordination of new priests by bishops became impossible, as did the sacraments that required the participation of clergy. With the world in this state, priestless Old Believer theologians came increasingly to locate religious authority and its transmission

14. ORKiR NB MGU, PV, 803, l. 257r. In some manuscripts this quotation is attributed to the *Book of the Faith (Kniga o Vere)*.

15. ORKiR NB MGU, PV, 803, l. 260v.

16. For the best recent review of the differences among the many "concords" of Old Believers, see Robson (1995, 14–41).

in the collective decision-making capacity of the people themselves (Robson 1995, 25). This theological move lent a particular social shape to the kinds of Christian moral communities that sought salvation along the priestless Old Believer path. Most notably, it removed the authority of a specialist, ordained, and self-perpetuating hierarchy to regulate ethical practice.

The organizational advice from Vyg appears to have been taken to heart in the Upper Kama. In 1994, more than two centuries after the "on pastors" letter from Vyg, Anastasia Ivanovna, 74, described an election to the office of spiritual father:

> For us, [a pastor] is picked by the people. My mother told a story about a man [near our village], a good man. They selected people who were worthy—not married, not a drunk, not a troublemaker. They picked worthy people, and people who were literate. This man was off helping someone build a house.... And they came and conferred [the position on him]. They took him away to be [a pastor]. He wailed and cried, but what was he going to do? He quit working on the house. They lifted him up and carried him off and made him join [klast' nachal]. Could he refuse? No, he joined. A young man—forty, thirty-eight years old. If he's a pastor, he's not allowed to have a woman. He's obligated to live alone.[17]

I return to elements of this story several times below, but for the moment I wish to emphasize the putatively democratic origins of religious authority in priestless Old Believer communities. Clusters of villages and hamlets in the Upper Kama were grouped into small religious communities, with an elected pastor tending to "spiritual affairs" (dukhovnye dela) for each. Pastors were chosen by the eldest generation in each community, with the participation of two or three spiritual fathers from neighboring villages. It is impossible to know how many pastors there actually were at any given time, but by the late nineteenth century the number was likely in the scores, spread about among the nearly three hundred population centers of Sepych Township and the surrounding townships. One manuscript, for instance, lists the spiritual fathers who attended a general council by baptismal name and village community represented, precisely the organization recommended in the letter from Vyg: "Gathered at a general council in the village of Grishek, in 1888, the following spiritual fathers, with the help of God, recounted the apostasy and lawbreaking of the heretic Maksim Zhdanov: 1. Sergei of Demino 2. Simeon of Sepych 3. Dmitrii of Bloshina 4. Ioann of Kuliga 5. Aleksei of Kirshino 6. Terentei of Zapol'e 7. Galation of Sevolozo 8. Savelii of Mal'tsevo 9. Petr of Grishino."[18]

---

17. AAL MGU, Video Archive 1994, 5. Communities of priestless Old Belief differed in their terminology for their spiritual leaders. In many places, the officeholder was called a *nastavnik*, or preceptor (Robson 2004), while in other areas and at other times, *dukhovnyi otets*, or spiritual father, predominated. In the present-day Upper Kama, the term *dukhovnik* (*dukhovnitsa* for women) is most common.

18. ORKiR NB MGU, PV, 1118, l. 672r.

The spiritual fathers of the Upper Kama also followed the guidance from Vyg in periodically meeting at larger councils to discuss and decide on matters of theology or discipline that affected all their communities. "Councils," wrote an Old Believer near Sepych in 1924,

> are as necessary in our lives as they were necessary in earlier times, because in the course of time there appear various misunderstandings [*razlichnyia nedorazumeniia*] that the intellect of one person and even of a whole community may not be sufficient to settle. Such a misunderstanding should be settled by a council. Disagreement with the decisions of a council leads to a falling away from the church.[19]

Ideally, then, pastors and councils collectively regulated the boundaries of the moral communities that chose and installed them; excommunications, penances, doctrinal disputes, and ritual purity were among their central concerns.

The two lists of spiritual fathers I have already excerpted illustrate the ways in which pastors' deliberations were located simultaneously in temporal and spatial vectors of obligation and authority. Temporally, the genealogy of spiritual fathers from Grigorii Iakovlevich to Maksim Grigor'evich situates pastoral authority in a historical chain extending back to Vyg and beyond. Spatially, the list of spiritual fathers assembled at a single council in 1888 identifies each with the small autonomous community that elected him. Together, these vectors depict an idealized Christian moral community in accord with itself, a vision of its members engaged in harmonious ethical practice and on the path to salvation. But this harmony, as I discuss in more detail shortly, rested on particular kinds of exclusionary power and required constant adjustment to the unpredictabilities of the material world. Moreover, even as pastors worked at this intersection of temporally and spatially derived authority over a moral community, they themselves also occupied a liminal position in the broader social landscape of the Upper Kama, one that both enabled their efforts to guide their small flocks and placed their own souls in considerable danger.

Worlds Apart: Laypeople and Elders

In Anastasia Ivanovna's account of the election of a pastor, excerpted above, the new spiritual father is immediately whisked away from his worldly task to begin a life of monastic prayer and ritual purity. That he was not even permitted to finish work on the house he was helping to build demonstrates the extent to which we must view the priestless Old Believers of the Upper Kama as

---

19. ORKiR NB MGU, PV, 1578, l. 2r–v.

Christian ascetics seeking salvation through withdrawal from the world. By the mid-nineteenth century, however, this withdrawal was largely confined to the eldest generation of villagers, while younger generations remained religiously nonobservant and heavily implicated in worldly affairs. Generation became a key category for the formation of different kinds of ethics and subjectivities in the Upper Kama: deferring ritual participation until late in life mapped a distinction between prayer and work as fields of ethical practice onto a social distinction between older and younger generations.

Pastors were doubly caught in the middle of this age-grade system. First, their primary task was to enforce the separation of prayer and work and thereby to enable the effective withdrawal and yearned-for salvation of the community of elders. Pastors heard confessions, meted out penances in cases of transgression, and, not at all infrequently, acted with their councils to temporarily or permanently excommunicate members. Second, they themselves were most often respected middle-aged men (at least until the late nineteenth century) who served as long as their health and good standing permitted. Their office put them in the unenviable position—as Anastasia Ivanovna intimated in her story—of adopting at middle age a set of grueling monastically inspired practices, including celibacy, otherwise reserved for the eldest generation of villagers. Newly chosen pastors had every reason to wail and cry; at least one I knew did the same (although she was considerably older than the pastor in Anastasia Ivanovna's story).

It is unclear precisely when and how the practice of deferring ritual participation arose—it is neither suggested in the eighteenth-century correspondence with Vyg nor common among other communities of priestless Old Believers. The Russian Orthodox missionary Lukanin, after a visit to the Upper Kama in the late 1850s, noted in the bulletin of the Perm Diocese,

> The Pomortsy [of Sepych] are divided into "laypeople" [*miriane*] and "Christians." "Laypeople"... are unbaptized and live as they like; "Christians" are baptized and should live as hermits and not associate—in food, drink, or prayer—with [Russian] Orthodox or even with Pomortsy laypeople. "Christians" alone are allowed at religious services, but "laypeople" are not. (Lukanin 1868, 258)[20]

Lukanin was very likely wrong in his observation that laypeople were not baptized until later in life. Ample evidence collected in archaeographers' early field interviews suggests that, at least in the last quarter of the nineteenth century, children were usually baptized by a pastor shortly after birth. From their early teenage years until marriage, children sometimes participated in religious services with the elders, where they often learned to read—less often

---

20. I am most grateful to Eugene Clay for sharing parts of Lukanin's writings about Sepych, serialized over nine months in the 1868 *Bulletin of the Perm Diocese*.

to write—Slavonic texts.[21] With very few exceptions, most then entered the world of laypeople for the majority of their lives, marrying, working, and raising their own families.[22] Later in life, after the death of a spouse, they might reenter the community of active religious participants, where they would strive to live out their days in observance of monastically inspired religious liturgy and discipline, made pure by a refusal to eat or drink with laypeople, even with younger generations of laypeople in their own families and villages. One elderly woman in the Upper Kama recalled the stages of her life for a visiting archaeographer in terms of the years she did and did not "pray." Born in 1904, she "prayed" until she was twenty-two years old, and she "didn't pray" again until she was sixty-five. At sixty-five, she joined the elders because she "already couldn't manage [*provorit'*], was living beyond her years."[23]

Lukanin's terminology also requires further explication, for it does not always match the vocabulary of local manuscripts and speech. The community of religiously active elders in each village went by the name *sobor,* or council; the same term referred to the general gathering of pastors elected from the many individual communities of the Upper Kama. The appellation *sobornye* (those of the council) was likely used more often than Lukanin's term "Christians" to describe observant Old Believers. Often, those of the council were simply called *stariki*—the elders. Most younger and middle generations probably did self-identify as Christians, but this meant little in terms of religious practice beyond helping to facilitate the ritual lives of elders already active in the council and, occasionally, listening passively at services. The elders of the council could also, in my experience, be called *nimirskie,* "those not of the world"—a phrase nicely evocative of the transcendence they sought to achieve. *Miriane* or (more commonly) *mirskie,* which I translate as "laypeople," is still more complicated. Most literally and broadly, it means "those of the world," but it has also been employed in various other Russian contexts to refer to nonbelievers and, in some cases, to members of the Russian Orthodox Church (because of its close links to the worldly state).[24] At least until the twentieth century, "laypeople"

21. The most common books for teaching were chasovenniks, kanoniks, teaching psalters, and azbukas, which together comprise just over a quarter of the Upper Kama manuscript collection (see Pozdeeva 2001, 12).

22. There are rare instances, from the nineteenth-century as well as the contemporary Upper Kama region, of children's never leaving the *sobor* and dedicating their lives to strict religious practice usually associated with elders.

23. AAL MGU, Perm-Verkhokam'e Field Diaries, 8, l. 10, 25.

24. *Mir* could also refer to the small agricultural communes of Russian serfdom. Clay (2004, 7) translates Lukanin's use of *miriane* as catechumens, which would suggest that the Old Believers of the Upper Kama had simply lengthened the Christian catechumenate—the prebaptism period of learning and training—to a period of decades. This seems to be a very good explanation for Lukanin's take on the matter, given his use of the term "Christians" and observations about the deferral of baptism. All available oral and written evidence, however, suggests that Lukanin somewhat misunderstood the practices he was reporting on. I am grateful to Cathy Wanner for helping me to clarify these points.

best captures the baptized, believing, but largely nonobservant characteristics of this stage of life.

This particularly sharp and ritually marked generational divide in the Old Believer Upper Kama is best seen as an intensification of, rather than a departure from, more widespread practices in Russian religious history. After all, a host of notable figures—among them Ivan IV ("the Terrible") and Anika Fëdorovich Stroganov, the "original" Stroganov, who died in 1570—took monastic vows or entered monasteries near the end of their lives. This practice is also consonant with the broader Eastern Orthodox theology of salvation, which developed outside the shadow of Augustine and the attendant debates on faith, good works, and justification so prominent in the Christian West. With a much less negative and absolute view of the Fall and original sin than the West, theologians in the East, notably Maxiumus the Confessor and, later, Gregory Palamas, concentrated on the ways in which human beings could themselves participate in the process of self-transformation that would mitigate the effects of sin and lead to deification—returning to become one with God.[25] While ultimate decisions would be rendered only at the Last Judgment—and baptized laypeople in the Upper Kama were thus not thought to be entirely excluded from chances of salvation—there was historical precedent and theological support for picking up one's pace on the road to salvation through a life of prayer in old age.

It is likely, I argue below, that the rise of deferred ritual practice was an adjustment that enabled Old Believers of the Upper Kama to maintain their strict, ascetic religious practices while avoiding the prying eyes and more overt persecutions of their landowners and state officials. If this is so, the most likely time frame for its entrenchment in local expectations would be the 1830s–1850s, during the inauguration of the Russian Orthodox mission and general hostility to Old Believers under Nicholas I. We have, however, only later accounts of what deferred ritual practice meant for relationships with these powerful outsiders. In 1890, for instance, the organs of self-government (*zemstva*) in Perm Province completed a detailed household survey that included Sepych and most of the rest of the Upper Kama. Perhaps accustomed to Old Believers in other areas of Perm Province, where religious objections to the authority of the state could interfere with the collection of their economic data, the census takers were pleasantly surprised by the cooperation of the peasants in Sepych Township:

> As for economic information, in this regard the population had no reason to be secretive, since from the point of view of life beyond the grave, earthly [*zemnoe*] property has no meaning. Naturally, among Old Believers there are people who

---

25. For a concise summary of the theology here, see, for instance, Pelikan (1977, 10–16). The writings of these and other Orthodox theologians and church fathers were well attested in the manuscripts and early printed book collections of the Upper Kama.

hold great authority, and they did not interfere in the economic significance of the census [by raising] any religious reservations. They tried to facilitate its success. (Krasnoperov 1896, 159)

The spiritual fathers, "who hold great authority," were, it would seem, so convinced of the division between religious practice and worldly production and exchange that they did not mind the statisticians' interest in local household economies. The surveyors also noted the withdrawal of elders, reporting that many households "did not show their old men and old women, because of some religious prejudice [*predubezhdenie*]." Nor, they added, did most households show their young children, although the surveyors attributed this not to the fact that children might also have been religiously active but to a "superstitious" fear that being counted in the survey would make them susceptible to pox (ibid.).

Although the snapshot reports of missionaries and zemstvo statisticians give a basic idea of the importance of generational distinctions for patterns of social organization and ethical practice in the Upper Kama, they do not provide many details about how this generational boundary was crossed in the course of individual lives. We know from an array of later oral accounts that anyone who had been baptized into the Pomortsy faith could attend services as a layperson (*khodit' po-mirskii*). Beyond physical presence, however, laypeople's involvement was limited to standing at the back of the service; participation in the prayers and rituals of the service was strictly limited to members of the community of elders. When a layperson judged himself or herself prepared to take up the strictures of the council—often after an invitation from the elders and a period of regularly attending services as a layperson—the ritual of *priobshchenie* (joining) marked the transition. At least insofar as it is possible to extrapolate from twentieth-century practices, the joining ritual itself appears to have been quite simple. It involved nothing more than completing the set of opening prayers and bows, known as a *nachal,* and from that day forward moving to the front of services to pray with the elders.[26] Of course, the apparent simplicity of the ritual itself masks the immense changes in every aspect of life that joining the community of elders indicated. Moving to the front of services also meant moving from a younger to an older generation, from being in the world to preparing to leave it, and from a life of work to a life of prayer. It meant resolutely departing one moral community—with its associated expectations about appropriate and inappropriate practices—for another.

I should emphasize at this point that my discussion of expectations about the kinds of activities and relationships appropriate to different generations is not

---

26. In local parlance, *klast'/polozhit' nachal,* or, literally, to "put/lay down an opening prayer."

meant to imply that elders spent all their time in prayer or withdrawn from the world of younger generations. Clearly they did not and could not, as the elderly Old Believers I knew would have been the first to admit. My concern thus far has been to describe the distinctive cultural expectations, social structures and institutions, and understandings of moral community that were thought to enable salvation for the Christians of the Upper Kama. These are necessary but far from sufficient elements of my approach to ethics. In practice, the vagaries and caprices of this world always found ways to intrude on the careful constructs of harmonious doctrine and structure. It was, therefore, the ongoing practical struggle of pastors and councils to keep the fallen world at bay, a task at which they quite often judged themselves—and others—to have failed.

In order to fully appreciate how the arrangements of moral community and social structure I have described thus far figure in the formation of ethical practices and subjects in Sepych, we need a more developed picture of the specific topics and relationships with which elders, laypeople, and their pastors wrestled. What was it that they worked to regulate? How and to what end? What could happen if they failed? What, in short, were the locally salient materials of ethics and how were they linked to the creation of certain ethical subjects?

The Underdetermined Nature of Material Practice

For Christians of all stripes, both the possibility of salvation and the many sins that threaten to derail it are inextricably caught up in fields of material practice (see esp. Keane 2007). The sermons, teachings, and writings that help to transmit Christian doctrine and ethics enter the world materially, as sensible things: books are written and circulate; sermons are preached and prayers are uttered; bodies are moved in ritually prescribed motions; churches are built. This materiality is unavoidable. It is how Christianity—and everything else—moves between and among human beings. Once in the sensible world, however, the material practices associated with Christianity encounter a myriad of other sensible things that must be reckoned with. What objects, words, and modes of embodiment should be cast as external, dangerous, or inimical to Christianity? What should be done with them? Should they be tolerated? Shunned? Transformed?

The paths that the sensible things of Christianity travel and the meanings they acquire are underdetermined—especially over time. The scribes who produced the manuscripts on which this chapter is based could hardly have predicted their works' route from Old Believer libraries in the Upper Kama to archives in Moscow to microfilms available worldwide. Nor, of course, could they have predicted the associated shifts in meaning and context—from religious texts to legally protected monuments of Russian national culture to sources for a historical ethnography of ethics. It is precisely because the encounters, paths, and meanings of material practices routinely escape even the best intentions of their authors that the stakes can often be quite high in efforts to control them—by freezing their conceptual or physical locations, for instance, or by keeping them apart from other material things thought to be associated with improper or corrupting ethics.

Both material practice and efforts to control its effects in the world are embedded in historically formed moral communities and relations of power and inequality. Material practice, in other words, is underdetermined but not wholly indeterminate—it takes place within, and helps to create, partially shared and partially discordant ideas about which practices lead to the formation of ethical relationships and subjectivities and which do not. The discussion of pastors, elders, and laypeople above has begun to describe the expectations about the kinds of moral communities in which material practices in the Upper Kama were situated. We can now deepen that picture and chip away at some of its neatness and all-too-easy abstractions by turning specifically to the kinds of material practice that most often aided and vexed pastors in their never-ending efforts to regulate and maintain the separation of the worlds.

Taking up the materials of ethics central to the ethical repertoire of the Upper Kama also enables me to more precisely position my arguments in this book against views of Russian Old Belief—and of rural Russia more broadly—that trade in what might be called overdeterminacies. These are understandings of Old Belief as bearing elements of essential Russianness; of peasant communes as traditional and largely isolated from broader Russian society; and of a unified, largely homogeneous category of the peasantry, as opposed to the aristocracy.[27] I am especially leery of the alleged dichotomy between Western individualism and Russian collectivism that so often underpins these ideas. As Oleg Kharkhordin suggests (1999), it is far more productive to ask about the *practices* of fashioning individuals and collectives than to begin from (and usually end with) abstract categories of individualism or collectivism. Among the priestless Old Believers of the Upper Kama, we could easily identify material practices that work to create what some would call "collectivizing" and "individualizing" modalities of subjectivity. Yet we might go still further and wonder whether the terms "individual" and "collective," even when cast as a continuum of practices, best capture the ways in which people come to understand themselves and one another as human subjects and aspire to participate in moral communities.[28] In the Upper Kama, limiting the discussion to

27. See Burbank (2004, esp. 10–14) for a succinct yet powerful statement of how studies of the Russian countryside have begun to move beyond these and other conceptual dead ends. For a parallel argument about the importance of conceptualizing religion in Russia as a set of lived practices, see Kivelson and Greene (2003).

28. Kharkhordin (1999, 9–13), closely following his reading of Foucault, understands the investigation of practice to focus on diffuse discursive formulations—what he often calls "background

these terms would impose external categories and miss the most interesting contingencies and crosscurrents of ethics as a field of underdetermined material practice. With an eye toward underdetermination, then, I introduce below the central materials of ethics that the residents of the Upper Kama have lived with—and through—from the eighteenth century to the twenty-first.[29]

SPACES, PRAYERS, AND RITUALS

One basic and very significant element of material practice in the Upper Kama has been the organization of space, the channeling of people as they moved through the landscape they inhabited. The early Old Believers of the Upper Kama spread themselves thinly over the land, so much so that observers from the nineteenth century to the present have consistently noted the correspondence of an extremely high number of population centers with a low average population per center. Sepych Township grew from twenty-two to fifty-three population centers in the thirteen years between the censuses of 1782 and 1795, with many of these settlements composed of only a few homesteads belonging to members of extended families (Pushkov 1999b; Ponosov 2003). A century later, there were close to three hundred separately counted settlements in Sepych Township alone (Chagin 1998b, 267).[30] Indeed, despite Soviet-era resettlements, significant elements of this very old landscape were still evident in twenty-first-century Sepych, especially the linkages between family names and small villages or hamlets. I have visited Krasnosel'e with the Krasnosel'skiis, stopped to swim in the pond at Mal'tsevo with the Mal'tsevs, and cut hay on the fields that used to be Fedoseevka with the Fedoseevs.[31]

Both the material organization of elders' ritual lives and their everyday efforts to avoid the worldly relationships of younger generations were intimately

---

practices"—that heavily circumscribe the possibilities for speech or action in any particular circumstance. Although I, too, wish to account for the persistence and transformation of particular ethical formations over the long term, I believe such a project must include careful analysis of what, in Kharkhordin's terms, might be called "foreground" practices: the underdetermined material practices constituting ethical subjects and communities in particular times and places.

29. The varieties of materiality and material practice on which I focus below are those I understand to be most prominent and significant in the Upper Kama. Other nonconformist religious groups in Russia came to emphasize other kinds of materiality in their dissent, such as the ritual modification of the body among Skoptsy ("castrates"). As Engelstein (1999) argues, castration and its representation had important implications for historical consciousness and perceptions of the past among both Skoptsy and professional historians. See Herzfeld (1990) for a highly original semiotic argument that turns, in part, on the distinction between particular local icons and their absent prototypes or reproductions.

30. Like the number of settlements, the overall population figures for the Upper Kama show steady growth. The Russian Orthodox missionary Lukanin reported 2,866 Old Believers in Sepych Township in 1857 (1863, 45), a figure that corresponds well to the 3,038 suggested in a survey of the population in 1855 (Vologdin 1895).

31. On the demographic history of the Upper Kama, see also Pushkov (1999a, 2005a, 2005b), Chagin (2001), Shilov (2001), and Bezgodov (2005b).

related to this highly dispersed, "surnamed" organization of the countryside. Pomortsy elders followed neither the cenobitic model of group living apart from the world within the walls of a monastery (such as that in Vyg so well described by Crummey 1970; see also Iukhimenko 1999) nor the fully eremitic model of individual hermits set far apart from other human interaction. The closest model is the Eastern Orthodox arrangement of monastic life in settlements, or sketes (*skyty*), in which each member of the community lived separately—in this case, with their own families and often in natal villages— but all came together for prayer services and occasional meals. There were several dedicated prayer houses (*molebnye doma*) in some of the more populous settlements of the Upper Kama, but in most villages the elders simply gathered to pray facing the icon corner in the home of one of their number (see also Chagin 1992, 163; Smilianskaia 1997, 123). The living space of the home was temporarily transformed into ritual space, with only the elders permitted to move and pray within it and the younger generations temporarily expelled from the room in which prayers were offered. (In the twentieth century, at least, they were often expelled only as far as the kitchen, where they prepared food for the elders.)

The elders of the Upper Kama came together far more frequently for liturgies in these spaces than they did for the disciplinary and doctrinal councils described in the on-pastors correspondence with Vyg. In the larger councils of elders, there was often a division of labor between the spiritual father or pastor—who tended to matters of doctrine, baptism, penance, and general order—and the specialist in the rituals of the liturgy (*ustavshchik*). In smaller communities and more recently, these roles have often been combined. Elders gathered on religious holidays and days commemorating deaths, as well as for the baptisms or funerals of anyone—layperson or elder—in their villages and communities. Whether alone in their separate households or gathered with other members of the council, many also prayed the morning and evening cycles of daily prayers that have long been the hallmark of Christian monasticism. In group liturgies, participants who were literate in the old texts shared responsibility for reading and singing the liturgy.[32]

Certain that the reforms of the seventeenth century had inaugurated the rule of the spiritual Antichrist, priestless Old Believers did not practice those Christian rituals that could be performed only by ordained priests. There remained only those sacraments that could, according to long Christian practice,

---

32. Around two-thirds of all the manuscripts described or collected by archaeographers in the Upper Kama were liturgical, with Gospels, Apostles, trebniks, mineis, and triodions the most common. Together, these books provided nearly all the prayers and hymns necessary for priestless Old Believer services. Gospels included the text of the four New Testament Gospels; Apostles, the Acts of the Apostles and the Epistles; trebniks, prayers and rites for all occasions; the twelve mineis, the order of services for each month of the year; and triodions, prayers and hymns for the portions of the church year that varied with the date of Easter (see Pozdeeva 1996, 18–19).

be performed by laypeople when necessary: baptism and penance. On most occasions, neither of these sacraments performed by spiritual fathers took place within the regular liturgies of the council. In liturgical services, there were thus few moments that ritually and materially manifested differences among the gathered elders. In fact, the reverse was true. The role of a pastor in a service, I was told, was simply "to light the candles" in front of the icons at the beginning of the service and then begin the recitation of the opening prayers. To be sure, knowledgeable pastors often coordinated the rituals of the services by assigning roles, but nearly all the readings, hymns, prayers, prostrations, and crossings were undertaken by all members in unison or specifically arranged roles. Other significant relationships and responsibilities lay just beneath the practicalities of the service. In addition to rotating among members' homes as spaces in which to hold the liturgies, manuscripts and printed editions belonged to the religious community as a whole rather than to individual members. Termed *sobornye* (belonging to the council), they were cared for by the currently serving pastor and passed on at the end of that pastor's term. Council money was pooled to purchase candles, incense, or needed service books for the council as a whole.

The importance of elders' communal liturgical rituals and the significance of the boundary between laypeople and elders were connected. In the context of the elders' collective liturgies, prayers offered by one person who had fallen into sin could render ineffective the prayers of the entire gathered council of elders. Ritual contexts, in other words, created a mode of interconnected subjectivity among the assembled elders, such that the transgressive state endangering the soul of one could spread via contagion to the rest of the community of Christians. As was the case with pastors, one person fallen from the path could, if he or she prayed with other elders, lead everyone into darkness. Confession and penance, both of which were highly elaborated and frequently practiced in the Upper Kama, were thus designed to keep both individual elders and the small communities to which they belonged on the path to salvation.[33] Pastors heard confessions and meted out penances on behalf of, and, if necessary, in consultation with, the community of elders. Lesser offenses might require a certain number of bows in front of the icons; one elderly man in the Upper Kama recalled that a penance of hundreds of full prostrations a day for a week or more was not out of the ordinary—a difficult proposition for the elderly and infirm.

Although the most serious or unusual matters of discipline warranted the summoning of a general council of pastors from the surrounding villages, elders' transgressions were, for the most part, handled at the local level by the

---

33. The archaeographical collection of penitential texts from the Upper Kama is particularly large and includes copies of the *Trebnik* (which contained many penitential prayers); the *Skitskoe Pokaianie*, or *Hermit's Repentance;* and a large collection of penitential spiritual verse.

members of each community of elders, with the participation and guidance of their pastor. Serious transgressions, such as participating in a worldly marriage ceremony, might warrant excommunication from the community, after which the offending elder could not rejoin until penances were completed and a certain amount of time had passed. In the meantime, the expelled elder was to remain outside the interconnected subjectivity created by ritual occasions, lest his or her fallen state threaten the souls of other elders. Death during the time of expulsion meant that an elder's soul would not be prepared for heaven—thus making the prospects for salvation far more uncertain (although not, according to most, out of the question). In the Upper Kama, as among many groups of priestless Old Believers in Russia (see Paert 2004b), confession and penance thus retained their dual roles as a means of rehabilitation for those who had stepped off the path to salvation and as a way to mark and maintain the borders of the moral community from which they had been temporarily expelled.[34]

All these aspects of the ritual and prayer lives of elders could, I suppose, be shoehorned into an argument about the use of material practices in forging nonindividualist, collectivist subjectivities as a condition for salvation in the priestless Upper Kama. This would not be entirely wrong, but it would miss many of the other material practices—some of them individualizing—on which they depend. Moreover, to dwell on these distinctions above all others misses significant aspects of the ways in which residents of the Upper Kama themselves encountered and sought to avoid the world. These encounters occurred most regularly in their own households and revolved around the everyday materials of food and drink.

FOOD AND DRINK

Recall that Lukanin, the Russian Orthodox missionary who visited Sepych in the early 1860s, observed that "Christians"—his term for elders—did not interact with laypeople in relations of food, drink, or prayer. On occasions when elders gathered in homes to pray in the Upper Kama, the younger generations hosting them would prepare and serve a meal at the conclusion of the service (called a *trapeza,* after the communal meals in monasteries). In order to help keep the elders' consumption practices away from those of laypeople, elders arrived with their own individual dishes and spoons so as not to eat with the

34. These more public and communal dimensions of penance had, in the mainstream Russian Orthodox Church, fallen out of common practice by the mid- to late nineteenth century, taken over by the expanding disciplinary apparatus of the state (Freeze 1993). That such practices remained part of the background expectations and discourse of the Russian state lies behind Kharkhordin's innovative argument (1999, 35–74 and passim) that the injunctions to "reveal, admonish, and excommunicate" characteristic of medieval Russian Orthodoxy endured into the Communist Party practices in the Soviet era.

utensils of the lay household they were visiting.[35] Food was prepared separately for the elders, using cookware held separate from that used by laypeople. Elders ate together at the conclusion of the religious service, served by members of the younger generation; laypeople in attendance or hosting ate at a second, later seating, in many cases after the elders had already departed.[36]

This separation of the material practices of food and drink extended beyond the context of prayer services into everyday life as well. The modified semieremitic organization that predominated in the Upper Kama was particularly challenging for elders concerned with ritually preparing their souls for death by ensuring against the mixing of different kinds of material practices and contamination by the things of this world. As I have already noted, elders continued to live in their own households after joining the council, rather than in a monastery with one another or by themselves as hermits. This residence pattern placed in excruciatingly close proximity precisely those material practices that the elders had staked their salvation on holding apart. Anyone who has spent any time at all in an agricultural community knows that material practices involving food and drink are simply omnipresent. The production, exchange, storage, and consumption of food course though the space of the entire household and entangle all its members on a day-to-day basis. Over an agricultural cycle, multiple extended families are drawn into interconnected webs of working together in the fields, exchanging foodstuffs with one another, and eating and drinking together at festivals and other rituals.

Separating elders' food and drink from those of laypeople is thus a particularly dramatic way to mark their separation from the world. It also verges on the impossible, for a lifetime of intimacy and familiarity does not bear easy separation. In the small stove and at the table were the foods of the world that elders could not eat and dishes they could no longer use. Across the house—often across the room—from their celibacy were the sexual relationships of the next generation or generations. (One elder I knew, who considered herself to have given up on most of the taboos separating her from younger generations, nevertheless refused to sit on the bed in which her daughter and son-in-law slept.) All around, in the house and in the garden, hour by hour, were the material affairs of the world in which the younger generations participated

35. This practice, often called *chashnichestvo*, was not uncommon among priestless Old Believers (see, e.g., Paert 2004b, 284). The relationship of taboos to social organization was a classic topic in various incarnations of structuralist anthropology (e.g., Radcliffe-Brown 1952; Douglas 1966; Lévi-Strauss 1966). Although I certainly take some inspiration from that literature, especially as it concerns the relationship of morality and society (esp. Durkheim [1890] 1997, 1973; Valeri 1999), my primary concern is with material practice rather than social organization or deep structures of the human mind.

36. Chagin (2005) usefully traces the different practices associated with baking and eating bread through various rituals and exchanges in the Upper Kama. In some cases, for instance, the same stove could be used by elders and laypeople if the elders' fire was lit by embers from another fire.

fully and from which older generations sought distance. If the younger generations I knew are any guide to past practices, they were not always particularly
patient with the careful ritual prohibitions and worries of their parents and
grandparents.

MONEY AND LABOR

Taking up the indeterminacies of material practice also enables me to begin
a discussion of the ethics of worldly production and exchange in the Upper
Kama. Studies of Old Believers too often skip over the concrete ways in which
material practices judged to be on the outside of true Christianity work in
practice. It is easy to cast the rituals and prayers of a community of Old Believers against monolithic abstractions like modernity, the state, globalization, or
the world. After all, many Old Believers themselves do this with alacrity. But
our analyses should not rest here. Attending to the messiness and unpredictability of the full spread of material practices in particular times and places—
which Old Believers also do with alacrity—adds crucial dimensions to our understandings of how various ethical relationships and subjectivities are created
and transformed. If, for instance, one wants to piece together an ethical life by
cloistering oneself from the world, it matters a great deal how one understands
the world to manifest itself materially, how those manifestations change, and
how the resulting dilemmas are hashed out in practice.

Money, monetary exchange, and labor were issues of particular concern and
danger for ascetic elders in the Upper Kama. When the material practices to be
regulated and properly arranged moved outside the household's or commune's
food and drink, money often became the medium through which people interacted with one another. As a general form, money is a material incarnation
of a state's attempt to exert sovereignty over transactions among the people
it counts as its own. Money works by generating equivalencies and potential
transactions among the most disparate of objects and relationships; anything
is potentially transformable and alienable when brought into relationship to
the state's money. Although it need not be, money can easily be understood to
carry traces of the long, unknowable, and potentially dangerous chain of transactions that brought it to one's hands. As Keane shows with particular clarity
(2007, 270–84), currency objects and the assumptions about agency, subjectivity, and ethics that they often carry are thus prime candidates to become
significant axes of dispute among religious groups.

As Keane's analysis would suggest, money and labor in the Upper Kama
were important, and often contested, materials of ethics. Money, for instance,
entered into a debate, held sometime in the mid- to late 1850s and published in
1868, between the Russian Orthodox missionary Lukanin and an Old Believer
in Sepych. Nestled among many intricate disputes about the nature of the Antichrist, sacraments, and Christian and Russian history, there is a discussion

of whether religious books could be bought and sold and whether it was appropriate for the person performing sacraments to accept money. The missionary Lukanin argued in the affirmative on both counts, suggesting that money changed hands only to compensate for materials and labor. Such transactions, he argued, did not mean that the Word of God or the sacrament of baptism was itself being sold: "Any person values his labor, and no one is going to work for free; no one is going to give the materials necessary for publishing a book for free either" (Lukanin 1868, 444). His Old Believer interlocutor in Sepych, however, refused to accept this line of argument, insisting that these transactions did indeed imperil the true faith by bringing corrupting worldly money into a direct exchange relationship with the divine. The acceptance of money in exchange for sacraments and sacred books was, in this view, one more reason that the Russian Orthodox Church had slipped from the true path to salvation.

Other evidence also points to the salience of money and labor as significant, and often threatening, materials of ethics in the Upper Kama. As Pozdeeva (1982, 64) has shown, writings about money are quite common in the Old Believer manuscript record from the Upper Kama. Likewise, the brief comment by census takers in 1890 that households in Sepych Township "did not show" their elders is good evidence that religiously active Old Believers withdrew from the broader relations of production and exchange that were of so much interest to zemstvo statisticians. Well into the twentieth century, I was told, some elders steadfastly refused to accept pensions from the Soviet party-state.

Beyond elders' avoidance mechanisms, though, the worldly relationships of money and labor were central to the formation of laypeople's ethical sensibilities in their lives as serfs on the Stroganov estates. The material practices, moral communities, and everyday ethics of laypeople have been invisible in much of what I have covered so far, a consequence of the paucity of adequately local sources about serfdom for the period up to the middle of the nineteenth century. By the 1830s, however, we begin to get sporadic but substantial reports from Sepych about relationships of production and exchange in this corner of the northeast non-black-earth region. One brief example should be sufficient to illustrate, at least for the moment, my general insistence that material practices deemed by elders (and many scholars) to be outside Old Belief are in fact crucial arenas for the generation of ethical sensibilities and moral communities in Sepych—including those of the elders themselves. Attention to the actual movement of money and labor in particular cases also illustrates the ways in which peasant practices of production and exchange should be seen not as parts of a traditional system but as elements in fields of ethical practice and contestation that extend far beyond the Upper Kama.

In the summer of 1849, a serious hailstorm destroyed the crops of thirty-two families in the Sepych agricultural commune. At around the same time, a fire completely gutted a number of houses and grain stores in the nearby

Putino commune. These unexpected hardships generated a detailed paper trail of discussions about the proper obligations and relationships of serfdom that stretched from Sepych and Putino all the way up to Count S. G. Stroganov at his central office in St. Petersburg.[37] The serfs of Sepych and Putino appealed to the local offices of the Stroganov estates in the town of Ochër to ask for a reduction in the quitrent (*obrok*) that they owed the Stroganov family that year. Unable to grant such a reduction themselves, the officials in Ochër appealed to the next higher level of authority—the offices of the Stroganov landholdings in the Urals, based in the town of Il'insk, near Perm. The office answered definitively that no reductions or discounts should be given under any circumstances because it was the collective and exclusive responsibility of the agricultural communes themselves to meet their payments each year. Unanticipated losses caused by misfortunes such as hail and fire should be absorbed by the rest of the agricultural commune, not passed on to the Stroganovs. When the local officials in Ochër objected and appealed again on behalf of the residents of Sepych and Putino, citing the extreme poverty of the communes in question, the entire matter was forwarded to Count Stroganov himself. The count carefully looked over all the details and wrote back that "this one time, out of extreme mercy" he would grant a discount on obligations to the agricultural commune in Sepych. (Noting the bureaucratic confusion about the matter, he also ordered a full-scale review of policies for handling such requests across the family's landholdings in the Urals.)

This correspondence is interesting in the context of my preliminary discussion of material practice for two reasons. First, the correspondence points strongly to some of the central material practices through which the moral communities, ethical sensibilities, and inequalities of Russian serfdom were constructed: money, goods, and, not least, letters among bureaucrats. Second, it demonstrates in broad strokes the two primary circuits of exchange in which the serfs of the Upper Kama participated: responsibilities to one another in the context of a peasant commune and obligations to their landowners. These are, of course, the well-known structures of Russian serfdom, but we also see them here as material practices set in motion by unforeseen and unpredictable events. The events following the hailstorm and fire are undetermined: contested, negotiated, and worked out along connections and levels of bureaucracy extending all the way from Sepych to St. Petersburg. All manner of different expectations and claims about ethical obligations and how they should be realized through material practice enter into this single debate: serfs to one another in an agricultural community, different layers of estate bureaucracy to peasants and to one another, and the Count Stroganov himself to both his offices and his serfs. This correspondence suggests, in sum, that these sets of

---

37. See RGADA, f. 1278, op. 2, d. 2159, as well as the partial summary in Pushkov (2005a).

relations were never constructed and experienced in the same ways, much less in ways that usefully support the overdetermined abstractions so often foisted upon Russian peasants.

In introducing the materials of ethics that have long been central in the Upper Kama, I have sought to emphasize the ways in which material things and their movements could present ethical dilemmas and difficulties that demanded resolution on an ongoing, practical basis. What should be done about the threats to a council's ritual purity posed by a single elder's transgressions? How could the omnipresence of laypeople's food and drink in a peasant household be avoided? What was the appropriate response to unfortunate events like hailstorms and fires? The answers to these questions are not usefully rendered in overdetermined abstractions such as the inherent traditionalism of Old Belief, a peasant "mentality," or the famous "collective obligations" (*krugovaia poruka*) of peasant communes. They are matters of interconnected, underdetermined ethical practice to be traced and explored in as fine a grain as possible. To bring together the several strands of material practice I have been discussing and show the importance of attending to a quite local ethical repertoire as it unfolds, I turn next to several episodes in which the ethics of local Old Belief clashed with the moralizing discourses actively propounded by the tsar, Russian Orthodox Church, and Stroganov family on interlinked matters of central concern to all: marriage, sexuality, and the laboring households of serfdom.

"On Marriage"

Expectations about generation in Sepych have often intersected with expectations about gender, about the construction of women and men and the proper relationships between them.[38] Among priestless Old Believers, as well as in Eastern Orthodoxy more broadly, marriage was often the overarching rubric given to a plethora of issues and debates about gender and sexuality that extended far beyond the Christian sacrament (Paert 2003; compare Levin 1989, 10). Marriage was, for instance, an important topic in Old Believer theology. What were the natures of male and female human beings, and what was their purpose on earth in a world ruled by the Antichrist? What constituted proper sexual relations in and out of marriage? What was the role of marriage as a worldly and economic institution, especially when Old Believers looked past their own lives to the future of their communities? How should Old Believers respond to state attempts to regulate marriage and sexual practices?

---

38. "On marriage" is a marginal colophon, presumably added by an elder near Sepych, in a manuscript description of the priestless Old Believer debates on marriage discussed in this section; see ORKiR NB MGU, PV, 803, l. 539r.

These widespread dilemmas took on specific valences as elements of the ethical repertoire of the Old Believer Upper Kama. Marriage practices in Sepych, especially by the mid-nineteenth century, were suspended among the teachings of Old Believer theologians, the Stroganovs' interests in extracting labor and money from their lands, and the growing hostility of the state apparatus and Russian Orthodox Church to Old Believer marriage practices during the reign of Nicholas I. Debates and practices that fall under the "on marriage" rubric illustrate not only a crucial element of the ethical repertoire I have been exploring but also the ways in which ethical practice in the Upper Kama has been shaped at the intersection of very large-scale vectors of power. Here, as in so many other domains of life, the ambitions of Sepych's Old Believers to design and live by a set of precepts that would facilitate transcendence of a tainted world were nevertheless entangled in underdetermined flows of worldly material practice. In this case, the materials of ethics at hand were often human bodies: in sexual relationships, in laboring couples and families, and in the overarching question of whether there would continue to be new generations of priestless Old Believers in the world at all.

Marriage and sexuality were central to the ascetic aims of priestless Old Believer theology as it emerged in the formative years of Old Belief. In their mid-eighteenth century letter to the Upper Kama on the role of pastors, for instance, the Vyg fathers lamented, "O, spiritual fathers, how can you give your blessing to marriage?" They exhorted the Old Believers of the Upper Kama to "live chastely, that is, unmarried [*bezhenno*]."[39] The sacrament of marriage, in other words, had gone the way of all the other Christian sacraments that required an ordained priest; celibacy was to be preferred in the short time remaining before the end of the world. The monastic ideals of the generation of Pomortsy fathers in the north who composed this letter proved hard for the peasants of the Upper Kama to follow. Even the official views of Pomortsy theologians moderated in later years, as it proved difficult to simultaneously endorse full celibacy and to reproduce their own communities.[40] The Pomortsy view of marriage, then, or at least the one that emerged from the centers of Vyg and later Moscow, gradually shifted from the dim view enunciated in the on-pastors letter to a qualified endorsement, and in some cases even careful sacramentalization of marriage (see Paert 2004c, 560). By the early nineteenth century, wedding

---

39. ORKiR NB MGU, PV, 803, l. 263r–v.

40. The changing Pomortsy views on marriage and sexuality featured in already sharp disputes within and among groups of priestless Old Believers, disputes that were sharpest between the 1760s and the 1830s (see Crummey 1970, 115–23; Pera 1986; and, above all, Paert 2003). The Old Believers in and around Sepych were familiar with these broader debates on marriage, as well as with the nineteenth-century moderation in the central Pomortsy views, as summaries of these debates appear in several historical miscellanies from the Upper Kama. See, for example, ORKiR NB MGU, PV, 803, l. 310r–330r; 529r–39v. On broader Orthodox views of sexuality and marriage, see esp. Levin (1989).

ceremonies and the institution of marriage were permitted in Pomortsy communities across Russia, including in and around Sepych. Pomortsy elders and spiritual fathers in the Upper Kama, however, as firmly convinced as ever that the Nikonian reforms had eliminated the possibility of all sacraments from the world, did not preside over wedding rituals or even, in all cases, bless them. In contrast to many other priestless communities, elders in the Upper Kama were strictly prohibited from participating in wedding ceremonies and rituals.

Because none of these marriages were sanctified through the rituals of the Russian Orthodox Church, they were officially designated as civil marriages (*svodnye braky*) by the Russian state.[41] In rural areas such as the Upper Kama, these marriages were also intricately caught up in the institutions and rhythms of serfdom, for the laboring married couple (*tiaglo*) and its associated household comprised the most basic unit generating income for serf owners. Regulating and registering marriages could thus be an important aspect of administering an estate. Thus by the middle of the nineteenth century there was ample potential for conflict between, on the one hand, the local Old Believer position permitting marriage but not its sacramentalization or registration in the Russian Orthodox Church and, on the other hand, the interests and projects of the Russian state and its landholding aristocracy. When especially sharp conflicts about marriage practices arose in Sepych in the mid-nineteenth century, they did so precisely on the terrain where moralizing discourses met practical ethics.

I suggested in the introduction, following Corrigan and Sayer (1985), that one important element of the study of ethics is attention to the ways in which states or other powerful institutions can adopt a language of morality as a means to control or mobilize their populations, often in the face of perceived threats. By defining and seeking to enforce particular notions of morality, state officials project and attempt to achieve a coherence that might otherwise be exposed as fragmented and contingent. Russia during the reign of Nicholas I (1825–55) is a prime context in which to explore such moralizing discourses in Sepych, for Nicholas's campaigns against Old Believers and other religious dissenters were often couched precisely in the language of morality and proper family life (see also Paert 2004c). Furthermore, the active participation of Count S. G. Stroganov in the imperial commissions and St. Petersburg court life of the era meant that the Stroganov landholdings in the Urals—heavily populated by Old Believers—were among the main proving grounds for the tsar's efforts to reshape Russian morality. Linked offensives against Old Belief, civil marriage, and "sexual licentiousness" in the Upper Kama were carried out in earnest in the late 1840s, but their proximate origins lie in earlier decades, and their echoes reverberated for many years to come.

---

41. Only in 1874 did some Old Believer marriages receive a modicum of official state recognition.

Nicholas was, of course, hardly the first of the Romanovs to be concerned with the marriage and sexual practices of Russian subjects.[42] But as Richard Wortman has argued, the rule of Nicholas was nevertheless a departure from earlier projections of the tsar's power in that it "made the family a central symbol of the moral purity of Russian autocracy [such that a] violation of family morality would throw into doubt the moral foundations of autocratic rule" (1998, 82; see also 1995). In addition to the positive exemplars provided by the tsar's own family life that Wortman discusses in great detail, this reformulation of the basis of autocratic rule meant that violations of family morality across the empire became a threat demanding elimination. As the influential Metropolitan Filaret put it, marriages outside the Russian Orthodox Church simply "did not provide the basis for a good family."[43] Priestless Old Believer marriages were considered among the most dangerous and subversive, for many did not employ any sacramental rituals at all (as, for example, priestly Old Believer weddings did). For the vast portions of the rural population living on estates not directly administered by the Russian state, transforming the Russian family meant working not only through the revitalization of the Russian Orthodox Church but through serf owners and their extensive legal and administrative bureaucracies.

Here, Nicholas's new family-values campaign joined forces with landholding families' existing practice of issuing detailed and lengthy instructions for the bureaucratic, legal, and moral administration of serfs on their land. The premise of these sets of instructions was simple: that the maintenance of "moral order" on estates was fundamental to the generation of profits through quitrent and corvée labor.[44] In 1837, the Countess Sofia Vladimirovna Stroganova issued a new set of instructions for the family's landholdings in the Urals (the previous set dated to 1812).[45] After outlining the general administrative structure of the estates, it described the division of each region (*okrug*) into several agricultural communes and, at a lower level, into individual households with work teams of married couples. Her instructions also included extensive sections on religious (i.e., Russian Orthodox) and civic morality (*nravstevennost'*), as well as listing specific offenses against good order and the punishments that they should receive—from whippings with a birch rod to exile in Siberia.[46] "All

42. See the discussions of church control over marriage and sexual practices in Freeze (1989, 1990) and Kaiser (2003, 2006).

43. Quoted in Paert (2003, 200).

44. See esp. Melton (1990) on the linkage between instructions and profits from quitrent (*obrok*) or corvée labor (*barshchina*) to the maintenance of good order among serfs. Melton terms this arrangement "enlightened seigniorialism" and relates it to broader European attempts to create "well-ordered states."

45. See Kut'ev (2004) for an excellent and useful narrative history of the Stroganovs' administration of their estates in Perm Province.

46. RGADA, f. 1278, op. 2, d. 4421.

of my people," wrote the Countess, "are obligated to follow the Law of God and to...take part in the holy sacraments."[47] Accordingly, the instructions demanded and expected marriage for all serfs on the Stroganov estates and elaborated in special detail the punishments for extramarital sexual activity and licentiousness (*raspustvo*). They went so far as to include a yearly monetary fine for any family that had not yet married off those daughters who had turned twenty years old. Marriage, of course, meant the sacrament of marriage in a Russian Orthodox church—not the civil marriages and peasant wedding ceremonies that predominated in and around Sepych.

The Countess Stroganova's instructions on morality and good order in her lands may well have formed the basis for fines or even arrests of priestless Old Believers in the Upper Kama starting in 1837. If they did, we have no record of such punishments. In the middle of the 1840s, though, there was an explosion of prosecutions for marriage violations and sexual licentiousness across the Perm region and especially in Sepych. The reasons for this sudden concern with marriage and sexual morality were several. In the first place, there was the general shift to a vision, discussed by Wortman, of the Russian autocracy as rooted in moral family order. More specifically, Nicholas I's regime was shaken by the Polish Uprising in 1831 and several episodes of peasant unrest in Perm Province a decade later—episodes in which Old Believers played an important role (Paert 2004c, 563–64). Regulating Old Believer marriages and family structure thus appeared a particularly good way to shore up an autocracy that understood itself to be under threat.[48] At the same time, also at Nicholas's urging, a concerted mission against Old Belief in Perm Province had finally begun in 1830. A church was built in Sepych in 1833–35, providing at least the possibility for Russian Orthodox marriages and supervision of sexual practices. The church eliminated any excuses about the lack of a priest that local residents might have used to avoid sacraments in earlier years.

In 1846, Count S. G. Stroganov replaced his aunt at the helm of the family landholdings in Perm Province and promptly accepted an invitation to join the tsar's Secret Committee on Old Belief, formed in St. Petersburg in 1825.[49] The secret committee had outlawed Old Believer civil marriages in 1839, and Count Stroganov immediately began writing to his administrators in the Perm region asking for reports on morality, the number of civil marriages in each

47. Ibid., l. 39.
48. Paert provides an account of this period that focuses on the actions of the Holy Synod and tsar's secret committee (2003, 193–205).
49. RGADA, f. 1278, op. 2, d. 1533. On the founding of the secret committee in the reign of Aleksandr II, see Pera (1990). Although the secret committee was not especially active in the 1820s, it did dispatch a secret envoy to the Perm region to snoop on the situation of Old Believers in the Stroganov lands and report back to St. Petersburg (Nechaev [1826] 1894). Crummey (1970, 198–218) tracks the secret committee's offensives against the Vyg Monastery, which resulted in its destruction and the dispersal of its community in 1855.

region, and the efforts that had been put in place to end them.[50] Apparently not encouraged by the first reports he received back, Count Stroganov composed a supplementary set of instructions for the Perm landholdings, specifically designed to combat as many forms of extramarital sexual activity as possible. Point 1 of these new instructions, for instance, read, "It is forbidden for the heads of household...to take girls or women of unsatisfactory conduct into their houses in the guise of a lodger or a housekeeper." The remaining points—twenty-five of them in all—explicitly prohibited an extensive array of other possible arrangements whereby men and women of any age could find themselves sharing a residence with anyone other than their official spouse and immediate family members. The instructions also specified the punishments that were to be administered for those violating each of the points; they ranged from warnings and fines for first offenders to arrests and beatings for second offenders. Military conscription or exile to Siberia was prescribed for multiple offenses.[51]

Count Stroganov dispatched these orders in September of 1846 and requested periodic reports on the number of serfs who had been found guilty of each of the offenses.[52] By spring of 1848, he received statistical reports showing that nearly seven hundred of his serfs in the Perm region had been deemed licentious enough to warrant one of the punishments outlined in his supplementary instructions.[53] Sepych, however, appears to have demanded special attention. It was the only town in the vast Stroganov landholdings for which local officials drew up a special list of eighty-seven unmarried bachelors, listing their ages and precise reasons for not being married (which ranged from poor health to poverty to military service to the "desires of women").[54] Sepych was also among the only places that provided Count Stroganov, in 1848, with a detailed case-by-case accounting of each one of the thirty "depraved peasants" that had been caught in the struggle with licentiousness and how each incident had been resolved.[55] In each incident, not only were the appropriate punishments administered, but what the report termed "lovers" (*liubovnitsy*) were separated, usually with the girl returned to her parents' care. In several cases, men about to be charged as serial offenders fled to Siberia rather than face punishment in their home commune. The report does not make distinctions among, or allow any

50. See, for instance, RGADA, f. 1278, op. 2, d. 4855, l. 3.

51. RGADA, f. 1278, op. 2, d. 4604, l. 1–6.

52. Among several other letters emphasizing the importance that Count Stroganov placed on the battle with licentiousness and his expectations for full enforcement and reports, see RGADA, f. 1278, op. 2, d. 4855.

53. Statistics on civil marriages and sexual immorality take up a substantial portion of the correspondence between the Stroganovs' head office in Il'insk and St. Petersburg during this period. See, e.g., RGADA, f. 1278, op. 2, d. 463; f. 1278, op. 2, d. 4685; f. 1278, op. 2, d. 4666; f. 1278, op. 2, d. 4197, f. 1278, op. 2, d. 4672a, l. 23–ob.

54. RGADA, f. 1278, op. 2, d. 4670, l. 98–100.

55. RGADA, f. 1278, op. 2, d. 4604, l. 7–10.

insight into, how the immoral lovers themselves regarded their relationships. As a civil marriage cemented in a peasant wedding ceremony but not registered or sacramentalized? As an unmarried cohabitation combining sexual relationships with household labor?

The struggle with licentiousness in Sepych demonstrates how visions of morality set out by the tsar and caught up in much larger reorganizations of the ways in which the Russian autocracy conceptualized its rule manifested themselves in the Upper Kama. Count Stroganov, moreover, had ample reason to collaborate with the tsar's campaign on his lands. As Stephen Hoch (1986) has so persuasively argued, landowners' control over their serfs rested less on direct power than on a tacit alliance with family patriarchs in the villages. These family patriarchs, who substantially controlled marriage choices and alliances in their extended households, created a stable laboring environment that made (at least notionally) for steady profits for their landowners. Count Stroganov, new to the administration of his family's landholdings in 1846, had every reason to take up the tsar's cause against what he would likely have seen as unruly, immoral family behavior interfering with the collection of quitrent payments from the serfs of the Upper Kama.[56]

But how did this large-scale mid-nineteenth-century attempt to regulate ethics in Russia fare when it encountered the already-existing sensibilities and expectations about ethics, moral community, and ethical practice that were particular to Sepych? Although the ways in which residents of the Upper Kama responded to and creatively manipulated the campaigns against civil marriage are not visible in the Stroganov archives, we can discern their general shapes from other, albeit less easily dated, sources. It is tempting to posit that the campaigns of the 1830s and 1840s *created* the distinction between laypeople and elders: that, in other words, the Old Believers of the Upper Kama found that the best way to adapt to the joint thrusts of landlord, church, and state was to separate the worlds of marriage and labor from the ascetic practices of priestless Old Belief as thoroughly as possible. Such a direct causality seems, however, less likely than a gradual process of hardening generational distinctions that proceeded in tandem with the increasing regulation of rural Russia in the longer course of the nineteenth century. At the very least, however, we can say that the morality campaigns of the 1840s accentuated processes already taking place in priestless Old Believer theologians' debates on marriage and, at the same time, transformed them in conjunction with a whole suite of local ethical expectations.

Marriage in the Upper Kama, as I have already hinted in the discussion of pastors, evolved in dynamic interaction with other aspects of the local ethical

---

56. This alliance between landowners and tsar should not be taken for granted. A century earlier, the Demidov family's interest in maintaining their skilled Old Believer laborers in their Urals factories clashed with Anna I's campaigns against Old Belief (Hudson 2002). See also Bowman (2003).

repertoire. Much of the temporality of the divide between laypeople and elders emerged from transitions in and out of married life and prohibitions on mixing the distinct fields of ethical practice indicated by each status. Those young teenagers who did attend religious services with the elders did so only until they married or, at any rate, until they took up the relationships of worldly production and reproduction. It was usually only after the death of a spouse that those in older generations made the decision to rejoin the community of elders. That is, a refusal of sexual relationships joined the refusal of food, drink, money, and labor as a material way in which elders sought to reorient their everyday practices away from what they understood to be this world and thereby to create the conditions of possible salvation. The most frequently noted manifestation of this separation was that elders in the Upper Kama were not even allowed to attend lay wedding services (except perhaps for watching from the doorway, according to some accounts) or to sing wedding songs. They often received strict penances if they violated this taboo, and full participation in wedding services could result in temporary excommunication from the religious community. Chagin recounts the story of one elderly man, a greatly esteemed conductor of weddings, who delayed his entry into the community of elders until he was eighty-three because, in his own words, he "wanted to live it up a bit more, to carouse at weddings" (*khotel eshche zhit' vvoliu, guliat' na svad'bakh*) (1998a, 286).

In the absence of elders, the weddings of laypeople in the Upper Kama were variants of the more general wedding customs of the peasant regions of the Urals—typically three-day affairs involving multiple feasts, initially separately for bride and groom and then, after the first day, together with extended families and many guests.[57] Worobec (1995, 162) shows that, across rural Russia, it was the communal recognition of the union between bride and groom celebrated in the peasant wedding ritual (*svad'ba*) that was more valued than the Russian Orthodox rites of wedding (*venchanie*). This was even more so in priestless Old Believer communities of the Upper Kama, where the minor role elsewhere reserved for the Russian Orthodox priest, whether performed at a church or in the home of the groom, was altogether absent (at least until the construction of Sepych's mission church in 1833–35). In place of a religious functionary and sacrament, couples in the Upper Kama who chose to get married bowed to their parents and asked for blessings. The best man (*bol'shoi druzhok*) also played a correspondingly larger role in these weddings, organizing all the events and moving the wedding from one stage to the next (Chagin 1998a).

In the era of campaigns against civil marriages, one of the primary responses to the Stroganovs' morality campaigns in Sepych, it seems, derived from this

57. For more detailed accounts of wedding ceremonies in the Upper Kama, see Nikitina (1982, 106–11), Chernysheva (1982, 132–38), Makashina (1992), and Chagin (1992, 1998a). Descriptions of marriage rituals more broadly in the Urals can be found in Aleksandrov (1989).

local expectation that marriage was squarely a matter of "this world" and of little concern to the elders. Although this lack of regulation of marriage and worldly sexuality by proper religious authorities (and therefore a low marriage rate and, in the eyes of state officials, rampant licentiousness) attracted the attention of those concerned with bringing proper morality to Sepych in the first place, this very same indifference on the part of elders provided a convenient response that would satisfy the state: getting married in the Russian Orthodox Church. More than a few couples did just this. Indeed, Stroganov officials charged with carrying out the campaign against civil marriages often warned that the fact that Old Believers were agreeing to get married in the Russian Orthodox Church did not mean that they had truly given up their schismatic ways. In fact, many Old Believers in Perm Province went so far as to purposefully hold their weddings in Russian Orthodox churches far from their homes, the better to ensure that they did not have to become regular members of a parish community.[58] On one occasion in 1862, church officials in Sepych summoned the police to arrest an elder who had prohibited a young girl from marrying in the church, demanding instead that she enter a civil marriage (see Chagin 1992, 2001). The very fact that Sepych's Russian Orthodox priest summoned the authorities in this case suggests that a good number of couples did, in fact, marry in Sepych's Russian Orthodox church in the period between 1846 and 1862.

In most cases, all available evidence suggests, this strategy for appeasing demands for a new morality and family structure did not produce much loyalty to the Russian Orthodox Church among the local population. Nor, if some of the stories I discuss in chapter 2 are true, did they cut down on what authorities deemed licentious behavior. Many local Old Believers, after marrying in the Russian Orthodox Church, simply went about their worldly lives as before and joined the priestless elders when the death of a spouse ended their worldly marriage. A worldly marriage in the Russian Orthodox Church might not have thrilled the priestless elders, but neither did it, in and of itself, prohibit joining them. After all, everyone who joined the community of elders had been living in the world for decades. Although likely a common tactic in the aftermath of Nicholas I's campaigns against marriage, this practice also does not seem to have outlasted the morality campaigns themselves. By the 1890s, the metrical books for the Russian Orthodox church in Sepych (which record baptisms, marriages, and funerals) listed over a dozen marriages each year. Almost none of the surnames listed, however, is among those that have been common in Sepych for centuries.[59] Those who married in Sepych's church were, as several

---

58. RGADA, f. 1278, op. 2, d. 1543.

59. See, for example, AOAVR, f. 112, op. 2, d. 5; 15. I have found nothing to suggest that late-nineteenth-century Old Believers in Sepych married in Russian Orthodox churches elsewhere in the Perm region.

oral accounts of the church's influence indicate, far more often outsiders coming to Sepych for market days in the postemancipation period.

IN exploring debates, practices, and campaigns associated with the broad category of marriage in the Upper Kama, I have traced two intertwined sets of transformations in local ethical sensibilities. The first of these was a theological decision to permit marriage and sexual reproduction in the world at all, one in which the Pomortsy Old Believers of Sepych joined the rest of their concord throughout Russia. The second transformation, far more particular to the Upper Kama and caught up in the morality campaigns of Nicholas I, involved folding marriage and worldly sexuality into a strict division of the worlds designed to preserve the possibility of salvation through asceticism in the face of steadily increasing contact with, and regulation by, outsiders.

However much these aspirations failed in the untidiness of material practice, I am arguing, they also had important implications for the shape of local ethical expectations about gender and generation. The most crucial artifact of the ways in which debates about gender and generation played out in the early history of Sepych was a significant degree of separation between biological and social reproduction. Biological reproduction became resolutely an affair of the married middle generations, immersed as they were in the relationships and material practices associated with the labor, money, food, drink, and sexuality of this world. Significant elements of social reproduction, however, shifted to the generation of elders and its relationships with pre-marriage-age children. Knowledge of the prayers, rituals, and texts of Old Belief was, it seems likely, passed on to younger generations while married members of the middle generation labored in the fields: religious education and instruction in Church Slavonic by elders went hand in hand with child care. Then, upon marriage, the embodied practice of many of these Old Believer rituals—and therefore the practical, material construction of the subjects and communities they worked to create—would enter a period of dormancy that could stretch for decades until the elders beckoned anew. Outsiders wanting to remake ethical relationships and subjects in Sepych have often not understood that crucial aspects of local social reproduction and central arenas of self-fashioning had long since been evacuated from the worldly relationships and materials of ethics associated with marriage and labor in the world. If the mid-nineteenth-century campaigns to install a new kind of morality in Sepych did not cause this evacuation, then they certainly solidified its usefulness in the absorption and diversion of powerful attempts to reshape the ethical field of the Upper Kama. If one could have a Russian Orthodox marriage and subsequently join the elders, then why not join the elders after a socialist marriage?

Each of the elements of the ethical repertoire of the Upper Kama I have introduced here will return, in new configurations and contexts, in later chapters.

Although none of these elements on its own is without precedent or correlate in Russian history, I have argued that the moral communities, ethical subjects, and materials of ethics orienting life in and around Sepych began to articulate into a specific, identifiable repertoire between the arrival of Brother Grigorii from Vyg in the early eighteenth century and the morality campaigns of Nicholas I and Count S. G. Stroganov in middle of the nineteenth century. In tracing the genesis and early history of this ethical repertoire, I have drawn frequent attention to local visions of Christian harmony and aspirations for achieving salvation from a fallen, frustratingly mercurial world. Although such aspirations, visions, and successes are central—and underappreciated—aspects of ethics, focusing too much on them partially obscures the relationships of power and inequality, discord and disagreement, that also suffuse human attempts to reflect on and construct ethical lives. Particularly dramatic evidence of these dimensions of ethics in the Upper Kama comes from the postemancipation period.

2 *Faith, Family, and Land after Emancipation*

> In the end times, there will be many gods…and eight thousand
> divisions in the faith…just like a net woven across the world by
> the devil to catch Christian souls so that they cannot know true faith
> and baptism and repentance. And the people will be in great confu-
> sion and discord and schisms, and they will not know where to come
> to know the true faith.
> — *On the Division*, a manuscript written in the Upper Kama in 1888[1]

In 1888, after twenty-two years of rancor, the priestless Old Believers of the Upper Kama divided against one another in a bitter schism that would endure through the Soviet period and into the twenty-first century. Although differences of opinion and interpretation had flared many times before, they had largely been contained by the decentralized structures of conciliar authority in place in the Upper Kama, supplemented by occasional intervention from the Vyg elders in the north. In the decades following the emancipation of the serfs in 1861, however, ripples of disagreement about religious authority, sexual morality, and the proper relationship between the worlds of work and ascetic prayer exploded into a full-scale schism.[2] Beginning in 1866, elders and laypeople were forced to take sides—sometimes against friends, relatives, and neighbors—in an expanding dispute between two influential spiritual fathers and their flocks. Despite several attempts to convene general councils that would quell the acrimony and "put anger in its place," by

---

1. ORKiR NB MGU, PV, 1118, l. 653v–54r. This passage likely refers to the apocalyptic imagery in Matthew 24.
2. By the time controversy struck the Upper Kama in the postemancipation period, the northern settlements of priestless Old Believers, led by Vyg, had been largely silenced by the same state campaigns against Old Belief that affected the Upper Kama during the reign of Nicholas I. The Preobrazhenskoe Cemetery complex in Moscow, a successor to the Vyg settlements as the center of priestless Old Belief, did not rise in influence until the early years of the twentieth century. In 1866–88, the Old Believers of the Upper Kama were left to discern the true Christian path to salvation on their own.

1888 the two factions had traded polemical manuscripts containing multiple anathemas, detailed accusations of heresy, and vicious diatribes born of a Christian community's broken dreams of harmony. The Maksimovskie (mak-SIM-ov-ski-e), as one group came to be called, took their name from the spiritual father Maksim Zhdanov; the Dëminskie (DYO-min-ski-e) took theirs from the village of Dëmino, a center of opposition to Maksim not far from Sepych (see map 2 in the introduction).

This *razdel,* or division, as it was still called when I lived in Sepych, occurred in the same years as the more general turmoil permeating the Russian countryside after Aleksandr II's emancipation of the serfs in 1861. In these decades, the former serfs of Sepych Township were struggling to adjust to shifting relationships of nascent agrarian capitalism, including land reform, marketization, new possibilities for wealth accumulation, and the creation of new organs of local government. These worldly dislocations of the postemancipation period were, I suggest, intimately related to the schism between Maksimovskie and Dëminskie elders. Along with generations of townspeople and villagers in the Upper Kama, this chapter asks how and why the schism of 1866–88 happened. Was it the result of stubborn disobedience to the authority of a local council of spiritual fathers, as some maintained at the time? Did it begin, as others countered, with one spiritual father accumulating vast amounts of wealth and inappropriately mixing worldly and spiritual affairs? Or was the whole dispute, as later generations of townspeople in Sepych insisted when I inquired, "over a woman"?

The surviving accounts of the schism agree on very little, making it impossible to offer a single, unified retelling of what Maksim Zhdanov and his fellow spiritual fathers fought over, let alone how their falling out was related to the broader transformations of the immediate postemancipation era. I use this overabundance of explanations for the schism for two related purposes. First, in the course of working through the available written and oral sources, I develop my own understanding of the roots of religious discord in the postemancipation Upper Kama, one that rests not on a consensus view of what happened but on the shifting expectations about ethical practice that informed the positions and opinions advanced by all sides. Second, the events of the schism serve as a route into my principal goal of continuing to elaborate the elements of the ethical repertoire of townspeople in Sepych. The schism, in sum, opens a window onto the comprehensive transformation of the moral communities, materials of ethics, and kinds of ethical practice that had organized relationships and expectations in the Upper Kama for the preceding century and a half. The ethical regime of serfdom was coming to an end. A wide array of forces extending far beyond the Upper Kama now intersected to inform struggles over the emergent ethical regime of the postemancipation years.

A word on the sources I employ in this chapter is necessary. Our current understandings of the Russian countryside in the pre- and immediate postemancipation periods are heavily informed by scholars' creative analyses of state surveys and statistics, ethnographers' and geographers' questionnaires, administrative and bookkeeping records of landholding families, and material from the township (*volost'*) court system. Although I make some use of survey, census, and limited ethnographic data from the local organs of self-government (*zemstva*), many of my claims rest on a pair of sources that offers uncommon—if not unique—glimpses into the ethical worlds and struggles of a Russian peasant community after emancipation. As the disputes of the 1860s crystallized into schism, both Maksimovskie and Dëminskie factions of elders composed lengthy documents indicting and anathematizing the other side. These manuscripts are locally termed *podlinniki o razdele,* or "original documents about the division" (the phrase is as awkward in modern Russian as it is in English). Although the Old Believer scribes of the Upper Kama copied and recopied hundreds of texts composed elsewhere, the two manuscripts about the schism are far and away the lengthiest known texts of entirely local composition. The Maksimovskie text is over five thousand words, the Dëminskie still longer at around seven thousand. The several surviving editions of each, most of them stitched into historical miscellanies, are written in careful semi-uncials, with pervasive archaisms, Church Slavonicisms, and citations to Scripture, church fathers, and canon law.[3]

Given the high literacy of these peasant authors and their audiences at the time, and thus the peculiarity of my key sources, I should reiterate at this point that my goal is not to generalize from Sepych and the Upper Kama to the Russian peasantry or even to Old Believer peasant communities. The Russia-wide spread of literacy as a catalyst for religious and social change in the postemancipation period is thus of less consequence for the case I discuss here than in many other areas of rural Russia (Brooks 1985; Chulos 2003). Rather, I aim first to particularize—to explore the fine grains of ethical life at a particular time and place and to situate them at the convergence point of much larger processes. It is precisely through this level of ethnographic and historical detail that broader, although not necessarily generalizable or representative, propositions about ethics can be usefully generated.

3. As is usually the case when dealing with manuscripts, there are subtle differences among the surviving versions of each manuscript, the results of shifting orthographies and what paleographers call "scribal error." These differences, while of great importance for linguistic and paleographic analysis, are not significant for the arguments I make here. I have compared versions as much as possible in the passages I translate, but I rely primarily on the Maksimovskie version published as Smorgunova (1982) (see also ORKiR NB MGU, PV, 1996) and the Dëminskie version at ORKiR NB MGU, PV, 1118, l. 653r–73v. To cut down on clutter, I do not provide page-level citations for every quotation from the manuscripts below. Although my archaeographer colleagues collected versions of these manuscripts in the Upper Kama as early as the 1970s, they have to date published almost no sustained commentary on or analysis of the manuscripts themselves.

The Maksimovskie Account of the Division: Disobedience, Interconnected Subjectivities, and Contagion

The version of events recounted in the Maksimovskie manuscript attributes the division to the refusal of elders from the village of Dëmino to obey a series of general councils composed of elders from all over the Upper Kama. The Maksimovskie manuscript begins:

> On the splitting of our true Orthodox Christian Pomortsy faith. There has been a division with those from Dëmino and Kuliga, in the year 7374 from the creation of the world, the ninth indict, the year 1866 from the birth of Christ. It first began near the town of Sepych in the community headed by the spiritual father Maksim Grigor'evich and Tat'iana Petrovna.[4]

The manuscript then alternates between narratives of specific alleged transgressions and the deliberations and rulings of six councils called, ultimately without success, to bring the elders from Dëmino into line. Because of its focus on matters of religious discipline and authority, the Maksimovskie account sheds further light on some of the configurations of power that shaped patterns of ethical practice and boundaries of moral community in the Upper Kama. I have already discussed the ways in which pastors' power derived not from a hierarchical institution (such as a priesthood) but from election by the members of a small community confirmed and blessed by neighboring pastors already in office. As the Maksimovskie manuscript makes clear, much of pastors' power following installation rested on their authoritative interpretation of religious texts. But what did it mean to issue authoritative interpretations—and to enforce them—in a radically decentralized and resolutely council-driven structure of religious authority? The years following emancipation, the Maksimovskie manuscript suggests, pushed decentralized religious authority in the Upper Kama up to, and then beyond, its breaking point.

---

4. The dating of the schism is somewhat unclear. Both Maksimovskie and Dëminskie manuscripts begin with the dispute in Dëmino in 1866 (a date confirmed in both manuscripts by the additional dating from the creation of the world and the reference to the ninth indict; fifteen-year indict cycles function as calendrical "check digits"). However, the Maksimovskie version has all six councils taking place in the course of a single summer, while the Dëminskie version places the final council in 1888. It would be easy to see this 1888 date as an error (scribal or otherwise) except that these manuscripts are not given to this kind of error: every single one of the dozens of citations to Scripture, canon law, and church fathers in both manuscripts is absolutely precise across multiple copies. Moreover, the Church Slavonic numbering system does not leave 6s looking at all like 8s. I have opted to see the schism as gradually hardening over two decades, but my overall analysis would not be substantially undercut if everything did indeed happen in 1866. No known additional sources provide confirmation of either date.

IN the spring of 1866, according to the Maksimovskie manuscript, the spiritual father Grigor'evich of Dëmino, his companion Petrovna, and another elder, Davyd, celebrated the service for the Annunciation of the Blessed God-Bearer (as Eastern Orthodoxy terms Mary) at the home of Gerasim Maksimovich on the Friday before Easter.[5] The three had also agreed to celebrate Easter—services would have begun the Saturday evening before Easter Sunday—at Gerasim Maksimovich's house. Between the two holiday services, however, the three elders were called away to sing the funeral canons for someone who had died nearby. Following the funeral services, Grigor'evich and Petrovna returned to Gerasim Maksimovich's house to rest and then begin preparations for Easter. Davyd, however, returned to his own house. When it came time for the Easter services, Davyd did not return as had been agreed. Instead, and contrary to the original plans, Davyd's mother arrived to summon Grigor'evich and Petrovna to Davyd's house for the service. After a brief quarrel, with Petrovna angrily claiming, "They already have all of the food and drink prepared here...it isn't good [to move now]," Grigor'evich prevailed, and they all went to Davyd's house for the Easter services. A second quarrel broke out when Davyd, for reasons that are not described, forbade Petrovna's young niece to sing in the choir. Petrovna, we are told, spent the whole Easter service in tears as a result of Davyd's arrogance.

In order to address these issues, Grigor'evich and Petrovna called for a general council of spiritual fathers in the week following Easter. On the day of the council, several of the elders encountered Davyd at the market and summoned him to attend. Davyd asked, "What will the council be about?" They responded, "Come and you'll find out." When the council began that evening, however, neither Davyd nor Grigor'evich was in attendance. The gathered elders and spiritual fathers sent one emissary and then another for Grigor'evich, and he was finally brought to the council. Davyd did not come at all. The council then opened its deliberations by selecting Maksim Egorovich (Zhdanov)—later to become leader of the Maksimovskie—as reader. Apparently setting aside whatever disputes the council had been called to address in the first place, Maksim stood and read from the Canons of the Third Ecumenical Council, as written in the *Kormchaia Kniga*: "If a metropolitan or a bishop refuses and does not come to a council, then he wants to plan or plot something, and then let

5. More fully, Maksim Grigor'evich, Tat'iana Petrovna, and Davyd Ivanovich. I follow the manuscript and common practice in many areas of rural Russia in using only patronymics to refer to Maksim Grigor'evich and Tat'iana Petrovna. In the present case, this also avoids the confusion that might potentially arise from the fact that the primary spiritual fathers involved in the schism were both named Maksim—Maksim Grigor'evich on what was to be the Dëminskie side, Maksim Egorovich Zhdanov on what would be the Maksimovskie side. "Companion" is my awkward term for Petrovna's relationship to Grigor'evich. The nature of Petrovna's dealings with Grigor'evich, Davyd, and Maksim Zhdanov is unclear from the manuscripts, although see my discussion below on the pivotal role that later stories of the schism appear to have assigned to Petrovna.

him be excommunicated," and "If a layperson shall go against the council, let him be excommunicated; if a cleric, then let him be stripped of his rank."

The manuscript's narrative continues: "Maksim Egorovich read these laws, walked out from behind the table, sat on the bench, and said, 'How do you decide this matter, fathers and brothers, according to the laws or not?'" Everyone gathered at the council—elders and some laypeople—agreed, saying, "How can we go against the laws? We must keep Davyd in order." Davyd, they decided, was to be excommunicated for not obeying the summons to attend the council. The council members then turned to Grigor'evich, Davyd's pastor and spiritual father in Dëmino, and asked whether he was in agreement. Although with some hesitation about his ability to control Davyd, Grigor'evich responded in the affirmative: "As the laws excommunicate, so too do I excommunicate." The elders brought the council to a close and reiterated their charge to Grigor'evich to "keep your [spiritual] child [Davyd] in order" and not pray with him or accept him at services during the period of his excommunication.

At this point, some readers may be skeptical that things really unfolded in this way, or that a disagreement over where to hold an Easter service or absence from a council could really lead to excommunications or a full-blown division in the faith. If things were really this sensitive and elders this touchy, how could the community have held together for more than five minutes, much less 150 years? My response is *not* to argue that Old Believers were particularly strict about such matters of church law and ritual and should therefore be taken at their word that these offenses were very serious. In fact, as I discuss shortly, many laypeople and elders in the Upper Kama itself—both at the time and more recently—were also skeptical of this account. Thus we do not need to decide between taking religion seriously (i.e., accepting and analyzing what some would see as outlandish or illogical religious statements at face value) and coming up with external causes or explanations that religious practitioners themselves might not recognize. These different styles of explanation are already at play in the ethically saturated debate in question. We can take religious claims seriously *and* adduce certain other explanations without departing from the field of local understandings.

With this brand of analysis in mind, I want to linger on the first council described in the Maksimovskie manuscript, for it points to central aspects of the ways in which religious authority over the formation of ethical subjects and the maintenance of Christian moral communities was conceptualized and practiced in the Upper Kama (even if not always very completely or very successfully). The internal logic of the Maksimovskie account is significant even if many in the Upper Kama themselves considered its narrative only a partial or heavily redacted version of the events that led to the schism of 1866–88.[6]

---

6. Here I take some inspiration from Michael Cherniavsky's classic treatment of Old Belief (1966), which insisted on the importance of attending to the precise language and logic of Old

As portrayed in the Maksimovskie manuscript, all six councils of 1866–88 closely followed the general Eastern Christian practice of collective deliberation as a means to reach authoritative decisions on moral and doctrinal matters. The elders gathered near Sepych in the week after Easter conferred in the same manner as bishops and metropolitans had done for more than a millennium. They read, weighed, and applied a triad of textual authorities: the writings of church fathers, Old and New Testament Scriptures, and the pronouncements of earlier councils—especially the Seven Ecumenical Councils (see esp. Pelikan 1974, 23). The canons of the Third Ecumenical Council read out by Maksim Zhdanov in 1866, for instance, were a quite appropriate basis on which to excommunicate Davyd. While the first two ecumenical councils (in 325 at Nicea and 381 in Constantinople) codified aspects of Christian doctrine, the Third Ecumenical Council, held at Ephesus in 431, was called mainly to pronounce anathemas on the heretic Nestorius and his followers. Bishops who voiced their support for Nestorius by not attending the council were stripped of their rank. So, too, in this logic, could Davyd be excommunicated for refusing the summons to council he had received in the market earlier that day. Indeed, it was only through reference to these kinds of authorities that Davyd could be properly excommunicated—removed from the moral community of ascetic Christian elders and returned to the world.

Robert Crummey has rightly suggested that it is useful to see groups of Old Believers as "textual communities" (1993b, 707; see also Stock 1983). Although Crummey's work has concentrated on the formation of an early Old Believer canon in the seventeenth century (1994), the later Old Believers of the Upper Kama were just as devoted to the preservation and interpretation of a corpus of Christian writings (see also Brooks 1985, 25–26). Archaeographers who combed the area around Sepych in the 1970s and 1980s cataloged and collected thousands of old Cyrillic printed books and manuscripts, many no longer in use at the time (Ageeva et al. 1994; Pozdeeva 2003). Their brilliant scholarship on "book culture" (*knizhnost'*) has proven that many Old Believers in the Upper Kama were inveterate bibliophiles. They lovingly preserved pre-Nikonian books and manuscripts; assembled and maintained communal libraries; hand bound diverse texts together into thematic miscellanies; and copied, recopied, and restored old editions.[7] Indeed, the work of individual copyists such as the prolific "Master Sergei," whose work dates to the mid-nineteenth century, can often be discerned by comparing the scribal hands and

---

Believer theological discourse. My analysis, however, is directed toward local expectations and struggles rather than Russia-wide shifts in religious and political theology.

7. This is a massive and enormously impressive body of scholarship. For overviews, see Pozdeeva (1982, 1992, 1996, 1998, and 2001). On citationality, see Kobiak (1992); on the intersection of oral and written traditions, see Smorgunova (1992); on libraries, see Rovinskoi (1999); on marginal inscriptions in manuscripts, see Pozdeeva (2005); on reading and singing, see Makarovskaia (2005) and Pozdeeva and Makarovskaia (2008).

marginal notations of manuscripts written in the Upper Kama (see esp. Smilianskaia and Kobiak 1994).

The relationship of Old Belief as a textual community to the shaping of ethical practice in the Upper Kama is of most interest to me here. As is evident in the
Maksimovskie recounting of the first council of 1866, the power to discipline
and shape ethical subjects like Davyd and to police the borders of a Christian
moral community like the one in Dëmino was substantially located in texts
as they were authoritatively interpreted and applied by pastors and councils.
Precisely which texts were adduced as evidence could be an item of dispute,
as could the motives or probity of particular elders or pastors (as we shall
see shortly). And, of course, a whole council could be assailed as illegitimate.
But both Maksimovskie and Dëminskie manuscripts agreed that the ultimate
sources for the making of proper Christian selves and communities lay in a
correct, conciliar reading and interpretation of the textual guidelines set down
by Holy Scripture, church fathers, and preceding councils. As Grigor'evich put
it succinctly at that first council in 1866, "As the law excommunicates, so too
do I excommunicate."

This textual dimension of ethics in the Upper Kama rested on a particular
materiality and a particular kind of historical consciousness. To participate
in a council was often to write oneself into Christian history, to leave a material record at once full of citations to the past and durable enough to guide
the deliberations of future councils.[8] In addition to their elaborate citational
apparatus, for instance, both manuscripts about the schism carefully situate themselves in Christian time and space in order to accomplish this task
effectively. The Dëminskie section analogous to the Maksimovskie opening
quoted above reads, for instance, "We describe the division [razdelenie] of the
faith in the year 1866, the ninth indict, Perm Province, Okhansk region, in the
area around Sepych Township... in the domain of the spiritual father Maksim
Grigor'evich and the deaconess Tat'iana Petrovna."[9] The division of 1866–88

---

8. Chagin has written extensively on historical consciousness in the Upper Kama and elsewhere
in the Perm region (1999). However, he poses the central question of historical consciousness as
"What do the peasants know about history?" I prefer not to assume an "objective" existing history against which peasant knowledge can be measured and instead to inquire into the various
ways that people in the Upper Kama came to understand and encounter any kind of past. Although
the manuscripts about the schism of 1866–88 are the most dramatic instances in which the Old
Believers of the Upper Kama wrote themselves into Christian history as they understood it, more
everyday practices such as inscribing books (e.g., Pozdeeva 2005) and writing births and deaths
into a family psalter accomplish a similar task. Relying on field research among Old Believers in
Canada, David Scheffel has proposed the "iconic principle" as the dominant mode of knowing
the past in Old Believer communities: "[A]ll representations of orthodoxy must be authenticated
copies of ancient and unchanging models" (1991, 224). Although I find this analysis instructive
for understanding attitudes toward manuscripts in the Upper Kama, it does not completely explain
how past, present, and future met and mingled around Sepych—even among elders.

9. ORKiR NB MGU, PV, 1118, l. 654r. Not all councils left material traces, but at least several
called in the mid-twentieth century did. For a priestless division in neighboring Viatka Province

3. Old printed books set out in preparation for a priestless service, 1994.

was so wrenching, so pivotal, and the ethical stakes understood to be so high that both groups poured an enormous amount of energy into leaving a detailed, material, historically situated account of the other side's transgressions and the deliberations of councils. The manuscripts, then, reveal a particular kind of ethical reasoning and accounting to which both sides resorted in a tumultuous time. Nevertheless, for all their animosity, the manuscripts' modes of calling the other side to account are remarkably similar in their styles of textual argumentation, in their very materiality, and in their ways of knowing Christian past and present. We shall see later on that other elements of ethics in the Upper Kama at the time rested on quite different materialities and brands of historical consciousness, but let us first return to the events of the summer of 1866 as told by the Maksimovskie.

Three days after the general council at which Davyd was excommunicated, Grigor'evich went again to Davyd's house for a service commemorating the death of one of Davyd's family members. Grigor'evich, however, mentioned nothing to Davyd about the excommunication, and the two prayed together. Only after the service, as they rose from eating to depart, did Grigor'evich say to Davyd, "Now, Davyd Ivanovich, you are on your own. The council has

---

that left similar documents, beginning with time and place and including similar kinds of evidence, see Iserov (2004, 82–85).

forbidden me to pray with you." As it happened, other elders were also attending the commemoration service, and one of them challenged Grigor'evich on the wisdom of not mentioning the excommunication to Davyd before the two had prayed and eaten together. Grigor'evich is reported to have replied, "If we had not accepted Davyd [at the service], he would not have fed us."

Reports of what had transpired at Davyd's house quickly made it to the participants at the first council, who, "in great sorrow," summoned a second council a week later to reckon with Grigor'evich's disobedience. At this council, Maksim Zhdanov and the gathered spiritual fathers again consulted the sacred texts. They found it written in both the *Kormchaia Kniga* and the *Kniga o Vere* (*Book of the Faith*) that if a Christian prayed with someone who had been excommunicated, he or she must also be expelled. They cited as evidence Canons 33 and 39 of the Council of Laodicea (held in ca. 363–64), which expressly forbade praying and feasting with heretics and those whom the church had excommunicated. But just as the council prepared to expel Grigor'evich for praying and eating with the already excommunicated Davyd, Grigor'evich objected and begged them to reduce his punishment. Instead of excommunication, he offered to be "a simple elder [*prostets*]" and promised, "I will no longer attend to spiritual affairs." The council heeded his request and decided not to excommunicate him, appointing a certain Ivan Mikhailovich to be pastor in Dëmino and ruling that Grigor'evich could assist as an elder but could neither baptize children nor act as confessor.

The second council turned out to be no more effective in quelling the dispute than the first. The laypeople of Dëmino promptly objected to the decision of the general council to remove their pastor. Elected representatives from among them addressed the third, fourth, and fifth councils that were called to deal with the expanding and deepening divide. Each time, the gathered spiritual fathers consulted the sacred books, debated the issue, and attempted to put an end to the rift by finding laws and precedents that would either isolate Grigor'evich more effectively or, as many laypeople demanded, permit his forgiveness and reinstallation. Grigor'evich, despite his initial vow to become a simple elder, continued to baptize and hear confessions on demand. On at least one occasion, it seems, he did so with the tacit permission of a member of the general council. Eventually, a sixth and final council was held in the village of Viatkini, but by this time Grigor'evich and several of his sympathizers refused to attend. The spiritual fathers, including Maksim Zhdanov, promptly pronounced anathemas on all the absent spiritual fathers. They justified their decision with a lengthy list of citations to authority—by far the longest in the manuscript—distilled from two full days of study, prayer, and deliberation.

The last portion of the Maksimovskie manuscript describes what happened after the sixth and final council in Viatkini. The excommunication of several elders and spiritual fathers at once meant that if the rulings of the council were to be followed, those wishing to remain in the Christian community could not pray with any of those who had been cast out. This prohibition, however, was rapidly overwhelmed by the intense and interlocking web of prayer services and ceremonies in which elders from all over the Upper Kama participated. In addition to the daily and holiday services celebrated in home communities like Dëmino, there were always baptisms, funerals, and memorial days for extended family members or friends from other parts of the Upper Kama; indeed, the Maksimovskie manuscript, with all its comings and goings, provides a good sense of the enormous amount of time that elders were expected to dedicate to prayer and ritual. In this environment, it rapidly became impossible to keep track of who had prayed with or bowed to whom, on what occasion, and in which village. Contagion was swift. The Maksimovskie manuscript briskly traces some of the connections along which schism spread and then states bluntly, with evident anger and resignation, "That's how they mixed everything together [*vot" i smeshali vso*]." Soon after the council of Viatkini, the Maksimovskie and Dëminskie began to hold their own councils, and, despite some final, poorly received overtures from each side, the pastors of the entire Upper Kama gradually fell into two separate and contentious Christian communities.[10]

The Maksimovskie version of the schism is, then, an account of the disobedience of Davyd, then Davyd's spiritual father Grigor'evich, then the village of Dëmino, and finally whole swaths of the Upper Kama. In describing these events and councils, the Maksimovskie manuscript affords considerable insight into expectations about the relationship between the creation of ethical subjects and the maintenance of moral communities among elders in the Upper Kama. On the one hand, the account is extremely council-centered, emphasizing the primary and robust role of members of a Christian community in maintaining collective purity and thereby the possibility of salvation in a fallen world. On the other hand, chances for salvation are presented as extremely fragile, threatened by the potential for contagion within the interconnected subjectivities created by ritual occasions. Grigor'evich was stripped of his role as spiritual father at the second council not primarily because, like Davyd, he disobeyed a council but because he ate and prayed with someone who had been excommunicated and returned to the world. Similarly, the schism of 1866–88 raced through the Upper Kama following the sixth council because elders on different sides continued—wittingly or unwittingly—to pray with one another. In the heightened stakes of material contexts like prayer and meals, the fallen state of one elder's soul could transfer to another, threatening the entire community if that second person was not speedily isolated from the community of elders as well.

10. This situation was further exacerbated by the erosion of ties with coreligionists in the north, who might have intervened, and by the weakness of the local Russian Orthodox mission, which did not pose a significant threat against which to rally.

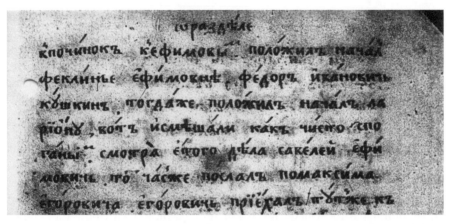

4. An extract from the Maksimovskie manuscript "On the Division," charting the course of schism as elders prayed with those who had been excommunicated. ORKiR NB MGU, PV, 1996, 7v. Reproduced courtesy of UMI/Proquest Microfilms.

The Maksimovskie manuscript also brings into sharp relief some of the limits of priestless Old Believer attempts to preserve a single, pure, Christian moral community by means of decentralized councils rather than a hierarchy of clerics. In addition to the problems caused by contagious subjectivities in ritual contexts so dramatically illustrated in the rapid spread of the division following the sixth council in Viatkini, there was the enduring problem of the laypeople of Dëmino. Although not themselves active in the prayers and rituals of Old Belief, middle-generation laypeople could easily grow attached to the pastors who baptized their children, sent their dead parents off to hoped-for salvation, and, in general, served the spiritual needs of their communities. The process for electing and installing a pastor, that is, could encounter problems when run in reverse to expel a spiritual father like Grigor'evich. The general council of spiritual fathers from all over the Upper Kama could, in the abstract, strip one of their number of his authority but not, perhaps, without running into substantial opposition from the members of the community that pastor served. In other words, the practice of allowing pastors to be chosen with the advice of the villages they served also provided mechanisms by which attempts to discipline those pastors could be contested by an entire flock, not only the pastor in question. A whole village or section of the Upper Kama had to be cut off, rather than a single deviant pastor.

Finally, I suggest that the Maksimovskie manuscript as a whole, in its narrative, its evidence, its accusations, and its emphases, illustrates one important way in which Old Belief in the Upper Kama could be presented—both to its own adherents and to outsiders. The one true faith appears, in this manuscript, to be a self-contained, self-regulating system almost entirely untouched by shifting material practices in the surrounding world. Save for basic coordinates in time and space, worldly markets and moral communities are mentioned only in passing. The local bazaar is merely the place that Davyd happened to be when the elders called him to council; the laypeople of Dëmino are spiritual accomplices to Grigor'evich's disobedience, not members of a postemancipation agricultural community struggling with its own deep ethical transformations. We might say, then, that the Maksimovskie narrative of the schism participates in elders' ascetic ideals by avoiding the potential corrupting influence of material practices judged to be on the outside of a moral community of Christians in search of salvation. As valuable as this kind of account is for the ways in which it illuminates some of the material practices through which certain Old Believers strove to avoid the world (through the formation of textual communities, for instance), it is precisely the ways in which this project of pure separation must fail that interest me in this study of ethics. But the interest is not mine alone. The influence of other, more worldly, patterns of material and ethical practice on elders' ability to sequester their fragile communities has been a topic of considerable interest to residents of the Upper Kama as well, both at the time of the schism and in the century and a half since. Along with the Dëminskie manuscript and some widespread oral accounts of the schism, there were a great many other factors at play in the division of 1866–88, factors related to the rapid transformations taking place across rural Russia in the last third of the nineteenth century.

The Dëminskie Account of Division: Ancient Heresies and the Mixing of the Worlds

The Dëminskie manuscript differs from its Maksimovskie counterpart not simply in its account of the events and causes of the schism but in its overall narrative structure. Whereas the Maksimovskie narrative alternates steadily between specific alleged transgressions and councils summoned in response, the Dëminskie version recounts the six councils as one of only several ways to catalog the many heresies of Maksim Zhdanov—a list so long, it claims, that "there isn't enough time to relate them in detail" (*nedostanet" vremeni podrobnu ispovesti*). The Dëminskie manuscript, although just as determined as the Maksimovskie account to ground its anathemas in textual sources, also points beyond the communities of elders and their authoritative texts into the wider turbulence of the postemancipation years in the Upper Kama. It offers some initial clues as to how the transformations of the 1860s–80s might have created ethical dilemmas for Old Believer elders and their ascetic attempts to hold the relationships of this world apart from the moral community of Christian elders seeking salvation.

After a brief introductory section (including the eschatological imagery quoted in this chapter's epigraph), the Dëminskie narrative opens with the familiar dispute over where to hold the Easter service in the spring of 1866. But events rapidly take a different turn than in the Maksimovskie telling. Petrovna, the manuscript asserts, improperly exceeded her place as a woman and interfered in negotiations between men (Davyd and Grigor'evich) about plans for the Easter service. After Davyd put her in her proper position and the service was held at his house, Petrovna went outside her home community to find a spiritual father who would excommunicate Davyd in retaliation. She found such a supporter in Maksim and through her "devilish women's charms" (*zhenskaia lest'*) convinced him to convene a council of spiritual fathers from all over the Upper Kama.[11] At this first council, Davyd was excommunicated, as Petrovna had hoped he would be. In the Dëminskie version of events, however, Grigor'evich did not go on to pray with Davyd and wait until after their meal to inform him of the council's excommunication. Rather, the manuscript relates that Grigor'evich refused outright to accept that Maksim's council had the authority to excommunicate someone in another village community. Grigor'evich continued to pray with Davyd quite intentionally and with the ardent support of laypeople in and around Dëmino. Not backing down from this challenge to his authority, Maksim then attempted to have Grigor'evich himself excommunicated at a second council. After further escalation, further councils, and further illegitimate attempts by Maksim to extend his own power over another autonomous council of elders, the dispute ultimately concluded in a lasting division.

The Dëminskie manuscript is less concerned with the deliberations of Maksim's councils than it is with the sins and heresies of Maksim himself. Most of its pages are taken up with evidence that Maksim fell into multiple ancient heresies, among them the Montanist heresy of placing women in positions of religious authority (*zhenovlastiia*) and, for reasons that are less clear, the "Armenian heresy."[12] Maksim was also, we are informed by the Dëminskie account, guilty of sorcery, theft, incest, and the violation of numerous rules regulating marriage. The accusation most frequently hurled by the Dëminskie, however, was that by attempting to exert authority over members of another self-governing Christian community, Maksim was guilty of the ancient Roman heresy of arrogance (*samoliubiia*). The Dëminskie manuscript begins as follows:

> A description of Maksim's and Ivan's falling away from the general apostolic conciliar church, and witness to their crimes from the Holy Scriptures. Like the bishop of ancient Rome, their power is cut off [*sovlastiiu svoeiu ogranichen"est'*].

---

11. On peasant women as temptresses, see especially Worobec (1990).

12. Montanus was cast as a heretic by the church fathers in the second century on the grounds, according to most accounts, that he preached a charismatic form of Christianity that influenced the theology of Tertullian. His two closest followers, however, were women, and it is this element on which the Dëminskie manuscript fixes (see below). There is no indication that Maksim Zhdanov advocated the theological positions associated with Montanus or, for that matter, the dualist theology of the Armenian heresy. The point seems to have been to associate Maksim with as many heresies as possible.

One of its dozens of similar accusations reads, "And this [Maksim] Egorevich did not want unity, he wanted a division. In order to reconcile, he wanted to be the most senior, just like the pope of Rome [*byt' emu stareishinoi iakozh papazh" rimskii*]." There are also several accusations of *papezhestvo*, or "being a Pope."

The Dëminskie manuscript, then, presents its own take on the proper authority and structure of councils. Here the emphasis is not on the authority of councils or the consequences of disobedience (as it was in the Maksimovskie account) but rather on the overriding importance of decentralization and self-governance in matters of priestless Old Believer spiritual affairs. In this view, Petrovna should not have gone outside Dëmino with her complaint, and Maksim should not have interfered in a spiritual matter internal to another community of Christians. Maksim was guilty of attempting to excommunicate "someone else's sheep, the child of someone else's pastor." All of Maksim's councils were thus illegitimate and lacked the authority over Davyd and Grigor'evich that they claimed. This position, as the manuscript makes clear, is amply supported in the rulings of ecumenical councils and the writings of church fathers. Indeed, an account of the falling away of the Roman church—attributed to the claims of primacy by the Bishop of Rome—has a prominent place in the 1650 edition of the *Kormchaia Kniga* that the Dëminskie were likely consulting as they compiled their evidence against Maksim. In part, then, the schism of 1866–88 replayed a very old line of debate and dispute in Christendom, one central to the high-stakes question of how Christian subjects and communities should be formed in the quest to stay on a path to salvation: Where is proper authority vested and how is it exercised?

In support of its accusations of heresy, the Dëminskie manuscript introduces a great deal of background evidence for Maksim's depravity and illegitimacy. Unlike the Maksimovskie account, much of this evidence is drawn from outside the dispute about Easter and the cascading crises of religious authority it provoked. Among the most dramatic and detailed of this evidence is the following:

> And then this Maksim, a sorcerer and apostate, began to steal from the small religious communities [*sobory*]. Wherever there are icons and books he takes them and adds them to his own.... The shameless robber expands his land as if he were prince of this world [*kniaz sego mira*], accumulates many slaves and servants...and hosts many feasts.... And he insulted and broke up many councils with such violence, and offended the less powerful. And violently takes and forever buys [*nasil'no otbiraia i navechno otkupiaia*] land ownership from many farmers.... If farmers [*zemledel'tsy*] began to refuse to give the robber their farms, because there would be nowhere for them to subsist, then he forbade them baptism and confession.... At a holiday service, he drove the poor and lowly from the porch outside.

The allegations show that in the eyes of the Dëminskie, Maksim fell prey not only to a range of ancient heresies but to other worldly temptations as well.

Moreover, these temptations are immediately recognizable as tied to the characteristic transformations of the Russian countryside after emancipation: increasing social stratification and shifting patterns of labor, exchange, and land-ownership. As in the pre-emancipation period discussed in chapter 1, these worldly relationships entailed their own patterns of ethical practice and moral communities—all of which elders and pastors sought to avoid in their attempts to become true Christians deserving of salvation. According to the Dëminskie, Maksim Zhdanov was failing rather spectacularly at the task of separation in the 1860s. Rather than detaching the worlds of work and prayer, Maksim was "taking for himself worldly and godly power" (*privlachaia sebe mirskuiu i b[o] zhiiu vlast'*), and in doing so, he was leading his followers astray. Unlike the allegations of the Maksimovskie manuscript, these charges point beyond the concerns of Old Believer elders and their manuscripts—they can be evaluated in light of zemstvo statistics and census reports. These surveys were, after all, designed specifically to chart the dynamics of certain worldly material practices among the peasantry, especially the movements of food, labor, and money.[13]

TSAR Aleksandr II issued his decree emancipating some 23 million Russian serfs on February 19, 1861, bringing what I have been calling the ethical regime of serfdom to an official close and ushering in an era of uncertainty and unrest across the empire. Nearly all the fundamental categories and patterns of rural life were renegotiated in the subsequent years, beginning with land ownership. In the western Urals, the Stroganovs continued to receive redemption payments from what the postemancipation land settlements termed "temporarily obligated" peasants, but the family was also working to shift its income base from agriculture to factory operations.[14] So long as the redemption payments were made, the Stroganov family bureaucracy took a decreasing interest in the workings of peasant villages that, like Sepych, lay further from their industrial centers. There were to be no more instructions, no more careful—even personal—attention to the details of peasant life of the kind to which Count S. G. Stroganov was so devoted in the mid-nineteenth century. Legal oversight of peasant life was transferred to the township court system, and beginning in the middle 1860s, organs of local self-government assumed administrative and state functions.

In this environment, the peasants of Sepych Township did not miss new opportunities to actively reshape the relationships by which they defined themselves

13. Pozdeeva (1982, 62; 1996, 10) and Chagin (1999, 45) both note that the division of 1866–88 took place in circumstances of growing economic inequality. One of my claims in this chapter is that we can be a good deal more specific than this.

14. See, for instance, RGADA, f. 1278, op. 2, d. 2229, and, more generally, Gorovoi (1954). Compare also Vargin" (1899) on the status of agriculture in the Okhansk region by the turn of the twentieth century.

with respect to one another and their former owners. When a peace mediator arrived with a drafted land settlement in April of 1862, for instance, the peasants of Sepych Township held him hostage for three days, threatening him and refusing to sign the settlement unless the proposed payments were significantly reduced. They did not sign until two weeks later, after ten of their ringleaders were jailed and a detachment of Cossacks was summoned to supervise the agreement.[15] In 1863, commune leaders apparently conned or bribed a land surveyor sent by the Stroganov family to lower the size of redemption payments for the entire township on the basis of a short, guided stroll through especially poor land in one corner of Dëmino. When the proposed reduction was questioned and investigated at a higher level, the resulting report castigated both the surveyor and the peasants of Sepych Township, who, it claimed, had only "very weak respect" for the land settlement they had signed.[16]

The peasants had good reason for their discontent: V. P. Pushkov has calculated that the postemancipation redemption payments owed to the Stroganovs in 1862 increased by almost 65 percent over the quitrent owed in 1856, while land itself decreased marginally (by 2.5 percent) (2005a, 267). Moreover, the peasants of the Upper Kama soon owed taxes to the zemstvo over and above their payments to the Stroganov family (see Kotsonis 2004). These heavy obligations and the new kinds of practices they demanded helped to place enormous pressure on the moral communities and patterns of ethical practice that had long been common in the Upper Kama. Nevertheless, as these examples from the very early 1860s show, the residents of the Upper Kama continued to reshape and negotiate the emergent worldly communities and relationships in which they participated—an important reminder in view of the fact that the extant statistics do not capture this practical dimension of social and cultural life.[17]

For all the massive changes taking place around it, the peasant commune with its collective organization and responsibilities remained the fulcrum of postemancipation rural life. The reforms of 1861 devolved land ownership from serf owners to newly created supravillage "agricultural communities" (*sel'skie obshchestva*) rather than directly to peasant households or to older

---

15. Gorovoi (1951, 104–5). For comparable incidents elsewhere in the Urals, see also Druzhinin (1949, 1963).

16. RGADA, f. 1278, op. 2, d. 2168, l. 127–30v. See also Pushkov (2005a, 265–68).

17. Zemstvo statistics have long served scholars of the Russian peasantry and the "agrarian question," from Lenin and Chaianov to the surge in Western scholarly interest in the Russian peasantry in the 1980s and 1990s. The most recent wave of scholarship making use of zemstvo data has drawn attention to the ways in which economists and statisticians "constructed" peasants in certain ways, rather than reflecting an already-present peasant society and culture (Frierson 1993; Kotsonis 1999; Darrow 2001). Although I am in general quite sympathetic to the theoretical stance adopted in this scholarship, I believe it is still possible to use the collected data to discern meaningful changes in the circumstances of peasant life.

village-level peasant communes.[18] Male household heads in each agricultural community elected officials who were responsible for the allocation of rights to land, the collection of taxes and redemption payments, the maintenance of law and order, and the upkeep of roads and bridges on their territories. By the end of the 1880s, there were fifteen agricultural communes in Sepych Township, each composed of several villages and hamlets. Peasant families in these communes produced wheat, oats, winter rye, and barley for their households and for sale at the periodic markets in Sepych or in other townships in the district. They labored now to generate income to pay the Stroganovs, the zemstvo, and, particularly as the 1880s progressed, themselves. Many households began to supplement work on their plots of land with either handicraft production or small-scale industry such as smithies or mills. Some—we do not know how many—sought increased income through labor migration to Stroganov factory towns to the east.

These are the local incarnations of the Russia-wide changes in the postemancipation peasant commune that historians have studied in detail; they need not be fully rehashed here. However, one question that has seldom been addressed seems to have been among the most pressing in the Upper Kama in the period of 1866–88: What happened when neighboring communes interwoven by ties of family and faith changed in quite dissimilar ways as the transformation of the Russian countryside unfolded? Sepych, most likely the original home of Maksim Zhdanov and his supporters, and Dëmino, only a few kilometers away and home to Davyd, Grigor'evich, and the other Dëminskie, encountered precisely this kind of rapid differentiation.[19] Zemstvo statistics paint quite different pictures of the two agricultural communities initially involved in the schism of 1866–88, lending some credence to the kinds of allegations lodged against the spiritual father Maksim Zhdanov by those from Dëmino.[20]

18. Historians have debated which peasant communities were relevant at this point—these new agricultural communities or older, village-level communes (Grant 1976; Lewin 1990). The evidence in the case of Sepych does not shed any new light on these dilemmas, for the zemstvo statistics adhere faithfully to state classifications in terms of agricultural communities, while the Maksimovskie and Dëminskie manuscripts about the schism do not offer this sort of information about the organization of the world of laypeople. In the case of Sepych Township, then, it is does not appear possible to determine the extent to which these larger agricultural communities superseded older village-based communes, a fact that limits the claims I can make about the postemancipation period itself.

19. It is clear from both manuscripts that the Dëminskie hailed originally from the village of Dëmino and were later joined by other communities in the Upper Kama. As for Maksim, the manuscript record is silent; we have only the word of later generations of local Old Believers that Sepych itself was an early stronghold of Maksimovskie Old Belief. Intermarriage and migration within the Upper Kama make it impossible to read later settlement patterns back into the time of the schism with any degree of confidence. In Russian Orthodox areas of the countryside, the once-tight link between agricultural and local religious communities (parishes) had already been ruptured in the eighteenth century (Freeze 1976), making the kind of dispute I discuss here less likely.

20. What details we have about the 1860s–80s in Sepych come largely from a detailed census and economic survey carried out by officials from the Perm provincial zemstvo in 1890–91.

To be sure, Sepych and Dëmino began the reform period in different positions—Sepych was the township seat—but the transformations of the postemancipation period seem to have accentuated these differences and changed their dynamics. By the 1880s, many of the households in and around Sepych had ridden the wave of marketization that swept much of the Russian countryside in the decades after emancipation. Sepych itself was fast becoming a significant hub in the livestock, grain, and small-industry markets of the countryside straddling the border of Perm and Viatka provinces. In 1890, there were 263 people in the Sepych agricultural community and 172 in the Dëmino community. Nonagricultural production was an activity of only 31 villagers in Dëmino (about 1 in 5), who brought in 632 rubles among them. In Sepych, however, fully 131 people (half the population) took up some form of nonagricultural work, earning 3,092 rubles in 1890. (By contrast, in 1858 there were few artisans of any sort in this area of the Stroganov lands; see Vologdin 1895, 205; 218). Sepych's 27 small traders tallied 1,026 rubles in 1890; Dëmino counted no small traders at all. In 1857, there were two mills in all of Sepych Township—both in or near Sepych.[21] By 1890, Sepych was home to four mills and five smithies, while in the Dëmino agricultural community there were no mills and two smithies, both of which were less profitable than their counterparts near Sepych. "Maksimovskie," a Dëminskie Old Believer reported to an archaeographer, "were always richer."[22]

Residents of the Sepych agricultural community also spent more money at markets on vegetables, evidence that they relied less on their own plots for food and had greater cash reserves. Over twice as many households in Sepych as in Dëmino bought cucumbers at a market, for instance, and those households spent nearly four times as much on cucumbers as did households in Dëmino. Villagers near Sepych were more far more likely to have rented supplementary land from poorer villagers and more likely to have participated in government credit programs than their counterparts in Dëmino. The town of Sepych was home to a small weekly market and a massive three-week market each October. The October market was attended by buyers from as far away as Glazov in Viatka Province and livestock speculators and profiteers from still farther away. Although villagers from Dëmino would certainly have attended markets

---

Over the course of several months, more than fifty survey workers, aided by local schoolteachers, went from household to household in each of the township's communes. Their goal was to produce an exhaustive catalog of social and economic activities in the entire region that would serve to guide the government credit schemes intended to modernize the countryside. Data from the household survey, with accompanying commentary and analysis, were published in 1896, along with data from the other townships of the Okhansk region of Perm Province. Pushkov's (1999a) analysis of this data compares the Old Believer population of the Upper Kama with the neighboring Russian Orthodox townships; I am concerned here with differences *within* the Old Believer population.

21. RGADA, f. 1278, op. 2, d. 8579, l. 2v–3.
22. AAL MGU, Perm-Verkhokam'e Field Diaries, 13, l. 42.

as well, the scope and presence of such significant markets in Sepych could only have contributed to the perception that Sepych was becoming a center of worldly economic exchange. Indeed, later generations of residents of the Upper Kama frequently referred to Sepych in the postemancipation period as a "rich merchant town." Similarly, local historian E. F. Klimov (2003, 36) notes that residents of Sepych came to call some of their neighbors in the village of Sokolovo "the upper poor people" (*verkhota-bednota*), a reference to the slightly higher elevation and the much lower standards of living in the agricultural communes to the west of Sepych.[23]

All this evidence points to comprehensive and divergent restructurings of many of the kinds of ethical practices and moral communities that had characterized life in the Upper Kama for well over a century. Particularly in Sepych itself, the materials of worldly ethics—the food, labor, and money exchanged by laypeople—flowed in new, wider, and faster currents. Markets expanded and intensified the relationships in which families participated, for exchanges no longer took place primarily within individual communes or between communes and serf owners but among traders and travelers of all sorts who made their way to Sepych. Some families in town discovered that after they had paid their rents and taxes, there could still be money left over to reinvest or diversify their sources of income, perhaps by renting additional land from poorer villagers on the outskirts of Sepych. In sum, what local expectations had long cast as the relationships and moral communities of this world were growing in scale and in proximity in the emergent ethical regime of the postemancipation years. Moreover, they were doing so more in Maksim's home of Sepych than in Dëmino. Could the elders continue to hold the materials of this world at bay in order to assure their salvation?

There is some evidence that they could and did. The zemstvo surveyors, for instance, reported in the introduction to their lengthy report that many households in Sepych Township refused to permit elders to be counted or questioned by the representatives of the state. But the accusations in the Dëminskie manuscript also point to a more complex, and more troubled, picture. Although some of the Dëminskie allegations clearly critique Maksim's alleged accumulation of wealth in and of itself, they are most indignant when claiming that Maksim mixed the materials of ethics through which domains of spiritual and worldly power were constituted. Recall, for instance, the claim that Maksim was expanding his land "as if he were a prince of this world." In the eyes of those from Dëmino, the great sin of Maksim Zhdanov was not, or at any rate not only, that he was getting rich. In the priestless Old Believer Upper Kama, still more serious was the fact that Maksim baldly attempted to exert

---

23. For all the statistics cited in the above two paragraphs, see Krasnoperov (1896).

simultaneous control over the worlds of work and prayer, fields of material and ethical practice that a great deal of ritual and other energy had long gone into keeping separate. The charge that Maksim acted like "a prince of this world" was less about Maksim acting like a *prince* of this world than acting like a prince of *this* world while also serving as pastor.

How true were these charges against Maksim? We have little reason to doubt them, and they fall well within the scope of common peasant-on-peasant crimes documented by studies of the township court system after emancipation (Frank 1999). But they also have their specific resonances in the Old Believer Upper Kama. In the chaotic postemancipation years, maybe Maksim was unable to mediate between the worlds of laypeople and elders, as pastors had long been asked. Perhaps he, his family, and his commune could not afford to remove a middle-aged man from the worldly labor force and still hope to meet their exorbitant obligations to the Stroganovs and the zemstvo. In this scenario, Maksim, unexpectedly elected a spiritual father at middle age and chosen because he was respected and well connected in Sepych, might have found it impossible to give up his expanding worldly contacts and take up the life of elders, whose very purpose was to reorient their relationships away from the materials of this world. Perhaps Maksim, as the Dëminskie manuscript suggests, attempted to resolve these dilemmas by uniting the worlds. He might, for instance, have utilized the connections afforded by his faith to foster emerging mercantile exchange and credit networks, as did so many Old Believers elsewhere in the Russian Empire after emancipation (as in West and Petrov 1998)? Perhaps Maksim even came to see the rise of Sepych in spheres of worldly exchange and production as a marker of the superiority of Sepych's council of elders, thus succumbing, at least in the Dëminskie view, to the Roman heresy of asserting primacy over other Christian communities. Beyond the accusations of the Dëminskie manuscript, we have little aside from the circumstantial yet compelling evidence provided by zemstvo statistics that some combination of these scenarios might well have come to pass.

At the very least, we can say with some certainty that the conditions of the postemancipation period and the transformations associated with the rise of agrarian capitalism created new and deep dilemmas for both elders and laypeople in the Upper Kama. In particular, the agricultural communes of Sepych and Dëmino changed in quite different ways over the years between the emancipation of 1861 and the final break of 1888. The Dëminskie manuscript reveals some of the ways in which these emerging worldly differences put enormous pressure on the shared faith that had long united the many population centers of the Upper Kama. Whether or not Maksim actually stole from poorer religious communities or shamelessly expanded his land is in some sense irrelevant. The accusations of the Dëminskie manuscript demonstrate that the worldly moral communities and materials of ethics out of which they were

5. An extract from the Dëminskie manuscript on the schism of 1866–88, locating the falling away of the Maksimovskie in Christian time and space: "We describe the division of the faith in the year 7374, the ninth indict, Perm Province, Okhansk region, in the area around Sepych Township." ORKiR NB MGU, PV, 1118, 654r. Reproduced courtesy of UMI/Proquest Microfilms.

constructed were changing. They were, moreover, changing in ways that made accusations against Maksim intelligible and plausible to their intended audience: those elders and laypeople who allied themselves with the dissent of Davyd and Grigor'evich from Dëmino.

In his study of peasant labor migration in villages near Moscow in the late nineteenth century, Jeffrey Burds (1998, 186–218) argues that religious denunciations and anathemas were most often leveled at those peasants closely identified with change. In the cases he explores, this meant labor migrants earning money that destabilized the older ties of village communes. The Dëminskie manuscript makes clear that Old Believer communities were not immune from the dynamic Burds describes. The Dëminskie focused many of their charges against Maksim specifically at his participation in the patterns of change in the Russian countryside as they appeared in the material forms of money, labor, and food. Within this context, their anathemas followed an ethical logic particular to priestless Old Belief in the Upper Kama, including accusations about mixing the worlds, clashes over decentralized and conciliar authority, citations to the *Kormchaia Kniga,* and others. Something similar holds true for other significant agents of change in the postemancipation countryside: women. The Dëminskie manuscript, after all, laid much of the blame for the schism of 1866–88 at the feet of Petrovna, with her impudence and her "devilish women's charms." Similarly, Maksim stood accused not only of straying into the world by accumulating land and wealth but also of partaking in pleasures of the flesh forbidden to pastors. Indeed, it is these explanations of the schism that are lodged most solidly in the memories of today's residents of the Upper Kama.

Later Stories of the Division: Marriage, Sex, and the "Woman Question"

When I lived in Sepych at the turn of the twenty-first century, townspeople still spoke of the origins of the division between Maksimovskie and Dëminskie, often during conversations about the construction of a new church in the town center in the 1990s. The new church's affiliation with a hierarchy of *priestly* Old Believers from the nearby city of Vereshchagino presented Maksimovskie and Dëminskie alike with renewed impetus to reflect on the genesis of their communities—in good part because the differences that had divided the priest-less groups for over a century were becoming increasingly irrelevant in the post-Soviet period. Like the manuscript accounts, these stories of the division in 1866–88 began with a dispute between spiritual fathers. However, even those few townspeople who had read the manuscripts did not usually follow the texts in suggesting that the discord was rooted in Grigor'evich's disregard for the authority of councils or Maksim's attempts to combine spiritual and worldly power. One elderly woman suggested simply, "There were two spiritual fathers...and they split up [*razdelilis'*]. It's said that they didn't get along for some reason."[24]

Others in town were less circumspect about what, according to the stories their parents and grandparents had told them, had come between the two spiritual fathers. The most common explanation for the division was also the most succinct: "over a woman." Here is the story summarized for a visiting archaeographer in 1974: "The Dëminskie faith is Pomortsy. The Maksimovskie faith is also Pomortsy. They just split up; they fought because of a girl [*iz-za devki*]. One fell in love, the other fell in love, and there you have it, they split up."[25] Anastasia Ivanovna, a Dëminskie elder whose account of the election of a spiritual father I discussed in chapter 1, spoke of the division in similar, but more detailed, terms in 1994.

> [A pastor] is not allowed to have a wife....Take Grigor'evich. He was around forty and part of the faith, was attached to the community of elders [*otnosil k vere, soborosviazanym byl*]. Since he didn't have a wife, he had a worker...a worker plus some [*rabotnitsa s prirashcheniem*]. And it seems that against the rules of marriage Davyd made a trip to the hayloft with that worker. And then Maksim up and excommunicated that Davyd and pulled the community apart.[26]

It is difficult from the distance of a century and a half to sort out who might have been cavorting in a hayloft with whom circa 1866. Anastasia Ivanovna's

---

24. AAL MGU, Video Archive 1995, 10. Townspeople frequently gave the names of the two spiritual fathers as Dëmo and Maksim, assuming that both groups drew their names from pastors.

25. AAL MGU, Perm-Verkhokam'e Field Diaries, 2 (part 2), l. 10.

26. AAL MGU, Video Archive 1994, 5.

description of Petrovna as "a worker plus some" indicates a sexual relationship between Petrovna and Grigor'evich, one forbidden for a pastor. It would not have been at all rare for a priestless Old Believer spiritual father to skirt expectations about marriage by employing a female "cook" or "worker" who was also a mistress (Paert 2003, 79). And might sex have drawn the spiritual father Maksim into the dispute as well? Some stories I heard suggested just this, hinting that Petrovna slept with Maksim rather than (or in addition to) Davyd. These stories pick up, perhaps, on the Dëminskie manuscript's assertion that Petrovna used her devilish woman's charms to convince Maksim to call a council and excommunicate Davyd. We do not, however, need to know all the details to surmise that the postemancipation countryside presented new possibilities and dilemmas within the set of issues that priestless Old Believers had long debated under the rubric of "marriage" and zemstvo statisticians had begun to call "the woman question." I showed in chapter 1 that questions of marriage and celibacy, men's and women's sexuality, and the gendering of religious authority had long been central to ethical practice and the shaping of moral communities in the Upper Kama. In the postemancipation period, gender and sexuality were again important, especially as domains in which transformations of the material and ethical practices of this world put pressure on the ascetic elders in ways that fanned sparks of disagreement into full-blown schism.

At least since the mid-nineteenth century in the Upper Kama, the social divide between laypeople and elders corresponded—in residents' expectations, if not always in their practice—with a divide between married and unmarried life. Celibacy had long been among the chief challenges for middle-age pastors, who were expected to uphold many of the elders' taboos while themselves most often belonging to the age cohort of the middle generation. Accusing a pastor of engaging in sexual relationships was thus one more way to allege the inappropriate mixing of the worlds.[27] The Dëminskie manuscript does just this. Juxtaposed with its allegations that Maksim exploited the less well-off in Sepych by accumulating wealth and land in this world are assertions of sexual transgressions:

> And [Maksim] builds many houses and stays in them with whores [s bludnitsami]. And has two whores, one named Fotina and the other Anna, and does everything according to their wishes like the heretic Montanus, and fornicates with them [s nimizh blud" tvoriashe]....And makes deacons of his whores.

And elsewhere:

> We also introduce [privodim v lichnost'] a description of when this fornicator blessed his whore Mavra Osipovna to attend to spiritual affairs. And then

27. As Chulos (1995) notes, accusations of clerical debauchery were common in Russian Orthodox areas of rural Russia as well; they took on a particular set of valences in the priestless Old Believer Upper Kama.

fornicated with her [*prebyval s neiu v bluide*], not considering it a sin. . . . Osipovna was a wet nurse for Fotina Fëdorovna. And this fornicator, wanting to get his fill [*khotia nasytisia nesytyi*], began to scheme about how to charm this Fotina into fornicating with him.

To hold the office of spiritual father and also to engage in sexual relations violated the separation of the worlds just as being both a prince and a pastor did. Scholars have often noted that there was a double standard in the Russian countryside when it came to marital infidelity and sexual promiscuity: while women were often publicly shamed and dishonored for engaging in sexual relationships outside marriage, men suffered few consequences (see esp. Worobec 1991, 197; Glickman 1996, 222). The fact that the Dëminskie manuscript castigates Maksim for violating local expectations about marriage and celibacy as much as—indeed, more than—any of the women involved indicates that there were interesting, if atypical, dynamics in the Old Believer Upper Kama in the years after emancipation.

Some of these dynamics can be glimpsed in the various portions of the Dëminskie manuscript excerpted above. Maksim, for example, is accused not just of mixing the worlds by engaging in worldly acts of fornication but of succumbing to other explicitly gendered heresies, especially by placing women in positions of religious authority (which the Dëminskie manuscript terms *zhenovlastiia*). Recall, too, that the Dëminskie manuscript presents the Easter dispute in 1866 as a disagreement initially caused by Petrovna's inappropriate intervention in negotiations between two men, compounded by her effort to enlist Maksim in the excommunication of Davyd. I suggest that the anointing of women to pastoral roles, Petrovna's alleged overassertiveness, and the purported sexual transgressions of nearly all the participants in the division should be seen as local instantiations of a single, larger phenomenon: widespread challenges to patriarchal authority in peasant families and rural communities following emancipation. I thus take inspiration from the arguments of historians who have seen the refiguring of gender roles in the countryside as a key aspect of the era of Great Reforms (Engel 1990; cf. Wagner 1994). These insights, however, require some adaptation to understand transformations of the ethical practices and expectations of the Old Believers of the Upper Kama.

Changes in the Old Believer family were also, it turns out, of great interest to the zemstvo surveyors and statisticians who spent much of 1889 in Sepych Township. Among the items they measured and compared was the marriage rate, which they concluded stood at 55 percent of men and 46 percent of women of working age—a figure much lower than that for the Russian Orthodox areas of the Okhansk district they surveyed. But we also have reason to question a marriage rate even this high, given that the surveyors may have been using data gathered from the metrical books of the local Russian Orthodox church. If they did, they likely captured only those priestless Old Believers who had their worldly marriages registered in the local Russian Orthodox church.

This common tactic for avoiding fines or arrests, which seems to have evolved in the midst of Nicholas I's campaigns against Old Believer civil marriages (see chapter 1), did not translate into lifelong, or even short-term, affinity with the Russian Orthodox Church or its visions for proper married life. Indeed, in the narrative commentary attached to their report and statistical tables, the surveyors seemed to doubt their own figures on the marriage rate. Their impressions bear quotation at some length:

> The woman question among the sectarian population, at least in Sepych Township...has extraordinary importance for everyday life. The point is that there are no constraints on the making and annulment of marriages. No one even finds it necessary to register a marriage in the books kept for that purpose [in Sepych's Russian Orthodox church?]...These annulments are initiated by peasant women, who appear to change husbands frequently—in some cases, three or four times in a single year. These loose women [perebezhentsy] have even received a special nickname among the peasants—"warriors" [ratniki], for some reason. These literate women, after the breakup of their first marriage, usually avoid subsequent marital cohabitation, joining the ranks of those privileged [villagers] who fulfill "spiritual needs" in various religious rituals and, in this way, gain for themselves some material means and a great deal of well-known respect. These same women, who receive the name "little nun" [chernichka] in recognition of their ascetic way of life, also teach children how to read and write.[28]

The report seems to confirm an increasing number of women pastors in the Upper Kama as well as the fact that the struggle with licentiousness and associated efforts to strengthen and sacramentalize priestless civil marriages in the 1830s and 1840s were not particularly successful. Indeed, many of the forces driving those earlier morality campaigns had subsided, if not disappeared altogether. So long as their cash rents were paid, the Stroganov family had little further reason to closely regulate family life and sexuality in their villages; likewise, much of the fire of the early years of the Russia-wide mission against Old Belief had gone out by the last decades of the nineteenth century. At the same time, emancipated but "temporarily obligated" peasants were confronted with new demands for diverse and intensified engagements with the worldly material practices of money and labor. The higher income necessary to pay rents and taxes meant that they increasingly entered larger capital and labor markets—especially in a quickly transforming town like Sepych. As numerous scholars have noted, both nonagricultural household labor at home and (predominantly male) labor out-migration placed peasant women in more active roles in their households (esp. Glickman 1984, 1990, 332–35; Worobec 1991, 184–87; Engel 1994). In the Old Believer Upper Kama, these demands for

---

28. Krasnoperov (1896, 187). See also Meehan-Waters's (1992) study of Russian Orthodox peasant women who took up various kinds of religious life in prerevolutionary Russia.

intensified worldly activity likely also made it increasingly hard for elders to make the decision to leave worldly relationships behind for a life of asceticism. Extending the office of pastor to include women could relieve some of this pressure to produce and exchange in the world until later in life.

All these shifting vectors of force in the Russian countryside help account for what the surveyors of the late nineteenth century noted were the increasing prominence and respect accorded women in matters of spiritual affairs.[29] We can, then, understand the Dëminskie manuscript's railings against these transformations of gender and sexuality in part as a heated response from defenders of the patriarchal peasant family, which had, with support of tsar and lord, exercised far greater control over village life prior to emancipation (see also Frierson 1990). It is, once again, perhaps not surprising to see this position staked out by the elders from Dëmino, a village that participated far less directly in the intensification of capital and labor markets than did the Maksimovskie stronghold of Sepych. Even if the priestless Old Believer Upper Kama remained substantially patriarchal after emancipation, it is nonetheless evident that circumstances in Sepych placed women in a far greater and far more legitimate role as religious authority figures and stewards of moral communities than was the case in most other places.[30] As later stories, manuscripts, and surveys combine to demonstrate, these changes both reflected and helped to create yet another type of pressure on the elders of the Upper Kama.

This same trio of sources suggests a still more precise mechanism for the role of gender in the events of 1866–88, one that also helps account for why stories of the schism passed down through the generations most frequently emphasize the "over a woman" explanation. It is not a coincidence that redistributions of land and property in peasant families and the schism between Dëminskie and Maksimovskie went by the same name: division. Nor is it a coincidence that in both cases disputes among younger men in a family were often attributed to the provocation and agitation of women.

Russian peasant families could be unmade in various ways (see esp. Worobec 1995, 76–117). Divorce, clearly common in the Upper Kama, was one, but just as intriguing for the purposes of thinking about gender and schism were household divisions. In a division, a large patriarchal household unit incorporating parents, sons, and sons' wives split into smaller independent units, usually composed of elder and younger sons with their wives and children. One of the most significant functions of these agricultural communes was, as during the

---

29. The Maksimovskie manuscript lists, in passing and without particular comment, several women among the pastors gathered at the councils it describes. The Dëminskie manuscript does not do this, except in its accusations about Maksim promoting "whores" to attend to spiritual affairs.

30. The significant role of women in priestless Old Belief has often been noted (e.g., Crummey 1970, chap. 6). As the outright misogynism of the Dëminskie manuscript indicates, however, this aspect of Old Belief should not be overemphasized or taken for granted.

period of serfdom, to periodically reallocate and equalize the land tended by each of the commune's constituent households. This process took place either through a general repartition of all the commune's land or, more commonly, through a partial repartition of a single village. Equality in portions of land was usually achieved by some combination of assigning households multiple strips of land on fields of different quality and reassessing land requirements based on changes in household composition since the previous repartition.[31]

In Perm Province, as elsewhere in Russia, the rates and causes of divisions within peasant families were items of particular interest to many observers of Russian peasant society (see Frierson 1987). Among the economists who pored over the data collected by zemstvo statisticians across Russia, the answer to this question was important. To critics of state policy, a higher rate of divisions after the end of serfdom pointed to the increasing individualization and commercialization in the countryside and the imminent death of the "traditional" large patriarchal family household (Fëdorov 1979; Milogolova 1987). To others, a steady or declining rate of divisions could be used as evidence that the patriarchal family and the commune of which it was an integral part were flexible enough to withstand the challenges of new forms of production and exchange. It was in this intellectual environment that the household surveyors in Sepych Township trained their attention on divisions.

Divisions in peasant households seem to have been plentiful in Sepych Township after emancipation.[32] Of the 380 divisions that took place in the decade of the 1880s, the report listed the following causes: 246 were attributed to disputes among men in households; 11 to the initiative of women, including stepmothers and young brides; 37 to overly close living quarters caused by additions to the family; 67 to young families wanting to split off and set up their own households in new hamlets; and 19 to other reasons, many of which were disputes between mothers-in-law and daughters-in-law (Krasnoperov 1896, 187).[33] In all of Sepych Township, the length of time between repartitions was gradually lengthening and the negotiations becoming more contentious, which

31. For a review of early scholarship on divisions and land reallotment, see Aleksandrov (1990). For additional background on the makeup of peasant families, see Czap (1978, 1983).

32. Unfortunately, the report does not provide any basis, statistical or anecdotal, on which to compare the number of divisions in the 1880s with those of earlier decades or periods. As Frierson (1990) notes, divisions were on the rise in Russia more generally; elsewhere (1987, 37) she cites statistics that give the total number of divisions in European Russia for 1860–80 as 116,229 and for the decade of the 1880s alone, 140,355. Chagin (1992) provides figures suggesting that households in the Upper Kama remained somewhat smaller than in many non-Old Believer areas in the late nineteenth century, but this does not in and of itself suggest a greater or lesser number of divisions.

33. On the issue of daughters-in-law and their often contentious relationships with the members of the patriarchal family into which they married, see especially Farnsworth (1986). For similar catalogs of reasons for divisions elsewhere, see Worobec (1995, 87–90, 97–103), and compare Burds (1998, 34–37).

might suggest that more-well-off peasants worked to delay the repartitions that would have re-equalized their land holdings with those of less-well-off peasants (ibid., 165; cf. Worobec 1995, 26). But the report then went further, drawing on the opinion of the chief census taker for the township to interpret the important matter of household divisions more closely:

> The formal reason for divisions is attributed to the younger generation of men, but, looking more deeply into the difficulties that make up the soil in which the mass of divisions arise, the Old Believers of Sepych Township, and probably of other counties in the Okhansk region, have every right, indicating the root of the question, to say: "*cherchez la femme*" [look to the woman]!(Krasnoperov 1896, 187; emphasis in original)

There is a striking similarity between this explanation of household divisions, which the head statistician attributed to information picked up through interviews, and local explanations of the schism. Can it be a coincidence that the Maksimovskie version of the schism is entitled simply "On the division" (*O razdele*)? It begins, "On the splitting [*rassechenii*] of our true Orthodox Pomortsy faith. There has been a division with those from Dëmino and Kuliga...." The Dëminskie manuscript, untitled in existing versions, nevertheless frequently uses the term *razdel* to refer to the schism. The passage that corresponds roughly to the above part of the Maksimovskie account reads: "We describe the division [*razdelenie*] of the faith in the year 1866, the ninth indict, Perm Province, Okhansk district, in the area around Sepych Township." It claims elsewhere that "this [Maksim] did not want to unite, he strongly wanted to have a division [*razdel*]."

There were, that is, two sorts of fissions in the Upper Kama in the postemancipation period, both of which were locally understood as "divisions." Both sorts involved disputes between men of the younger generation that ended in lasting splits within families, whether individual peasant households or the family of the "one true Orthodox faith." Furthermore, a good deal of local commentary points, in both types of divisions, to a significant, if underspecified, role played by women in disputes among men (see also Frierson 1987, 46; Tian-Shanskaia 1993, 127–28). How are we to understand this overlap, given that the evidence at present allows no firmer conclusions about the causes of family divisions than it did in the hands of nineteenth-century statisticians themselves? We might see family divisions, long a part of rural life but on the rise in the postemancipation period, as part of a conceptual model of a moral community and its trajectories in which the course of the schism was understood. Leaps from family to faith and back again were, in fact, constantly made by residents of the Upper Kama themselves, as the title of the Maksimovskie manuscript intimates. It is not difficult to see the decentralized priestless religious communities of the Upper Kama as patriarchal peasant families writ large. This is, in fact, precisely what the Vyg fathers did in their mid-eighteenth-century letter on pastors to the Upper Kama when they insisted that priestless communities organize themselves into flocks of "ten or twenty sheep," headed by multiple pastors in communion with one another, with "Christ as the head" (see chapter 1).

It would have made eminent sense for cleavages in the faith to follow patterns that were structurally similar to those for cleavages in families. Even as the dueling spiritual fathers and councils hurled citations from church fathers and ecumenical councils at one another, those in the Upper Kama who were not so well-versed in religious texts might have looked elsewhere for explanations about what was happening to their moral communities in the transformations of the postemancipation period. They found them, perhaps, in the same place they often found explanations for family divisions: the role of women in a patriarchal and patrilineal society that was under threat. Furthermore, it is entirely reasonable that this version of the schism survives primarily in oral form, passed on to current generations in the Upper Kama by parents or grandparents who were alive at the time of schism. A division over a woman was the way laypeople understood disputes that their pastors saw—at least for the purposes of exchanging durable written anathemas—as matters of theology, doctrine, and ancient heresy. In yet one more way, the attempts of these Christians to escape the materiality of this world and chart a path to salvation elsewhere were thwarted by the numerous other varieties of material practice at a particular historical juncture.

Viewed in long-term perspective, the aftermath of emancipation was a moment at which local ethical sensibilities and expectations were heavily strained and fiercely disputed. It would not be the last such moment, but the schism of 1866–88 was a signal event for the Christians and moral communities of the Upper Kama. The venom of the division would influence the lives of elders and laypeople for more than a century, coloring the ethical dilemmas of both Soviet and post-Soviet periods in significant ways. As if anticipating a long and bitter struggle, the Maksimovskie manuscript concludes with a final glimpse of a Christian community rent from within and a defiant challenge to the Dëminskie faction:

> Then [the Dëminskie] began to write a document, where they judged our pastors, Maksim Egorovich [Zhdanov] and Ivan Nikferovich and added them to all the ancient heretics, to those who have been expelled, and to the lawless, and called them on the left hand of Christ. [The Dëminskie] judged without God and condemned us all to be set on the left side [*postavit' na levu storonu*].
>
> Only they could not send us there [*tol'ko posadit' ne mogli*].[34]

34. "On the left side of Christ" is presumably a reference to Matthew 25, where Jesus speaks of separating people at the last judgment "as a shepherd separates the sheep from the goats." The sheep, to his right, were to be welcomed into the Kingdom of Heaven; the goats, to his left, were to be cast into the eternal fire.

The scars of the division ran deep on the Dëminskie side as well. Well into the twentieth century, it was said by Dëminskie elders that, upon his death, the earth refused to accept the body of Maksim Egorovich Zhdanov.[35]

CHRISTIANITY, its adherents would agree, holds out the possibility of salvation from a fallen world. Yet Christians the world over have long held differing conceptions of what precise combination of words, deeds, subjective states, and institutions—to name just a few elements—properly accomplishes humanity's part in this transcendence. Despite these many different paths to salvation, both classical and contemporary anthropological studies of Christianity have focused almost exclusively on Protestant and, to a somewhat lesser extent, Roman Catholic forms of Christianity. Yet Christians in the Orthodox East have often differed substantially from their Western counterparts—in their conceptions of virtue and vice, their understandings of worldly and otherworldly powers, and their efforts to properly construct moral communities and human subjects worthy of God's salvation (see also Hann 2007, Hann and Goltz in press, Rogers in press). Part 1 has explored these and other elements of ethical life as they ebbed and flowed in one community of Eastern Christians over two centuries. I conclude by drawing attention to some of the ways in which these particularities of the Upper Kama are situated within broader fields of Christian ethics and practice. Briefly sharpening these distinctions not only provides a corrective nudge to the neglect of Eastern Orthodoxy in studies of Christianity but also helps to bring into focus elements of the ethical repertoire of the Upper Kama that will be central to the arguments of subsequent chapters.

Anthropologists, Joel Robbins has argued (2007), have not paid sufficient attention to the experiences of the Christians they study. Rather than taking Christians' accounts of totalizing conversion and radical temporal discontinuity seriously, he suggests, anthropologists have too often relied on analytic categories (such as "culture") that emphasize long-term continuities over the inherently rupturing experience of becoming Christian. Robbins proposes that temporal discontinuity is a fundamental Christian experience, especially in the contexts of conversion and eschatology, and that it should therefore be an important focal point for improved anthropological scholarship on Christianity. Yet both Robbins's arguments and those he critiques are deeply entwined in a particular variant of Christianity: evangelical Protestantism in European colonies and postcolonies. Indeed, a large literature has grown up around conversions to Christianity in the context of nascent capitalism; Peter van der Veer sums up a central proposition of much of this scholarship succinctly: "[I]t is under capitalism that the entrepreneurial bourgeois self with his urge for self-improvement becomes the bearer of modernity....I would argue that both Catholic and Protestant missions carry this new conception of the self...to the rest of the world" (1996, 9). The process of joining a Christian community via conversion, in this view, has often been the crucible in which new, capitalist subjects are made (see also Comaroff and Comaroff 1991). Western Christian conversion, in short, appears at the center of some recent and influential theories of modernity, subjectivity, power, and political economy.

Nonetheless, we must also recognize that these issues have articulated differently in many non-Western, noncolonial Christian contexts. They certainly have in the Upper Kama. The coming of agrarian capitalism in the postemancipation period, to give but one example, was associated not with conversions but with a local schism in which both sides vociferously asserted continuity. Indeed, despite all the transformations I have discussed in chapters 1 and 2, few if any in the Old Believer Upper Kama would ever claim to have "converted" to anything. Narratives and experiences of continuity and discontinuity are correspondingly configured differently than they are in so many studies of the Christian West. In and around Sepych, idioms of identity and difference over time have more often centered either on reclaiming the true faith of the past, as in the arrival of Brother Grigorii in the Upper Kama in 1730–31, or on heresy and schism, in which others fall away from the true Christian path but one's own faith persists unchanged. The discontinuity of joining the community of ascetic elders has thus been framed by an encompassing experience of continuity. The life-altering decision to answer the summons of the elders has been understood as a return to the ritual lives and Slavonic texts of childhood—and of ancestors—rather than as a radical break with one's own past (such as, for instance, that associated with becoming "born again" in Protestant circles).

As Robbins recognizes, the layering of continuity and discontinuity in Christian communities is a matter for empirical ethnographic and historical investigation, not generalization. If an anthropology of Christianity is desirable, however, it must find a way to build conversations about continuity and discontinuity—and thus of ethical subjectivity, moral community, and historical consciousness—that do not revolve around conversion. Conversion narratives offer only a limited model of Christian subjects' relationships to communities of practice, one in which communities are largely stable and subjects are mobile. Expanding our conversation to include schism reveals another common configuration, one in which the boundaries of a community shift around a subject whose practice is unchanged. We would benefit, in other words, from attending more closely to the many cases of intradenominational quarrels in both Western and Eastern Christianity that, like the division of 1866–88, have set the borders of an aspiring moral community in motion over Christian subjects who loudly assert their experience of continuity in a discontinuous world.

Viewed from the perspective of a second major strand in the recent anthropology of Christianity, however, the dilemmas with which Old Believers of the

Upper Kama wrestled were not so different from those habitually encountered by Christians the world over. The incursions of an unpredictable and under-determined material world on human beings' best efforts to escape its grasp were as confounding in and around Sepych as elsewhere in Christendom (see esp. Cannell 2006; Keane 2007). Chapter 1, for instance, traced a vision of a particular kind of Christian community, a "spark of true piety" insulated from the fallen, sinful world and perpetuated along an unbroken chain of decentral-ized, masculine authority. A version of this same dream of separation from the world was evident in the Maksimovskie manuscript's description of the schism of 1866–88 as a matter of internal pastoral discipline having nothing to do with the rapidly transforming Russian countryside.

In both serfdom and emancipation, however, my analysis led out of these care-fully constructed ideals and, via the persistent untidiness of material practice in the Russian countryside, to quite specific ways in which Christianity in the Upper Kama was implicated in and shaped by a range of objects, institutions, and ethical sensibilities that its adherents would have considered well off the path to salvation. In the eighteenth and nineteenth centuries, the ascetic aspi-rations of Sepych's early peasant Old Believers were partially reformulated by the coordinated campaigns of state, Russian Orthodox Church, and Stroganov family. While the Maksimovskie manuscript bracketed out the changes taking place in this world by focusing on purely doctrinal and internal disciplinary matters, the Dëminskie manuscript and oral accounts of the schism pointed precisely to the ways in which the shifting materialities of the post-emancipa-tion countryside created quandaries that could not be resolved and tensions that could not be contained. These manuscripts articulated their own com-petition in part by positioning themselves differently in a very common set of Christian dilemmas and disputes about how to pursue the ascetic withdrawal necessary for salvation amid the materially underdetermined and historically shifting currents of this world.

The approach to ethics I outlined in the introduction and have been illustrating across part 1 captures both of these central arenas of concern for Christians—continuity/discontinuity and attempts to transcend a fallen world—and places them in relationship to each other. I have therefore written of ethical subjects and moral communities in the Upper Kama, as well as of the underdetermined ways in which each can be made and unmade through various materials of ethics. I have described times when these elements cohered into a fairly stable configuration—an ethical regime—and times when all-encompassing transfor-mation demanded equally all-encompassing rearrangements. Throughout, I have sought to chart the formation and early history of a specific ethical reper-toire, a suite of malleable, recombinant, often bitterly disputed sensibilities and expectations about how to live an ethical life to which residents of the Upper Kama have returned again and again. Parts 2 and 3 will show that they did so even as many in Sepych ceased to think of themselves as Christians altogether.

PART II

The Generations and Ethics of Socialism

The entire purpose of training, educating, and teaching the youth of today should be to imbue them with communist ethics.... [T]he generation of people who are now aged fifty cannot expect to see a communist society. This generation will be gone before then. But the generation of those who are now fifteen will see a communist society, and will itself build this society. This generation should know that the entire purpose of their lives is to build a communist society.

—V. I. LENIN, *The Tasks of the Youth Leagues,* 1920

3 *Youth*

Exemplars of Rural Socialism

The Soviet era in Sepych opened with bloodshed. In August of 1918, as civil war raged in the western Urals, rebellions against Soviet power broke out in the factory cities of Izhevsk and Votkinsk, some 150 kilometers to the south of Sepych in Viatka Province. The Bolsheviks responded by placing all of Perm Province on a war footing and issuing mobilization orders to former soldiers and officers who had returned to their villages in the western reaches of the province. In Sepych and the neighboring townships, however, the mobilization did not succeed in raising many new troops for the Red Army. Instead, it sparked a violent uprising that went on for five days, left hundreds dead or maimed, and reverberated across the Upper Kama—and indeed across the Urals—for decades to come. The events of the Sepych Uprising, with their sudden and stark brutality, pose some pointed questions about what it means to think ethnographically and historically about ethics in the Soviet period. How, in short, does a historical ethnography of ethics deal with violence and its aftermath?

On the night of August 17, hours before mobilized soldiers and officers were to present themselves in the center of Sepych, a small band of rebels, probably including members of the Social Revolutionary Party, cut the telegraph wires connecting the seats of Soviet power in the central border region of Viatka and Perm provinces.[1] At eight o'clock the next morning, they and some fifty

---

1. Many of the details of the Sepych Uprising are clouded by the conflicting and heavily politicized memories of later years. For the events of August 1918 themselves, I rely mainly on the narrative pieced together by Bezgodov (2005a) and some of the many recollections penned by A. E. Zhdanov, held at VRKM, f. Sepych Uprising, dd. 287-V, 373-V, 393-V, and 1993. See esp. Figes (1989, 321–53) on peasant uprisings during the civil war; on the Red Army mobilizations of

others from assorted villages of the Upper Kama entered Sepych and easily disarmed its small detachment of Red Guards. The township representatives of Soviet power were not in their offices that day—it was Sunday—so the insurgents roused them from their homes, brought them to the center of Sepych, and summarily executed several of them. Other communists and their families, eventually nearly a hundred, were placed under guard in a locked granary. The leaders of the uprising called a general public meeting of the gathering soldiers and peasants (many of whom had come to Sepych for a large market that day), where they received broad support for their actions and immediately repudiated the Bolsheviks' mobilization orders, declaring instead their allegiance to the tsarist People's Army. The rebels then set about fortifying and expanding their position in Sepych, seeking to link up with other disaffected soldiers and peasants in the nearby countryside and beyond. By August 19, no fewer than six neighboring townships had joined the uprising, expelling or arresting representatives of Soviet power and contributing soldiers, horses, and weapons to a motley militia that, at its height, numbered close to two thousand men. Three hundred or so organized into a cavalry squadron, while the rest armed themselves with the crude weapons of a peasant rebellion: axes, pikes, crowbars, pitchforks, and the occasional old revolver or pistol. Local blacksmiths were ordered to turn out more arms.

The Bolshevik leadership in Perm grew alarmed at the scope of the uprising gathering in the west of the province, for if the rebels of Sepych linked up with elements of the White Army in Viatka Province, the Bolsheviks in the Urals could be effectively cut off from much of European Russia. The Red Army committed some of its last reserves from Perm and struggled to recruit loyal troops from the region in order to quell the disturbances in and around Sepych. Meanwhile, in the early-morning hours of August 22, several Bolshevik sympathizers in Sepych itself managed to free and arm the prisoners held in the granary. The escaped captives promptly set upon and detained the leaders of the uprising in Sepych's Russian Orthodox church, which had been serving as a headquarters and observation point. When heavily armed Red Guards dispatched from Perm, Okhansk, and Vereshchagino finally arrived in force to occupy Sepych later in the day on August 22, they encountered little resistance. Many of the insurgents were already melting back into the remainder of the terrified population, rejoining relatives who had spent days hiding in forests or potato cellars.

An investigative commission from Perm arrived in Sepych on August 25. Its report documents some of the staggering violence that enveloped the region in the summer of 1918. The investigators found that around fifty communists had been murdered in the course of the uprising, thirty-three of them cast into

---

1918–20 in particular, see Figes (1990). On the civil war period as, in part, a set of struggles over whether Bolsheviks had consolidated the "moral authority" to rule, see Raleigh (2002).

a shallow common grave near the center of Sepych. Most of the bodies discovered by the commission had been viciously mutilated: arms and legs broken, ears and noses cut off, eyes gouged out and torsos sliced open, heads split with axes and crowbars. As a result of its hurried inquiries, the commission tracked down and executed eighty-three people whom it judged to be the main instigators of the Sepych Uprising, among them officers and soldiers, many peasants, and the Russian Orthodox clergy who had allowed their church to be used as a headquarters and its bells to be rung as signals.[2] The commission's report does not, of course, mention the incidents of violence earlier in the summer of 1918 that had primed Sepych Township for an uprising against Soviet power in the first place. Throughout July and early August, bands of Red Army soldiers had passed through Sepych Township repeatedly. As they enforced the Bolsheviks' asserted monopoly over grain—they were likely particularly attracted to the many wealthy merchant households of Sepych (Mosheva 2004, 4)—they stole, raped, and shot indiscriminately at villagers; took the last stores of grain from the poorest of families; and, according to one written complaint, "struck fear into the entire area."[3]

What places, then, do violence, fear, and brutality have in this historical ethnography of ethics?[4] Some remarkable recent studies of ethics in anthropology focus precisely on violence, suffering, and pain as points for the creation of subjectivities (Kleinman et al. 1997; Asad 2003; Das 2006); others have explored the effects of symbolic or structural violence on persons and communities (Farmer 2004; Nagengast 1994, 111). My goals and conceptual language are somewhat different from this literature. I ask throughout part 2 how moral communities seek to regenerate themselves in the wake of acts of violence exacerbated by the complicity of their own members (for socialist societies, see especially Siu 1989; Mueggler 2001). Ultimately, I aim to situate the Sepych Uprising and other episodes of violence in the Soviet-era Upper Kama within a much broader and much longer-term set of ethical ebbs and flows. This, after all, is just what townspeople themselves sought to do.

It is in good part because of events like those surrounding the Sepych Uprising that some observers cannot abide the words "ethics" and "socialism" in the same sentence. Yet this is precisely the juxtaposition we must make if we are to understand the place of violence in an ethical regime that, for all its periodic

2. GAPO, f. 656, op. 1, d. 30, l. 5r-v. On the executions, see also GAPO, f. 732, op. 2, d. 160, ll. 11–12. Some investigations of the leaders of the Sepych Uprising continued into the early 1920s; see VRKM, f. Sepych Uprising, d. 3741.

3. GAPO, f. 656, op. 1, d. 30, l. 6.

4. By posing this question at this point, I do not imply that violence was absent from the pre-Soviet Russian countryside, since there is plentiful evidence of beatings and cruel punishments at the hands of commune, state, and landlord. Moreover, as Peter Holquist (2002) has shown, the brands of violence and terror frequently ascribed to the Bolsheviks were not uncommon in Europe at the time and not limited to the period after World War I in Russia.

paroxysms of cruelty, far more often rested on the shaping of moral communities and ethical subjects in much less absolute ways. To be sure, the murders and executions of the Sepych Uprising echoed throughout the Soviet period in Sepych—in charged personal recollections, sporadic newspaper articles, school lessons, library exhibits, NKVD interrogations in the 1930s, and a monument to the fallen communists of 1918 erected atop their common grave. One particularly gruesome photograph of executed insurgents lying in neat rows in the center of Sepych was even made into a Bolshevik postcard in the early 1920s. But in the end these echoes of the Sepych Uprising comprised only a fraction of the many ways in which the residents of the Upper Kama combined elements of a much older ethical repertoire with new possibilities in their attempts to fashion ethical lives in vastly transformed configurations of culture, society, and power.

Socialism's Ethics

My discussion of the Soviet period in Sepych does not offer a comprehensive portrait or analysis of Soviet or socialist ethics. However, I begin by briefly describing the broader currents of scholarship on ethics in socialist societies in which my claims about the particularities of the Upper Kama are situated. This approach presumes that there is utility in treating the Soviet period as a whole, despite the evident differences between, say, the 1930s and the 1970s in rural Russia. Although a good deal of historical detail is lost in this strategy and I do not claim that my analysis of any particular epoch approaches the nuance of more specialized studies, there are also some substantial benefits. For one thing, this approach remains faithful to the markers by which townspeople in Sepych usually divided their own history and charted their own pasts in our conversations: the period before the revolution; "Soviet times" (which usually were said to have ended with Gorbachev's perestroika rather than in 1991); and the present, post-Soviet, period. At the same time, this approach enables me to continue to work with the analytic unit of an ethical repertoire, using permutations and fluctuations in the highly localized expectations and practices of the Upper Kama to suggest some ways in which we might revise and extend our understandings of Russian history on a larger scale.

I subscribe, broadly, to an understanding of socialist societies that places primary analytic weight on the ramifications of a centrally planned economy, "rational redistributive" organization, and the drive to increase party-state control over the means of production (rather than, say, on the implications of one-party rule).[5] At the level of ideal types, socialist societies are usefully

5. On this understanding of socialism, see Konrád and Szelényi (1979), Kornai (1980), and Fehér, Heller, and Márkus (1983), especially as synthesized and sharpened by Verdery (1991, chap. 2).

conceptualized as "wealth in people" systems. Wealth in people refers to a mode of accumulation analogous to but quite different from the accumulation of wealth in capital so central to capitalist systems. In socialist contexts, the importance of collecting people was a response to the widespread shortages created by socialist central planning. In order to make ends meet in conditions of unremitting shortage, socialist citizens trafficked in all manner of horizontal and vertical rights and obligations outside the official plan. Built up over time, these rights and obligations created networks that could be deployed for purposes as varied as meeting quotas at a large enterprise or obtaining scarce products to put on the dinner table. To advance in this system one accumulated not capital but people—in the shape of rights and obligations circulated through larger and larger networks. Successful managers of socialist enterprises, for instance, were those who could most adroitly wheel and deal in networks that extended far beyond their own firms.[6]

But what constituted success in a society that relied on bargaining, cooked books, and backroom deals as an intrinsic part of its existence? Surely not something like the "real" production figures so fetishized by Western economists. One interesting outcome of the confluence of networking, ongoing state schemes to induce harder labor, and the general importance of collecting wealth in people is that socialist societies around the world have been populated by what I think of as "socialist exemplars": citizens and groups of citizens lauded as models of correct, successful socialist behavior or morality or, on the other hand, derided and shamed for nonsocialist conduct. How this exemplar status—whether positive or negative—was achieved often depended less on actually overfulfilling the plan, say, than on having the connections and contacts that enabled one to access the scarce resources that made overfulfillment possible in the first place. More simply, it could rest on having a friend in the regional accounting office willing to add a few zeros or move a decimal point. As untold numbers of socialist bureaucrats and administrators can attest, wealth in people could evaporate as quickly as wealth in capital on Wall Street, leaving once-proud enterprise directors or party members out in the cold (sometimes literally).[7]

Within this general framework of socialist circulation and reputation making/breaking, anthropologists and social historians have turned their attention to

6. Humphrey's ([1983] 1998) monograph on collective farms in Buryatia was the first to draw attention to the Soviet system as a "hierarchy of administrative rights held in practice" and to identify the importance of this organization for the flow of vertical and horizontal exchanges. I prefer "wealth in people" to "rights in people" because I think it more accurately captures obligations as well as rights (see esp. Verdery 2003, 61–63; Dunn 2004;) and because "wealth" draws attention to the importance of accumulation. See Guyer (1995b) for an example of the ways in which anthropologists have analyzed wealth in people in African contexts.

7. On exemplars in the Soviet Union as they relate to the aspects of socialism as I understand it here, see, for instance, Kotkin (1995) and Siegelbaum (1988, 1998). In other socialist contexts, see Anagnost (1997), Rofel (1999), and Montoya (2007).

varieties of practical and everyday ethics in socialist societies. These scholars' guiding question has been, What kinds of human beings and social/cultural/ linguistic groups are created in socialist systems and what kinds of exchanges facilitate the relationships that make those people and the communities into which they are clustered? Their answers have been considerably more nuanced than those of most Western political scientists and economists, for whom the scenarios described above verge on a dystopic nightmare of social embeddedness. Classically, anthropologists' answers have revolved around connections made and goods flowing outside the plan. Humphrey's ([1983] 1998) pathbreaking monograph on a Siberian collective farm, although not directly concerned with ethics as such, was the first to theorize the importance of "manipulable resources": goods that flowed outside official channels and enabled enterprise directors and ordinary citizens to make do (and make friends) when elements of the plan did not fall into place as intended (see also Ledeneva 1998, 2006; Dunn 2004).

Informal gifts, networks, and bargaining have been central to theories of how socialism worked in practice. However, these very common and very important practices are not the end of the story when it comes to the creation of moral communities and ethical subjectivities in socialist societies. Indeed, in my view, all the attention to network building and "informal economies" has, especially among anthropologists, obscured some significant dimensions of the practical ethics of lived socialism.[8] I suggest that Soviet-era Sepych allows us to add some further, intersecting dimensions to our understandings of socialist ethics, among them population resettlements and the associated reorganization of the landscape; the unintended local consequences of explicit efforts to inculcate moral visions of New Soviet Persons (including both labor incentives and antireligious campaigns); and the implications of socialist labor and consumption patterns for ritual and religious life. Although hardly in the ways anticipated by theorists and planners in Moscow, all these vectors of transformation intertwined to shape the field of ethical transformation and competition in and around Soviet-era Sepych. Attending to these dimensions of socialist ethics does not necessitate jettisoning a general analytic emphasis on the ramifications of centralized planning, rational redistribution, and their attendant shortages and work-arounds. Rather, my arguments about the Soviet period work precisely to situate this broad range of socialist transformations of ethics within the wider "laws of motion" (Verdery 1991) of socialist societies summarized above.

---

8. Among anthropologists, the intersection of language and performance has been a particularly fruitful domain in which to extend the study of Soviet ethics and subjectivities beyond informal economies (e.g., Lemon 2000; Yurchak 2006). Nikolai Ssorin-Chaikov's analysis of official gifts to Soviet leaders makes a similar point: anthropologists should move beyond "informal practices" in analyzing what he calls "the social map of the state" (2006, 360).

Applied to the Soviet-era Upper Kama, this analytic framework reveals again and again the significance of generational distinctions in the socialist countryside. "Generation" most frequently refers to age cohorts—groups shaped by moving through a set of common experiences together, such as Yurchak's "last Soviet generation" (2006) or David Ransel's three generations of village mothers (2000).[9] As should already be clear from my discussion of the preevolutionary period, I approach generation in a somewhat different manner: as a set of cultural and social expectations about the fields of practice appropriate to age-defined groups, such as older masters and younger apprentices in the early Soviet print shops studied by Diane Koenker (2001) or, in the Upper Kama, elders and laypeople. So although I discuss several socialist-era cohorts in Sepych over the course of these chapters, I have in mind these generationally defined fields of ethical practice and subjectivity when I claim that the primary way in which Soviet socialism transformed local expectations in Sepych was by widening and hardening generational distinctions. In Sepych, young, dedicated collective farmers of the 1940s often became, later in life—and to the ongoing surprise of higher-level party organs—ascetic elders in the 1970s. This socialist-era shape of generational distinctions and transitions is attributable, in good part, to expectations about generation extending well back into Sepych's pre-Soviet past. Yet it was also enabled—even fostered—by the generational characteristics of the Soviet socialist ethical regime itself. Among the most consistent of these over time was the movement of the rural population. Attention to long-term patterns of resettlement in the Upper Kama thus permits an initial, wide-angle view of generations and ethics in the context of rural socialism.

Resettlement and the Spatialization of Generations

In the decades of serfdom and emancipation, the high number of villages, hamlets, and agricultural communities spread throughout the Upper Kama was one important factor in shaping the local ethical repertoire. The dispersed configuration of agricultural settlements had long been tied to the decentralized organization of local religious communities; this decentralization in turn helped to channel the ways in which the marketization that followed emancipation created new possibilities for some—like Maksim Zhdanov and his followers in Sepych itself—to a greater degree than for others. The twentieth century recast this entire arrangement of the countryside. Indeed, the movement of the rural population into cities, towns, and centralized villages was one of the most consistent dynamics of the Soviet period. In 1926, the Sepych rural soviet included 114 separate population centers—a conglomeration of villages, settlements,

9. See Rofel (1999) for one of the best applications of generational cohort analysis to understanding the workings of a socialist system.

and scattered independent farmsteads. Their populations ranged from 6 to 150 residents; Sepych itself counted only 254. By 1972, there were but twenty-nine population centers in the Sepych rural soviet. During my primary fieldwork in 2001, only twelve remained. Sepych had grown to around 1,437 residents, with just over 300 people in the remaining outlying villages.

THE LONG ARC OF SOCIALIST RESETTLEMENT

The most intense waves of resettlement and centralization in the Upper Kama began with initiatives from above, as part of socialist plans to maximize productivity in the agricultural sector and transform the Soviet economy as a whole through urbanization and industrialization.[10] These campaigns differed markedly in method, from the violent removal of wealthy peasant families in the early 1930s to more gentle inducements in the 1970s. In many cases, in fact, younger rural residents needed little overt prodding from above to leave smaller villages and settlements for the very different kinds of communities to be found in centralized farming operations or growing socialist cities (Pallot 1979). Whether the result of forced resettlement, voluntary movement, or some combination thereof, all these peregrinations unfolded within the general context of programs designed to increase state control over the means of production and more effectively redistribute resources throughout the socialist system.

In the Upper Kama, the influence of prerevolutionary agricultural communities on population patterns and movements had already declined somewhat by the beginning of wholesale collectivization in the fall of 1928. The Stolypin reforms of the early twentieth century and the hybrid "state capitalist" economy of the New Economic Policy (NEP) (1921–28) fostered the appearance, if never the entrenchment, of independent farmsteads (*khutory*) and some small experimental "socialist communes," the average size of which was a mere eleven households in the Vereshchagino district.[11] The collectivization campaigns of

10. For this section, I have relied a great deal on the excellent local histories of the Vereshchagino district published by V. G. Mel'chakov through the Vereshchagino department of cultural affairs (1993, 1994, 1996, 1998). I have also drawn on the local history research carried out by E. F. Klimov (2003) as well as on the staff of the Vereshchagino and Sepych local history museums. Compare Paxson's descriptions of a changing rural landscape in the Russian north (2005, 28–49 and passim), and see Bezgodov (2005a) for part of the story I tell here from the perspective of a single village in the Upper Kama. For a different approach to the spaces of socialist agriculture, see Lampland (1995, chap. 6).

11. For those of an entrepreneurial bent who chose to work them, farmsteads combined the multiple strips of land tended by a peasant household of the postemancipation era into a single substantial holding either on the edge of or not far from a village. Independent farmers often built a new house or small settlement on this land. The number of population centers in the Vereshchagino region actually grew in the period of farmsteading. Mel'chakov (1996, 19) cites a figure of 134 farmsteads in the Vereshchagino region by 1926, 110 from the era of the Stolypin reforms and 24 from the NEP period.

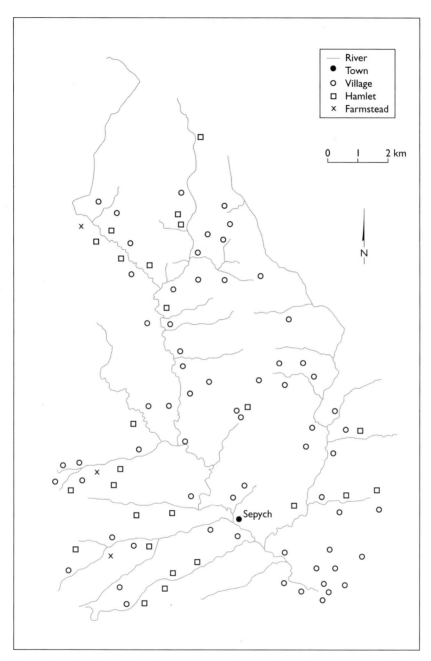

3. Approximate location of population centers in the Sepych Rural Soviet in 1926, before collectivization. The map does not show an additional eighteen settlements between four and nine kilometers to the southeast of Sepych.

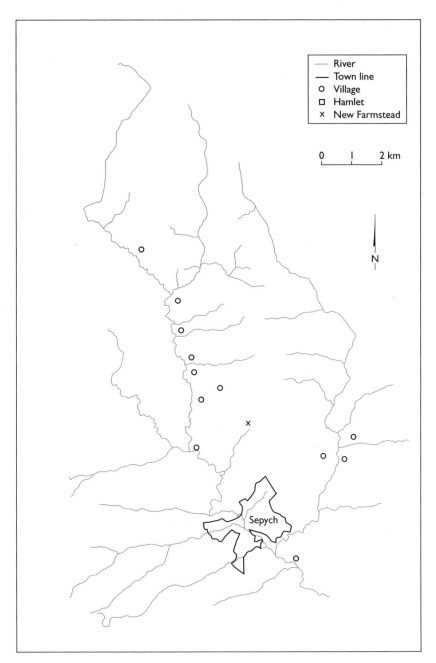

4. Remaining population centers in the Sepych Rural Administration as of 2001. Sepych grew substantially over the twentieth century and was, in 2001, home to more than three-quarters of the population of the Sepych Rural Administration.

the late 1920s and early 1930s sought to eliminate both farmsteads and the early, largely ineffective socialist communes and to replace them with collective farms (*kolkhozy*), in which land was to be held and worked communally by all members. By 1932, nearly all the peasants in the Vereshchagino district had joined collective farms by one route or another. A small number steadfastly refused to join the collectives, and these independent farmers (*edinolichniki*) continued to live on their farmsteads, often with nominal membership in the collective farm or with only one member of a household registered in the collective farm (see Fitzpatrick 1994, 152–62).[12] Although the collectivization drive was certainly heavily resisted, in and around Sepych as across the Soviet Union, early collectivization did not seriously challenge the village-level and slightly larger units of organization that had long been the primary units of affiliation for peasants. In other words, establishing these first collective farms often involved not the physical relocation of peasants to another village but rather the reconceptualization of existing village boundaries and property relationships in an effort to reincorporate the small settlements and farmsteads that had cropped up along their edges.

Collectivization did, however, depend heavily on the massive, forced removal of peasant families from the local countryside altogether. Dekulakization—the deportation of "rich peasants" (kulaks) and any other families unfortunate enough to attract that label—hit the Upper Kama particularly hard.[13] Much of the intent of collectivization and dekulakization was not simply to move peasants into larger, collectivized villages but to shift them out of the countryside altogether, into the labor-hungry industrial sector of the Soviet economy (some of it in labor camps).[14] For the same reasons that the Red Army was drawn to the large grain stores of Sepych in 1918, the once-wealthy Old Believer peasants of

12. There was, at first, a far greater proportion of these edinolichniki in the Upper Kama than elsewhere in rural Russia, perhaps indicating a higher degree of refusals to join early collective farms among Old Believer merchants in the area (S. A. Dimukhametova, I. V. Pozdeeva, personal communication). The early Soviet household books for the Siva district, to the north of Sepych in the Upper Kama, confirm that these stand-alone farmsteads were home to only the eldest residents. In 1940, for example, there were only five remaining edinolichniki (down from scores in 1938) in the Siva district; their average age was nearly 68. See POKM, f. 18742, dd. 60, 72.

13. On the specific course of dekulakization in the Urals, see Mialo (1988), Hughes (1994), Papkov and Teraiama (2002), and Leibovich et al. (2004, 71–76). At the very western edge of the Urals, the area around Sepych was not directly affected by the labor camps and "special settlements" commonly associated with the Urals in the 1930s (see, e.g., Pervukhina, Bedel', and Slavko 1994). Many of the techniques of resistance and avoidance to collectivization documented by Viola (esp. 1996) are well attested in Sepych, among them killing livestock, burying valuables, and self-dekulakization.

14. Harris (2002) sees campaigns against "wreckers" and "saboteurs" in the Urals as closely related to regional bureaucrats' attempts to bargain and evade the plan handed to them by the center: when a plan could not be fulfilled, targeting specific wreckers was one way to shift responsibility. See also Harris (1999, esp. 105–22) for a broader view of the Urals region in the early Soviet system.

Sepych and the surrounding areas were prime targets for district party officials seeking to fill deportation quotas in the early 1930s.

The young communists in charge of identifying and relocating kulaks in the Vereshchagino district found in the Sepych Uprising a convenient source of supporting evidence. Not for the last time in the Upper Kama, even peripheral participation in the violence of August 1918 returned to sow yet more violence. The deportation orders for E. Kh. Silkin and his family, for example, begin by listing their extensive property before the revolution and their exploitation of labor by hiring help and then introduce as aggravating evidence Silkin's alleged role in the Sepych Uprising. Deported on June 22, 1931, amid the drive to collectivize, Silkin was later arrested, tried, and shot in the fall of 1937—on the evidence of a counterrevolutionary career beginning with the Sepych Uprising and his prior dekulakization.[15] One elderly woman succinctly summarized the effects of dekulakization as follows: between those wealthiest families who were deported and those who hurriedly left of their own accord, "not a single one is left."[16] Only a few in present-day Sepych remember direct relatives who were permanently deported, a consequence of the fact that the most common unit of dekulakization was the entire family rather than a single individual. Rather, memories cluster around former neighbors and more distant kin; "Our kin [rod] are scattered all over Siberia," one friend told me. Thus were many of the most established families of the Upper Kama eradicated from its older moral communities as one especially violent part of socialist efforts to make new ones.

Collectivization and dekulakization—and especially their attendant violence—are often viewed by scholars as the singular and diagnostic events of rural Soviet socialism. However, from the perspective of many townspeople in Sepych, concerned as much with the rehabilitation and reconstitution of moral communities over the long term as with attempts to destroy them, these dislocations of the early 1930s blend into subsequent periods of movement within and out of the Soviet countryside. A second major period of resettlement began in the Upper Kama in 1940, as it became apparent to regional planners (themselves responding to initiatives from further above) that still-extant individual farmers and farmsteads were interfering with plans to increase the collective farms' productivity. In late June of 1940, the regional party and executive authorities decreed that any village with fewer than ten households would be considered a farmstead (khutor) and its population forcibly relocated to a nearby village by late July (that is, within a single month!). Seventy households in the Sepych rural soviet, and just over a thousand in the twenty-six rural soviets of the Vereshchagino district, were slated for immediate resettlement. With no time for building new houses, the plans simply called for the peasant huts to be

15. GOPAPO, f. 641/1, op. 1, d. 15543, t. 1, l. 59; t. 3, l. 28, 41. See also Leibovich et al. (2004, 100–102).

16. AAL MGU, Video Archive 1995, 6; see also AAL MGU, Video Archive 1994, 1.

dismantled, transported, and reassembled back in the village. Fully implement-
ing this effort proved impossible in many cases, particularly with the other
demands on collective farm members during the summer months. As a result,
the deserted buildings of former farmsteads often dotted the fields around collective farms for years to come, their residents likely having moved in with
relatives or simply left the countryside altogether.

A third round of village resettlements came in the mid-1970s, again in conjunction with attempts to increase productivity in the agricultural sector of the
Soviet economy. By this point, there were already few traces of older agricultural communities: the small village-based collective farms of the early collectivization period had given way to massive, multivillage farming operations. It
was with these economies of scale in mind that the Council of Ministers' decree
of March 20, 1974, "On Measures for the Further Development of Agriculture in the Non-Black-Earth Zone of the USSR," foresaw the near-complete
disappearance of small rural villages by 1989.[17] Planners hoped to begin this
process by resettling 170,000 families across the Soviet Union in the five-year
period between 1976 and 1980. This time, the planned resettlement was not
carried out nearly as swiftly as the elimination of independent farmsteads in the
1940s. Services such as schools and medical stations in rural villages, painstakingly built in earlier times to educate and care for even the most remote Soviet
citizens, were steadily shut down. Massive funds were pumped into construction projects to build houses for those moving to larger rural centers from villages designated "unpromising" (neperspektivnyi).

In and around Sepych, many villagers again left for the cities, and abandoned
peasant huts and outbuildings again covered the landscape for a time. One by
one, these structures were dismantled, their territories plowed into new fields.
In 1976, State Farm Sepych's official plan included a list of fifty-two population centers in the enterprise's purview. According to the plan, which meticu-
lously projected a closing year for each, forty-eight of those villages were to
be closed by 1989 (the target date set by the Council of Ministers' decree).
Remaining would be only Sepych itself, a large and as yet unnamed village
that would combine the neighboring villages of Dëmino and Krivchana, and
the remote Upper Lysvy, which was home to its own separate logging enterprise (lespromkhoz) (State Farm Sepych 1976, 132–34). Based on the population figures given for each village, the plan projected the gradual relocation of
1,198 villagers and 355 families.

When the Soviet period came to a close, State Farm Sepych had fallen short
by around a dozen villages in its efforts to fully centralize the once highly

17. On the Soviet theories of agricultural production that lay behind resettlement plans in
and after the Khrushchëv era, see esp. Pallot (1979). Grant (1995, 120–43) utilizes the analogous
resettlements on Sakhalin Island to illustrate both the remaking of indigenous identities in the
Brezhnev period and the aesthetics of ruins so often central to tropes of modernity.

dispersed population. Nevertheless, the very fact that the movements and residence patterns of people in and around Sepych were now being planned and coordinated—if not always successfully—by a mammoth state enterprise speaks to the scope of the transformations that had taken place over the course of the Soviet period.

A SPATIAL AND GENERATIONAL GRADIENT

From the perspective of residents of the Upper Kama, these resettlements were central to the refiguring of both generations and ethics in the socialist period. For those who remained in the Upper Kama throughout the Soviet period, an important distinction grew up between the centralized villages toward which younger generations had gravitated and the more remote villages in which older generations had often been born and sometimes still lived. Younger generations usually moved first, for their labor was more important in the grand enterprises of Soviet agriculture; many then commuted to take care of their parents or grandparents back "in the village." In these more remote villages, further from the prying eyes of the socialist state, elders often practiced the prayers and rituals of Old Belief with a greater degree of impunity. This pattern was repeated over the course of the twentieth century, such that elderly residents of outlying villages in the late Soviet period had often themselves relocated from still further-flung villages in their youth.

S. A. Moshev, born in the now-abandoned village of Teplënki, recalled that he walked twenty kilometers to work at the Machine Tractor Station in Sepych each Sunday for fifteen years, returning to his home village every Friday evening to visit his wife and family. He and his wife, now elderly, had long since moved to Sepych itself when I knew them.[18] If, in the official Soviet terminology, "unpromising" villages such as Teplënki were "closed," it was not uncommon to hear townspeople in Sepych say that a village had "died," or, indeed, that the countryside had died. "The villages died...like people in the war," reflected one elderly woman I knew. The association between Old Believer elders, themselves preparing for death, and the disappearing villages of the countryside around Sepych was as available and potent as the association between laboring youth and the centralized divisions of State Farm Sepych.

This was not, however, a forgotten landscape. "They herded us like livestock," reflected one friend in Sepych, as he pored over a list of population centers in 1926 that I had obtained from the local museum. He promptly challenged his wife to a competition over who could locate more of the villages on the list; each of them confidently placed well over half of the 126 villages enumerated, despite the fact that no more than a dozen still stood.

18. AAL MGU, Video Archive 1995, 9.

As the attention they and others lavished on my photocopies suggests, nearly seven decades of forced and voluntary resettlements had not entirely erased the numerous pre-Soviet villages from the landscape. Rather, this geography of steadily disappearing villages continued to serve as a grid for the formation of moral communities in the Soviet and post-Soviet periods, although neither in the ways it had in the postemancipation period nor, to be sure, entirely in the ways envisioned by the architects of socialist resettlement.

To learn to live in Soviet or post-Soviet Sepych—whether as child, husband or wife from out of town, or visiting anthropologist—was gradually to assimilate the history of resettlements as a basic part of getting around. Long after they had been plowed over into fields or become clusters of abandoned and decrepit houses, many villages continued to serve as sites of navigation through the countryside. Veteran tractor and combine drivers could rattle off the names of former villages for many kilometers around; directions to everything from picnics to cow pastures relied heavily on knowledge of an earlier geography of dispersed settlements. The many walks and tractor rides I took along the packed-dirt roads crisscrossing the Sepych rural administration were often accompanied by running commentaries on which villages had stood where, which socialist modernization drive had transformed them from populated settlements into pastures or hayfields, and who the last residents had been. I learned to recognize the spots where villages were likely to have stood, nestled in the bends of streams or between copses of pine and birch. Occasionally, I was told, a potato cellar from a long-abandoned village would turn into a sinkhole under the tall meadow grass, pulling in a tractor axle during July mowing.[19]

In nearly all cases, stories about these invisible villages included stories about Old Believer elders who had continued to live there after their children had moved to a more central village or to Sepych. For these older generations in the Soviet Upper Kama, this spatialization of generations is particularly evident in *sinodik-pomianik* manuscripts from the twentieth century. Sinodik-pomianiki were lists of the dead to be prayed for, cataloging the baptismal names of deceased elders according to the village-based community of Maksimovskie or Dëminskie to which they belonged. One lengthy sinodik-pomianik, written largely in the 1960s and given to archaeographers in 1979, provides a useful example. Each page is carefully divided into four columns giving baptismal name, date of death, month of death, and "notes." "Notes" often included patronymic names or years of death (unlike days and months, years were not

---

19. Note that the memories of closed and merged villages in the Soviet Union vary and are likely linked to a range of local factors. For example, Humphrey ([1983] 1998, 141) describes the *forgetting* of analogous earlier settlements in Soviet Buriatia, a process she attributes to the kind of "structural amnesia" that British Africanists once described for patrilineal systems. Compare also Crate (2006, 187–90).

necessary for determining when to hold memorial services). The first several pages of the manuscript, entitled "spiritual fathers," contain lists of names and dates with no specific village affiliation. They are presumably all or most of the spiritual fathers of either the Maksimovskie or Dëminskie concord (in this case, it is not conclusively clear to which group this manuscript belonged). The remaining pages organize deceased elders by village. In all, thirty-two villages and hamlets are covered in the fifty manuscript pages; table 1 shows a partial entry for the village of Batalovy.[20] After the many pages of dead cataloged by village, there follow lists of the names of still earlier adherents to the faith, including ancient church fathers and the Old Believers from the Pomortsy monastic settlements in the north who traveled to the Upper Kama in the early eighteenth century: "Grigorii, Avvakum, Gavriil...."[21]

Of the thirty-two villages mentioned in the manuscript, only around ten were still extant in the mid-1970s. It is unclear precisely when the village of Batalovy was abandoned. Its name does not appear in State Farm Sepych's plan for the future resettlement of outlying villages in 1976, which suggests that it was likely already empty at that point, several years at the very least before the manuscript was discovered by archaeographers. In the sinodik-pomianik, however, generations of Old Believer ancestors from Batalovy were remembered and placed among the ranks of the dead from neighboring villages, the spiritual fathers of the Upper Kama, the first Old Believer settlers from the north, and the ancient church fathers. Part of the task of living generations of Old Believer elders was to maintain relationships with all these inhabitants of the other world, to pray for their salvation, and to prepare themselves to join them after death. A note on the cover of one sinodik-pomianik reminded younger generations, "Write me in here too, when I die, and leave it to my kin."[22] In the Soviet period, writing oneself into history through manuscripts—a significant element of the creation of Christian textual and moral communities in the pre-Soviet period—also meant writing oneself into a rapidly shifting organization of material space. It meant recalling those elders whose villages could only be imagined in the ever more sparsely populated Soviet landscape.

Resettlement also radically transformed the circles in which those older townspeople and villagers who took up the practices of Old Belief moved. Although councils of elders remained based in villages and small groupings of villages throughout the Soviet era, resettlement and centralization steadily reduced the number of these communities. The net result, by the end of the Soviet period, was far fewer councils of elders and therefore fewer pastors. During the 1990s, there were only a handful of elderly pastors in place to challenge those

---

20. For other village-based lists of the dead, see ORKiR NB MGU, PV, 1423, 2005, and 2049.
21. ORKiR NB MGU, PV, 1419[1], l. 41r. These names correspond to the genealogy of spiritual fathers in the early Upper Kama discussed in chapter 1.
22. ORKiR NB MGU, PV, 1423, 1r. See Ageeva et al. (1994, 132).

Table 1. Excerpt from an Old Believer Sinodik-pomianik Mansucript

[Name]	[Day of death]	[Month of death]	[Year of death]
Timofei	6	April	1902
Vassa	11	August	
Elena	26	November	
Andrei	1	April	1924
Marfa	4	July	1946
Anastasia	8	December	
Anna	9	December	
Irina	11	May	1939
Tat'iana	21	January	

Source: ORKiR NB MGU, PV, 1419[1], l. 10r.
Note: In the original manuscript, the dates are given in the Church Slavonic manner, with letters standing for their numerical equivalents. The years, when noted, are given in the modern style.

new outsiders who began to vie for the religious allegiances of townspeople. Resettlement of large portions of the population also advanced a process that was likely under way to some extent even before the Soviet period: the rupture of the original association between Maksimovskie and Dëminskie factions and particular geographical subregions of the Upper Kama. Recall that the schism of 1888 had much to do with the postemancipation fortunes of the agricultural communities in which Maksimovskie and Dëminskie were based. As villages were closed and their populations moved in the Soviet period, there soon came to be *both* Maksimovskie and Dëminskie councils of elders in most larger villages, each group conducting separate services, electing its own pastors, and offering baptisms and funerals to its members from the younger generation. Religious affiliation does not appear to have influenced patterns of resettlement; after all, most people moved during their laboring years, long before the age at which they might have considered devoting their energies to the active practice of Old Belief.[23]

In sum, the reorganization of the populated landscape was a central pillar of the socialist organization of economy and society in all its multiple modes: official and unofficial, violent and voluntary, planned and chaotic. Resettlement—especially the resettlement of youth—was clearly and directly tied to socialism's characteristic labor shortages and central planners' perpetual attempts to overcome them through the further rationalization of production and redistribution. Viewing the long sweep of resettlement in the Soviet Upper Kama through these characteristics of socialism begins to highlight just what

---

23. Communities of Maksimovskie and Dëminskie Old Believers also spread, along with some of the rural population, to the urban district center of Vereshchagino.

was socialist about the refashioning of ethics and generations in the twentieth-century Upper Kama. Although the surrounding landscape remained one of the key materials of ethics, as it was in the periods of serfdom and emancipation, it was transformed anew. Family relationships, labor patterns, religious practice, and, indeed, consciousness of local history itself stretched out across the material landscape in a generational gradient, radiating outward from the ever-expanding center of Sepych.[24] The remainder of part 2 explores additional Soviet-era transformations that intersected with resettlement and contributed to the overall sharpening of generational distinctions in the ethical regime of socialism.

Socialist "Incentives to Labor" as Moralizing Discourses

Intersections of labor, money, and ritual played a central role in my analysis of serfdom and emancipation in the Upper Kama, particularly as these materials of ethics figured in the making and breaking of kinship and community bonds. The instructions issued by Countess S. V. Stroganova in 1837, for instance, carefully spelled out the proper arrangements of labor, money, and (Russian Orthodox) ritual for the family's Perm landholdings on the model of a European "well-ordered state." They did so, moreover, in a language of morality that, when later amplified by Count S. G. Stroganov and combined with Nicholas I's own moralizing campaigns against religious dissenters and civil marriages, had important implications for the ways in which residents of the Upper Kama encountered ethical dilemmas about everything from rent payments to sexual relationships. A century later, elements of the Soviet party-state were similarly occupied with generating moralizing discourses about how labor, money, and ritual should be arranged in and around Sepych—this time in the aid of building the world's first socialist society. This was a task that, although it pervaded all aspects of life, focused special attention on younger generations.[25] Like the Countess Stroganova's instructions, however, these moralizing

24. Comparative analysis should reveal a great variety of experiences and reformulations of historical consciousness linked to Soviet-era resettlements. Uehling (2004), for example, brilliantly uses the example of the Crimean Tatar deportations and resettlements of the late 1940s to explore the ways in which Soviet communities and understandings of history could be shaped by longing for a homeland lost through forced resettlement.

25. The literature on Soviet youth is particularly instructive on the ways in which Bolsheviks conceptualized the role of young generations and created institutions such as the Komsomol to realize these visions (e.g., Fitzpatrick 1978, 21–27; Viola 1987, 37; Tirado 1988, 1993, 2001; Pilkington 1994). Anne Gorsuch's (2000) description of Bolshevik specialists in matters related to youth as "moralists" fits well with some of my conceptual language here. Although I do touch on the Komsomol below, I also cast a wider net in exploring how younger generations were formed in Soviet-era Sepych, including many kinds of ethical practice not directly connected to "youth" in Bolshevik language. It is telling that there is next to no developed scholarly literature on what it

discourses of the Soviet party-state were transformed as they encountered the field of practical ethics in the Upper Kama. Accounting for the continuities and discontinuities that comprise these transformations requires attention to the shape of socialist moralizing discourses themselves, to the ethical repertoire they encountered in Sepych, and, as with ethical consequences of resettlement, to the facets of the socialist mode of production within which this encounter unfolded and to which it lent shape.

Philosophy departments in Soviet universities and Communist Party schools churned out a substantial body of literature on socialist morality, much of which was incorporated into specific projects directed at regulating and transforming the population, especially its youth.[26] The ways in which morality was conceptualized in Soviet discourse is neatly summed up in an entry in the second edition of the *Great Soviet Encyclopedia*:

> *The Moral-Political Unity of Soviet Society*—the unity of economic and political interests; the commonality of views, goals, and moral and spiritual makeup of workers, peasants, and intellectuals of the USSR, fighting under the leadership of the Communist Party for the victory of communism.[27]

Projects aimed at creating this moral unity—the classic moral language of the modern state (Corrigan and Sayer 1985)—spanned all aspects of life that the Communists hoped to see transformed. Ethical transformations in the Soviet-era Upper Kama are best introduced by focusing on a single example that is particularly well illustrated by twentieth-century Sepych: party-state moralizing visions aimed at reshaping labor and exchange through what became widely known and talked about in Soviet society as different kinds of incentives to labor. "Material incentives to labor" (*material'nye stimuly k trudu*) referred to mixes of cash and noncash salaries paid to Soviet workers, whereas "moral incentives to labor" (*moral'nye stimuly k trudu*) applied to the awards, rituals, socialist competitions, unpaid voluntary labor, and other enthusiasm-generating devices designed to induce harder work for the sake of brigade, enterprise, district, and, ultimately, communism on the world stage. I thus take

meant to be old in Soviet-type societies, despite the fact that most of the young people of the early Soviet period that are the subject of these studies of revolutionary youth did in fact age.

26. Rosenberg (1990, 15–49) groups together a range of early Soviet writings on the emergence of communist morality and ethics, including Lenin's address to the Communist Youth Leagues from which the epigraph to part 2 is drawn. Stites (1989, 115–23) links early Soviet attempts to establish communist morality to long-running utopian currents in Russian history. See also Iakuba (1970) on socialist law and morality and DeGeorge's (1969) overview and extensive bibliography of Marxist-Leninist moral philosophy (including discussions surrounding the 1961 *Moral Code of the Builder of Communism*). Field (1998, 601–3) provides an excellent summary focused on the Khrushchëv years.

27. *Bol'shaia Sovetskaia Entsiklopediia*, 2d ed., s.v. *Moral'no-Politicheskoe Edinstvo Sovetskogo Obshchestva*.

a cue from Martha Lampland's (1995) study of socialist Hungary by asking how labor was conceptualized and exchanged around Sepych and what those exchanges meant for the refashioning of ethical subjects and moral communities in the Soviet period.

The Soviet phrase "moral and material incentives to labor" presents some terminological difficulty for my analysis, for in it, as so often in the study of socialist and postsocialist societies, cousins of my own conceptual vocabulary stare back from my fieldsite. The phrase "material incentives to labor" emerges, for instance, from Soviet debates and discussions about relations of production in the writings of Marx and Lenin. "Material," in this interpretation of Marx, describes arrangements of labor, money, and commodities upon which rise the institutions and states of consciousness characteristic of a particular stage of history. From the perspective I adopt in this book, however, a wedding, with all its modes of embodiment, dress, ritual speech, and so on, is just as validly described as having a materiality as is a labor process. Indeed, a key part of my argument in these chapters is that these elements of Soviet socialism in practice are central to the movement of not only goods, but also items with different kinds of materialities, such as rituals. I thus adopt a different view of these sorts of rituals than is conventional in the literature. Most studies ask some variant of the question, "Did Soviet citizens actually believe in what socialist rituals represented?" or "Were new rituals effective in replacing pre-Soviet rituals?" (Binns 1979, 1980; Lane 1981, McDowell 1974). From my perspective, questions of belief and efficaciousness are less relevant than the ways in which these rituals could be used to create obligations in the overall Soviet system of exchange, circulation, and accumulation that encompassed other materials of ethics as well.

The interaction of these multiple materials of ethics is, as I showed in my discussion of ritual, labor, and money in the prerevolutionary period, far less given in advance—and its historical trajectory far less predictable—than in the readings of Marx that lie behind Soviet incentives to labor. My understanding of "material," in other words, is both broader and less deterministic than orthodox versions of historical materialism; the tricky part is that important players in the situation I am analyzing *were* strong base-determines-superstructure historical materialists (at least in their programmatic writings). It is important to study their language, plans, and goals as moralizing discourses that influenced Sepych in the twentieth century. Without belaboring this point or tracing manifold lines of descent from Marx but still wishing to emphasize the space between Soviet analytic vocabulary and my own, I leave the terms *material'nye* and *moral'nye* in transliterated Russian when I refer to the Soviet usages of these terms. By contrast, I continue to use the analytic terms "material" and "moral" as I presented them in the introduction and have used them thus far in my analysis. This device, admittedly somewhat cumbersome, allows me to trace how significant socialist discourses of morality were constructed and introduced to the socialist population while at the same time avoiding potential confusion deriving from the fact that these Soviet terms are loaded with Marxian assumptions about the nature of materiality and morality that are quite different from my own.

At the level of socialist theory, then, material'nye and moral'nye incentives to labor were carefully elaborated in Soviet moral philosophy and scrupulously linked to the writings of Lenin and Marx.[28] They can be traced directly to visions of the New Soviet Person and the kinds of relationships that socialist visionaries deemed appropriate to the construction of a noncapitalist society. Indeed, the issue of how to interest the population in the construction of socialism was arguably *the* problem facing socialist party-states. Boiled down, the Marxist-Leninist argument for material'nye and moral'nye incentives to build socialism ran as follows. Socialist societies were founded on a critique of the immorality of alienated labor and its central role in class formation. They aimed to achieve a further stage of human history in communism, during which it was thought that workers would, of their own volition, labor for the benefit of society at large. Until that stage was reached, however, it was the role of the party-state to provide incentives for socialist citizens to labor for the good of society and the march toward communism. A considerable amount of party-state energy went into attempting to design and implement modes of compensation to laborers that were not exploitative *and* would help in the creation of new kinds of persons who, eventually, would not need incentives to work for the good of the collective. Thus were born theories and practices of material'nye and moral'nye incentives. As socialism progressed further in the direction of communism, the proportion of material'nye (cash and noncash) incentives would, in theory, gradually be replaced by moral'nye (award-based, ceremonial) incentives. Ultimately, when communism was attained, the field of material'nye and moral'nye exchanges between party-state and laborer would disappear altogether. True communists would labor for society as a whole without any incentives at all, the state would wither away, and the vanguard party would no longer be necessary. The famed slogan "from each according to ability, to each according to need" encapsulated this vision as an idealized relationship of exchange.

Clearly, these visions did not play out as planned and were not widely shared, but neither did they simply vanish at the level of practice. Rather, they were distilled into step-by-step action plans and projects and placed in the hands of enterprise directors and Communist Party officials in places like Sepych. The intricacies of Marxist-Leninist theories of incentives were of little concern to these officials and bureaucrats *except* for the crucial fact, as the next sections show, that material'nye and moral'nye incentives offered a plethora of ways for skillful

28. On the Soviet socialist theory of moral and material incentives, see Laptin (1962), Karinskii (1966), Shcherbak (1973), and Rekovskaia (1987).

administrators to alleviate perpetual labor shortages, build networks, and collect people into moral communities that did not, in the end, much resemble the visions handed down in theories of material'nye and moral'nye incentives. In conditions of socialist shortage, enterprise directors constantly found themselves in the position of needing to wring extra hours out of their workforces and of struggling to find enough laborers to achieve something approximating production quotas. They could draw some of these incentives from outside the formal, planned economy (by hoarding or trading goods, for example), as Humphrey so cogently argued ([1983] 1998, 217–24). But directors who desperately needed labor had at their disposal not only these "manipulable resources" to exchange with workers or to grease the palms of those above them but also a much broader spread of possible enticements that derived directly from moralizing discourses about the construction of New Soviet Persons, including material'nye and moral'nye incentives. The recognition that party bureaucrats and managers drew on these grand socialist visions as well as on manipulable resources or "socialist gifts" to accumulate wealth in people is significant because it offers a way to think about how Soviet citizens inhabited and diverted certain moralizing discourses of the socialist party-state without requiring us to abandon the analytic importance of central planning, with its characteristic shortages and improvisations mediated by the administrators of socialist enterprises.

In and around Sepych, these general tendencies of socialism intersected with an array of more local categories and practices, central among them a vocabulary that revolved around the term *khoziain* (variously, master, owner, administrator, boss, man of the house; pl. *khoziaeva*). Although *khoziaistvo*—the domain commanded by a *khoziain*—was a common term for peasant household in this part of the Urals well before the revolution, it received a substantial boost in the early Soviet period. Anxious to avoid bourgeois capitalist terminology, Soviet visionaries preferred *khoziaistvo* (economic organization) to *ekonomika* (economy) to refer to the national economy (Humphrey [1983] 1998, 78). Soviet economic production was, in significant ways, to be conceptualized as household production writ large (see also Jowitt 1992, 127ff.). At the highest level was the *narodnoe khoziaistvo* or "people's economic organization." Soviet agriculture as a sector was *sel'skoe* (rural) *khoziaistvo,* and the collective and state farms constituting the sector were, respectively, *kollektivnye khoziaistva* (or *kolkhozy* for short) and *sovetskie khoziaistva* (or *sovkhozy*). In many areas of rural Russia, including Sepych, individual households continued to be termed *khoziaistva,* as they were in the prerevolutionary period. Thus, in Sepych as elsewhere, the official tiers of the party-state administration bore the label *khoziaistvo* at each level from the unionwide "people's economic organization" right down to the rural household.

Although not in official terminology, those who administered these nested domains were often called their khoziaeva. In this term and the everyday activities of those to whom it referred resided many of the practices of administration, property rights, and power characteristic of socialist systems more broadly. Ken Jowitt (1992, 143), for instance, echoing Alexander Gershchenkron's earlier formulation (1966, 310) suggested that the primary tendency within the Soviet system was for the "*khoziaistvennik* to become a *khoziain*"—the economic administrator/functionary to become the owner. State or collective resources in one's administrative domain, that is, had the tendency to become one's own resources, redirected into channels outside the plan. Indeed, the ability to accomplish such transformations—impossible shortage into successful subsistence, contradictory demands from above into improvised local solutions—were central among the elements that made one into a proper khoziain of a particular khoziaistvo.[29] I focus below on the ways in which various khoziaeva in and around Sepych made use of material'nye incentives in the era of collective farming (1930–65) and moral'nye incentives in the era of state farming (1965–91).[30] Tracking the permutations of these incentives fleshes out what new materials of ethics younger generations encountered, and what kinds of moral communities they were able (and unable) to build, as they moved or commuted from the Upper Kama's dispersed villages to the centralized farming operations of socialist agriculture.

Material'nye Incentives: From Labor-Days to Monetization (1930–65)

The collective farms meant to replace village communes and farmsteads existed in various forms and at various scales in Sepych from 1930 to 1965. By the late 1930s, the peasants of the Sepych rural soviet were organized into no fewer than twenty-eight separate collective farms, most of them named, like the agricultural communities of old, after the village at their center. Stand-alone farmsteads and some independent farmers—still an officially recognized and legal

29. There is a great deal more to Russian khoziain terminology than I can cover here. Paxson (2005), for instance, provides a sustained and rich discussion of the metaphysical and otherworldly dimensions of khoziain concepts in rural Russia. See also Hachten (2005) on khoziaistvo in the middle Soviet period. In other parts of the socialist world, the common language of material'nye and moral'nye incentives was refracted through other local vocabularies; see, for instance, Humphrey ([1983] 1998) on Buriatia and, further afield, discussions of the *zadruga* state in Eastern Europe (Verdery 1996, 64).

30. I do not mean to imply by my organization of this chapter a rigid temporal distinction between material'nye and moral'nye incentives to labor. My decision to treat material'nye incentives from 1930 to 1965 and moral'nye incentives from 1965 to 1991 derives from the kinds of archival material that are most available about Sepych and the topics upon which the townspeople I interviewed chose to focus. Festivals, socialist competitions, days of volunteer labor, and so on were all crucial elements of early Soviet rural life as well. On the range of activities that fit under the general category of moral'nye incentive in the era before State Farm Sepych, see, e.g., Siegelbaum (1998) and Petrone (2000). Stites (1991) explores Soviet rituals in the 1920s in part through the works and designs of Anatolii Lunacharskii, the famous commissar of enlightenment.

status in those days—dotted the edges of the farms. In the mid-1950s, the twenty-eight collective farms around Sepych were consolidated into five larger farms, and names from socialist central casting replaced the village names of the first generation of collective farms: Stalin, Kirov, Molotov, Victory, and, in Sepych itself, Lenin's Path. In 1959, as part of yet another round of mergers, Lenin's Path subsumed its neighbors and much more besides, becoming one of only four collective farms in the entire Vereshchagino district, each covering the territory of what had been scores of early collective farms.[31]

My conversations about collective farming in Sepych were thus peppered by dizzying accounts of movements and mergers that quickly surpassed my ability to keep comprehensive track of even small families or villages. Everyone seemed to be moving from remote to central villages, often in several stages and, not infrequently, via a long stretch in the military or in one or another city. At the same time, the borders of collective farms and their subdivisions were also constantly on the move, expanding or shrinking with little warning to incorporate new villages and groups of villages or to shed others.[32] Within this perpetually shifting, amoebic material landscape, memories of collective farming usually turned to the kinds of exchanges that took place between households and the collective farm or the state. I learned, in particular, to inquire into memories of monetary and nonmonetary compensation for labor, for moral communities and practical ethics in the era of collective farming were fashioned largely out of what laborers received in exchange for their hours in the fields—that is, out of material'nye incentives.

In their accounts of collective farming, townspeople almost always pointed to the absence of money in all manner of exchanges: the taxes collected by the state in agricultural products, the in-kind payments collective farmers received for their work, and the grain that they or their parents secreted away from the collective farm in the bottoms of their shoes. This was all evidence, they said, of "living poorly," of possibilities reduced by what they regarded as insufficient means of exchange. Older townspeople often drew attention first and foremost to an aspect of material'nye incentives called the labor-day (trudoden'). In the organization of collective farm labor across the Soviet Union, at least

31. These movements and mergers were, in fact, related strategies to increase productivity in the agricultural sector. Collective farm amalgamation was intended to reduce the ratio of farm administrators and office staff to workers and to capitalize on economies of scale, although mergers did not always represent an improvement for the combined farms or their divisions. Humphrey ([1983] 1998, 150) notes that amalgamations did not necessarily change the relations of production or the division of labor in collective farms—hence my argument below holds across these changes in scale.

32. It is notable that townspeople's memories of mergers and acquisitions were usually much hazier when it came to the shifting borders of rural soviets, the units of civil administration in the Soviet countryside (see, e.g., Slatter 1990). This haziness likely corresponds to the more general weakness of this vector of party-state power, at least in comparison with Communist Party organs and socialist enterprises like state or collective farms (see Humphrey [1983] 1998, 119–26, 300–372).

before the 1960s, the amount of labor expected of and compensated to collective farmers was measured in labor-days.[33] Labor-days were designed with the goal of moving Soviet workers into properly nonexploitative relationships with one another and with society as a whole; they were one part of the grand plans to create relationships appropriate to New Soviet Persons. Because both labor and compensation were to be equally distributed among members of the collective farm—in the stage of building socialism, the slogan ran "from each according to ability, to each according to work"—labor of different kinds and skill levels had to be brought into equivalence. The labor-day system aimed to accomplish this, requiring those in more difficult or higher-skill jobs to work fewer actual hours than those allotted lower-skill tasks. Until the mid-1950s, the labor-day norms for various farm occupations were set at the national level, and the directors of individual collective farms were not permitted to alter these norms for their members. As labor shortages continued, though, the hours required to achieve a single labor-day, and the sum of labor-days necessary to meet yearly quotas, increased.

Labor-day compensation to members of a collective farm was to be paid out of the collective farm's central account but only after all other debts and obligations had been settled. In many areas of the Soviet Union, this meant that there was rarely enough—if any—cash on hand to cover more than a tiny fraction of what was owed to the members of the collective farm for their labor-days. The difference was usually made up in set quantities of grain, meat, or other products. For instance, in Sepych in 1964, by which time collective farm chairmen had been granted a degree of flexibility in setting the rate of compensation for labor-days in their enterprises, the chairman of Lenin's Path announced that tractor drivers who worked nights would receive, in addition to their money, a kilogram and a half of grain per labor-day, half a kilogram more than those working the day shift. Those hearing the announcement would likely have been skeptical of the promise of money, but the director clearly thought that an increase in grain allotments would add to the number of members willing to work at night.

The noncash payment of labor-days had several important implications for the social relations of younger generations in and around Sepych, implications that had little to do with the lofty goals of equality that labor-days were designed to advance but everything to do with how actual moral communities were and were not made on collective farms. As has been widely noted for most of the rural socialist world, much of the real agricultural productivity took

33. Compare Creed (1998, 86–91) and Kideckel (1993, 112) on Eastern Europe, although detailed comparisons are difficult in part because it is far harder to collect and analyze rich memories of early collectivization in the former Soviet Union, where collectivization began decades earlier than in Eastern Europe. The archives of Sepych's early collective farms burned in the late socialist period. Cash compensation for labor in the Soviet agricultural sector was not guaranteed until 1966, when it was also made the first (rather than the last) obligation to be settled by collective farms in each accounting period (see Clarke 1968, 160–61).

place on the small subsistence plots allotted to collective farm workers rather than in large socialist enterprises.[34] In Sepych, noncash payment facilitated and enhanced production on these domestic plots (see also Humphrey [1983] 1998, 267–99), for payment in quantities of grain, for instance, could handily be used to feed domestic livestock. With no developed agricultural markets for the purchase of inputs, payment in agricultural goods rather than cash could thus be turned to some personal advantage (compare Creed 1998, 94–97, on rural Bulgaria). Noncash payments actually exacerbated labor shortages because they gave collective farmers more reason to devote their time to personal plots rather than to work on collective farm lands.

Despite all the migration and resettlement characteristic of the era, then, one of the key materials of ethics—in-kind payments—functioned largely to keep the everyday scope of exchanges quite small and to undermine the development of allegiance to the collectives envisioned by socialist planners of material'nye incentives like the labor-day. Without the greater degrees of exchangeability associated with money, the transactions of collective farmers in Sepych were limited to those with the state, the collective farm itself, and the closely associated household plots. In Sepych and the former merchant towns of the Upper Kama, this reduction in the scope of social relations was a far cry from the large markets and high degrees of cash turnover associated with the preevolutionary and NEP eras in which early collective farmers had grown up.

Considering the practical uses of these material'nye incentives to labor in Lenin's Path also throws some light on the ways in which enterprise directors, acting in their capacity as khoziaeva, used labor-day payments not so much with an eye toward creating new sorts of socialist morality among their workers, as they were intended, but as a means of collecting wealth in people—the center of gravity of socialist ethics. In many rural areas of the Soviet Union, collecting people often meant not just amassing far-flung networks but also struggling to keep villagers from leaving a particular collective farm (see Humphrey 1983 [1998], 300–316). Lenin's Path was not considered an exemplary collective farm; indeed, it often served as a negative exemplar for the whole region. In 1965, an entire special issue of the Vereshchagino district newspaper devoted to Sepych began its lead article, entitled "Serious Blunders: Why the Fallow Isn't Plowed in Sepych," with a question:

> Who in the Vereshchagino district is further behind than anyone else in the grain yields, productivity of livestock, the sale of agricultural products, and other measures? Those in Sepych. And it has been that way for many years.[35]

---

34. On the importance of rural domestic production in the Soviet Union, see Humphrey [1983] 1988, 164–74), and compare Creed (1998), Kideckel (1993), and Lampland (1995) on those Eastern European states that followed the path of rural collectivization.

35. "Ser'eznye promakhi: Pochemu v Sepyche ne vspakhany pary," *Zaria Kommunizma*, July 24, 1965, 4.

The failure of Lenin's Path to meet its quotas (or to bargain or fudge them successfully) meant that it frequently appeared in the pages of the district newspaper under similar headlines intended to shame its members into greater productivity.

When the chairman of Lenin's Path was given a chance to account for the poor state of his enterprise, he pointed immediately to problems with both amount and kind of material'nye incentive, summing up the difficulties of keeping workers in the collective farm this way:

> One of the main reasons is the lack of people's material'nyi interest in society work. Payment is too low. The average labor-day costs 67 kopeks, but [in Lenin's Path] field workers received only 25. In past years we gave out even less. It isn't a coincidence that nearly 300 healthy able-bodied men and women have left the collective farm in the past five years.... We are considering how to raise the material'nyi incentive for collective farmers.[36]

It is worth noting that this quotation appeared in the official newspaper of the local party organs. In general, the newspaper spoke in the moralizing language of socialist construction; its headlines were filled with exclamation points about the bright communist future and encouragements to work harder for the socialist motherland. The material'nye incentives the director sought to increase were not in and of themselves antisocialist. Nevertheless, his comment is a frank acknowledgment of the importance of using the strategies designed for the lofty goals of constructing New Soviet Persons simply to hold enough labor in the collective farm for it to function. In the case of Lenin's Path, then, visions of New Socialist Persons constituted through certain kinds of noncapitalist exchange were diverted into the relationships of actually existing socialism. Moreover, we see these material'nye incentives caught up in the director's failed attempts to collect people, hold labor in his farm, avoid the negative exemplar status handed down by his district newspaper, and, in general, be an effective khoziain of the domain he oversaw.

Before the chairman of Lenin's Path had much time to contemplate the changes in the structure of material'nye incentives he alluded to in his interview, his collective farm was dissolved and reorganized into two state farms. Until 1965, there had been only one state farm in the entire Vereshchagino district. In the summer, one former member of Lenin's Path told me, the state farm used to graze its cattle near Sepych on occasion, and townspeople could not believe how big and healthy they were. "We all wanted to be a state farm," she said, the envy still evident in her voice. On August 17, 1965, they got their wish. Another member of Lenin's Path recalled that she was out in a collective farm field haying on that day. When she returned home, she heard that the

---

36. "Chestnyi trud—kliuch k pod"emu arteli," *Zaria Kommunizma*, February 18, 1965, 1.

head of the collective farm had received an unexpected phone call from the district center. All the collective farms in the Vereshchagino region were to be immediately transformed into a system of nine state farms. Lenin's Path would be divided into State Farm Sepych and State Farm Sokolovo.

The district newspaper began to run a series of articles instructing the local population in the differences between collective and state farms, the first of which—published only two days after the conversion—was entitled "State Farms—the Leading Socialist Enterprises in the Countryside." Others followed: "State Farm Party Organizations," "The Organization of Labor in a State Farm," and "Payment of Work in State Farms."[37] It was this final topic that townspeople I knew remembered most about the switch from a collective to a state farm. They became waged employees of the state rather than members of a collective farm that contracted with the state to meet production quotas. In the state farm, all means of production, as well as all that was produced, were also the property of the state, without going through the sales or contracts that were necessary in collective farms. The labor-day was abolished, replaced with a set of cash-based compensation systems that included bonuses for work above the norm. Dispersed out of state budgetary allocations to agriculture, which were on the rise, rather than out of the collective farm general account, salaries began to be paid with a good degree of regularity in Sepych.[38] By the middle of the 1970s, State Farm Sepych, in contrast to its struggling predecessor, Lenin's Path, was regularly overfulfilling its plans and setting the standard for other state farms in the district. The fame of its exemplary director spread throughout the Urals.

Townspeople's memories of the transition from collective to state farm organization underscore my points about material'nye incentives and their implications for the making of different kinds of moral communities among socialist laborers. In contrast to the period of collective farms, the state farm era was recalled by townspeople in Sepych as one of rapid monetization and a correspondingly expanded set of social relations and moral communities. Changes in the mix of monetary and nonmonetary remuneration—both understood as material'nye incentives to labor—had important implications for the

37. "Sovkhoznye Partiinye Organizatsii," *Zaria Kommunizma*, August 21, 1965, 4; "Organizatsiia truda v sovkhoze," *Zaria Kommunizma*, August 21, 1965, 3; "Oplata truda v sovkhoze," *Zaria Kommunizma*, August 26, 1965, 3.

38. Durgin (1964) gives a comprehensive overview of the monetization of Soviet agriculture in the 1950s and 1960s, relating it to theoretical and policy debates about labor, value, and cost accounting at the highest levels of the party-state establishment (see also Morozov 1965). Durgin's prediction that fuller monetization would lead to the replacement of administrative control of the agricultural sector with control via price levers and incentives was not borne out—as the discussion of State Farm Sepych below shows. Money and prices in socialist systems, in short, should not be assumed to behave as they (are assumed to) behave in capitalist systems. For an example of the many how-to case studies of farms transitioning from in-kind labor day payments to full monetization, see Zinochkin (1960).

kinds of relationships in which those who received them could participate. Cash salaries widened the circuits of exchange; noncash salaries shrank them. The alternation between these different modes of compensation points to an important dynamic in relationships of exchange concentrated in this world, one that stretched back to the era of serfdom and continued into the postsocialist period. Indeed, local history in the Upper Kama was often understood by townspeople in Sepych as alternating between periods of monetization and demonetization as they created widening and shrinking circuits of exchange and interaction.

To summarize my argument thus far, cash and in-kind compensation for collective farm work, calculated through the labor-day system, provided key materials of ethics out of which socialist workers could fashion relationships and communities from the 1930s to the 1960s. These materials of ethics were distinctly socialist in multiple ways. They were closely linked to grand visions of communism on the march through the elaboration of material'nye incentives to labor in Marxist-Leninist philosophy and economic policy. At the same time, they were caught up in—and aided in the constitution of—actually existing socialist moral communities, especially those associated with labor shortages, struggles to keep collective farms running, and the attempts of khoziain figures to accumulate wealth in people and achieve positive exemplar status.

We have also begun to glimpse some of the ways in which these socialist transformations of ethics were received and incorporated into longer-term expectations and sensibilities in and around Sepych. First, there were important generational dimensions to the paths along which material'nye incentives flowed, with the younger generations who moved to centralized villages most closely involved in the system of labor-days. At least in the 1930s and 1940s, older generations in more remote villages were somewhat more insulated from these changes on still-peripheral farmsteads. Second, we are now in a position to see more clearly a centuries-long oscillation between periods of monetization and demonetization in the Upper Kama, one in which the cash deficits of the era of collective farming and the turn to monetization in the 1960s appear along with the rapid monetization of the postemancipation era and the equally rapid demonetization of the post-Soviet period. All these points about cash vs. noncash material'nye incentives will be central to my arguments about Old Believer elders in the Soviet period, the subject of chapter 4. Just as the periods of marketization and monetization following emancipation in the 1860s–80s heavily influenced the schism between Maksimovskie and Dëminskie elders, the extreme shortages, demonetization, and correspondingly shrunken circuits of exchange in the period of collective farming lent important shape to elders' responses to this world in its early socialist manifestations.

Moral'nye Incentives in the Era
of State Farm Sepych (1965–91)

The Brezhnev era was not one of stagnation in Sepych. In the late 1970s, the local state farm, specializing in milk and meat production, was the largest in the Vereshchagino district. It spanned over fourteen thousand hectares of land and employed around seven hundred people throughout its six divisions, one in Sepych and the remaining five in nearby villages. Beginning in the early 1970s, State Farm Sepych was led by Andrei Petrovich, a young member of the Communist Party from a local family who had previously worked as a grain storage manager and then a brigade leader in Lenin's Path. Under his leadership, State Farm Sepych gradually began to reverse the negative exemplar reputation that had dogged it predecessor collective farm. By the early 1980s, State Farm Sepych was a highly regarded state farm, not only in the Vereshchagino district but across the Urals. The district newspaper no longer upbraided its leadership and workers but instead began to cite Sepych as a model for the other local state farms. Frequently enough, State Farm Sepych was alone in the district in meeting its yearly quotas—testament in part to higher productivity, but perhaps more significantly to the charisma, connections, and steadily increasing wealth in people held by its director. "His *best friend* was the head of the regional executive committee [*oblispolkom*]," one friend emphasized to me, in one of our conversations about the differences between the Soviet and post-Soviet periods in Sepych.

Soviet media outlets above the district level started to take note of Sepych in the late 1970s. Correspondents from the national monthly *Rural Life* ran periodic articles about what one correspondent began to call the "Sepych phenomenon"—the enthusiastic participation of young people in state farm labor. For some reason, in contrast to the trend across the Soviet countryside in the years of collective farming, young men and women in Sepych were marrying, staying in town, and working for the state farm. Enterprise and school directors, as well as all manner of party officials, wanted to know how Andrei Petrovich and his colleagues had stemmed the tide of migration out of the countryside. There were always visitors in Sepych in those days, one local party member recalled to me; when there weren't visitors, the director was off in Perm, working his contacts hard to divert more resources to Sepych, to transform its successes into still greater productivity and recognition. Although the switch to cash salaries that came with the state farm era in Sepych was significant for townspeople, it was not exclusively the change in material'nye incentives to labor that produced the Sepych phenomenon. This generation of young socialist workers emerged in large part from the consequences—intended and unintended—of a powerful khoziain's successful use of Soviet moral'nye incentives to labor: the range of programs, rituals, festivals, and socialist competitions designed to simultaneously increase agricultural productivity and fashion new sorts of noncapitalist subjects and moral communities.

Liudmila Ivanovna, a former Komsomol member, remembered her job as one of the main organizers of Communist Party-sponsored activities in Sepych largely in the vocabulary of collecting and transforming people. In our conversations she was insistent that her job was first and foremost to shape socialist subjects oriented toward society and the success of the local state farm. Her primary task, she told me on several occasions, was "get to people" (*dobrat'sia do liudei*) and "work with people" (*rabotat' s liud'mi*), spreading the message about the importance of working hard to bring fame to State Farm Sepych and its region. Luidmila Ivanovna's mother, who was never a party member, once asked why she spent so much of her energy working for the party. Her response, she recalled, was that she did it "for people, to work with people." She was always going around with the director in the summer to see how workers were doing in the fields and barns and to give them "moral support" (*moral'naia podderzhka*) so that they never thought they were "unnecessary" (*nikomu ne nuzhny*). We didn't "get to" everyone, she said to me once, but they did get to many, and tried hard for the rest.

Liudmila Ivanovna's work with people was, I came to understand, a special instance of the more general category of "society work" (*obshchestvennaia rabota*) (see also Humphrey [1983] 1998, 352). As examples of Soviet-era society work, townspeople frequently cited voluntary summer harvest brigades before or after their regular work shifts (the famous Soviet *subbotniki*) and groups of youth who brought firewood to elderly townspeople; a disposition toward society work was a key criterion for admission to the ranks of the Komsomol. At the higher ranks of the Komsomol and the party, where the organization of cadres was a primary task, a kind of meta-society work prevailed, what Liudmila Ivanovna described as work with people. If society work referred to the socialism-building tasks in which all citizens were expected to participate, then party members' work with people ensured that an extra shift of society work in the hayfield at four in the morning actually had a sufficient number of workers or that the firewood actually got delivered. In short, to organize everyone else's society work was to work with people.

Some dedicated Communist Party activists in Sepych worked tirelessly and sincerely to build socialism above all else. But even for them, both society work and work with people were of necessity part of the vocabulary through which they participated in socialism's characteristic informal connections, coalitions, and networks—important raw materials for socialist moral communities. For citizens, to participate in society work was often to expect something in return (or, more often, to have already received goods, favors, access, and/or recognition) from the party member organizing the work. For a party member, to work with people was to be skilled at organizing and deploying reluctant labor, often by diverting resources from further up the party-state bureaucracy and doling them out as enticements. In extreme cases like that of Andrei Petrovich, being associated with the successful and famous domain he commanded was enough to entice all manner of society work out of townspeople. "Work with people," Liudmila Ivanovna told me, brought "fame to our region, to our state farm." In sum, one did not need to believe in or even think much about the lofty ideals of building socialism to participate in society work or to work with people. Both kinds of work were, however, integral to the wealth-in-people networks on which the socialist sense of belonging to a moral community rested. In Sepych, under the guidance of Andrei Petrovich, Liudmila Ivanovna, and others, moral'nye incentives to labor were central to these efforts.

On an afternoon when she was visiting Sepych and again months later when I visited her at home (now in a nearby city), Liudmila Ivanovna outlined the elements of the regime of moral'nye incentives to labor that she and others had collaborated to design in Sepych. It all began, she said, with the close ties between State Farm Sepych and the local school. New cadres for the farm were drawn from the school, and the farm's recruiting efforts were concentrated on the cultivation of young workers. Andrei Petrovich allotted tractors, combines, and eighteen hectares of land to the school. Older schoolchildren—initially just young men but increasingly young women as well—gained experience and training while harvesting the school cafeteria's own food each year. The fact that Liudmila Ivanovna began with the school in each of our conversations, whether with the director's frequent visits or with the apprenticeship programs she instituted, underscores the extent to which the efforts of the party-state emphasized younger generations.

Despite its centrality, the school was only one site where moral'nye incentives to labor were offered in Sepych. The Soviet House of Culture, or "club," was a second such place. Liudmila Ivanovna recalled with special fondness the two kinds of rituals that she helped develop for the club, both of which were variations on wider Soviet rituals in the later Soviet period (see Lane 1981, 109–29). She and others planned elaborate "initiations" into field work and farm work (posvashcheniia v khleborobie i zhivotnovodstvo), in which the newest ranks of schoolchildren joining the state farm would be initiated by those who were retiring in the same year. Other club rituals honored "labor dynasties" (trudovye dinastii), families in which three generations had devoted years of service to socialist agriculture. These evenings would begin, Liudmila Ivanovna recounted, with cars sent out from the central office to collect all the family members from their scattered homes and bring them to the club, where they would be escorted to the stage in front. She or another party leader would then describe the accomplishments of each family member to the gathered workers. They would add up the total years that all twenty to twenty-five people in the family had worked, someone would bring them bread and salt, and Andrei Petrovich would present them with gifts from the state farm.

6. Sepych's former Russian Orthodox mission church, now a House of Culture.

When she hosted these events, Liudmila Ivanovna said, it was her job to try to induce a feeling of envy into those in the audience, to try to make them want to be like the people on the stage. This was an important part, she said, of working with people, or as we might phrase it, acting as a khoziain by instilling obligations in others in order to accumulate wealth in people. Note, in the context of my more general argument about the place of ethics in the socialist mode of production, that these rituals were a way of creating obligation that did not revolve primarily around gifts trafficked in the informal economy. They were materials of ethics that derived, rather, from the practical use of quite overt and official means to create New Soviet Persons out of the younger generations in the audience. Moreover, they were intimately connected to the process of making new socialist exemplars—people, families, and entire enterprises that others would aspire to emulate.

By far the most successful (and most consequential, in the long term) means of accumulating people in State Farm Sepych were marriages among members of the younger generation. In the summer of 1980, a film crew from Perm spent nearly a month in Sepych, shooting a film for regional television about the successes of State Farm Sepych. Partway through the project, I was told,

the director of the film decided that the unifying thread of the scenes and interviews should be the high number of weddings celebrated each year in the state
farm. One young couple, both state farm employees, planned to get married
in the near future, and they moved the date of their wedding so it could be incorporated into the filming. Thus was born *Sepych Weddings,* a fifteen-minute
film about State Farm Sepych, its director Andrei Petrovich, its workers, and,
most of all, its plentiful weddings.[39]

The film opens at an outdoor wedding, with the sounds of folk music and
brief shots of wedding guests, a bride and groom welcomed with bread and
salt, and a young man who will shortly be identified as Andrei Petrovich. Over
these images, and with the music still playing in the background, the female
narrator begins, "It's polite to consider love something deeply personal, but
you'll agree that twenty weddings a year in a single town speaks of something
else, not only love." Wider images of Sepych then follow the opening credits: workers unloading a hay cart, boys playing in a small pond, teenage girls
laughing and splashing one another with water from a well, muddy streets
lined with half-finished duplex houses, and finally the kindergarten under construction. The narrator continues:

> Sepych is often called the depths of the Perm region, fifty kilometers from the dis-
> trict center, much farther than that from the regional center. State Farm Sepych is
> large, and working hands are probably the most critical problem. It's a town like
> any other town, except it differs in that there are many children here, of all ages. A
> decade ago you wouldn't have seen this picture—Sepych was nearly given the sen-
> tence of "unpromising town." Then everything started to change. A whole settle-
> ment grew up in a single Five-Year Plan—Komsomol Street, Youth Street. For the
> most part, it is young families who receive these new apartments. And it turns out
> that families in the state farm don't wait more than a year for housing. On Youth
> Street, there are already twenty-three children. The kindergarten is Project Number
> One, and therefore state farm director Andrei Petrovich is most often found here.

These introductory segments set the tone for the film as a portrait of hard and
successful labor on the fields of rural socialism, one in which the active participation of young generations is critical.

---

39. *Sepych Weddings* was shown frequently on regional and then national television at the time
and later won an award in Vladivostok. When I lived in Sepych, I watched the copy of the film
I had made with different audiences on the rare occasions when time and the presence of a VCR
coincided. Surprisingly, the film still appeared on regional television from time to time even during my fieldwork, although I never saw it broadcast. On views of private and public life in official
and unofficial Soviet discourse about morality as it relates to marriages and divorces in particular,
see Field (1998). My analysis supports Field's contention that couples did not usually employ the
language of communist morality in making decisions about marriage and divorce; when they did,
they most often appropriated this language for their own ends. However, I do see the kinship
and community ties that resulted from these marriages and celebrations in State Farm Sepych as
important elements of socialist ethics in practice, for they added enormously to Andrei Petrovich's
wealth in people and Sepych's exemplar status.

Sepych Weddings glorifies youth at every turn, from young women and men on tractors to the toddlers in the new kindergarten. Youth Street and Komsomol Street (named after the Communist Youth League) are indications of the focus on successive younger generations of townspeople in socialist construction. The film's single brief shot of an elderly man cutting hay with a scythe—a sharp contrast to the powerful new tractors driven in other scenes—only emphasizes the importance of youth. As he slowly cuts hay in a field by himself, the narrator fills in what purport to be his thoughts on the matter of generations and the importance of focusing on youth: "As long-time resident Sysoi Ignatevich says, 'An old tree holds by its roots, but a young growth always demands a great deal of attention.'" Older generations, the film implies, will hold firm in their commitments to the socialist future, but younger generations still needed to be fashioned into New Soviet Persons. This purported statement, as will become clear in the next chapter, is more than a little ironic. In Sepych, younger generations ("young growths") did indeed receive a great deal of attention and became immersed in the relationships of rural socialism. Older generations ("old trees"), however, did not always hold by the socialist or communist roots set down in their youth. In old age, more than a few in the Upper Kama worked precisely to abandon those roots and take up the ascetic practices of priestless Old Belief.

After its opening sequence and place-setting scenes, *Sepych Weddings* turns to the subject of labor in State Farm Sepych. "It isn't a coincidence," the narrator begins this segment, "that young women occupy such a central place. They're a great help to the director, in work and leisure time—they're everywhere. And they keep the bachelors in town." Women, that is, are useful means to solve the problem of labor shortage, both by contributing their own labor and by marrying young men and raising families in the state farm. The film goes on to focus on "Brigantina," one of the first young women's tractor brigades in the Urals in the late Soviet period.[40] Over one of the shots of a Brigantina member plowing a field, the narrator comments:

> It's considered that this isn't [long-term] work for young women because in front of them lies married life, families. Naturally, they won't stay for long, but they work out their time and ignite the interest of others.

The film thus notes specifically that the women's tractor brigades for which Sepych was gaining fame in the Urals were only temporary work for young women. Their real task was to get married and reproduce.

Indeed, within the staid conventions of Soviet propaganda films, *Sepych Weddings* does its best to eroticize farm labor. The scenes of women's award-winning

---

40. Although it had connections to Union-wide initiatives to address farm labor shortages by encouraging women to take on new roles in state and collective farm labor, Sepych's Brigantina was a novel approach in the Urals at the time, and most attributed it to the active encouragement of Andrei Petrovich. On Soviet women's tractor brigades, see Bridger (2003).

labor in the fields are followed by a scene of town nightlife, set at an outdoor dance floor built in a small wood at the edge of town by the local Komsomol. The dance floor and similar youth events, the film implies, are where Sepych's many young marriages have their origins. From the dance floor, *Sepych Weddings* jumps back to the images of a wedding with which it began. It also returns to its central message, which is to combine successful work in the fields, Sepych's al fresco nightlife, weddings, and new houses full of young families into a glowing portrait of young lives dedicated to socialist agriculture. The role of the director of the state farm was central in all of this. He not only coordinated and directed all labor in State Farm Sepych, but he also presided at its weddings. At the conclusion of each, he presented the newlyweds with keys to a new duplex in the state farm. Liudmila Ivanovna recalled that the newlyweds were also given the use of the director's car for the day.

The film records Andrei Petrovich's toast at the featured wedding in full:

> My dear comrades, friends, and guests. Here we are, gathered together again to celebrate the most recent wedding—here are our guests of honor, Liza and Misha. We should say today that, if we take two years ago, 1979–1980, there were fifty weddings in the state farm, then this is already the eighteenth wedding this year. So it is a great pleasure for me to wholeheartedly congratulate our dear newlyweds and wish them great happiness, great success in their work, and, most important, wish that they live well. The very, very best wishes to you and good luck in your lives. Comrades, raise a toast to the newlyweds.

The director's toast, and the fact that he presided over every one of the weddings he mentioned, is more indication of his direct involvement in using socialist rituals to collect wealth in people, bring fame to State Farm Sepych, and enhance his standing as a powerful khoziain. Note in particular his emphasis on the *number* of weddings in the state farm, the size of the wealth in people that he and local party organizers had accumulated in the previous years. Along with the party members like Liudmila Ivanovna who helped organize the weddings, the director was using the tools of socialist construction that coupled marriage and work in a state farm as means of collecting people and creating an exemplary socialist enterprise, one that would attract still more resources from the center.

Notably, they were using "folk traditions" to do it. *Sepych Weddings* is full of references to local wedding rituals. It concludes, for example, with a slow-motion shot of the bride and groom "going for water," one of the rituals of the folk wedding long practiced in Sepych. On the last day of the three-day wedding ceremonies, after the bride and groom were already married, it was customary for them to go with their guests to the river, returning with buckets of water from which they served everyone in attendance. In actual weddings, the most commented-upon part of going for water was (and remains) the effort to drench one's friends and family as thoroughly as possible. The much more sober *Sepych Weddings,* however, shows only the bride and groom returning from the river, surrounded by friends, with the bride carrying two buckets full of water. The narrator's final comments conclude with a gentle direct address to the bride:

> Weddings in Sepych go on deep into the winter. Sepych weddings speak of love and harmony—not for nothing do old Russian customs live on here. Happiness is in your hands. Carry it. Don't spill it.

The slow-motion shot emphasizes the extent to which the narrator's words slow down time and attribute an endless traditionality to the wedding ritual.

One particularly useful way to understand this aspect of *Sepych Weddings* is through the lens of Gail Kligman's discussion of folk weddings in socialist Romania (1988). Kligman points out that, contrary to their theoretically forward-looking and antinationalist agendas, socialist states often found presocialist, traditional folk customs associated with rural life-cycle rituals a productive way to mobilize the allegiance of citizens around affiliations of national identity (see also Lane 1981; Rausing 2004, 136–45). Kligman's analysis fits well with the concluding scene of *Sepych Weddings,* the film's predominantly folk-music soundtrack, and many of the narrator's comments.

First, it is a very particular kind of tradition that State Farm Sepych's wedding ceremonies drew on, one devoid of religious content. The wedding rituals of the Upper Kama were the rituals that had long had the *least* to do with local priestless Old Believer practice. In the nineteenth century, many younger generations were so distanced from the practices of local Old Belief that they even married officially in the local Russian Orthodox mission church. Elders and pastors were prohibited from attending weddings, which proceeded according to a variant of the Russian folk wedding. In this case, the state farm's wedding rituals did not present problems of extricating elements of secular national culture allegedly preserved by peasants from their religious origins, as they did in Kligman's Romanian Orthodox context (1988, 280–81). In the priestless Old Believer Upper Kama, weddings, marriages, and sexual reproduction had long been matters of this world that concerned pastors and elders primarily as things to be avoided on pain of excommunication.

If we consider the full spectrum of points at which practices intended to shape New Soviet Persons might have tangled with ethical sensibilities prevalent in the Upper Kama before socialism, wedding rituals and marriages were a point of very minor friction. This is one way in which the locally significant generational divide between worldly and otherworldly affairs created the conditions under which socialism did and did not transform ethical sensibilities in Sepych. In this case, the conditions made for a *lack* of conflict. To put this in the terms I outlined in chapter 1, local expectations about ethical practice separated central aspects of social reproduction from biological reproduction, locating the former in relationships between eldest and youngest generations and the latter in relationships among middle generations of marriageable age. To aim efforts at transforming social reproduction and the durable creation of socialist subjects at marriage-age generations, as socialist wedding rituals did by design, was to miss much of the target in and around Sepych.[41]

Second, returning to Kligman, we can add to her analysis additional mechanisms by which the socialist party-state made use of (and even invented) folk traditions. Kligman's analysis concentrates on the ideological level, on national folk traditions as a technique of propping up the legitimacy of the socialist state (see also Verdery 1991). *Sepych Weddings* itself, as an item of propaganda shown repeatedly on Soviet television, should probably be seen in this light. But the actual weddings of Sepych, as remembered by townspeople and portrayed in the film to some extent, point to an additional, more local way in which party-state bureaucrats made some use of what we might call folk-socialist weddings. In Sepych, weddings were wrapped up in the whole range of moral'nye incentives to labor on the farm directed at younger generations. Whatever use the deployment of folk traditions had at the level of creating national ideologies in Sepych and elsewhere, their practical use on State Farm Sepych was to further the farm and local party leadership's accumulation of wealth in people and pursuit of exemplar status in the socialist society surrounding it. Sepych's folk socialist weddings accomplished these goals with spectacular success (some subsequent divorces and disenchanted departures aside), and with results that were evident well into the postsocialist period.

MY analysis of *Sepych Weddings* dovetails in part with Alexei Yurchak's (2006) argument that the ritualized speech acts of the Soviet party-state were not, at least in the late socialist period, primarily evaluated for or experienced through their truth content. Rather, Soviet citizens pivoted off these elements of moralizing discourse—"deterritorialized" them, in Yurchak's poststructuralist phrasing—as part of the process of creating meaningful ethical lives, lives that depended on socialist discourses but were by no means fully circumscribed by them. Yurchak's clear and careful formulation has considerably advanced our understandings of how Soviet socialism worked at the level of discursive practice and, in his examples, for the world of late socialist youth in urban centers.

---

41. This situation is vastly different from the one in Ukraine, where many Baptists took their dedication to hard, honest worldly labors into socialist factories, with the paradoxical result that some were simultaneously lauded as "Stakhanovites" and arrested for violation of laws against the practice of religion (Wanner 2007, 83–84). Note also the difference between Sepych and the Buriat case explored by Humphrey, in which Buriat weddings were central to local notions of kinship and social reproduction and thus made for a much higher degree of friction in the Soviet period ([1983] 1998, 382–401).

Some questions, however, remain. What to make of the fact, for instance, that different socialist citizens had very different levels of success at deterritorializating party-state moralizing discourse, with important implications for their own lives and those of others surrounding them? The failures of the collective farm Lenin's Path and the great successes of State Farm Sepych point to one answer: that the diversion of the moralizing discourses of material'nye and moral'nye incentives was intimately caught up in efforts to collect wealth in people and to achieve exemplar status in the broader socialist mode of production and circulation. So, too, as I have shown, were differential modes of labor compensation like labor-days and cash salaries. Rituals, gifts, labor, money, and in-kind compensation, that is, all mingled with one another as materials of ethics utilized in the practical construction of socialist moral communities and ethical subjects among younger generations. Moreover, significant social distinctions of the sort that largely fall outside the scope of Yurchak's linguistic and discursive analysis both helped to shape and were shaped by these interactions. It mattered a great deal whether the subjects created through the diversion of socialist moralizing discourses in Sepych were men or women, young or old, positive or negative exemplars, or holders of greater or lesser wealth in people.

How, we might ask next, did the ethical lives crafted by these particular socialist citizens and groups of socialist citizens draw not only upon new kinds of practices characteristic of the ethical regime of socialism but upon an older repertoire of expectations and sensibilities? To explore more fully the importance of generations in Soviet-era Sepych, we must turn from the youth of this chapter to Sepych's elder generations of Old Believers and their relationships oriented toward the other world. This interest in elder generations is not mine alone. In the early 1980s, the local party activist Liudmila Ivanovna was asked a question about religion at a regional Communist Party conference in Sverdlovsk, where she was giving a presentation entitled "Raising Young People in the Labor Traditions of State Farm Sepych." She answered, quite sincerely, that in Sepych the Communist Party had no problems with religion: the one church had been closed long ago and there were no priests or other churches for fifty kilometers in any direction. However, in the very same summer that the television crew from Perm was filming *Sepych Weddings*, scholars from Moscow State University were trumpeting their discoveries in and around Sepych: hundreds of Old Believer manuscripts and scores of older villagers who still actively used them. Many of those who donated their manuscripts to Moscow State University were, in fact, the parents and grandparents of the young women and men driving tractors and getting married in *Sepych Weddings*.

The next chapter deals with these successive generations of older townspeople. It shows that despite their attempted avoidance of the world, elders' ethical dilemmas in the Soviet period were deeply caught up in the shapes of rural socialism, both those connected to resettlement and incentives to labor and those, introduced in the next chapter, that had to do with antireligious campaigns, the remaking of textual communities, and the effects of socialist patterns of circulation and consumption on elders' ascetic attempts to renounce the world. The young men and women of *Sepych Weddings* will, however, return in later chapters. In the 1990s, after the end of the Soviet Union, the former young party members and workers of *Sepych Weddings* were moving into leadership positions in the privatizing state farm and the civil administration, worrying about how to cope with the changes brought by decollectivization and massive devaluation in the Russian countryside. They fondly recalled earlier means of accumulating wealth in people—the means by which they were convinced to marry and labor in State Farm Sepych—and wrestled with new and knotty dilemmas about how to deal with demands for the accumulation of capital. In the 1990s and into the next decade, the young men and women of *Sepych Weddings* were also turning forty-five, fifty, and fifty-five years old. Many had buried their parents and seen their own children grow up to leave Sepych for work in urban centers. Some of the most active members of the much-heralded youngest generation of exemplary socialist workers in State Farm Sepych began to consider withdrawing from this world and increasing their chances of salvation. But they did so in yet another reconfigured ethical field, one vastly different from that of either their parents or their grandparents. I pick up their story in part 3.

4 *Elders*

Christian Ascetics in the Soviet Countryside

On a June day in Sepych, in the lull between the all-out labors of sowing and haying, three middle-aged women came to visit the house in which I was boarding. I had, by that point, grown accustomed to such unexpected visits from townspeople who wanted to meet the foreigner living in Sepych. We sat in the living room for a couple of hours, drinking coffee and asking questions of one another. Upon learning that I was interested in Old Belief, one of the women immediately launched into a story that, she said, would illustrate for me what religion was like in the Soviet period. There was a picnic one day, she went on to recount, out in the woods somewhere far from town. At this picnic were several schoolchildren, a schoolteacher, and a few elderly townspeople (*stariki*). At one point one of the elders abruptly turned to the teacher and asked, "Do you believe in God?" Here my guest assumed the posture of the teacher in her story. She looked to one side of the living room couch, as if to the children, then to the other, as if to the elders. She looked at her lap, paused, and then glanced again to the children on one side and to the elders on the other. "No, I don't believe," she said finally, quoting the teacher. Shifting back into narrative mode, she explained that the elders did not question the teacher any further, but that he later took them aside and admonished them, "Of course I believe in God. Never put me in that situation in front of children again."

Our conversation quickly moved on to other topics. At the time, I took the story to be about the difficulty of publicly avowing belief in God in Soviet times, especially in front of potentially loose-lipped schoolchildren. This was a frequent enough recollection of the Soviet period and not, of course, particular to Sepych. Even as I wrote up my notes the next day, however, I began to wonder whether the incident of the picnic was not a bit apocryphal. In a social universe where everyone knew nearly everyone else—by some distant kinship

tie or shared school class at any rate—almost all stories came with some oblig-
atory discussion of who did what, when, and where. Yet this story had taken
place in an unspecified wood near Sepych, at some vague Soviet time, with an
entirely unidentified cast. I have since come to agree, however, that the picnic
story, apocryphal or not, is aptly illustrative of a central set of ethical dilemmas in Soviet-era Sepych, especially in my guest's vivid embodied portrayal of a
middle-generation schoolteacher caught, uncertain and temporarily speechless,
between the younger and older generations on either side of him.

In turning to consider Old Belief in the Soviet period, I should emphasize that
I do not think religion in Soviet society is best approached by regarding it as resistance to state power or as an arena of robust Russian traditions. The category
"religion" itself, in fact, may obscure more than it reveals. In the case of Sepych,
we would do some considerable injustice to local understandings and experiences if we were to impose these categories on the shifting currents of ethical
practice. Finding religion and tradition in Sepych, for instance, is just what different wings of the Soviet party-state sought to do, with varying results and degrees of success. The perspective I adopt here, in contrast to that of some studies
of tradition and religious resistance, reveals that Old Believer elders seeking the
narrow path to salvation in the twentieth-century Upper Kama were every bit as
implicated in the distinctive characteristics and movements of socialist societies
as were the younger generations of socialist laborers. There was no place entirely outside socialism from which to resist. Shortage, resettlement, and socialist incentives to labor affected old and young alike, if in different ways.

Readers should thus keep in mind that everything I describe pertaining to
elders was unfolding at the same time, across the same landscapes, and in the
same households as the more youthful transformations discussed in the previous chapter—a point to which I return throughout. Moreover, the local practice of deferring participation in the rites of Old Belief until late in life meant
that most elders had themselves been directly and deeply involved in the material practices of building socialism on collective and state farms at earlier stages
of their lives. At any one point in the Soviet period, in other words, youth and
elders faced each other across a widening generational divide; over the decades, many crossed that divide themselves. In the last analysis, I suggest, the
ethical regime of socialism in the Upper Kama paradoxically helped to sustain
crucial elements of local Old Belief rather than eliminate them.[1]

---

1. The approach I take here also departs from other common approaches to religion in the
Soviet period. I do not, for instance, find the musty question of whether communism is a kind of
religion to be very helpful, inasmuch as it most often rests on definitions of "religion" and "communism" that are highly abstracted from social and cultural practice. However, a number of recent
scholars have recast this question and fruitfully revisited it in specific historical circumstances,
noting ways in which various Bolshevik activists and sympathizers drew on aspects of religion
familiar to them in the aid of advancing revolution (e.g., Steinberg 1994; Hernandez 2001). Although variants of this argument are often made for "sects" in particular (Engelstein 1999; Etkind

Skirting Soviet Secularization

The moralizing discourses undergirding Soviet efforts to secularize society were, like material'nye and moral'nye incentives to labor, carefully and thoroughly linked to writings on the development of socialist society and consciousness in the Marxist-Leninist canon. In practice, however, antireligious efforts differed significantly from labor incentives in that they were almost always lower priorities for the party-state: they received less funding, were pursued with less consistency and intensity over time, and garnered far less prestige among party bureaucrats than, for example, work in the vaunted industrial sector of the planned economy. Like all aspects of the party-state, the administrative units that housed efforts to regulate and eliminate Old Belief changed over time, from the Commission on Cult Issues (1928–38) to the Council on Religious Cults (1945–66) to the Council on Religious Affairs (1966–90). I refer to this shifting set of administrative units, including their interactions with other units of the party-state (from schools to local organs of Soviet power when they addressed religion) as the "Soviet religion bureaucracy," although I do not wish this title to convey coherence of goals or methods (see also Wanner 2007, 35).[2]

In all its different instantiations, the Soviet religion bureaucracy repeatedly faced a conundrum familiar to social and cultural theorists: defining religion and secularism.[3] Did religion lie in physical church buildings? In the specialists officially representing a church or analogous body? In attendance at collective rituals? In personal belief? In some combination thereof? At different times and in different places, Soviet antireligious campaigners and bureaucrats looked for religion in each of these places and implemented schemes to root it out—at which point they faced other problems. How could they know when and whether religion was being replaced by secularism? How does one reliably measure religiosity? In the context of my overall argument about ethics, note especially that all these possible locations for and measurements of religion had material correlates: church buildings, religious specialists, embodied rituals, and verbal or nonverbal expressions taken as evidence of internal belief states. They were thus every bit as subject to the vagaries and indeterminacies of material practice as anything else. That is, just as material'nye and moral'nye

---

2003; Zhuk 2004; Coleman 2005; Paert 2005), I found no developed evidence to support it in the Upper Kama. Recall, for instance, that the rituals of *Sepych Weddings* were *not* drawn from local Old Belief.

2. On the structure of Soviet administrative bodies charged with regulating religion, see esp. Anderson (1991) and Warhula (1992).

3. Peris (1998) makes particularly adept analytic use of the problem of defining religion as it was confronted by the League of the Militant Godless in the early Soviet period. See also the recent approaches to Soviet-era religion taken by Young (1997) and Husband (2000), each of whom poses useful questions more useful and complex than those framed in terms of religious resistance.

incentives to labor—other important material aspects of building socialism—took unexpected twists and turns in their encounters with local expectations and practices in the Upper Kama, so too did Soviet drives to regulate and eradicate religion.

What is notable about the Soviet religion bureaucracy's efforts in and around Sepych is the extent to which their most overt dimensions often missed their targets, a partial consequence of some stark disparities between the ways in which party-state organs conceptualized religion and the ways in which residents of the Upper Kama were accustomed to fashioning ethical lives in and beyond this world. The material manifestations of religion that interested representatives of one or another agency concerned with religion often did not, in other words, appear or operate as expected in the Upper Kama. In fact, the domestic, decentralized, and largely deferred nature of local Old Belief had prepared residents for many of the most significant Soviet campaigns to define, regulate, and eliminate religion. For example, in light of the youth-focused environments of collective and, especially, state farming, it was highly advantageous that local expectations already associated the active, visible cultivation of ethical selves and communities in pursuit of Christian salvation almost exclusively with members of the eldest generation. The continued practice of priestless Old Belief in Sepych through the Soviet period is attributable at least as much to the specific material contours of the Soviet religion bureaucracy's campaigns as it is to the strength of so-called Old Believer traditions in the face of persecution.[4]

SPACES

One mainstay of Soviet attempts to control—and ultimately eliminate—religion was the regulation of religious buildings and other sacred places that were focal points for the formation of relationships among religious practitioners and with beings inhabiting another world. Indeed, central officials concerned with administering religion often took the number of churches open or closed as an important diagnostic of the progress of antireligious efforts. A 1937 report from the Sverdlovsk region (of which Sepych was a part at the time) noted that of just over 1,000 religious buildings in the region before the revolution, only 340 were still open. The Vereshchagino district counted 12 churches, all of them either Russian Orthodox or associated with the communities of priestly Old Believers well to the east of Sepych in Vereshchagino and Ageevo.

4. On antireligious campaigns in the Urals more widely, with a focus on the Russian Orthodox Church, see especially Agafonov (2003), Viatkin (2003), and Nechaev (2004). There is almost no scholarly literature on Old Belief in the Urals (or elsewhere, for that matter) during the Soviet period. A notable exception is Paert's analysis of oral interviews about the Stalin period conducted in 1990 (2001b, 2004a), which suggests many themes similar to my own analysis. See also Ageeva et al. (1997).

Because they did not meet in church buildings, priestless Old Believers in the Upper Kama escaped the gaze of this report and a great many others like it.[5]

The bells in Sepych's Russian Orthodox mission church were taken down and presumably melted in 1936, likely in a wave of church closings across the entire region.[6] However, as might be expected from the ineffectiveness of the Russian Orthodox mission in Sepych in the nineteenth and early twentieth centuries, the closing of Sepych's Russian Orthodox church had little effect on the local practice of Old Belief in the Upper Kama. Few if any of Sepych's Old Believers had attended the church; it served mainly the outsiders who came from other parts of Perm and Viatka provinces to Sepych's precollectivization market days. The handful of townspeople who remembered the church before its transformation into a grain storage facility told me that their parents had once or twice taken them to look inside but that, as one put it, "our kind went around to houses" to pray.

Although there were no priestless Old Believer churches to close in the Upper Kama, there were several houses of prayer (*molebnye doma*), including one in Sepych itself. I was told by townspeople that Sepych's house of prayer had burned to the ground in 1936—the possibility of arson was not mentioned—and that the others had gradually been closed by local Soviet authorities or left behind by departing villagers. Significantly, these small houses of prayer did not leave any of the archival traces that churches did. Moreover, in my conversations with townspeople about the Soviet era, the memory of these houses of prayer also seemed slight—the absence or closing of dedicated religious buildings was never presented to me as interfering with priestless Old Believer practice. In villages where a priestless Old Believer house of prayer had been closed by Soviet authorities, the local elders and pastors easily returned, it seems, to meeting in one another's houses. In communities without the resources to construct a house of prayer, after all, services and councils had long been held in elders' homes (as, for instance, recounted in the polemics between Dëminskie and Maksimovskie factions in the late nineteenth century).

Sepych's Russian Orthodox church was, like many other rural churches, originally transformed into a grain storage facility for the local collective farms.

---

5. GARF, f. 5263, op. 1, d. 1551, l. 3–3v, 30. Figures on the number of active church buildings—and procedures for opening and closing churches—were a staple of reporting and internal circulation among the Soviet institutions concerned with religion. On churches and Old Believers throughout the Soviet Union, see, for instance, GARF, f. 6991, op. 3, d. 1, l. 34–37; op. 4, d. 1, l. 39; d. 68. In the Vereshchagino district of the Perm region in particular, see, among many others, GARF, f. 6991, op. 3, d. 25, l. 162–63; d. 813, l. 4–5, 25–26, 33; d. 814, l. 22–27, 68–69; op. 4, d. 360.

6. On the mid-1930s closing of churches in the towns of Voznesensk, Ochër, and Siva—all of them in or near the Old Believer areas of the Upper Kama—see GARF, f. 5263, op. 1, d. 1552, l. 73–76v; d. 1556, l. 116–116v; d. 1553, l. 174; d. 1730, l. 33–33v. See also Mel'chakova (2003) for a wider view of this era in the Perm diocese of the Russian Orthodox Church. It is not certain, in fact, that a Russian Orthodox priest was stationed in Sepych between 1918 and 1936 at all, following the execution of the local priest for his participation in the Sepych Uprising.

As Sepych's collective farms grew and increasingly built their own facilities, the church was overhauled yet again, this time into a Soviet House of Culture. A stage rose in place of its altar, and rows of seats filled the nave; eventually local party activists added a movie screen, a sound system, and a large annex to be used for additional gathering space. From the perspective of Soviet planners and propagandists, at any rate, the construction of such Houses of Cultures would speed the path to communism both by reducing the influence of religion and by building allegiance to the goals and new moral communities of socialism.

These goals were made explicit in Sepych by a report to the Council on Religious Cults in 1952, which attributed ongoing religious activity among the population—including the continued presence of young children at "secret" gatherings—to the lack of effective party lectures and activities and the dismal condition of Sepych's club. The report recommended urgently updating the club's library, installing a radio receiver, and constructing an inviting place for reading groups and performance rehearsals.[7] As we have already seen in Liudmila Ivanovna's memories of her time as a party organizer in the heyday of State Farm Sepych, the refurbished House of Culture did indeed host many socialist rituals and coordinate other moral'nye incentives to labor. But neither these rituals, with their focus on laboring younger and middle generations, nor the closing and remaking of the Russian Orthodox church building itself, had their intended effects on local Old Belief, whose largely elderly practitioners had preferred to shun church buildings for centuries. In the Upper Kama, sacred space, as well as the high-stakes rituals and modes of transformation that could take place within it, was anywhere the elders gathered; it was not in bricks and mortar that could be demolished or converted to other uses.

SPECIALISTS

A closely parallel effort by which the Soviet bureaucracy sought to regulate what it understood to be religion was by eliminating or tightly controlling the specialists who facilitated it. On some occasions, this meant arresting, deporting, executing, or otherwise removing priests or other specialists from the communities they served. More often, it meant working to co-opt or redesign the hierarchies and institutions into which religious specialists were organized. Like church buildings, those people classed as religious specialists had to be officially registered; they were often called in for meetings with representatives of the religion bureaucracy to report on the activities of their group. Additionally, each parish or analogous religious community was expected to register itself. As part of the registration process, religious groups would name councils of

---

7. This report on the state of Sepych's club was made to the central offices of the Council on Religious Cults in Moscow in late 1953 as part of the Perm region's quarterly reporting on religious activity in the region. See GARF, f. 6991, op. 3, d. 815, l. 107–11.

twenty members (called *dvadtsatki*) who would serve in an advisory role and place their names on record as officially responsible for legal use of the religious buildings and property. These "twenties" were intended to create a check on the power of official clergy and a second official vector of power through which the religion bureaucracy could monitor the activities of groups.[8] Thus, even ordinary correspondence between the priestly Old Believer parish in Vereshchagino and the Old Believer archbishopric in Moscow—acknowledgment that a publication had been received, or requests for building repairs—passed through the offices of the Soviet religion bureaucracy.[9]

As in the case of religious buildings, the priestless Old Believers of the Upper Kama were relatively well positioned to deflect these Soviet attempts to administer religion and ultimately secularize society. Recall that spiritual authority in the Upper Kama had long been far more diffuse than in the Russian Orthodox Church or groups of priestly Old Believers. Indeed, in the eighteenth- and nineteenth-century Upper Kama, decentralized priestlessness was defined precisely in opposition to the hierarchical structures of these groups. Rather than being ordained by a hierarchy of specialists, pastors in the Upper Kama were chosen from within their own community of elders in consultation with two or three pastors from neighboring communities. At the time of the schism of 1866–88, this arrangement proved debilitating, for the lack of a generally accepted hierarchy meant that one or another pastor could not easily be removed from office without angering his flock. Heresy could spread swiftly through the decentralized councils of elders. In the Soviet period, however, the decentralized, democratic, nonhierarchical nature of local religious authority meant that those pastors removed forcibly by agents of Soviet power could be quickly and quietly replaced from within. The disappearance of pastors—I discuss several cases shortly—was thus not so devastating a blow to the formation of ethical relationships with the other world as it was for other religious groups.[10] The means by which a community of elders could reconstitute itself after the

8. These registration procedures were carefully elaborated and periodically revised at the highest levels of the Council on Religious Affairs in accordance with current Soviet laws on religion. See, for instance, GAPO, f. r-1204, op. 1, d. 1, ll. 1–12; GARF, f. 6991, op. 6, d. 4, l. 47–50. On the role of the twenties—an administrative structure apparently often misunderstood by regional-level administrators themselves—see GAPO, f. r-1204, op. 1, d. 4, l. 107–9. For an example of registration documents for priestly Old Believers in the Vereshchagino district, see AOAVR, f. 1., op. 1, d. 381, l. 1–3; d. 382, ll. 96–97.

9. GARF, f. 6991, op. 4, d. 52, l. 123–25.

10. See also Wanner (2007, 39) on similar dynamics in Ukrainian Baptist communities. Seeking to register individual groups was not the only strategy pursued by the Soviet religion bureaucracy. In one case, the Council on Religious Cults worked in concert with the High Council of Old Believers in Lithuania to help form and organize an All-Soviet Center of Priestless Old Belief. In other words, where there was no hierarchy, one option was to work actively to help create one, the better to observe and influence it. On this and similar collaborations—which did not touch the Upper Kama—see GARF, f. 6991, op. 3, d. 11, l. 31–32v; d. 47, ll. 22–26, 45.

removal of a pastor were, in other words, nonhierarchical and more or less impervious to being co-opted by the Soviet religion bureaucracy.

As we might expect from this mismatch between the Soviet institutions designed to implement the moralizing visions of a secular society and the resolutely nonhierarchical sensibilities and practices of the Upper Kama, the archives of the various agencies comprising the Soviet religion bureaucracy reveal a decades-long and ultimately unsuccessful attempt to register the priestless communities in and around Sepych. In report after report, it is clear that district- and region-level officials were made well aware of the prayers and baptisms taking place in this corner of the Vereshchagino district, largely by reports from local Communist Party officials or schoolteachers.[11] Just as clearly, however, they did not have the tools, connections, or local leverage to discern with any reliability or regularity who was leading these groups, much less to register and monitor them in accordance with Soviet laws on religion.

One report, from 1950, accounted for its own shortcomings with the excuse that "the believers [in and around Sepych] notify each other about the days of prayer secretly, so to find the place that a group of them gather is not possible."[12] This is not, quite simply, an excuse that could be used in the case of a hierarchy that relied on the use of a dedicated building for worship or included registered members who reported directly to the Soviet religion bureaucracy. Frustrated in their attempts to register priestless groups, yet often under pressure to show progress in the war with religion, these officials could often do no more than track down particular elders who confessed to participating in unregistered religious activity, sternly remind them of Soviet laws, and extract a promise not to continue to attend service or baptize children.[13] The former head of the Council on Religious Affairs for the Perm region confirmed for me in an interview that registering small groups of priestless Old Believers was one of his largest and most consistent headaches during his time in office.

DEFERRED RITUAL PRACTICE

With respect to both spaces and specialists, then, priestless Old Belief in the Upper Kama simply did not manifest itself in ways that organs of the Soviet

---

11. See, for a representative sampling, GARF, f. 6991, op. 3, d. 815, ll. 9, 52–53, 106–14; d. 814, l. 68–69, 76–81v; op. 6, d. 305, l. 100; d. 549, l. 34; d. 794, l. 26–29; GAPO, f. r-1204, op. 2, d. 3, l. 12. In 1961, a onetime inventory of all registered religious communities in the Soviet Union—likely an accounting in preparation for Khrushchev's crackdown on religion in the mid-1960s—listed twelve priestless communities of Old Believers in all of the Perm region (GARF, f. 6991, op. 4, d. 360). In fact, there were likely more than twelve priestless communities within easy walking distance of Sepych.

12. GARF, f. 6991, op. 3, d. 814, l. 51–53.

13. See, for instance, AOAVR, f. 1, op. 1, d. 300, l. 117–117v. As I discuss below, there were several instances of fines being levied on priestless Old Believers living in the city of Vereshchagino, but I came across no reliable oral or archival evidence of fines in the rural areas around Sepych.

state were primed to recognize. A variation of the same dynamic took place with respect to the common practice of deferring ritual participation until late in life—a practice that, I argued in chapter 1, crystallized during the campaigns against local Old Belief under Nicholas I and Count S. G. Stroganov. In the context of deferred ritual practice, how could one tell the difference between a believing—but not practicing—layperson and an ordinary Soviet atheist? This question perpetually vexed party-state operatives when they turned their eyes to Sepych, for the internal belief states that were of some interest to the religion bureaucracy were impossible to discern except by means of some material manifestation: a verbal confession of belief, say, or participation in a ritual. Yet in the Upper Kama, it was precisely these manifestations of religious practice that priestless Old Belief had long deemphasized for its middle, worldly generations. Like churches and a hierarchy of specialists, the everyday material practices of religion anticipated by the Soviet religion bureaucracy were often simply not recognizable enough to battle effectively in the Upper Kama.

Even as it confounded antireligious campaigners, who knew that religious activity was taking place in Sepych but could not discern its contours, deferred practice also lent particular shape to the communities and possibilities of the socialist period for the residents of the Upper Kama themselves. It was, for instance, not as inconsistent as it might seem at first blush for some townspeople to spend their worldly lives in the service of socialism but then withdraw into the ascetic communities of priestless Old Belief upon retirement, just as prerevolutionary Old Believers had temporarily satisfied the demands of worldly power by marrying in the Russian Orthodox Church. Indeed, nearly all the active Old Believer elders I knew in Sepych were former members of the local collective or state farms or had worked in other sectors of the socialist labor force. In the later Soviet period, elders-in-waiting had often been model Soviet citizens and occupied relatively high positions in the local Soviet bureaucracy earlier in their lives; a few were even members of the Communist Party.

Did they actually believe in God in their Soviet-era laboring days? After asking this question too many times myself, I have come to see it as less than useful, for it placed me in the same conceptual and definitional traps that ensnared representatives of the Soviet religion bureaucracy (compare Needham 1973). How does one define or apprehend a belief state? Far more is revealed, I have come to conclude, by watching how others, such as the Council on Religious Affairs, struggled with the question of belief in and around Sepych. At the same time, we can note how townspeople's inheritance of expectations about deferred ritual practice allowed them to take advantage of outsiders' misperceptions of what religion looked like.

Consider the example of Evdokia Aleksandrovna, whose life course aptly illustrates some of the ambiguities of deferred ritual practice in the Upper Kama during the Soviet period. Born into a Dëminskie family in one of Sepych's outlying villages in 1915 and never married, she had moved several times over the years and spent most of her life as a member of one or another of the collective farms that predated State Farm Sepych. She had also worked for almost a decade, including the years of World War II, in a military airplane factory near Perm. During my time in Sepych, Evdokia Aleksandrovna lived alone in a small house on the edge of Sepych. She had become an active elder in Sepych's Dëminskie community after her retirement in the 1970s and subsequently joined the town's new community of priestly Old Believers in 1994.

In the 1960s, while still a layperson, Evdokia Aleksandrovna had served as the elected chair of Sepych's rural soviet, a position that, while it did not require membership in the Communist Party, implicated her deeply in the rural socialist bureaucracy—including its monitoring of religion. Among the tasks allotted to rural soviets was the surveillance and regulation of religious activity in their territories; it was they who provided much of the raw material out of which higher levels of the party-state bureaucracy, including the regional offices of the Council on Religious Affairs, fashioned their reporting and plans for future work with the population. Although Evdokia Aleksandrovna did not speak to me of the episode herself, the archives of the Council of Religious Affairs in Perm recount a visit by some of these higher-level authorities to the Vereshchagino district during her tenure as representative of the rural soviet in 1963. After reporting briefly on the two priestly Old Believer churches in the eastern Vereshchagino district, the report turned to rural areas:

> It is clear that, in the Vereshchagino district, especially in the group of settlements around Sepych, Borodulino, Sokolovo, Vedenichi, and others, the religion of Old Belief is preserved like nowhere else in the [Perm] region. [Several members of the leadership of collective farm Lenin's Path, local teachers, and engineers] affirm that religious services and rituals are held in the majority of houses in Sepych and other population centers.

> To the question, "Why does the executive committee of the Sepych rural soviet not conduct any work to conform with laws on religion and, at the same time, allows religious sects to actively function without interference?" the representative of the rural Soviet E[vdokia] A[leksandrovna] only shrugs her shoulders with embarrassment. [Others] answer that same question [by saying that] E. A. herself takes part in religious services, observes fasts, and so on: "You want her to conduct a war with sectarians, but Evdokia Aleksandrovna is herself the first one to pray."[14]

This report demonstrates the multiple implications of deferred ritual practice in the Upper Kama. In the first place, like so many other reports across the Soviet period, it reveals that officials from the religion bureaucracy were aware of a high level of religious practice in Sepych yet were largely unable to figure out how it worked and, in the end, were surprised and aggravated to hear that

14. GAPO, f. r-1204, op. 2, d. 6, l. 50–53.

their presumed local point person was not only not combating religion but, at least according to other townspeople, was actively participating in rituals. (Although she was not an active Old Believer elder at that point, Evdokia Aleksandrovna attended some services as a layperson, standing in the back but not praying with the elders. For those wishing to condemn her for whatever reason, even attendance without active prayer would have been sufficient evidence.)

The case of Evdokia Aleksandrovna also demonstrates that Old Belief in the Upper Kama during the Soviet period was not characterized simply by marginal, peripheral, or thoroughly resistant practice. Although it often took place in secret, it was not the realm of dissidents uniformly opposed to the party-state or even, in all cases, the Communist Party. Those who adopted the rituals of Old Belief late in life could occupy, as did Evdokia Aleksandrovna, central positions of authority in the administration of rural socialism. In fact, in numerous ways, the practice of Old Belief, and therefore the cultivation of certain moral communities and subjectivities understood to lead to Christian salvation, often depended heavily on the worldly connections and networks of socialism. After joining the Dëminskie community of elders and rapidly becoming one of its most respected members, for instance, Evdokia Aleksandrovna occasionally made use of the moderate wealth in people she had accumulated in her years in the world. In the early 1970s, she recalled, the spiritual mother of Sepych's Dëminskie community came to her and said she was afraid to summon the rest of the elders to her house for Easter. Evdokia Aleksandrovna went to the serving chair of the rural soviet, a middle-aged man, and said to him, "We want to pray on Easter—promise us that there won't be any persecution." She recalled his response: "Pray...quietly." In this case, her worldly contacts were useful even after she had joined the community of elders—she could intervene with younger officials whose respect she had gained in her earlier position.

Note, finally, that Evdokia Aleksandrovna's response to the direct question about her failure to adequately engage in antireligious activities was, according to the report, "a shrug." Like the schoolteacher's hesitant glances back and forth in the picnic story that opened this chapter, this shrug is telling, for it offers—or attempts to offer—no speech in response to a direct question that demands it. For believing laypeople and elders in the Upper Kama, the best response to antireligious campaigns was to avoid as many kinds of material evidence of belief as possible. Deferred ritual practice afforded them many, many ways to do this, but this strategy could break down when the questioning became too direct (in the case of the schoolteacher) or when it was answered by others with local knowledge that outsiders did not possess (as in the case of Evdokia Aleksandrovna).[15]

15. Evdokia Aleksandrovna's case is not strictly representative, for she does appear to have attended services as a layperson. For those middle-generation townspeople not inclined to attend services as laypeople, who preferred to put off all consideration of the other world until later in

For many others, the best answer was never to get themselves into these situations at all—being an atheist in the world did not, of absolute necessity, mean that one always would be. From the perspective of Soviet moralizing visions of New Socialist Persons, this was troubling, for it was assumed that proper socialization in socialist society would ensure against a person's taking up religion late in life. In the generational logic of the Upper Kama, however, even a high degree of participation in this world did not in and of itself disqualify one from religious practice at retirement. Deferred ritual practice, like decentralized and nonhierarchical organizational structure, meant that the priestless Old Believers of the Upper Kama did not need to confront as directly as other religious groups the roadblocks to relationships with the other world erected by Soviet secularization efforts. Centuries of avoiding the Russian Orthodox Church and tsarist state served the priestless Old Believers of the Upper Kama well, for they furnished institutional structures and expectations about the locus of subject formation that could slip past some of the main Soviet attempts to define and curtail religion. Although I have focused on their historical and ethical valences in the Upper Kama, these aspects of priestless Old Belief in and around Sepych are in fact quite representative of much religious practice in the Soviet Union. Without an ordained clergy, hierarchy, or crucial nondomestic buildings that channeled relationships with the other world, the Old Believers of the Upper Kama began the Soviet period where many religious groups ended it: without priests or religious buildings and with unordained specialists active in domestic spaces (Dragadze 1993).

Thus far I have followed the fate of Soviet antireligious campaigns in Sepych to trace the ways in which their expectations about the material manifestations of religion often missed local expectations about the formation of ethical subjects and communities. I have found it less productive to ask whether townspeople in Sepych actually believed in God in the Soviet period than to watch the traffic in different kinds of material manifestations and their connections and misconnections. One of the lessons of the argument so far is that the Soviet religion bureaucracy made a set of assumptions about religion, whereas residents in the Upper Kama were concerned not with an abstracted, measurable, definable category called religion but with a practical ethics worked out through a myriad of intersecting material practices and present in everything from kinship relations to the very landscape around Sepych itself. Shifting the angle of approach from religion to ethics opens my analysis beyond the Soviet religion bureaucracy to other organs and wings of the Soviet party-state, and to material practices characteristic of socialism more broadly, that influenced successive elder generations in the Soviet period.

---

life, it would have been even easier to avoid a confrontation between the ideals and practices of the this world in its socialist manifestations and those related to the other world.

Breaking and Making Textual Communities
in the Twentieth Century

My discussion of the formation of a local ethical repertoire in the Upper Kama in the eighteenth and nineteenth centuries gave special weight to manuscripts and printed books. Not only were these texts repositories of authoritative moral guidelines to be consulted, followed, and cited in all aspects of life, but they were also highly valued objects, material tracers of moral communities across space and time. In all these roles, they were touchstones for the development of historical consciousness: to possess, inscribe, and pass on books was to participate in—indeed, to write oneself into—Christian history. To a lesser extent than in previous centuries, twentieth-century Maksimovskie and Dëminskie scribes also produced and copied new texts. These twentieth-century scribes made use of the materials that were available to them, often flimsy Soviet school notebooks and shoddy pens or pencils. They also tended to copy only the minimal service and spiritual verses that were necessary for particular services—especially funerals—rather than reproducing whole volumes. With a few exceptions, Soviet-era manuscripts were shorter, less ornate, and less perfect in their Slavonic lettering and citation, especially as compared with the local manuscripts of the eighteenth and nineteenth centuries.[16] They were, however, no less central to the formation of moral communities, as demonstrated by the sinnodik-pomianik manuscript from Batalovy with which I illustrated the stretching out of generations across the changing physical spaces of the Soviet countryside.

The thousands of manuscripts and other Old Believer writings stashed in trunks and under beds in the Upper Kama remained largely invisible to representatives of the Soviet religion bureaucracy—yet another symptom of these agencies' difficulties in coming to terms with the practice of priestless Old Belief in Sepych and elsewhere. However, two other elements of the Soviet party-state—diametrically opposed in nearly every way—took a great deal of interest in precisely these textual materials of ethics, both old and new editions. For investigators from the NKVD in the 1930s, "sectarian" books, seized in sudden searches and arrests, were some of the firmest evidence for virulent "counterrevolutionary terrorist activity" in the Upper Kama. For university field archaeographers in the 1970s and after, ancient books and manuscripts discovered in and around Sepych were evidence of a still-extant Russian national tradition, one that had survived intact the horrors of the 1930s. In both cases, the materiality of these books and manuscripts, as well as the paths they traced and connections they enabled, continued to play a significant role in the

---

16. For one such exception, see the large Dëminskie volume dated to the 1920–60s at ORKiR NB MGU, PV, 1577.

formation and transformation (and sometimes the brutal destruction) of ethical subjects and moral communities among elder generations in the Upper Kama.

NKVD INTERROGATIONS AND ARRESTS IN THE 1930S

The decentralized, nonhierarchical, and deferred characteristics of priestless Old Belief worked best to shield elders in the Upper Kama in times of low or moderate overt antireligious activity. A 1937 letter from the Sepych rural soviet, filed in the archives of the Commission on Religious Cults, describes some of what transpired in more extreme, if also more uncommon, times. The letter, from Andrei Mal'tsev of the village Mal'tsevo to "Mikhail Ivanovich Kalinin... head of the government of the U.S.S.R. and defender of the rights of citizens and establisher of lawful order," begins by citing the "Stalin Constitution" of 1936. It goes on to register specific complaints:

> The main law that we wish to take up in our request here is Article 124, which speaks about the provision of free conscience to citizens, the freedom of religion [*svoboda otpravleniia religioznykh kul'tov*] [and] the freedom of antireligious propaganda for all. But it isn't turning out that way here. There is no antireligious propaganda of any kind, but at the same time our religious group—Old Believers or Pomortsy—has been driven underground. [Pomortsy], in truth, in all their rituals and laws, do not challenge [*idet v razrez*] Soviet power.... Our spiritual fathers are not hired by the religious group and do not go through a spiritual academy, but only must be able to read Slavonic and are elected by the people. They are not younger than fifty and have no income whatsoever.

After providing further evidence that the local Old Believers were uneducated, did not earn money for services rendered, and had no intention of interfering with Soviet power, the letter concludes:

> Therefore, in light of all that is summarized above, we ask Comrade Kalinin and his Central Executive Committee, on the basis of Article 124 of the Stalin Constitution, to [allow?] us to freely [practice?] because at the moment local authorities have driven us underground. They don't permit us to pray freely. Several leaders have been taken and sent it isn't clear where, with no basis. The rest have been driven underground, and so it turns out to be a complete persecution of the Christian faith and against all laws.[17]

Andrei Mal'tsev's letter illustrates several points. First, if any evidence is needed, the letter shows the wide gulf between Soviet constitutional decrees on the freedom of religion and the actual practice of forced secularization, at least in the later 1930s. Second, it demonstrates that priestless Old Believers themselves

17. GARF, f. r-5263, op. 1, d. 1544, l. 158–159r.

understood quite well some of the reasons Soviet authorities used to justify the removal of religious specialists: that they exploited the population by collecting money, that they challenged Soviet power, and that they took young men from the Soviet workforce. In rebutting these justifications, Andrei Mal'tsev's letter was very much in keeping with local expectations about separating this world from the other world. The ascetic pastors and elders in the Upper Kama had a much stronger claim to being exclusively concerned with otherworldly matters than did other specialists who caught the eye of the religion bureaucracy elsewhere in the Soviet Union. Third, the letter shows that these carefully argued rebuttals often did not make any difference in the Soviet system, especially in the turbulence and violence of the 1930s. The letter confirms the hazy stories I heard elders tell about the disappearance of some well-regarded pastors from the Upper Kama.[18]

Several years after I came across Andrei Mal'tsev's letter to Comrade Kalinin, I learned that the NKVD files on these arrested pastors, along with the files of thousands of other victims of Stalin-era repressions throughout the Perm region, had been declassified and made available to relatives and scholars. The files—I reviewed forty-five of them—are thick, painstakingly organized, and absolutely chilling to read. They tell of the ways in which books and manuscripts held in the Upper Kama became, in the 1930s, central elements in attempts to destroy the moral communities and histories they had so long helped to create. Most of the files include some combination of the following elements, in more or less the same order: a snippet of accusation by an informant or other incriminating information; an arrest record along with results of a search of the suspect's residence; a set of handwritten interrogation transcripts in question-and-answer format, including the testimony of other witnesses brought in to substantiate claims; scrawled signatures, or sometimes just inked thumbprints, of the accused certifying each answer and each page of interrogation; a typed, summary report on the entire file passed on to NKVD superiors; a clip from the minutes of the Sverdlovsk regional NKVD leadership pronouncing a sentence; occasional appeals or letters from worried relatives; and, near the end of the file, a slip of paper confirming that the sentence—transfer to a labor camp or, more commonly, execution—had been carried out. These final, faded forms, each containing only a single, mimeographed sentence with blanks for name, date, and penalty to be written in, are startling in their juxtaposition of bureaucratic efficiency and brutal finality. Many files conclude with a spare "was shot."

Andrei Mal'tsev's appeal to Comrade Kalinin notwithstanding, the late 1930s arrests and executions in the Upper Kama do not appear in these files as part of an explicit offensive against Old Belief; indeed, sectarianism appears as a

18. See also the brief account of the arrest of a pastor in AAL MGU, Perm-Verkhokam'e Field Diaries, 33, l. 45–47.

primary theme in many, but certainly far from all, of the cases. This is true despite the fact that the NKVD focused its efforts largely on elder generations: for the thirty files that I read in detail, the mean age of those arrested was 56.7, the median, 62.[19] Rather than focus exclusively on pastors or sectarians, NKVD investigators, working with local party officials and informants (who are referred to only by code names), cast about for any evidence that would support allegations of engagement in an array of anti-Soviet activities: a kulak past, spreading rumors about coming war, predicting the fall of the Bolsheviks, or agitating against collective farms. NKVD investigators and interrogators in the Vereshchagino region often relied on the testimony of friends and neighbors as witnesses, turning the intimacies of moral community into nightmares. "I know him well, as a fellow villager," said one of A. S. Pleshivykh's accusers. "As a close neighbor," began another.[20] The NKVD also relied heavily on direct confessions (surely coerced in many cases). For example, A. K. Moshev, shot on October 30, 1937, at the age of sixty-four, apparently stated to investigators during one of his interrogations: "I, as a former Old Believer pastor [*staroobriadcheskii pop (kerzhak)*], had authority among the population. That helped me carry out my counterrevolutionary work. Whether at home or not, I carried on anti-Soviet, counterrevolutionary conversations. I circulated rumors about war."[21]

These kinds of denunciations, accusations, and NKVD tactics were prevalent throughout the Soviet Union in the era of high Stalinism. Yet the Great Terror also took on specifically local characteristics in the Upper Kama, as NKVD officials devoted special attention to allegations of participation in the Sepych Uprising of 1918 and sectarianism. Some of the most common materials used by the NKVD to make a case for anti-Soviet activity in the Upper Kama were in fact quite particular to the region: religious books and other writings found during the search of the home of an arrested suspect. The file of I. S. Mezentsov, for instance, lists no fewer than twenty-seven sectarian books and manuscripts confiscated during a search of his home on August 26, 1936. His interrogations on August 27 and again on September 6 focused almost entirely on religious activity in and around his home village of Sokolovo, where he had admitted to being the head of an unregistered group of priestless Old Believers. Mezentsov, sixty-two at the time of his arrest, was eventually sentenced to five years of hard labor.[22]

The materiality of these confiscated books—their obvious endurance from a pre-Soviet past, their Church Slavonic lettering (in all likelihood, largely

19. Accusers, informants, and witnesses, although often anonymous and rarely described in detail, were almost without exception much younger. For the ten I could determine with some certainty, the mean age was 38.5, the median 36.5.

20. GOPAPO, f. 643/2, op. 1, d. 7457, l. 16, 20.

21. GOPAPO, f. 643/2. op. 1, d. 27532, l. 456.

22. GOPAPO, f. 641/1., op., 1, d. 15646, l. 4v, 64–66. For other such instances of seized religious books in the Upper Kama, see GOPAPO, f. 643/2, op. 1, d. 27532, l. 32, 34–38; d. 29494, l. 64.

unreadable by young NKVD agents from the city)—made them prime pieces of evidence for conspiracies and threats against the state. The case of A. E. Fedoseev, V. I. Fedoseev, and G. S. Patrakov is a particularly illustrative example of how Old Believer writings and texts could become, in the imaginations and interrogations of NKVD officers, compelling evidence of anti-Soviet conspiracies in the Upper Kama.[23] The trio was arrested in September of 1937 on suspicion of anti-Soviet activity and leadership of a "counterrevolutionary sectarian group" of twenty people based in the village of Nifoniata. A search of A. E. Fedoseev's house on September 27 yielded several religious books, a map of the village, and, on the icon shelf, a few sheets of paper on which, the officer leading the search noted explicitly in his on-the-spot report, was written, "Let us arise, brethren, let us ari—" (*vostanemte, bratie, vosta—*). Two and a half weeks later, on October 13, this apparent call to arms became the leading piece of evidence used by the Vereshchagino NKVD in summarizing for their superiors their proof that the three men from Nifoniata were indeed members of a secret sectarian group bent on overthrowing Soviet power. G. S. Patrakov was sentenced to ten years of hard labor on October 22, 1937. A. E. Fedoseev and V. I. Fedoseev were shot.

The few incriminating sheets of paper seized during the raid on A. E. Fedoseev's house were, unlike the large books, incorporated into his NKVD file, allowing us to discern at least some of their context before they went to Vereshchagino and Sverdlovsk to be used as material evidence of anti-Soviet conspiracy.[24] The file contains two short manuscripts, the first a lengthy copy of a penitential verse with several elaborate scribal notes on the final page, typical of copyists in the Upper Kama: "1923," "This book was written by Ivan Fedoseev" (perhaps V. I. Fedoseev's father?), and "written for laypeople." The second short text is a printed *azbuka*, or alphabet, designed to teach the rudiments of Church Slavonic. It is on the back of this text that the words, "Let us arise, brethren, let us ari" appear. What none of the NKVD personnel from Vereshchagino would have known was that these words are the opening of a popular and much-copied Old Believer spiritual verse: "Let us arise, brethren, let us arise / let us pray to God / our age is coming to an end, brethren / and the Last Judgment is being readied."[25] For those steeped in the textual and scribal conventions of the Upper Kama, such scribbled verses, like the scribal notes on the back of the other short manuscript on Fedoseev's icon shelf, were everywhere, hardly extractable as evidence of a conspiracy.

It was, it would seem, part of A. E. Fedoseev's great misfortune that an old Russian call to prayer before the Last Judgment could be read by suspicious,

---

23. GOPAPO, f. 643/2, op. 1, d. 27463.

24. See, for instance, GOPAPO, f. 643/2, op. 1, d. 6687, l. 38–43.

25. ORKiR NB MGU, PV, 2050, l. 11v. No fewer than ten independent copies of this spiritual verse have been found in the Upper Kama (Ageeva et al. 1994, 442).

uninformed NKVD eyes as a summons to worldly counterrevolution, something more on the order of "rise up, brothers, rise up." Indeed, when the NKVD
officer in Vereshchagino composed his report, he twice noted this phrase as
evidence before going on to introduce other evidence: the men's background
as kulaks and testimony that they had spread rumors about the coming end
of Soviet power. The report dutifully noted that the men from Nifoniata were
reported to have participated in the Sepych Uprising. Here, another instance
of the word *vostanie*—the Sepych Uprising (*Sepychëvskoe vostanie*)—served
to aid in transforming the words of elders' spiritual verse into a counterrevolutionary threat by recalling a history of hostility to Soviet power in the region.

As in the Sepych Uprising, the late 1930s in the Upper Kama were less notably a time for the creation of ethical subjects and moral communities than
for their destruction—a time when incentives, tools of persuasion, and attempts
to gradually mold new socialist communities were perceived to be under such
threat that the violent liquidation of older moral communities and ethical subjects appeared necessary and, in practice, spun out of control. We cannot know
whether the NKVD officers actually understood the old phrase in its context
and wished to spice up their reports or whether they read the Church Slavonic
"let us arise" as the more modern "rise up" out of ignorance. In the absence
of this phrase, they would likely have found additional incriminating evidence,
as they did for so many others in the Upper Kama. Ivan Fedoseev's arrest, de-
tention, and execution in 1937 did not, then, so much depend on the misread-
ing of an old spiritual verse as proceed through it. In the late 1930s—an age of
rumors, secret informants, conspiracies, and unsubstantiated accusations—the
tangible materiality of old books uncovered in a raid could be particularly
compelling evidence of an imminent threat to the establishment of socialism.
The distinctive materials of ethics and histories of the Upper Kama, that is,
colored even instances of their own annihilation.

BUT what if the jotted words on A. E. Fedoseev's *azbuka* really were a call to
worldly uprising after all? Perhaps, from the time of the Sepych Uprising in
1918 into the late 1930s, the corpus of Old Believer texts and verses circulating
quietly in the Upper Kama were, in fact, mined for inspiration in actual plots
to overthrow Soviet power. Perhaps the spiritual verse "Let us arise, brethren,
let us arise," was, in fact, the rallying cry of the Sepych Uprising, and the
imaginative link between an old, familiar spiritual verse and present-day political struggles was made not by (or not only by) a willfully ignorant NKVD
investigator anxious to fill his quota of counterrevolutionaries but by certain
Old Believers in the Upper Kama themselves. It would not be the first time in
Old Believer history that worldly instructions for the present moment were
extrapolated from ancient texts. Indeed, Lynne Viola (1996, 45–67) builds
her analysis of apocalyptic imagery in early Soviet peasant uprisings precisely

around such reinterpretations of old verses and texts, especially among peasant Old Believers.

Although it seems inconceivable that these old materials of ethics in the Upper Kama were not redeployed, at least by some, as elements of outright protest and even uprisings against Soviet power, no supporting evidence for Viola's scenario survives in otherwise plentiful manuscripts and memories from the Upper Kama. Those whom we know to have actively participated in the Sepych Uprising were of the middle, worldly generation of merchant families of the Upper Kama, less likely to have been directly informed by and acting upon the textual materials of ethics more closely associated with the generation of elders. Moreover, elders in the ascetic Upper Kama have far more often sought to withdraw from the world in all its incarnations than to rise up against it. Then again, Soviet power has been remarkably effective at eliminating traces of its early opposition in the Upper Kama, and we do not know enough about the losing side in and after the Sepych Uprising to make conclusive claims.

In the last analysis, however, and even if we grant a modicum of participation in actual and planned uprisings to Old Believer elders in the early Soviet period, it is abundantly clear that one of elder generations' more significant, longer-term tasks was the reconstitution of moral communities in the wake of socialism's occasional outbursts of violence—as opposed to active participation in them. Even the removal and execution of these pastors and elders did not radically disrupt or co-opt the decentralized, nonhierarchical structure of religious authority in the Upper Kama, for these pastors were quickly replaced from within their own communities. As the era of arrests and executions came to an end, the many surviving pastors and councils of the Upper Kama found some unexpected allies in their efforts to rehabilitate their moral communities.

FIELD ARCHAEOGRAPHERS IN THE UPPER KAMA

My discussion of older generations in the twentieth century has thus far concentrated on the fate of locally salient expectations and materials of ethics in the Upper Kama as elders encountered the Soviet religion bureaucracy and, in the 1930s, NKVD investigations, arrests, and executions. But not all agents of the sprawling Soviet party-state were uniformly bent on the regulation and elimination of religion. Not only did local officials in Sepych often look the other way and even quietly enable their parents' generation to pursue their otherworldly salvation, but Old Believers in the Upper Kama gained some new and unanticipated supporters in the late Soviet era: scholars from some of the Soviet Union's most prestigious university departments of history and philology. Beginning in the late 1960s, teams of these scholars fanned out across the Soviet Union each summer in search of ancient manuscripts and early printed editions. Historically Old Believer locales were their primary destinations.

In and around Sepych, expeditions from Moscow State University found more old texts than they had dreamed possible. To their surprise, the scholars also found themselves quickly and deeply implicated in lasting relationships with the elders they came to know on their expeditions. For their part, elders in the Upper Kama were at first baffled by and wary of these summertime visitors, but they eventually found archaeographers to be confidants and powerful patrons. In short, an unlikely textual-moral community grew up among urban scholars and rural elders in the late socialist period; ancient books and manuscripts—read, written, copied, discussed, exchanged, interpreted—were its connective tissue. In exchange for the patronage, validation, and friendship offered by field archaeographers, many elders sent their books and recollections off to Moscow and Perm, where they became the basis for a nation-based critique of the visions of socialist modernity. They were also the basis for the (at times very courageous) beginning of the study of religion in the late Soviet period (see Freeze 2001). Through friendships in the Upper Kama and their brilliant scholarship, archaeographers helped reshape what it meant to be an elder in the Upper Kama and, more broadly, what it meant to think and write about the Russian past and about religion in the Soviet period. Field archaeography is part of my story here not only because the relationships between outsider scholars and elders helped to refashion ethical practices in the Upper Kama in and after the Soviet period, but also because these relationships continue to illustrate elders' place in the broader ethics of socialism—both its wealth-in-people networks and its multiple, conflicting moralizing discourses. In this case, the larger moralizing discourse into which the elderly residents of Sepych found themselves inserted was a Russian national one, in contrast to the socialist visions their children and grandchildren were projecting in *Sepych Weddings*.

The historical subdiscipline of field archaeography had its first modern stirrings in the postwar period, as a number of Soviet historians, led by the renowned Novosibirsk academician M. N. Tikhomirov, began to realize that the descendants of early Old Believer communities might still possess very old Slavonic books and manuscripts. Finding these original manuscripts, scholars hypothesized, could revolutionize the study of Russian history, language, and literature in the postwar, post-Stalin years, when it was becoming politically possible to talk about Russian national history and traditions. In the winter months of the late 1960s, field archaeographers trawled through archives to trace the prerevolutionary movements and possible locations of Old Believer communities. They struggled with university administrators and Communist Party officials for permission to teach the classes and read the religious books that would enable them to properly study the manuscripts for which they searched. They negotiated with representatives from the national and local offices of the Soviet Council on Religious Affairs for information about and access to Old Believer locales. In the summer months, often on their own vacation time, they hiked kilometer after kilometer on foot, camped in forests, and, when necessary, requisitioned helicopters to access particularly remote areas once inhabited by Old Believers. By the early 1970s, telegrams from the most rural of post offices regularly crisscrossed the Soviet Union each July, notifying Moscow, Leningrad, and Novosibirsk of one exciting manuscript find after the next. Field archaeographers eventually left their calling cards in—and returned with tens of thousands of manuscripts and books from—nearly every former or present-day Old Believer community in the Soviet Union.[26]

In 1972, archaeographers from Moscow State University reported on their summer expedition to the Perm region:

> A group of Priestless Old Believers (Maksimovskie), who preserve and strictly observe not only the dogmatic but also the lifestyle particulars of the past (not using mechanical means of transport, not using tea, sugar, etc.) was discovered in the Vereshchagino district. They have a range of ancient books and manuscripts. Particularly interesting is the so-called Podlinnik that was obtained from the Maksimovskie—the unknown history of a schism of priestless Old Believers into the Maksimovskie and Dëminskie among the peasant population of the Sepych area in 1866. The schism is preserved to this day.[27]

A year later they observed:

> This year we began archaeographical exploration of the Sepych area of the Vereshchagino district, in which [we found] unique—for the European part of the USSR—conditions for work: the presence of a community attempting to preserve not only the particulars of the ancient rituals [kult'] but also elements of ancient lifestyle. Nearly 100 Cyrillic books were cataloged in this region, not less than half of them from the seventeenth century or earlier.[28]

Since those early reports, archaeographers from Moscow State University have added thousands of books and manuscripts to their Upper Kama territorial book collection—many of them in the first years, when it was not uncommon

---

26. It will come as no surprise to philologists and specialists in early Slavic literature that the Holy Grail of the early postwar field archaeography was a new copy of *The Lay of Igor's Campaign*, one that would prove the text's early authenticity once and for all (the connection is made explicitly in Tikhomirov 1948, 159). On early expeditions from Moscow State University, see Pozdeeva (1982, 1995), Smilianskaia (1995), and Smilianskaia and Kobiak (1994); from Novosibirsk, see Pokrovskii (1984, 1991, 1994); and from the Academy of Sciences Institute of Russian Literature (the Pushkin House), see Malyshev (1951) and the subsequent yearly updates in *Trudy Otdela Drevnerusskoi Literaturoi*. My discussion in this section is informed both by archival research and by many conversations with field archaeographers, some still active, some retired. The dozens of official field journals kept by expedition members from Moscow State have been particularly helpful in reconstructing the practice of field archaeography in the middle and later Soviet period. Although many archaeographers also kept personal journals, I limit my citations to official expedition diaries written with the knowledge that they would be archived and read by other scholars.

27. AAL MGU, Expedition Reports, PV, 1972.

28. AAL MGU, Expedition Reports, PV, 1973.

to return to Moscow with hundreds of books from a month-long expedition (see Ageeva et al. 1994; Pozdeeva 1982).[29]

The creation of a new textual community including Old Believers of the Upper Kama and scholars from Moscow began with cautious exchanges of manuscripts and old printed books. In their visits to the homes of elderly Old Believers, archaeographers always asked first and foremost to see whatever books the residents owned. They made inventories of each household's collection, eventually compiling a massive card catalog, and solicited the oldest and rarest editions for their growing library in Moscow. Although archaeographers collected many of these manuscripts and old printed books from young Soviet families who parted with them easily, other texts, often those considered the most valuable, were in the hands of Old Believer elders who still actively used them in services. In these cases, archaeographers often borrowed books, mailing them back after they had completed their study in Moscow. By the mid-1970s—the very same years that the laboring generations of State Farm Sepych were beginning to achieve recognition in the Urals—scores of letters and packages were traveling each year between elders in the Upper Kama and field archaeographers in Moscow.

For the Maksimovskie and Dëminskie elders in and around Sepych, their new annual visitors were, at first, a puzzle. Archaeographers were representatives of the state, belonged to the world, and collected valued manuscripts and books. Thirty years earlier, outsiders interested in manuscripts and books had spirited their owners away to NKVD prisons, many of them never to return. Yet at the same time, these new visitors were fluent readers of Slavonic texts, discreet champions of the rights of believers, and, in the far-flung rural areas of the Perm region, potentially very powerful patrons. From the beginning, it is evident that more than simple manuscript collection was going on in these expeditions. One letter, received by the Moscow State University archaeographical group in early 1973, gives a hint of the connections that developed through the traffic in Slavonic manuscripts and old printed books:

> It's Marina Vasil'evna writing to say hello to you and wish you good health and happiness in your work....I thank you 1,000 times for your attention and for sending me the book Nicholas the Wonderworker. I got it on the 3rd at 2 in the afternoon and sat reading past 1 in the morning. I read 135 pages and on another day I finished the rest. I will be able to send it back to you soon. I've also read and copied the whole service [*sluzhbu*] and can send that back to you....And now I'll need a psalter in the new printed style.[30]

---

29. These discoveries were hailed in regional and All-Union newspapers; see, among others, "Arkheografy vedut poisk," *Pravda*, April 1, 1974, 4; Iu. Andreotti, "Folinaty povedali," *Pravda*, November 19, 1976, 3; F. Medvedev, "Na stranitsakh—pyl' vekov," *Pravda*, February 17, 1978, 4; N. Mishina, "Neugasshie pis'mena: Drevnye knigi iz kollektsii MGU," *Pravda*, January 22, 1982, 3; L. Brutskaia, "Neischerpaemye sokrovishcha Prikam'ia," *Zvezda*, August 5, 1982, 2.

30. AAL MGU, Letter Archive, Incoming, 17/I/73.

These emerging relationships were facilitated by the fact that archaeographers dressed in the modest attire of Old Believers, complete with long dresses and head scarves. They often answered questions for the elders about which texts were to be read on which holidays. On many occasions, as Marina Vasil'evna mentioned in her letter, they found or loaned newer editions of service books—still in the old orthography—to trade for the centuries-old editions they were most interested in preserving in libraries. In many cases, newer editions collected from one family would be traded for older, less legible, but more historically significant (from the archaeographers' point of view) editions. In the off-season, back in their offices in Moscow, the archaeographers corresponded with their growing list of contacts, inquiring after books, health, family, and friends. They also struggled with university apparatchiks for permission to teach courses with content that could be termed religious and, on more than a few occasions, defended their very existence as a legitimate field of academic inquiry.

Like all moral communities, the textual community that grew up between archaeographers and Old Believer elders was laced with inequality and power relations. Despite all the indisputably warm interaction and correspondence that often attended the exchange of old books, for instance, archaeographers were not universally well received in the Upper Kama. Some elders avoided as many interactions—let alone exchanges—with archaeographers as possible, thus ducking the mutual obligations and expectations of moral community. The archaeographers' field journals tell of many occasions when the expeditions found that the elders on their list were not home. Not answering the door, I learned from some elderly townspeople in Sepych, seems to have been only one of the more common strategies of avoidance. One old woman told me that she hid from an expedition in her firewood shed, not wanting to have any more discussions about whether she would hand over the books she owned. She did an impression for me of archaeographers beseeching her to "give us the book, give us the book" and told me that a friend of hers had once asked only that, upon her death, her books not be given to the archaeographers. In Sepych in the 1990s, as some townspeople searched for the foundations of the Old Belief they were rediscovering, it was not uncommon to hear some indignation that the most valuable editions had been spirited away to Moscow.

Archaeographers, charged with collecting religious texts from communities of elderly men and women still using them, could be seen as representatives of the Soviet party-state in its modes of surveillance, acquisition, and centralization. Although clearly never the whole picture, neither was this a perception that archaeographers always tried to avoid. For example, each team traveled with letters of introduction from high-level university and party officials. In addition to documenting the legality of these expeditions, the letters served to impress on rural elders the considerable worldly powers of party and state that had brought these travelers to their doorsteps. Similarly, when archaeographers found themselves under attack by officials in the Soviet religion bureaucracy who asserted that expeditions unacceptably promoted the practice of religion, they could and did argue that their research was doing a service to the advance of socialism by removing religious texts from the population and helping to write the "correct"—secular—history of Old Belief. These kinds of claims, backed up by still more letters of reference, pacified numerous suspicions about archaeographers leveled by other wings of the party-state.[31] They were, as so often in the Soviet academy, a necessary cover for the quiet personal relationships and dedicated scholarly work that took place in the early, heady days of field archaeography.

Power moves along multiple vectors in moral communities, and elders in the Upper Kama, for all their efforts to hold to an otherworldly asceticism, were far from naive about the workings of socialist networks and the importance of collecting wealth in people. They quickly realized that among potential patrons, university scholars from Moscow and Perm were valuable prizes. As field archaeographers collected books, elders collected field archaeographers. According to an expedition story I heard more than once, one old woman in the Upper Kama kept herself busy while archaeographers pored over her books by updating her own card catalog—a record of the names and institutional affiliations of all the scholars who had knocked on her door over the years. The fact that an expedition all the way from Moscow State University had visited gave local Old Believers a way in which to defend themselves from provincial authorities who could be overzealous in enforcing Soviet restrictions on religious activity. When, for instance, the community of Dëminskie Old Believers based in Vereshchagino was fined for gathering on Easter, the archaeographers interceded on their behalf, writing from Moscow to inform local authorities that the fines were higher than the law allowed. The fines were reduced, and, it seems, word went out that the elders were to be left alone.[32]

Similarly, elderly Old Believers correctly saw Moscow as a place where items that simply did not exist in the Soviet countryside could be more easily obtained. They often wrote to the archaeographers with requests that extended far beyond the initial traffic in books and manuscripts. The Moscow State University Archaeography Laboratory's archives bulge with letters from Old Believers of the Upper Kama asking and thanking the archaeographers for

31. In 1972, for instance, officials in the history department at Perm State University were engaged in a back-and-forth struggle with the executive committee of the Communist Party in Vereshchagino, which had raised numerous concerns about the first archaeographical expeditions on their territory. See AOAVR, f. 1, op. 1, d. 300, l. 84.

32. For other examples of archaeographers intervening in local religious persecution and fines on behalf of Old Believer elders, see AAL MGU, Letter Archive, Incoming, 27/XI/72, 14/III/73, 20/III/73, 28/III/73, 5/V/74. Archaeographers also expanded their efforts to defend local elders by doing more general public relations work, including publishing newspaper articles in the region that carefully explained their work and insisted that all of Soviet society should be grateful to those who had carefully preserved these books. See, for instance, I. V. Pozdeeva, "Iz glubiny vekov," *Zaria Kommunizma: Organ Vereshchaginskogo Raionogo KPSS*, July 8, 1978, 4. Ageeva et al. (1992) describes archaeographers' own understanding of the obligation to reciprocate.

everything from eyeglasses to medicine to church calendars and even to baptismal crosses. This correspondence generated not only more contacts and books for the archaeographers, and not only shortage goods or patrons for the Old Believer elders, but also a great deal of mutual respect, admiration, and longing on both sides of this moral community. Numerous archaeographers told me how much they yearned for the start of the field season each year, not only because of the manuscripts they might find but because they had come to view the elders they visited as friends and living embodiments of Old Russia. "It's wonderful to return to old places," noted one expedition member on the first page of her diary at the start of a new field season.[33] Such feelings were often mutual. An elder from Krivchana, a village not far from Sepych, wrote to the archaeographers in May of 1980, "We received your letter and rejoice that you haven't forgotten us decrepit old women.... We still celebrate all the holidays and at each holiday we remember you. Forgive me, a sinner. Maybe you will visit again and I will still be alive. I'd like to see you. I'd like to talk with you. That's all for now."[34]

"WORD of your love of God and how much you submit to the holy laws has reached us in the Pomorskii monastic community.... We here rejoice...that in such a time, a spark of true piety has fallen in that remote corner." Thus read part of the letter of introduction that Brother Grigorii and his companions carried from the Vyg settlements in the north to the Upper Kama in 1730 or 1731 (see chapter 1). Recall that Brother Grigorii was engaged in Vyg's larger project of stitching together a unified Old Believer movement out of diverse communities of religious dissenters spread across Russia. This was an early invention of Old Belief in the Upper Kama. In the years following their own discovery of the same region over two centuries later, field archaeographers also came to be involved in a larger project—one for a different age than Brother Grigorii's. This project relied not on bringing new manuscripts, writings, and teachings to a remote corner of Russia and its environs but on centralizing them in Moscow. A copy of Brother Grigorii's letter, for instance, made the trip from the Upper Kama to Moscow in 1975.

The archaeographers' project was also, quietly and carefully, an exercise in the reclaiming of Russian national identity.[35] As archaeographers' relationships with local Old Believers deepened, their scholarship turned from an exclusive emphasis on books and manuscripts to broader studies of contemporary Old Believer life. Ethnographers and folklorists joined the expeditions in the late

33. AAL MGU, Perm-Verkhokam'e Field Diaries, 17a, l. 1.
34. AAL MGU, Letter Archive, Incoming, 5/31/82.
35. For an especially instructive discussion of the use of old manuscripts in the invention of history, see Lass (1988).

1970s and 1980s, producing studies of material culture, language, and ritual. With quiet circumspection and preferring the word "tradition" to the more politically risky "religion," these scholars wrote not only of a Russian past revealed through manuscript discoveries but of a past lived in the present as well—a living tradition (see esp. Koval'chenko 1982). Many came to argue that Russian national traditions were preserved—perhaps uniquely preserved—by Old Believer elders seeking the separation of the worlds in the Upper Kama district of the Perm region. Some of the best evidence of this preservation was, of course, centuries-old books and manuscripts still in active use—material markers of a deep Russian past extending into the present (Pozdeeva 1992, 1996).

It is no longer surprising to find national ideologies alive and well, and even proliferating, in twentieth-century socialist states (Verdery 1991; Slezkine 1994; Suny and Kennedy 2001). Nor is it surprising to find ethnographic, historical, and folkloric research on rural communities at the heart of these visions of national traditions preserved down to the present day (Kligman 1988; Hirsch 2005). In the early archaeographical exploration of the Upper Kama, however, we can see some of the concrete, material processes through which socialist-era producers of national ideologies worked as they carefully and courageously offered up alternate visions to a socialist present they found deeply flawed. We also see the meaningful, reciprocal, mutually constituting personal relationships that could develop in the course of expeditions to rural areas. At least in the Upper Kama, the national traditions of the socialist era were neither constructed out of thin air nor built on the backs of unwitting or easily forgotten rural people.

In my view, however, early field archaeography's focus on finding and preserving national tradition—born of a particular moment in the Soviet academy, crystallized in unexpectedly close relationships with Old Believer elders, and exemplified in the material durability of "book culture" (*knizhnost'*)—does not capture central aspects of Old Belief as lived practice in the twentieth century. Political necessity, personal preference, and scholarly methodology combined and reinforced one another to produce an archaeographical portrait of the twentieth-century Upper Kama with no space for mention of local collective and state farms, atheist lectures and antireligious campaigns, the worldly careers of those who became elders in the late Soviet period, or the laypeople who often lived with those elders who welcomed archaeographers. State Farm director Andrei Petrovich's father, after all, was a respected elder in Sepych.

My deep admiration for and debts to field archaeography are, by now, clear; moreover, my own fieldwork and archival research have also drawn me into meaningful relationships with the residents of Sepych and its environs.[36] My own

---

36. These interactions were, at least at first, heavily tinged by my association with Soviet scholars and their fieldwork, a phenomenon often noted by Western-trained anthropologists working in the formerly socialist world (e.g., Anderson 2000a, 135–37; Ssorin-Chaikov 2003).

entanglements, situated in quite different scholarly and political circumstances on a global scale, have produced a very different understanding of the Upper Kama. I round out my analysis of the Soviet period by bringing Old Believer elders back into explicit relationship with Sepych's younger, laboring generations. These generational threads are most usefully analyzed together, despite all the energies that have gone into holding them apart—whether those energies have been expended by visionaries of a socialist future making a propaganda film about local weddings, by Old Believer elders seeking their own salvation, or by field archaeographers seeking the salvation of the Russian nation.

Christian Ascetics in the Soviet Countryside

When I asked friends of middle and older generations about Old Belief in the Soviet period, their responses most often came in the shape of memories of their parents and grandparents. These recollections fall roughly into two groups: those that illustrate the steady feminization and geriatricization of Old Belief in the Soviet period and those that highlight dilemmas and conflicts resulting from elders' efforts to uphold ascetic prohibitions on eating and drinking with people of the world. In discussing each case, I show how domestic spaces and kin relations became key points for conversations and disputes about ethical practice and the constitution of ethical subjects appropriate to genders and generations. These disputes, stretching back to the periods of serfdom and emancipation, nevertheless unfolded through the specific, divergent materialities of ethics and moral communities that characterized the socialist period in the Upper Kama. They were intricately caught up in the larger processes and institutions of rural socialism in and around Sepych that I have discussed so far, including the resettlement of the countryside, moral'nye and material'nye incentives to labor, and the coming of archaeographers to the Upper Kama. They were much less influenced by the efforts of the Soviet religion bureaucracy or even by the NKVD arrests and executions of the Stalin era.

The Feminization and Geriatricization of Old Belief

I recounted above the story of Evdokia Aleksandrovna, a former head of the Sepych rural soviet who joined the Dëminskie group of priestless Old Believers after her retirement. As a member of the council of elders, she secured quiet permission from one of her successors at the rural soviet for the Dëminskie to gather for services without persecution. This later representative of the rural soviet, however, did not follow Evdokia Aleksandrovna from Soviet civil service into active religious practice upon his own retirement. When I met him in 2000, he had recently retired from the commercial farm where he had worked for some years after his time in the rural soviet. An active member of the Maksimovskie council once told me, "We've called him. It's time for him to join [the elders]." He, however, showed no signs of interest in taking up the austere strictures of Old Belief. By the middle of the Soviet period, few men did.

By the close of the Soviet period, priestless Old Belief in the Upper Kama was almost entirely feminized. Both Maksimovskie and Dëminskie participants were mostly women, their pastors were nearly universally spiritual mothers rather than spiritual fathers, and services took place in domestic spaces that had themselves become more closely associated with women than with men. Indeed, the association between active religious practice and old women was so strong in post-Soviet Sepych that middle-generation townspeople usually referred to religious occasions simply as times "to summon the old women" (*zvat' starushek*) rather than the older and gender-neutral phrase "to summon the elders" (*zvat' starikov*). Likewise, a spiritual mother I knew, quite elderly herself, could call a service to order with a gentle "Get ready, old ladies" (*gotov'tes', starushki*) and not worry about offending any men.

This Soviet-era feminization of Old Belief shaped some of the key ethical fault lines that ran through families and homes in the Upper Kama. Anastasia Ivanovna, a Dëminskie elder like Evdokia Aleksandrovna, retired from her post in the state farm central office in the mid-1970s and began occasionally attending services as a layperson (she was, at that point, still married). Her husband, Viktor Nikolaevich, was a well-respected member of Sepych's Communist Party and a brigade leader in State Farm Sepych. Viktor Nikolaevich, his family told me, was the kind of Communist who took his party membership seriously and believed the party was an agent of positive social change. "He didn't believe in God—he believed in the party," Anastasia Ivanovna said to me on one occasion. Her stark juxtaposition of God and the party points handily to the divergent materials of ethics and moral communities standing behind each side of this marriage: the party, socialist labor incentives and collectives, and this world for Viktor Nikolaevich; books, elders, and eventually archaeographers for Anastasia Ivanovna. In their marriage these distinctions were overlain with the distinction of gender, one that would not have applied in the prerevolutionary period, when older generations of both genders would much more frequently have reoriented their lives toward the other world by taking up the ascetic practices of priestless Old Belief.

Both Anastasia Ivanovna and her children were quick to explain to me that Viktor Nikolaevich's dedicated belief in the party did not translate into intolerance of the relationships with elders and inhabitants of the other world that his wife began to cultivate upon her retirement. Although at that point still a layperson and thus not subject to the ritual strictures and prohibitions of elders, Anastasia Ivanovna sometimes volunteered their house for services. Viktor Nikolaevich, I was told, did not object or criticize. On the contrary, he often volunteered to bring the elderly women to the service in his horse cart. During the actual prayers and subsequent meal, he would go about his own house-hold chores and, later in the day, take the other old women home. This he did faithfully until his death, always refusing to participate or think much about the other world himself. When Viktor Nikolaevich died, in the early 1980s, an iron red star was placed atop the marker at the edge of his grave. There were no prayers at his funeral, which was attended by party members from far and wide, including some from Vereshchagino. "He was a great man," said Anas-tasia Ivanovna, on one of the occasions when I visited his grave site with her. As the worldly ties and associations of her marriage faded, Anastasia Ivanovna became more and more active with the Dëminskie elders; she was eventually elected their spiritual mother.

Examples of the gendered distinctions of Soviet-era Old Belief could be easily multiplied. When, for instance, one of the unregistered communities of priest-less Old Believers in Vereshchagino was caught gathering illegally at Easter in the late 1970s, local officials elicited statements from those who were in atten-dance at the service, asking who had organized the service and why they had broken the law against unregistered gatherings. One man testified:

> I hereby certify that there is no leader among the Old Believer sectarians [Mak-simovskie] who are listed, or at least I don't know anything about [a leader]. I didn't participate in the meeting of the believers—that's my wife's work....I didn't take steps to disallow the meeting of believers because that might have led to a divorce.[37]

Although this husband might well have known more than he let on, it is not hard to imagine this precise situation; Viktor Nikolaevich would likely have said something similar. These are local examples of a pattern recognizable across the Soviet bloc: the disassociation of men from religious life as they identified more closely with public party positions, waged labor in the state farm, and the pervasive networks of socialist society. This was not, however, a symmetrical pattern. Women, while also associated with party building, agri-cultural work, and accumulating wealth in people—as much as men in many cases—were at the same time *not disassociated* from relationships that focused on elders' moral communities and carefully cultivated Christian subjectivities. In Sepych, these positions, as Viktor Nikolaevich's volunteer driving illustrates, could often be complementary rather than antagonistic, subsumed into a mar-ried couple's multiple obligations and divisions of labor.

One of the reasons for the lack of friction between Anastasia Ivanovna and Viktor Nikolaevich was, of course, deferred ritual practice. Even as she occasionally hosted the elders—but did not yet pray with them—Anastasia Ivanovna could still participate fully in worldly relationships until after her

37. AOAVR, f. 1, op. 1, d. 300, l. 188–89.

husband's death. Although such deferred ritual practice could smooth over relationships in a marriage and, in general, aided the Old Believers of the Upper Kama in skirting antireligious activity, this practice did not go untransformed by the Soviet period. With worldly demands from party-state and family stretching later and later into life, the age at which laypeople made the decision to join the council of elders increased dramatically over the Soviet period. This trend was particularly pronounced for pastors. The dueling pastors of the schism of 1866–88 were themselves middle-generation men charged with adopting the taboos, ascetic practices, and strict Christian practices of the generation of elders. This mediating role made them vulnerable to the temptations of worldly relationships—both carnal and acquisitive—just when they were supposedly withdrawing from such relationships.

As the Soviet period progressed, however, those elected to the office of pastor were more and more likely to already be members of the eldest generation. In my initial discussion of pastors, I mentioned that Anastasia Ivanovna gave the age of Grigor'evich as "around forty" in the late nineteenth century. Andrei Mal'tsev's 1937 letter to Comrade Kalinin about the disappearance of local spiritual fathers in 1937 claimed that those who were elected pastor in the Upper Kama were "not younger than fifty."[38] When archaeographers began to meet and interview local Old Believers in the 1970s, nearly all the pastors they encountered were already in their seventies, if not older. The role of pastor as mediator between the worlds of younger and elder generations was thus entirely eliminated by the end of the Soviet period. Although pastors continued to be the contacts for younger generations who requested religious rituals, they themselves were no longer of the middle generation. As in so many other ways, the Soviet period sharpened and exacerbated the differences among generations in the Upper Kama—in this case by eliminating the mediating role of pastors chosen at middle age. To some extent, as several of the previous cases indicate, this mediating role was taken up by middle-generation laypeople who—like the picnicking schoolteacher or Evdokia Aleksandrovna during her time as head of the rural soviet—were caught between obligations to both older and younger generations. But this role was characterized less by the assertive religious authority of a nineteenth-century pastor and more by quiet mediation.

These particular vectors of ethical transformation were largely the unintended consequences of shifting labor practices and gender ideologies in the quite worldly dynamics of Soviet socialism (see also Verdery 1996, 64–65). Throughout the Soviet period, labor shortages and their work-arounds, through both official moral'nye and material'nye incentives and the practical accumulation of wealth in people, placed ever-increasing demands on the labor power of men and women alike. Women, however, were not thereby excused from

38. GARF, f. r-5263, op. 1, d. 1544, l. 158–59r.

household and child-rearing labors—the oft-cited "double burden" of women under socialism. In Sepych, all these broadly socialist processes unfolded in an environment where ritual practice was already deferred for most and services were already held in domestic spaces. They were furthered, moreover, by generally shorter male life expectancies and the heavy male losses suffered in World War II.

Nevertheless, these processes were not unique to the Soviet period. They extended and completed processes that had begun in the postemancipation period, if not earlier, when heavy demands on worldly labor in the burgeoning labor and capital markets of the 1870s and 1880s—likely including male labor migration—had opened a space for women at the helm of religious groups and, in doing so, had confronted the authors of the Dëminskie manuscript with new dilemmas and the basis for accusations of heresy.[39] The role of women as heads of groups of elders—unthinkable at the time of the early-nineteenth-century genealogy of spiritual fathers from the Upper Kama and viciously contested in the schism of 1866–88—had come to be taken for granted by the end of the Soviet period. This transformation accorded women a great deal of authority in matters of textual and ritual interpretation, the maintenance of pure moral communities through the disciplines of penance and excommunication, and social reproduction through the rites of baptism. At the same time, however, that authority was located in an increasingly elderly segment of the population.

DOMESTIC RITUALS AND PRAYER SERVICES

Another common recollection of the ways in which the relationships associated with the other world of elders came into contact with the world of Soviet youth concerned prayer services. As I have already indicated, laypeople sometimes joined elders for important parts of the service, standing at the back of the rooms without praying. In Sepych itself, one of the largest towns in the Upper Kama, townspeople remembered that in the 1950s and early 1960s there would have been between twenty and twenty-five elders at an Easter service, with a full house of laypeople in attendance as well. Those who attended services usually arrived in ones and twos, only after it was already dark. They prayed with blankets covering the windows; most times, everyone was gone before sunrise. As the example of Evdokia Aleksandrovna and the younger head of the rural soviet showed, it was often the case that one or another elder could strike a deal with local bureaucrats to ensure that a prayer service would go uninterrupted, provided the elders were discreet. After all, those

39. The feminization of religion has been noted in other socialist contexts as well, such as Dragadze (1993), Bringa (1995), Ransel (2000, 164–83), and Northrop (2004). The feminization of religious leadership, as happened in the Upper Kama, was far less common than the feminization of laity.

local bureaucrats' parents were as likely as not to be among those gathering to pray.

Because these services often took place at night, children who grew up in the middle of the twentieth century frequently recalled their grandparents inviting other elders over to pray at their house. One woman, whose mother was the Dëminskie spiritual mother for a time, recalled that when the elders gathered at their house, she and her brothers and sisters were forbidden to pray. They were also forbidden to leave. They were told instead to lie on the stove in the room adjacent to the one in which prayers were being offered and listen until they fell asleep. She did not pray herself, she stressed to me. She was already a Young Pioneer at the time and was soon to join the Komsomol. She later worked for many years in State Farm Sepych. Another family of brothers and sisters, all of them now shareholders in the privatized successor to State Farm Sepych, told similar stories of their childhood in one of Sepych's outlying villages. Even before their mother retired and joined the community of elders, she sometimes hosted the Maksimovskie elders as a layperson. Her children told me with laughter that after the elders had left, and if their parents were not home, the five of them used to play "council." The eldest brother would be the spiritual father, and the younger children would be assigned other roles according to age: pretending to read from the service books, or singing, or simply standing in the back of the room bowing when their eldest brother commanded.

These youthful memories of elderly parents or grandparents are significant. Recall that it was not uncommon in the late nineteenth century for young boys and girls to be full members of the community of active Old Believers, sometimes even until marriage age, at which point they left for sexual, labor, and monetary relationships in the world until old age. During their early years of attending services with the elders and pastors, many children learned the prayers and rituals of priestless Old Belief and practiced reading Slavonic texts. When they rejoined the council of elders later in life, they had at least some practical knowledge of what it meant to extricate oneself from worldly relationships and to prepare one's soul for salvation. By contrast, none of the townspeople I knew remembered learning Slavonic texts or any of the prayers and rituals that were part of the services. This is significant because, in pre-Soviet times, as I have noted, it was often during their premarriage years of life in the community of elders that children learned much of the order of the priestless Old Believer service. They learned to understand and manipulate the materials of ethics in ways that would create possibilities for salvation. In the Soviet period, however, several generations of young townspeople worked their way through the socialist school system and its close connection to training cadres for the moral communities of State Farm Sepych and the relationships of this world. One net effect was that it became nearly impossible for grandparents to teach their grandchildren either to read Slavonic texts or to be more than passingly familiar with the rituals and prayers through which they communicated with those in the other world.

When those leaving the world of socialist agriculture made their decisions to join the communities of elders in the later Soviet period, it was with a much lower degree of personal familiarity with the practices, texts, and relationships they were electing to take up. Spiritual mothers in the late Soviet period, then, spent their time teaching the order of services to slightly younger members of their own generation rather than their grandchildren. Thus, although the practice of rural socialism only partially disrupted the *expectation* that those in the oldest generation should begin to wall themselves off from the world, it did break many of the specific material links of social reproduction between oldest and youngest generations. In the post-Soviet period, when those in middle and older generations began to think about the communities and subjectivities that led to salvation, they had memories of parents and grandparents of the sort I describe here. For the most part, they did not know how to read Slavonic texts, how to pray, or how, specifically, they were supposed to extricate themselves from the relationships of socialist accumulation and exchange that characterized earlier stages of their lives. Speaking with me in 2001, the recently retired woman who recalled falling asleep on the stove as the elders prayed reflected that, in retrospect, her mother had been wise. She had made the children listen to the services, and the sound of those prayers from the next room still echoed in her ears. But these were echoes, not the familiar embodied practices they might have been a century earlier.

SOCIALIST MATERIALS OF ETHICS AND THE SEPARATION OF THE WORLDS

In the twentieth century, as ever in the Upper Kama, elders' requirements for cultivating pure, Christian selves and communities that would enhance their chances of salvation were difficult to uphold in a material world at once stubbornly persistent and constantly changing. Yet something also changed about elders' ascetic strivings over the course of the Soviet period: the bitterly contested theological positions on display in the Maksimovskie and Dëminskie manuscripts of the postemancipation era faded as a means by which elders talked about themselves and distinguished themselves from one another. For both groups, a concern with correctly upholding the taboos on interaction with manifestations of the world supplanted debates about hierarchy, proper religious authority, and the role of women as pastors that were so hotly contested after emancipation. Although my archaeographer colleagues have tended to understand this change as evidence for the "decline of tradition" (I. V. Pozdeeva, personal communication), my different approach has led me to another explanation. I suggest that this Soviet-era shift to a near-exclusive concern with what had been a matter of no more than secondary importance—indeed, a matter of general agreement—in the schism of 1866–88 is tied to the elders' involvement in the specific movements and materialities of the socialist countryside. Supporting this claim requires both careful attention to how and when the issues of separating the worlds arose in the Soviet period and, as in my discussion of the postemancipation period, some educated guesswork.

The efforts of Old Believer elders to avoid worldly relationships of food, drink, money, and labor feature prominently in outsiders' and laypeople's accounts of local Old Belief in the Soviet era, as they did in the prerevolutionary period. Several former party-state officials from out of town told me, for instance, that they had quickly learned not to expect food, drink, or even well water from old women and men if they stopped near Sepych while touring the state farm's fields on a hot summer day. Middle-age townspeople I knew in Sepych had similar recollections of their parents' and grandparents' attempts to adopt an ascetic life in the countryside of the early and mid-Soviet period. One woman told me that in the 1980s, she dropped by her parents' house in their native village, found them away from home, and helped herself to a drink of *kvas* (a lightly fermented drink). The next day, her mother, who was an elder and a member of a Dëminskie council, became suspicious that something was amiss and called her daughter to ask if she had been there and touched anything. The daughter responded that she had indeed and described the flagon from which she had drunk. "Now you've spoiled it all!" (*Nu, ty vse ispogonila!*) shouted her mother in response when she found out which *kvas* her daughter had tasted.

From these accounts and others, it is clear that elders' refusals to exchange the basic materials of social interaction with both family and outsiders had much of their desired effect in marking their increasing separation from the affairs of this world. One woman remembered her grandmother to me:

> Do you understand what life "under direction" [*pod nachal*] means? It means you don't eat sugar, butter...if you joined the council [of elders], it meant you didn't go to the hospital, you didn't have any injections, that you refuse the world [*otkazyvaeshsia ot mira*]. My grandmother always had separate hot water from the rest of us in the sauna—it was a sin for her to use the same as ours. Everything was your own, and natural. No processing, no civilization at all. They went around to one another's houses to pray, bringing their service books and their own separate dishes.

Other friends told me of piles of dishes in their kitchens that they were not permitted to touch. Some, laughing, recalled that they touched the dishes simply to tease and provoke their grandparents—if elders' dishes were touched by someone from the world, the dishes would have to be washed in natural running water from a stream before they could be used again.

It is not surprising that these prohibitions feature prominently in the accounts of laypeople from inside and outside the Upper Kama; elders' avoidance strategies were, after all, explicitly directed at them. But questions of how to avoid the world also came to preoccupy and define elders themselves over the course of the Soviet period. At stake, as in earlier periods, was the ability to properly define and enter into ethical relationships considered appropriate to the formation of Christian subjects, moral communities, and the possibilities for salvation. What was different, however, was the elevation of these modes of self- and community-fashioning over others. Prohibitions on various kinds of exchange and interaction, rather than matters of theological debate or ritual practice, were frequently an item of central concern when elders gathered in council.

A list of the written decisions of a Dëminskie council of elders on March 9, 1960, includes the council's judgments on several issues that would have had implications for the daily rhythms of family life and the generational separation of the worlds: "The sauna is forbidden"; "Oatmeal from the market is not to be consumed"; "Inappropriate fish are not to be consumed"; and "Goat's milk is not to be consumed." These dietary and household restrictions are interspersed with other restrictions that pertained only to the elders and would have been largely invisible to laypeople: "There will be no Fedoseevtsy rituals"; "Icons of different faiths are not to be prayed to"; "New [post-Nikonian?] printed service books are not to be used for prayer." In other words, although matters relating to elders' lives of prayer were not absent from the council's deliberations, they were increasingly accompanied by, and even subordinate to, discussion of how to hold the world at bay properly. The decisions of this council concluded with an admonition applying more to avoidance than to rituals and prayers: "Do not forget that we have a monastic cell rule [*kileinoi monastyrskii obriad*]. Rid yourself of all that is forbidden....If you want to be in company with us [*v opshestve s nami*], do [*ispravte*] all that is written above."[40]

It is also evident from the few surviving twentieth-century council proceedings that matters of ritual and theology had, at least for many elders and pastors, ceased to be an obstacle to union between the Maksimovskie and Dëminskie. On several occasions, in fact, large councils of elders from all over the Upper Kama came together to discuss bringing an end to the divisive schism. As part of a series of large councils held in the first half of 1948—some of which included more than one hundred elders—the Dëminskie issued an appeal to the Maksimovskie:

> Loved ones, we should stop for a moment and look around: isn't it time to put an end to [*rastorgnut'*, lit.: annul] this excruciating devilish pride and make peace under the generous hand of our Lord Jesus Christ?...Our dear brothers! We have discussed the question of the baptism of Maksimovskie...and decided to accept

40. ORKiR NB MGU, PV, 1548, l. 1–2v. The manuscript contains only these short decisions of the council, with no notes on the deliberations or justifications that led to them.

it as true according to the first rule of Vasilii the Great in the *Kormchaia* [*Kniga*] because we have all church rituals in common.[41]

The manuscript goes on to recount that at least some of the Maksimovskie, under the leadership of a certain Mal'tsev, did not accept this offer of peace. Negotiations broke down and the schism continued. It is notable, however, that for those Dëminskie pastors who issued the appeal in the late 1940s—a time of postwar tolerance of religion in the Soviet Union—unity of ritual practice was sufficient reason for them to drop earlier anathemas against the Maksimovskie.

As these midcentury hopes for unity faded, the persistence of a divide between Maksimovskie and Dëminskie factions came to be explained and perpetuated by discussions of which group had the better, truer practices of avoiding the world. Some restrictions continued to be shared by both groups, including the standard prohibitions on eating, drinking, or sharing dishes with laypeople, which had their origins the prerevolutionary period. Other restrictions, however, became fiercely disputed as the kinds of worldly materials that could pose a threat changed. Members of the first Moscow State University archaeographical expedition in 1972 recounted to me that their first clue that they had discovered something interesting near Sepych was that an elderly woman walking by the side of the road refused the offer of a ride to her final destination. Maksimovskie elders, the archaeographers soon found out, were not permitted to use mechanized transport of any sort. They also refused to be photographed or recorded on cassette tape. Dëminskie elders, on the other hand, freely rode in cars and usually consented to appearing in photographs. Nearly every interview summarized in the archaeographers' early field journals identifies such prohibitions as central to the ways in which elders talked about themselves, their own faction, and their opponents. Similarly, when I asked about the differences between Maksimovskie and Dëminskie during my own fieldwork, elders and laypeople alike responded, without exception, by explaining that Maksimovskie were "stricter" and refused to ride in cars. Probing more deeply into the matter yielded not other disagreements but avowals that unity would be possible if only the other side were less intransigent about the correctness of its prohibitions on the world.

How, then, should we understand this emergence of concerns about the mixing of the worlds as the central front in the ongoing dispute between

---

41. ORKiR NB MGU, PV, 2285. Oral evidence suggests that there were hundreds of small gatherings of elders in the Soviet period. Minutes from only four survive in the manuscript record, either because of their importance or by coincidence of preservation and collection: ORKiR NB MGU, PV, 1578 (in 1924); 2285 (in 1948); 1548, l. 1–2 (in 1960); and 1685[5] (at some point in the second half of the twentieth century). Additional summonses to unity in the mid-twentieth century are discussed in ORKiR NB MGU, PV, 1579, entitled, "Unity with the Maksimovskie"; see also Ageeva et al. (1994, 240–45, 253).

Maksimovskie and Dëminskie in the twentieth century? The answer I offer relies not on tradition—perhaps in decay but strong enough to afford an arena of resistance to Soviet power through its taboos on worldly interaction—but on the full spread of materialities and ethical transformations of the socialist countryside. As I did in chapter 2 for the immediate postemancipation period, I suggest that new and reworked materials of ethics deeply influenced the practices of priestless Old Belief that were available, convincing, and enforced by the power of councils and pastors in the twentieth century. In the postemancipation period, I argued, shifting flows of labor and money created conditions that led to a schism in the one true Pomortsy faith. In the twentieth century, a new set of shifts transformed the Pomortsy faith yet again, this time into communities of opposed elders, largely women, concerned primarily with how to correctly uphold restrictions on exchange with the world, and with who was most successful in doing so. I offer four linked suggestions about how this transformation was shaped by the elders' experiences of, engagements with, and responses to the specific materialities of rural socialism.

First, the massive reorganization of the countryside associated with resettlement and collectivization ruptured the links between particular geographic subregions of the Upper Kama and the Maksimovskie and Dëminskie communities. In the decades after emancipation in 1861, the differential experience of new capital markets across communities fueled the dispute between elders that ended in schism. By contrast, as early as the 1930s and 1940s, forced and voluntary resettlement meant there came to be *both* Maksimovskie and Dëminskie councils in most larger, centralized villages of the Upper Kama, each meeting separately, each in communion with other councils of their faction spread through region. At the same time, collectivization, property appropriation, and dekulakization gradually evened out any of the remaining distinctions between the richer Maksimovskie, strongest in the old trading hub of Sepych, and the Dëminskie. If elders were to maintain distinctions between the factions, they would have to come up with different axes of comparison than the subregional distinctions and accusations of worldly acquisitiveness that prevailed at the time of the original schism.

Second, the material manifestations of Soviet efforts to regulate and eliminate religion, whether emanating from the Soviet religion bureaucracy or the NKVD, left preexisting structures of decentralized, conciliar authority largely intact in the Upper Kama. Even Sepych's many socialist weddings, a point of friction with religious authority in so many other places in the former Soviet bloc, did not make for much of a challenge to elders' religious authority or to local patterns of social reproduction. Although priestless Old Belief was indeed "driven underground," in the words of Andrei Mal'tsev's letter to comrade Kalinin in the late 1930s, elders continued to meet and discuss matters in periodic councils. Pastors, increasingly women and increasingly themselves members of the oldest generation, continued to enforce discipline through temporary excommunication. We have precious few accounts of the early councils of the Soviet period, but we might surmise without too much trouble that they, like the councils of the early postemancipation period, struggled with issues of how salvation-seeking Christians should respond to the changes in the world taking place around them.

Third, the general conditions of socialism in which these councils deliberated made it a great deal easier to argue that Christians should "rid [themselves] of all that is forbidden"—as the minutes of the council of 1960 discussed above demanded—than did broader patterns of exchange and circulation at other periods in the history of the Upper Kama. Socialism slowed the pace and reduced the scope of all manner of transactions. It privileged slower-moving personal connections (wealth in people) over faster-paced and wider-ranging money, made it nearly impossible to find items in stores, and necessitated constant resourcefulness and productivity in the household sector of the economy— especially when it came to food production in rural areas. This was especially the case in the Upper Kama in the epoch of material'nye incentives on local collective farms, when much of the countryside existed without cash and largely dependent on household plots.

It was precisely in these demonetized, intensely household-dependent years following collectivization that councils of elders would have had to deal most directly with how to handle the unfamiliar dilemmas created by the emergent socialist organization of the countryside. Socialism's shortages and shriveled scopes of circulation would have aided those elders who argued for (and enforced) ever stricter renunciation of the material world as the foundation of Christian ethical practice. Compared with the periods of intense marketization and expanding circuits of exchange in the 1860s–80s and again in the 1990s, the everyday material threats and temptations of an unfamiliar outside world were simply not as much in evidence in the 1930s and 1940s. It was precisely these reduced circuits of exchange that townspeople recalled as the most salient difficulties of the time. Through many debates, decisions, and excommunications taking place across the Upper Kama's decentralized councils of elders, we might surmise, strong prohibitions on mixing the worlds emerged as central to local Old Belief early on in the early socialist era. This was the case despite the fact that these prohibitions had been under such pressure from the expanding markets, wider and more intense circuits of exchange, and associated worldly acquisitiveness epitomized by Maksim Zhdanov in the late nineteenth century. In sum, the frequently heard complaint about socialism—that it failed to supply its population with desired, or even necessary, goods—seems actually to have *facilitated* older generations' efforts to avoid the things of this world as part of their attempts to sustain moral communities and subjectivities open to salvation.

Fourth, we must recognize that the implications of materials of ethics in the formation of subjects and moral communities are not just connected to the

literal presence or absence of objects. As theorists of consumption have powerfully argued, the connection between things and persons is also about the constitution of desire for objects. We might add to this that the desire in question
can also be to *avoid* those objects. In addition to its practical effects on patterns
of production and circulation, then, socialist shortage created endless worries,
desires, and discussions about the paths, availabilities, and fates of things—
particularly among women, who did the majority of provisioning in the Soviet
Union (Reid 2002). Even as younger generations in the Upper Kama—right
up to enterprise directors like Andrei Petrovich—perpetually sought out shortage items through their connections and networks, older generations of Old
Believers, increasingly women, tried to figure out how to avoid those objects.
This was especially the case in the era of state farming and moral'nye incentives, as monetization and the increasing fame of Andrei Petrovich and State
Farm Sepych brought ever more outsiders and unfamiliar objects into potential
contact with elders. Already primed to be concerned largely with taboos and
prohibitions from the early Soviet era, the Maksimovskie and Dëminskie councils of the later Soviet period found themselves making decisions about more
and more modes of mechanized transport, televisions, and archaeographers'
tape recorders.

Elders, we can conclude, worried about avoiding these objects every bit as
much as their lay children and grandchildren fretted about obtaining them.
Over the course of the Soviet period, this high-stakes arena became a prime
place for the articulation of differences between the Maksimovskie and Dëminskie as the significance and relevance of older distinctions faded. It no longer
made sense in the socialist countryside, as it did for many in 1866–88, to sig-
nify one's withdrawal from the world by avoiding and denouncing capital accumulation. Nor were the accusations of "being a prince of this world and also
a pastor" once leveled at Maksim Zhdanov likely to gain much traction, as
the role of pastor was reserved for elders and its mediating position between
generations became but a memory. Neither was there much to be gained in
trading accusations about the role of women as pastors, for nearly all pastors
had become women. Instead, a concern with consumption and its prohibition
became central to distinctions between Maksimovskie and Dëminskie and to
elders' efforts to live properly as members of either group.

In considering the emergence of withdrawal from consumption as the
key distinction between competing groups of elders, we must recognize that
socialist-era elders desired to withdraw not from just any world but from
the specific material arrangements of the *socialist* world. Their overriding
concern with avoiding certain objects—and avoiding them to precisely the
right degree—inverted (rather than simply repudiated) younger generations'
overriding concern with acquiring objects in conditions of pervasive shortage. Understandings of this ascetic withdrawal as resistance to socialism thus
fail to capture the extent to which Christian subject formation in the Soviet

countryside was, in fact, deeply colored by socialist subject formation. Indeed, the primary contours and vocabularies of Soviet-era asceticism emerged from precisely those worldly material practices and subjectivities that elders were seeking to leave behind.

To recapitulate, overt clashes between religion and the state were not characteristic of Soviet-era Sepych. Not only did a long series of party-state schemes to define and regulate religion in Sepych miss their mark, but more than a few elements of the party-state, including local officials and university scholars, worked quietly to facilitate the practice of Old Belief. Even the arrests and executions of the late 1930s did not dramatically alter local expectations, practices, and structures of religious authority. Rather, the key transformations of Old Belief in the Soviet period—feminization, geriatricization, and an overriding concern with prohibitions on engaging with the world—responded to and participated in the specific, shifting materials of ethics of the Soviet countryside. It was first and foremost at this level of ethical practice that age-old quandaries of what it meant to be a true Christian were hashed out in terms both old and new. The persistence of priestless Old Belief in the Upper Kama through the officially and sometimes militantly atheist Soviet period should not, then, be accounted for simply by pointing to the strength of Old Believer traditions and the deep convictions of their adherents in the face of persecution. This endurance argument is common and, on the surface, plausible. Strength of conviction in Old Belief as the path to true salvation is certainly part of the story, and specific Old Believers endured a great deal for the sake of their faith in the violent 1930s. Nevertheless, the totality of ethical transformations associated with rural Soviet socialism in Sepych did not overthrow but, paradoxically, *incubated* many townspeople's ability to make and traverse sharp distinctions between moral communities and ethical subjectivities defined by work and prayer.

What kinds of human subjectivities were characteristic of Soviet-type socialist societies? By what processes and through what powers were these subjectivities shaped? The intricacies of ethical transformations as they unfolded in Soviet-era Sepych, especially when viewed in the context of pre-Soviet history, offer some instructive pointers for ongoing discussions of this important issue. Two of my concluding pointers are methodological; the third is substantive.

In the first place, I have approached the formation of socialist subjects not as a stand-alone topic but as only one corner of the broader field of ethics—a field in which an array of materials of ethics and moralizing discourses circulates and helps to shape both ethical subjects and moral communities. By bringing many pieces of this constantly shifting puzzle into a single argument, I have sought to show that there was not one overarching way in which townspeople's ethical sensibilities were transformed in the Soviet period. There was never a single brand of socialist subject or socialist moral community in Sepych. Rather, the residents of Sepych were constantly engaged in ethical transformations and dilemmas on multiple, yet intersecting and interacting, fronts. Labor incentives and the work of archaeographers, for instance, are connected to each other not because they are part of some coherent socialist project but because each in its own way hooked into different aspects of ongoing conversations and shifting expectations about ethics in Sepych itself. At the same time, this approach showed the ways in which other potential vectors of ethical transformation did *not* have much of an effect in Sepych, especially overt antireligious campaigns and NKVD arrests in the late 1930s. If we are to comprehend socialist-era transformations in ways that are adequate to the experience of socialist citizens themselves, it will be instructive to look to such broad fields of ethical contest and confluence.

Second, each aspect of my analysis of the Soviet period has relied on understandings of the pre-Soviet past, of an ethical repertoire formed in the eras of serfdom and emancipation. This is not simply, I emphasize, a generalized Russian past or a Foucauldian "discursive formulation" (for example, Kharkhordin 1999) but a specific, historically formed, socially located, and culturally saturated constellation of expectations and practices about how to go about forming ethical subjects and moral communities. Significantly, this was a past that was often materially available to the ongoing present: worn into roads and fields, inscribed into old books and manuscripts, embodied in rituals. Viewing the transformations of the Soviet period in light of this history illuminates the stakes involved in Sepych's Soviet-era ethical reconfigurations. An appreciation of prerevolutionary arrangements of religious hierarchy and worldly marriage in the Upper Kama was, to recall but one example, crucial to my arguments about the ways in which certain Soviet moralizing discourses did not, in practice, seriously disrupt local expectations about social reproduction.

Finally, following both of these methodological paths has led me to the substantive conclusion of part 2: the continued salience and, in some cases, amplification of generational distinctions in Soviet-era Sepych. In part, this division between younger and elder generations as fields of ethical practice concerned with work and prayer was inherited from the prerevolutionary period. But the importance of generation was actively sustained in numerous ways—both intentional and unintentional—by the arrangement of moralizing discourses and materials of ethics within the Soviet socialist ethical regime itself. Not only did elders continue to understand Christian salvation as requiring withdrawal from the world, but various elements of socialism itself often facilitated the sharp distinction between generations on which this withdrawal depended. I noted this process at work in several ways. Through patterns of resettlement and collectivization, distinctions between older and younger generations were written into the landscape. Likewise, generational distinctions sharpened as the mediating role of middle-generation pastors faded—a consequence of increasing demands on male labor power and the difficulty of taking up religious practice before old age in the Soviet period. In a more intentional way, although with many unanticipated outcomes, collectivization drives and socialist incentives to labor focused largely on youth and middle generations; the work of archaeographers, by contrast, attended exclusively to the oldest generations of townspeople.

Each of these generational fields of ethical transformation in the Soviet period came with its own set of primary materials of ethics: money, in-kind payments, and labor rituals for youth and middle generations in socialist agricultural enterprises; books, manuscripts, letters, and ascetic rituals for older generations and their visiting scholars. Although each of these sets was situated within the overall socialist mode of production—especially its demands for collecting wealth in people in conditions of shortage—those trafficking in each set often strove mightily not to acknowledge the existence of the other. One of the most striking illustrations of this arrangement of generations is the fact that the film crew for *Sepych Weddings* and an archaeographical expedition from Moscow were in Sepych the very same summer, yet the subsets of townspeople with which each interacted were mutually exclusive. Moreover, the moralizing discourses produced by each group of outsiders, the kinds of subjects and communities they sought to project outward on the basis of their visits to Sepych, depended precisely on not mentioning the other generational group. The film crew's work focused exclusively on Sepych's youth and portrayed a bright, child- and labor-filled socialist future, while the archaeographers attended entirely to the town's elders and dwelt on the preservation of the Russian national tradition despite—indeed precisely as a carefully phrased challenge to—the modernizing aims of socialist agriculture exemplified by the town's youth. These outsiders' generationally inflected visits to town were but one more way in which the generational proclivities of socialism itself reinforced and contributed to the ongoing salience of expectations about the separation of the worlds in Sepych.

Townspeople in Soviet Sepych, then, followed their prerevolutionary ancestors in constantly navigating day-to-day dilemmas that arose from the close material and social proximity of strongly differentiated fields of ethical practice. It is, I have argued, in these intimate negotiations—among family, neighbors, and friends from near and far—that townspeople sought to fashion subjectivities oriented toward the moral communities of worldly socialism or to otherworldly salvation. Neither of these modes of socialist subject formation in Sepych can be fully understood by itself, not only because each presupposed and worked off the other in specific, identifiable, material ways but also because so many in the Upper Kama crossed the line between generations in the course of their own lives.

I do not mean to suggest that generational distinctions can be shown to operate in just this way across the socialist world, although I do wonder whether

Sepych presents an intensification, a limit case, of wider processes. Might we apprehend here, for instance, some of how Russian Orthodox churches continued to be populated with elderly women long after Communist Party officials had expected the "last" generation of elderly believers to die off? After all, we know very little about the lives of elderly Soviet citizens and long-term changes in the course of individual socialist lives, as scholars have more commonly followed socialist activists in focusing on youth and middle age. More generally, the case of Sepych may suggest a key way in which socialist subjectivities were unstable over time, a way not revealed by studies that focus on a particular slice of the Soviet period or assume, along with Soviet moralizers themselves, that human subjects, once formed in youth, are unchanging.

PART III

Struggles to Shape an Emergent Ethical Regime

Come now you rich
And weep
And wail
At the cruel sorrows
That are in store for you.
Your riches have rotted
And your clothes have been eaten by moths.
Your gold and silver has rusted,
And the rust will be evidence against you.
It will eat your treasures
And consume your body
Like the fire of the Last Days that you
have brought upon yourself.

— Priestless Old Believer Penitential Verse
   (see ORKiR NB MGU, PV, 1425, l. 6; James 5: 1–6)

5 New Risks and Inequalities in the Household Sector

The penitential verse that serves as the epigraph to part 3 was written for—and sung in—another age, yet the transformations it catalogs hint at the ethical debates and dilemmas pervasive in post-Soviet Sepych. The verse sets out the correlates and consequences of becoming rich, sorrows that are manifested primarily through changes in the nature of material objects—the rotting, rusting, and gnawing of moths and the corrosion of accumulated treasure. This corruption of things proceeds to consume human bodies and to become evidence for the flaws of human subjects and groups of subjects (the phrase "And consume your body" is singular, but the imperative "Come now, you rich" of the opening line is plural). Finally, the verse asserts that the linked corruption of objects and subjects interferes in the possibility of Christian salvation: the rich "have brought upon" themselves the end of the world or, at the very least, subjected themselves to sufferings of comparable gravity ("like the fire of the Last Days").

Similar assertions—that the attributes and transformations of material things both created and revealed the corruption of people—circulated widely in post-Soviet Sepych. Yet townspeople's most recent debates about the refigurings of subjects, objects, and moral communities have been much more multifaceted than the ineluctable chain of connections between worldly accumulation and the Last Days posited by the old verse. Among the most commented upon of the worldly objects circulating through post-Soviet Sepych, for instance, was moonshine (*samogon*). By 2001, it was already a source of abiding disdain in cities and occasional embarrassment in rural areas that moonshine had come to compete with rubles for the status of primary currency in the Russian countryside. To many, especially in urban Russia, moonshine and its effects on the mind and body were the quintessential markers of the decay—even the impending death—of the Russian countryside. Indeed, my urban acquaintances often worried that my fieldwork (and I, personally) would end up malformed, corrupted by too much moonshine. "Douglas, you haven't become a drunk out there in Sepych, have you?" was a standard question, only half-joking, whenever I set foot outside of town.

Moonshine did indeed lubricate my time in Sepych, but it did so in ways that traced the emergence of positively valued ethical subjects and moral communities as often as corruption and decay. In the busy warmer months, moonshine was compensation to workers after (and often during) the labor of domestic agricultural production—herding, slaughtering livestock, or haying. In the winter, social life slowed and slipped below ground, into the furnace rooms heating Sepych's public buildings. There men gathered for warmth and company, played cards, and discussed who among them would buy the next bottle of moonshine and who would sell it to him. Husbands hid moonshine from their wives. When they found it, wives rehid it from their husbands. Milk truck drivers from the privatized state farm, fulfilling requests from family and friends, often returned from their routes to urban processing plants with fifty-kilogram sacks of granulated sugar lashed to their trucks, a good portion of it for use in domestic bootlegging operations. Nearly everyone in town expressed some disapproval of the unemployed young men who worked odd jobs, charging their temporary employers only a bottle or two of moonshine. As one friend in Sepych put it, summing up a long conversation about exchange, "But, really, you know, everything here is done for a bottle."

It was, I came to understand, often in a moonshine idiom that townspeople experienced and discussed emergent kinds of ethical subjects, shifting axes of social stratification, ruptured moral communities, and soaring risks in the early postsocialist period. This chapter follows the paths carved by moonshine—especially as it interacted with rubles, labor, and U.S. dollars in the general context of decollectivization and global capitalist transformation—as an opening route into a much larger field of interrelated struggles and transformations in post-Soviet Sepych.[1] This was an ethical field that extended, as subsequent chapters show, beyond worldly moonshine, money, and labor to changes in the nature of relationships with the other world as well. The boundaries of this world were once again on the move, with another round of predicaments for those who sought out elements of a Christian life.

In characterizing Sepych's post-Soviet period in part 3 as a time of struggles to shape an emergent ethical regime, I have several things in mind. In the first place, I join most other anthropologists in avoiding the twin teleologies that have dominated Western scholarly and public conversation about Russia in the years since 1991: triumphalist predictions of a smooth and speedy

---

1. On the relatively neglected—at least in anthropology—topic of postsocialist labor see especially Dunn (2004) and Kideckel (2008).

transition to capitalism and democracy and, later, dire pronouncements about Russia's return to its true authoritarian nature. I see, rather, an array of ongoing struggles—by no means fully determinate or predictable—to reshape the people of Sepych as ethical subjects and as members of diverse, intertwined moral communities. The nature of these struggles is not at all well captured by the taken-for-granted categories and correlations presupposed by so much social science scholarship on the region (private property creates civil society, markets favor religious liberty, and so on), so I avoid measuring post-Soviet Sepych against dry indexes of marketization, democratization, or religious freedom.

My emphasis on emergence also reflects the ongoing uncertainty that attends so many aspects of life in Sepych. In the wake of revolution and collectivization, I argued in chapters 3 and 4, socialism congealed into a more or less stable configuration of ethical practices, materials of ethics, and moral communities in Sepych—an ethical regime. Although many aspects of socialist-era ethics continue to resonate in Sepych, their once-stable configuration has come to an end and has not yet been fully supplanted. To be sure, some of the staggering uncertainty and surreal unpredictability so vividly captured in early postsocialist ethnographies (especially Grant 1995; see also Verdery 1996; Burawoy and Verdery 1999) has now faded. Some possibilities have now been shut down and, barring truly enormous social, cultural, and political realignments, are unlikely to be reopened soon. Nevertheless, the processes I describe here are largely open-ended; they remain sites of struggle and transformation that have yet to cohere into a new ethical regime comparable to that of the socialist period.

Townspeople in Sepych are not alone in these struggles, for they are part of an era of worldwide ethical emergence closely associated with recent changes in the nature of capitalism. Townspeople in Sepych, like all former socialist citizens, encountered not some abstract, textbook version of capitalism after socialism but a set of very particular modes of accumulation, circulation, and power associated with what is often called "post-Fordist" capitalism.[2] These massive changes, however, cannot be fully understood apart from the ways they hook into and transform—and are transformed by—quite local ethical repertoires. The discussions of risk-bearing subjects, global financial crises, anticorruption campaigns, weak state organizations, religious revivals, and shifting rituals in these final chapters should, then, be at once familiar and strange: familiar because many scholars have taken up these topics as facets of the remaking of human subjects and communities in the contemporary world; strange

---

2. I draw here on a broad literature. On post-Fordism and general transformations of capitalism since the early 1970s, see especially Harvey (1989); on the financialization of capital of particular concern in this chapter, see Arrighi (1994) and LiPuma and Lee (2004). Verdery (1996) has argued that among the effects of these global transformations were the destabilization and eventual disintegration of Soviet and East European socialisms.

because, in my analysis of Sepych, they are heavily colored by centuries-long processes of ethical transformation quite different from those characteristic of the European colonies and postcolonies that remain among the most common contexts for the generation of anthropological theory.

Decollectivization, Involution, and Moonshine

The broader context of decollectivization in Sepych is crucial to understanding the ways in which materials of ethics such as moonshine circulated. The Yeltsin administration's first decrees on rural decollectivization came in late 1991; their many modifications and permutations gave rise to a range of fresh organizational possibilities in the post-Soviet countryside (Humphrey [1983] 1998, 444–81; Wegren 1998). The membership of State Farm Sepych voted for closed joint stock company (AOZT) status, which allowed the farm, renamed AOZT Sepych, to retain much of its Soviet-era brigade structure and permitted only current and former employees to hold shares, vote at meetings, and hope for yearly dividends.[3] Andrei Petrovich, director of State Farm Sepych since the early 1970s, was promptly and overwhelmingly elected director of the new enterprise.[4] Despite his considerable abilities and contacts, productivity levels and salaries in AOZT Sepych promptly plunged. There was never enough remaining at the end of the year for the initially much-discussed shareholders' dividends. Money virtually disappeared for months at a time. AOZT Sepych was nearly bankrupt for much of the 1990s, although not unintentionally so. Like other firms across the Soviet Union, AOZT Sepych tried not to register cash profits so as to avoid paying regional and federal taxes.[5] That is, the farm sought to circulate all manner of goods and services that, whatever else they could be exchanged for, did not register in cash in state accounts, which could be immediately garnished to pay back taxes. AOZT Sepych, for

---

3. Yulian Konstantinov (1997) terms this arrangement an "insiders' collective." It was one of the most popular choices for privatizing enterprises across Russia. In 2001, legal changes forced Sepych to change its name again, from AOZT Sepych to SPK (Agricultural Production Cooperative) Sepych. This change brought few if any immediate consequences for its organization or operation; for the sake of clarity, I stay with AOZT Sepych to refer to the farm in the post-Soviet era. There are likely to be substantial differences—confirmed by a great deal of anecdotal evidence—between interhousehold relations in Sepych, which chose to privatize into an AOZT, and interhousehold relations in former state or collective farms that elected to disband entirely into constituent households, leaving no input sources outside the household sector of production. For the same reasons, the case I discuss here is substantially different from Nagengast's (1991) analysis of labor exchanges and class in rural Poland, which was not collectivized.

4. On the continuing importance of directors, see especially Lampland (2002), Verdery (2003), and Allina-Pisano (2008).

5. See the partially contrasting treatments of this practice in Woodruff (1999) and Gaddy and Ickes (2002).

instance, arranged to pay taxes by supplying the local school directly with milk and meat.

Individual households, however, did not have the luxury of avoiding cash entirely—they needed at least some money. With the largest private employer in town paying salaries irregularly, with state agencies making their payrolls only slightly more reliably, and with the more general disappearance of Soviet-era social safety nets, townspeople in Sepych turned increasingly to their own barns and household plots for both food and income. Many townspeople, particularly the trained specialists who worked in Sepych's grade school, hospital, and state administration, never owned or learned to care for their own livestock in the Soviet period; they rapidly overcame their Soviet-era disdain for milking cows. In the 1990s, only a small handful of townspeople could rely on enough salary income to go without raising some combination of pigs, cattle, and fowl and growing potatoes on multiple scattered plots. Expanded garden fences and large new backyard sties were common sights in Sepych, evidence of the ways in which agricultural production continued to "involute" (Burawoy et al. 2000; see also Creed 1998, 246–262; Humphrey [1983] 1998, 2002, 164–74).[6] "We're all livestock breeders now," I was told on one occasion, despite AOZT Sepych's continued employment of several hundred townspeople across its divisions. In contrast to the Soviet period, when nearly all exchanges somehow involved State Farm Sepych, there was now a great deal more room for—as well as significance placed upon—transactions among households themselves.

A goodly number of these transactions involved moonshine, enough so that it is useful to see moonshine as something of an alternate currency—one circulating in a general post-Soviet environment that has been characterized as home to "some of the most curious nonmonetary payment schemes recently seen in the modern world" (Gaddy and Ickes 2002, 13).[7] Like the state's money, moonshine indexed certain kinds of connections, capacities, and the attendant creation of subjects and communities. In contrast to money, townspeople often

6. The issue of involution is related to debates about the return of the peasant after socialism (Creed 1995; Zbierski-Salameh 1999; Leonard and Kaneff 2002). To gain some sense of the issues at play in this literature, compare two studies of Romania: A. L. Cartwright's "return of the peasant" (2001) and Katherine Verdery's "death of a peasantry" (2003, 190–229). Caroline Humphrey ([1983] 1998, 446–53) discusses the many meanings that the term "peasant" took on in post-Soviet Russia. See also Susan Crate's (2006) analysis of the "cows-and-kin complex" in the Sakha Republic.

7. Although various sorts of alcohol changed hands all over Russia, likely only in rural settings did alcohol approach the status of currency (see also Hivon 1994 on vodka, and note Ssorin-Chaikov 2000, 345). Drinking during working hours and domestic labor fueled the urban stereotype of the drunken countryside, a stereotype that I challenge in this chapter. The common picture of rural Russians engaged in little but drinking moonshine day in and day out far overestimates the amount that was actually consumed in Sepych and far underestimates the amount of work that can be effectively completed with a bit of moonshine in one's system.

played up the local origins of circulating moonshine, noting that its provenance in the kitchens of their friends and neighbors bespoke a sense of communal trust that they did not always find present in monetary exchanges or even in the commercially produced bottles of vodka—often alleged to be of dubious quality—for sale in Sepych's stores. Moonshine was not particularly durable, despite its wide range of exchangeability. It demanded not further transformation or accumulation following exchange but, rather, consumption as an intrinsic element of (or very shortly after) exchange. As an object, any one bottle of moonshine was rarely long for this world—which meant that its accumulation, unlike that of money, could not be valued and that calculations of who had given whom how much could quickly become hazy.[8] Moreover, both moonshine and money in Sepych took on their greatest significance as townspeople struggled to bring them into equivalence with still another transactable: labor. In the negotiations over compensating the labor power that Sepych's growing private sector demanded, what was often at stake was whether labor could—and, as important, should—be exchanged for rubles, moonshine, reciprocal labor, or some combination thereof.[9]

Gendered Ethical Subjects: Moonshine and Money within Households

The intensification of domestic production characteristic of involution was reflected in everything from home-baked bread to home-thickened sour cream, and moonshine was yet one more dimension of the withdrawal of much of

8. Jennifer Patico has drawn attention to the more durable qualities of alcohol as a gift in urban St. Petersburg, counting it as one among a range of gifts that can be "saved for the right moment" by the receiver (2002, 361). This was rarely the case with moonshine in the rural setting of Sepych.

9. Attending to exchange objects is hardly a new strategy for coming to grips with postsocialist transformations. One line of investigation has paid particular attention to money, often tracing Russian variations on the discourse of alienation and decay available in many places where money circulates (Dinello 1998; Pesmen 2000, 126–45 and passim; Ries 2002; cf. Parry and Bloch 1989). A second set of researchers has focused on the proliferation of barter arrangements in the Russian economy (e.g., Humphrey 2002, 5–20; see also Cellarius 2000), in some cases engaging in productive discussions with economists also attempting to come to grips with post-Soviet demonetization (above all, Seabright 2000). A third cluster of scholars has concentrated on nonmonetary transactions in ethnographies of bribes, gifts, and informal connections accruing around access to goods and services (Ledeneva 1998, 2006; Patico 2002, 2008; Caldwell 2004; Rivkin-Fish 2005, 152–78). The arguments of this third group have generally been somewhat less oriented toward economic issues associated with barter and demonetization, illuminating instead the social construction of personhood and subjectivity through objects (Rethmann 2000; Ssorin-Chaikov 2000). In an innovative argument that has not received enough attention, Elizabeth Dunn (2004, esp. 94–129) showed that management in a postsocialist baby food factory began to treat workers as sets of qualities to be measured and improved—precisely the same view that management took of the objects (carrots, for example) that the workers processed.

Sepych's population from purchasing in stores (compare Creed 2002 on Bulgaria). The conflicts and complementarities of moonshine and money within a household, particularly in relationships between husbands and wives, form my first example of the ways in which attending to old materials of ethics in new contexts illuminates the shaping of new kinds of subjects after socialism. Although inputs from the circulation of both moonshine and money were important to domestic economies, the association of women with the higher exchangeability of money contributed to the widely held, if often contested, view that men were subordinate to women in the management of the household. Through households' exchanges of money and moonshine (and endless talk about them), new capacities for action and new, contested understandings of what it meant to be a woman or a man emerged in post-Soviet Sepych.

In contrast to the preponderance of store-bought vodka during much of the Soviet period—at least until Gorbachev's antialcohol campaigns of the mid-1980s—domestic moonshine production soared across rural Russia in the 1990s, reaching a level high enough to figure in the market forecasts of international sugar concerns.[10] The moonshine favored in Sepych's households was between 40 and 60 percent alcohol. It required relatively little to produce: granulated sugar, yeast, water, a pressure cooker of one sort or another, and, often, secret ingredients. Nearly all households with which I was familiar produced moonshine on occasion, but not all had a perpetual supply. As one friend from a somewhat wealthier family told me, "We prefer vodka for ourselves, but in the summer we always have moonshine around, for our helpers." Still fewer households actively sold moonshine to their fellow townspeople, a technically illegal activity that carried a heavy fine on the extremely rare occasions the law was enforced. Pegged to the market price of sugar, a half-liter bottle cost twenty rubles (sixty-five cents) in 2001, around one-third as much as store-bought vodka.

The occasions for consuming this moonshine were many but can be loosely classified into those marking hospitality for friends and family, those associated with sociability in the workplace (mostly, but not exclusively, male), and those accompanying hard labor in households.[11] Although there was a stronger

10. See, for instance, the *Czarnikow Russian Market Weekly Report* (2000). In 2001, the year of my primary fieldwork, moonshine was the drink of choice in Sepych, in contrast to many towns and villages closer to urban centers, where people were more likely to drink cheap, mass-produced grain alcohol (*spirt*). On my visits to Sepych after 2004, however, market conditions had shifted: *spirt* had become somewhat cheaper than, and as readily available as, moonshine. The least well-off townspeople in Sepych had correspondingly switched their allegiance, adding a new wrinkle to lines of inequality.

11. Post-Soviet drinking "at the table" (*za stolom*) has featured in several very instructive anthropological analyses (Ries 1997; Pesmen 2000, 170–88 and passim; Koester 2003). In these studies of Russian "drinking rituals," drinking often serves as a context for reflection on or creation of one or another kind of community, from the suffering Russian nation as a whole on down to small-scale drinking circles or one-on-one trading relationships. One goal of my argument here

association between men and alcohol, women's drinking was certainly on the rise in the post-Soviet era as well. Most women's drinking took place in the context of household hospitality and occasional workplace sociability, during which some women drank nearly as much as men. Most women I knew—although certainly not all—preferred vodka, cognac, wine, or champagne to moonshine on occasions such as birthdays or holidays; these women did, however, often drink moonshine in the contexts of household labor exchange. Whatever the occasion, no one ever objected to two or more different kinds of alcohol sitting on the table at the same time. Women did not moonlight as much as men did and thus did not figure as often in the relationship between moonshine and moonlighting I discuss below. The production of moonshine was not exclusively the domain of either women or men—depending on the household, husbands, wives, or both supervised the still. The exchanges enabled by these bottles, however, were often deeply gendered. In those households that regularly sold moonshine to other townspeople, for instance, it was usually wives who made the sales and kept charge of the cash proceeds. Husbands were less likely to sell moonshine for cash than to consume it with male friends, cementing relationships that ultimately led to nonmonetary inputs to the household.

Money, too, was a gendered item in Sepych's households. As others have noted, the involution and defensive strategies characteristic of much of the transition from socialism have transformed the roles of women and men in households (Pine 1996, 2002; Burawoy et al. 2000; Shreeves 2002). In Sepych, one element of this gendered transformation was that women most often controlled—or at the very least were engaged in ongoing struggles to control—the household's inflows and outflows of money. There were several reasons for this association between women and money. First, women were more likely be employed in the school, kindergarten, hospital, and culture department and hence to have access to comparatively reliable cash salaries from the federal budget throughout the year. Second, salaries from AOZT Sepych, the most likely source of cash income for men, varied seasonally and in kind. In 2001, they were lower on average than those of state-employed and usually female "budget" workers. At earlier points in the 1990s, AOZT Sepych workers were often paid not in cash but in agricultural products, construction materials, or commercial farm services, such as plowing. Third, even at the worst of times, state pensions were the most reliable source of money, and the much greater percentage of women over retirement age further amplified the association of money with women.

Although money competed with moonshine in many contexts, it also had a somewhat higher degree of exchangeability and portability than did moonshine. Women most often tended to those household expenditures that could be made only with rubles: large purchases of durable goods such as televisions

---

is to add to these studies a fuller consideration of the inequalities, exclusions, and emergent social fault lines also evident in shifting drinking practices.

or refrigerators, food purchased in stores, clothing and schoolbooks for children, electricity and telephone bills, and taxes. Women, that is, were more likely to both receive as salary and use in exchanges the currency with the highest degree of exchangeability, the most purchasing power, and the necessary payment for much-desired goods such televisions and other conveniences: rubles. Despite this, most women tried to maintain for their households only a moderate, defensive level of cash liquidity because bouts of inflation and devaluation meant that it was usually safer to transform rubles, whether from salaries or sale of domestic agricultural products, into more durable goods (Humphrey [1983] 1998, 459) or U.S. dollars.

Men, by contrast, were much more likely to be responsible for household inputs and outputs that involved moonshine rather than money. Men, for instance, spent a great deal of time with their friends conniving about how to steal from the commercial farm, collective activity that invariably involved drinking and payoffs in moonshine. These payoffs often had a generally agreed-on word-of-mouth price: a sack of grain stolen from the warehouse by a night watchman, for instance, cost two bottles of moonshine. In practice, distinguishing between drinking in this context, which brought inputs of various sorts into the household, and simply getting drunk at work with one's friends was often hard. Discerning the difference between these drinking contexts was of great importance to the wives who supervised household money. Although many women objected to their husbands' being drunk, they cared how men got drunk. If a man returned home from work so drunk as to be unable to complete the household tasks waiting for him and having spent part of his salary on moonshine to boot, he might find a very unwelcome reception from his wife. But the same wife would be more than happy to place a bottle on the table after the immediate family had completed a difficult day of household labor and would consider it her obligation to place far more than a single bottle on the table if her husband and his male friends or extended family members had just completed a set of arduous household tasks, perhaps stealing grain or firewood. In short, drinking as an element of household labor or labor exchange was not an outlay of money with only a hangover to show for it. Wives tolerated, encouraged, and often joined in this sort of drinking. A man simply getting drunk with other men at work, however, where bottles were often purchased on the spur of the moment, was useless and reprehensible in most women's eyes.

Many women's efforts therefore revolved around reducing the amount of money that men spent on moonshine with their friends so as to divert that money to household purchasing in stores or other contexts in which moonshine, despite the vast range of goods and services for which it could be exchanged, was of little use. Large and small battles about moonshine, money, and labor were common among the women and men I knew in Sepych and often came to a head over the amount of household monetary income men were permitted to spend purchasing and sharing bottles of moonshine with their coworkers. These battles ranged from the lighthearted—a husband I knew arrived home and informed his wife that the long summer work shifts would soon be over and she would be pleased to know that he would therefore be drunk less frequently—to the much more serious. I knew one couple whose relationship was strained to the brink of divorce in the 1990s precisely along the fault line between moonshine and money. The wife insisted on a greater degree of control over her husband's salary to provide for their young children in an economy in which, she argued, money mattered far more than it used to. Her husband, by contrast, insisted that he could not refuse to drink at work and hope to maintain his friendships, which provided another important source of inputs into the household through gathered helpers for labor projects and accomplices on thieving expeditions. In the end, the wife won the larger battle and greater control of their salary income. Another common compromise was for husband and wife to keep their own salaries while the wife kept charge of the much larger sums of money obtained from periodically selling livestock.

These conflicts extended to men's and women's alliances outside the household, as well. When men gathered to drink in the workplace, out of sight of their wives, they often had to pool pocket change to come up with enough for a bottle of moonshine or small amount of vodka (sold in Sepych's stores by the fifty- or hundred-gram shot). But coming up with the money was not always enough—the next step was properly lining up a purchasing relationship of appropriate social distance. That is, the gathered men had to elect a purchaser from their number and match him to a woman seller of alcohol (either a moonshine trader at home or a vodka saleswoman in a shop) who was not closely related to or good friends with the elected purchaser's wife. If she was close to the purchaser's wife, she was likely to be under orders not to let her friend's husband spend money getting drunk during the day. Relationships between wives and husbands were, then, often the point of conversion and contest between the currencies of money and moonshine, each with different degrees of exchangeability, both considered necessary for running a household.[12] Many marriages struggled to find a balance point between women's money and men's moonshine, struggles that were not aided by the unpredictably shifting levels of liquidity and exchange rates in the larger economy, as reflected in late salaries, in-kind payments, and inflation. Women's control of money enabled them to participate in a much wider array of exchanges than men could—including many exchanges outside Sepych. Men's moonshine networks, although locally potent, did not

---

12. Access to the inputs that accrued to the circulation of money and moonshine was one of the chief reasons widows, widowers, and divorced townspeople gave for remarrying swiftly (whether or not they did in fact remarry). Women said they found it much harder to negotiate with nonhousehold men for items to be stolen or for help with household work. Similarly, many men felt uncomfortable dealing with teachers and school administrators, tax officials, and other official contacts, especially those extending further from town.

extend far beyond the borders of Sepych. Many husbands resented their wives' attempts to control money, feeling that the greater purchasing power associated with money cast men in an inferior position in the household. In this way, the gendered subjectivities that moonshine and money helped to create were increasingly, if controversially, also an emergent axis of inequality.

As materials of ethics in post-Soviet Sepych, money and moonshine were thus differently gendered in the ways each currency featured in exchange for different sorts of household inputs. But moonshine, unlike money, could potentially feature in exchange for labor within the household itself. Most families strove to be selective about the amount and kinds of work for which they brought in outside help that would then have to be compensated or reciprocated. Wives, husbands, and children therefore divvied up the everyday tasks of attending to gardens and livestock and planned household chores around work and school. Hard work over and above the usual fare, such as herding the neighborhood cows (which families undertook by turns during the grazing months) or unloading and storing several tons of grain, might warrant a bottle of moonshine around the kitchen table after the labor was completed. Either women or men might recognize the completion of the work by opening a bottle for the family, whether from the household's own stash or purchased from a neighbor or family member down the road.

Depending on the household and the situation, these settings could slip back and forth between moonshine as contributing to commensality and moonshine as currency object exchanged for labor within households. A few glasses of moonshine and some food consumed together at table could, in some cases, mark satisfaction about work well done that might stand the household in good stead in the coming months. Grain stolen and stored could fatten a pig, which, when slaughtered and sold, would provide money to be rapidly transformed into a new refrigerator or television. In other cases, though, moonshine could serve as direct compensation for labor, and in households with particularly truculent men, a bottle at the end of the day could be used by wives as an incentive to get a solid day's work out of their husbands. Moonshine as object thus participated in the creation of different kinds of relationships and thereby subjects. This dynamic—between moonshine as fostering commensality and moonshine as compensation—underlies the uneasy equivalencies of money, moonshine, and labor in transactions among households to an even greater extent than within households.

The Strains of Mutual Aid: Extended Family and Close Friends

Given the burgeoning demands of domestic economies, very few households in Sepych could rely exclusively on their own capacity to labor, regardless of how much "self-exploitation" (Chaianov 1986) they engaged in (compare Creed 1998, 247). Households recruited the majority of assistance they required—and nearly all of the extra labor power—from other households in the private sector, either through mutual-aid arrangements with extended family and close friends or, as I discuss below, by hiring moonlighters. Moonshine and money—offered, haggled over, and ultimately exchanged in various proportions for this extra-household labor power—contributed powerfully to the constitution of new kinds of subjects and inequalities in post-Soviet Sepych. This increasing stratification of households was often understood to be a worrisome threat to familiar kinds of moral community, for it introduced new and unfamiliar differences in the kinds of ethical practice expected of various groups of townspeople. It mattered a great deal that different households had different capacities to transact different materials of ethics.

Aside from the increasing scale of nearly all household economies, multiple factors affected the proportions of labor for which households appealed to others for help. Some tasks, such as slaughtering a pig, haying, or building a new bathhouse, by their nature required more hands than most households could consistently muster. Moreover, there were also a great many households that did not match the local ideal type of married couple with coresident or nearby children. Sepych's large collection of middle-aged and elderly widows, for instance, found themselves relying a great deal on extended kin and neighbors. Even households that did match the local model family were, on occasion, largely beholden to others because of illness or other circumstances.[13]

When they needed assistance, households often turned first to grown sons and daughters who had married and moved out, particularly if they lived in Sepych or nearby. Children living in cities timed at least some of their visits home to coincide with the weekends when the most hands were needed in the countryside, especially during haying and potato planting or harvesting. The visitors enjoyed a weekend of fresh country air and, as more than one young man noted, the moonshine that flowed more liberally than in the cities, where their employers usually viewed drunkenness much more harshly.[14] Moonshine, sometimes homemade, sometimes purchased from others, was the sine qua non after (and usually during) hard household labor by friends or extended family members, whether they were two friends chopping firewood in December or over a dozen people haying in July.

13. Some minimal help with household work came from state agencies that, for example, provided free firewood vouchers for pensioners. The commercial farm was another source of official and unofficial inputs, in the form of patronage from those in leadership positions, "borrowed" equipment, or outright stolen goods (see chapter 6).

14. Visiting family members from the city also served as a handy conduit for selling pig or calf meat at better prices than were available locally, and many a car left Sepych after a long weekend laden with meat to be sold to urban friends or coworkers. On rural-urban kinship connections of this sort, see Eleanor Smollett's (1989) discussion of the Bulgarian "economy of jars."

This type of labor assistance, cemented by moonshine and commensality, was usually called *pomoch'*: "help" in any one instance but most accurately translated as "mutual aid" when referring to a general interhousehold practice.[15] On the evening before they planned a large task, the husband or wife in a household might go around to extended family members or close friends to collect help (*sobirat' pomoch'*), to invite helpers to join them at a certain time and place. Households could gather help for work that was typically male (slaughtering livestock), typically female (spring cleaning), or an affair for everyone (haying). Whether men or women collected the helpers, it was usually women who supervised the distribution of moonshine and food after the work was completed, as they often did for labor that took place within the household itself. When full meals were required—multiple full meals if a day of haying was the labor at hand—they were usually prepared by women. Households sometimes made special arrangements for kitchen help from friends or family on these days because all of the women in the household would be in the meadow. Whatever the precise arrangement, the household collecting helpers would then be expected to reciprocate at a later date, its members making their labor available to those who had helped them and sharing moonshine at their table. It was labor itself, in combination with moonshine and food consumed with family and friends, that was exchanged in mutual-aid relationships.

In conversation, townspeople often portrayed mutual aid as a centerpiece of interhousehold commensality and sociability, pointing out that difficult economic conditions necessitated helping one another as much as possible. Money never changed hands in mutual-aid relationships, and some suggested that mutual aid was a shelter from the harshness of unfamiliar kinds of labor markets and the money economy more closely associated with state employment or with hiring moonlighters. The moonshine-aided commensality and subsequent labor reciprocity associated with mutual aid blurred the lines between moonshine as hospitality for family and close friends and moonshine as direct, calculated payment for labor, a common means of compensating moonlighters. The moonshine of mutual aid, consumed in the context of sitting together after hard work, could refuse to admit labor as an object to be calculated and precisely compensated. Moonshine's nondurable quality lent itself to this possibility, for it was used up in the course of the evening, unavailable for further transactions (as money would be). In fact, the point at which enough moonshine had been consumed during and after mutual aid was also likely to be the point at which no one knew or remembered exactly how much had been consumed. Similarly,

15. I follow local speech in using the term *pomoch'* rather than the more standard Russian *pomoshch'*. Mutual aid, I was often reminded by scholars and occasionally by certain state officials outside Sepych, was a prerevolutionary Russian peasant custom. It would, however, be a mistake to identify present-day mutual-aid relations as simple reincarnations of the prerevolutionary institution, for the large-scale generalized reciprocity sometimes reported for the pre-1917 period was simply not a feature of post-Soviet Sepych.

the implied commitment to work off (*otrabatyvat'*) another's labor at some future time left room for varying claims on how much was to be repaid and when (although there was little doubt that moonshine would again figure in the deal). The kinds of subjects created at the intersection of these materials of ethics were, in the ideal, equal and unranked, with reciprocal and identical capacities for action that did not need precise calculation.

Denis, an employee of AOZT Sepych, was one of the more respected men in town in part because he owned his own minitractor, which he had purchased in the early 1990s with loans from extended family. With the loans long since paid off, the minitractor made Denis and his wife Katia independent in significant ways because they did not need to arrange for a tractor to plow their household plot, mow or rake their hay, or ferry potatoes back and forth from their far-flung supplementary plots. Most townspeople considered the minitractor a great boon not only to Denis and Katia but to their extended family as well. When I asked about the mechanics of haying, for instance, townspeople often pointed to Denis's family as an ideal model of successful mutual aid. Denis, I was told, would mow the hayfields belonging to each of the family's households, and all five households would take turns stacking and clearing one another's hay. After each day of work, everyone would sit at table drinking moonshine and eating, served by the wife or a daughter of the family whose meadow had been cleared that day. With so many households, and with sons and daughters visiting from the cities, Denis's family could put a large number of people on a hayfield at any given time. The means of transport were assured, and there was consequently little chance that haying would stretch out for weeks, allowing the hay to lose quality with the summer rains. In contrast to these public perceptions of Denis and his family, however, the actual practice of mutual aid in this case revealed a somewhat different dynamic, one of strained relations between households having newly unequal capacities to give and receive labor.[16]

As the haying season drew near, I asked Ol'ga, Denis's sister, how she and her husband, Leonid, were making arrangements to cut and transport their hay. Ol'ga surprised me by responding that she did not know how they were going to cope with haying. Leonid did not have access to a tractor at work, and hiring someone with a mowing attachment was getting more and more expensive, especially because everyone in Sepych was looking to hire the same tractors at the same time. Puzzled, and repeating what others in town had told me, I said that I thought Denis would cut the hay in return for Ol'ga's and Leonid's

---

16. During the July haying season, I worked with many of the families I knew to gain a varied perspective on haying organization and strategies. Judged in relation to the rest of the town, the tensions in Denis's family were relatively minor and evaporated shortly after the haying season. The description below is based on a substantial number of conversations I had before, during, and after the haying season as well as one day and one night during which I worked in the meadow with the households involved.

help on his hayfield. Ol'ga explained that the previous year, Denis had indeed cut their hay and helped them to transport it, but she did not know if he would agree to do it this year. She was getting more and more embarrassed at always asking Denis and Katia to help, not only with haying but also by lending their minitractor for other sorts of work. Laboring for them in return, she implied, was not really adequate repayment anymore. These differential capacities to exchange labor power were quickly caught up in the exchange of food and drink as well—throwing the ideal picture of mutual aid askew.

When the hot July haying days began, Denis mowed his own hayfield on the first day the weather permitted, and the news rapidly spread around town that haying had begun. Although I am not quite sure how and when the arrangement was finally made, Denis mowed Ol'ga and Leonid's meadow a day or two later. While the cut grass dried on the fields, both families began thinking about the arrangements for transporting it back to their haylofts. They needed to round up not only the helpers to physically heave the hay from the field to the cart and then from the cart to the hayloft but also the moonshine and food to sustain the haying team and provide for after-work commensality. On the evening of the third day after Denis had mowed their meadow, Denis and Katia set out to begin bringing back their hay. They told no one of their plans and did not ask Ol'ga and Leonid or any of the other households in their extended family for help. Denis had his minitractor to rake and pile the hay, and one of his good friends had brought a midsized truck to the field for use as a hay cart because the minitractor was not powerful enough to pull a cart by itself. Together with Katia and Denis's son, the group set to work, with the modest goal of bringing home one small load that evening.

Ol'ga, Leonid, and other extended family members found out that Katia and Denis were in the meadow only by accidental gossip. They dropped everything—including dinner—and headed straight for the hayfield, rakes and pitchforks in hand. With eight workers rather than four, the truck was filled in short order. Even so, more and more of Denis and Katia's extended family kept streaming over the hill, all of them uninvited, to work off their debt to Denis for having mowed their meadows already or in hopes that he would repay their labor by doing so in the near future. While one team stayed to continue stacking hay in the field, Denis and several of the men left in the full truck. Some stayed at Denis's house to unload the hay, while Denis himself ran to one of AOZT Sepych's garages to commandeer a full-sized hay cart and a more powerful tractor. By the time he returned to the meadow, there were over a dozen people stacking hay.

Shortly after midnight, and without explicitly asking for a single family member to help, Denis and Katia had nearly finished haying for the year. Katia served the helpers moonshine and what food she had around, and they all toasted the opening of the haying season until the morning hours. Despite not having asked for help, Katia found it hard to conceal her delight that the

7. Haying with helpers.

stresses of the haying season had disappeared so quickly. Knowing that Denis and Katia were not shy about asking for help on other, more minor, occasions, I asked Ol'ga why they had not collected helpers for haying. Denis and Katia, Ol'ga conjectured, wanted to remind other family members on the occasion of the most stressful work of the year that they did not need as much help as they could provide others with their minitractor. Denis and Katia could cast their participation in mutual aid as generosity, rather than the necessity it was for Ol'ga and Leonid.

Two days later, it was Ol'ga and Leonid's turn to bring in their hay. They asked Denis to help in the morning, rounded up several other helpers during the day, and waited for Denis's work tractor to arrive and take them to the meadow in the late afternoon. Although dependable to a fault, Denis did not show. After an hour of waiting, the gathered helpers began to ask Ol'ga and Leonid what the couple had done to offend Denis and Katia. Ol'ga replied that she thought she had made the proper invitation in the morning and that Denis had promised he would be there to help. You should go over there to ask again if you want your hay, came the helpers' advice. Ol'ga and Leonid were deeply embarrassed at the reminder that they always had to ask for help and distressed that their hay had already been rained on during the night. Instead of highlighting their dependence by asking for help again, they sidestepped the problem and set off for their meadow on foot to spread out the stacked hay so that it would dry faster. In the end, two other family members interceded, walking over to Denis and Katia's house to ask once again for help on behalf of Ol'ga and Leonid. The tractor and hay cart appeared shortly, with Denis and Katia in the cab. Denis and Katia drove the haying party to the meadow, left them the tractor, and walked off to weed their nearby potato plot, notably refusing to lend their labor to the haying itself. Hours later, when the cart was fully loaded, Denis drove everyone back to Sepych, the haying party exhausted atop the cart. Katia, who had not uttered a word to anyone all evening, was in the cab with Denis. The tractor stopped at the crossroads, and Katia jumped out and headed home, not going back to Ol'ga and Leonid's house to help unload or to sit eating and drinking with everyone else. Having withdrawn her labor, she withdrew from drinking and socializing as well. Denis sat and drank quietly in acknowledgment of his aid in procuring the tractor and hay cart and then went home for the night. Ol'ga, Leonid, and their other helpers worked through the night and, exhausted, finished unloading as the sun rose, so that Denis could pick up the tractor on his way to work.

After the end of the haying season, I spoke at length to several of those involved in this episode. Both sides offered detailed explanations that rested on the difficulties of adjusting to reforms since perestroika, and their analyses lend shape to this example of the ways in which the exchange of moonshine and labor in mutual-aid relationships helped to create lines of social stratification. Ol'ga interpreted Denis's failure to appear when asked in the same way that she interpreted Denis and Katia's refusal to ask family members for help in transporting their own hay: as a reminder of their greater degree of independence from circuits of exchange. By refusing to ask for help a second time when the tractor did not appear on schedule, Ol'ga and Leonid clung proudly to what independence they had, at the risk of diminishing the quality of their hay for the year. Every year, Ol'ga said, Katia wants to do her own hay by herself, just to show that she can—even though Denis would prefer to summon others and go to their aid as well.

Ol'ga and Leonid, on the other hand, had no choice but to ask for help and no strategy but to run to Denis and Katia's meadow without invitation in an attempt to erase their debt. Katia had a somewhat different story but one just as related to emerging social strata and new economic conditions. She confirmed that it was she, and not Denis, who had decided not to invite helpers to their meadow and she again who had temporarily barred Denis from going to help Ol'ga and Leonid in theirs. She pointed out that Leonid should be doing more to help his own household and that Ol'ga should not be relying on Denis when Leonid was such an ineffective husband. Her Denis, she said, worked hard at his job, was dependable at home, and earned extra money in the evenings on his minitractor. He also drank plenty, but he was doing his best to make his way and provide for his household in difficult circumstances. Leonid, she said, was one of those men who had not adjusted to economic changes, and he had still not learned that he had to provide for his household now in ways that he did not during the Soviet period. She did not want him dragging her family down with him. Ol'ga might well have agreed with Katia about Leonid's failure to adjust, but, as she pointed out, she still needed her hay and she did not have much choice but to ask her brother and sister-in-law for help.

Despite the egalitarian "language of help" (Humphrey [1983] 1998, 466; see also Caldwell 2004, 83–86), the labor exchanges of mutual aid frequently strained relationships in ways that highlight the formation of different subjects along axes of social stratification and inequality quite different from those that characterized the Soviet period. Before 1991, those who needed a tractor could frequently borrow one from State Farm Sepych through social networks or wealth-in-people ties (or, more rarely, by actually paying for it). After privatization, the new possibility of owning a reliable minitractor can hardly be underestimated, for it allowed connections to be left for other uses and some households to cast themselves as givers, rather than as takers, of all-important tractor time. A tractor added considerably to the capacity for work that certain households could offer. When haying had to be done (often by hand) in the uneven leftover meadows of the Soviet-era state farm, it would not have been feasible for a household to cope alone, as Katia and Denis now could. Socialist-era problems gathered around unequal access to decent hay in the first place, postsocialist problems around inequalities among households in their ability to deploy labor power and resources to cut their hay and bring it home. Exchanges of labor and moonshine—not always equal and not always voluntarily entered into—helped to create new lines of distinction and capacities for action in many extended families and among close friends. These distinctions become even more evident when mutual-aid arrangements are viewed in the context of moonlighting, which took on new dimensions as unemployment became an official category in the post-Soviet period.

Moonshine and the Moonlighting of the Unemployed

For the first time since the collectivization of agriculture in the late 1920s, labor power could legally circulate in the private sector, among Sepych's households themselves, rather than exclusively in relationships with the state-run farm, the apparatus of central planning, and the pervasive moral'nye and material'nye incentives of the Soviet period. Moonlighting was the chief manifestation of this new kind of circulation; it forms my third example of the kinds of subjectivities and inequalities that began to emerge as familiar materials of ethics began to trace unfamiliar routes through post-Soviet Sepych.

One afternoon in the spring, I ran into Katia in the center of town and, among other things, inquired about Denis. "I'll barely see him for the next couple of weeks," she replied. "He'll be at work during the day and moonlighting [*na shabashke*] until late at night." She added that Denis was not drinking at all at the moment. For one thing, he was driving all the time, answering calls from all over Sepych to plow household plots on his minitractor. For another thing, he was working outside the moonshine economy: he was earning money, rather than moonshine, for his work, most of which Katia took and saved for household purchases. *Shabashka,* in post-Soviet Sepych, referred to the wide range of labor that fell between mutual aid among extended family or close friends and official employment in an organization that was legally recorded in a labor book (*trudovaia kniga*).[17] *Shabas* is a variant of the Russian word for Sabbath, and *shabashka* originally meant time off from work for relaxation or simply quitting work at the end of the day. With the proliferation of the informal sector of the Soviet economy in the Brezhnev era, however, shabashka increasingly came to refer to all manner of work done outside one's regular employment. Unauthorized moonlighting could be prosecuted in the Soviet era, particularly as moonlighters typically worked harder on their after-hours projects than on their regular jobs and even on occasion offered their moonlighting services at their regular jobs (at higher than normal pay rates) to make up for their own failure to meet centrally planned quotas during working hours—a classic example of why enterprise directors like Andrei Petrovich were forced to come up with innovative tactics to deploy sufficient labor power through the creative use of material'nye and moral'nye incentives.

Moonlighting in postsocialist Sepych never involved reciprocal labor in the manner that mutual aid did. It was, however, exchanged for various combinations of moonshine and money. Evaluated in strictly economic terms, and taking into account the usual size of moonshine payments, money payments, and the cost of ingredients for moonshine production, paying in moonshine was cheaper than paying in money. Cost was, however, hardly the only factor in hiring negotiations, for the materialities of the transactables involved had important implications for how these negotiations proceeded—and for the ethical subjects they helped produce. The manifold possibilities for exchange point, once again, to the increasingly vertical relationships among differently situated households.

---

17. The barrier between *pomoch'* and *shabashka* was actually somewhat porous, although only in one direction. In practice, many of the mutual-aid relations discussed in the previous section could easily slip into the category of shabashka, but the moonlighting relationships of greater social distance were not normally referred to as pomoch'. I deal here only with moonlighting that took place in the private sector, that is, cases in which households hired moonlighting labor. The local state administration and other organizations also frequently employed moonlighters for tasks that ranged from repainting the town hall to snowplowing to renovating the school. In other parts of Russia, the term *kalym* is synonymous with *shabashka,* although the linguistic genealogy is quite different. Katherine Metzo (2001) traces *kalym* to the Kazakh term for bridewealth.

Denis's plowing work for those outside his extended family was highly regarded, in large part because it was considered proper moonlighting: evening or late-night work done to supplement a regular salary. Most in town also considered Denis's plowing technique to be excellent and therefore worthy of payouts in valuable money, particularly for such an important service as plowing a household plot. Denis could also charge money because the services he offered were relatively rare in Sepych. There were only a few private minitractors in Sepych, the larger tractors in AOZT Sepych were cumbersome to navigate on household plots, and the small hand-operated cultivators owned by many took too long to plow the average garden. The precise amount of money Denis charged for plowing a standard plot (seventy rubles, or just over two dollars) was always paid on the spot, with none of the imprecision of moonshine or reciprocal labor anticipated at a later date that attended mutual aid.

At least nominal full employment was a centerpiece of Soviet social policy. As unemployment became an official category and possibility in the post-Soviet period, the term *shabashka* expanded from Denis's kind of moonlighting, loosely analogous to Soviet-era moonlighting, to cover odd jobs that newly unemployed workers did to support themselves. Moonlighting, in other words, could for the first time in the post-Soviet period be one's regular occupation, and this sort of moonlighting without a regular job was as suspicious as Denis's moonlighting was respected. It was doubly so when unemployed moonlighters exchanged their labor not for rubles but for bottles of moonshine that they took with them rather than consume with their employer. In 2001, unemployment in Sepych hovered unofficially at around 15 percent of the able-bodied population, and debates raged over whether unemployed men were unemployed because they were so often drunk or drunk so often because they were unemployed. Either way, the association between the moonlighting of the unemployed and bottles of moonshine was strong. Those young men, and a smaller number of women, who offered to work on private household plots for moonshine on a regular basis were often termed "bums," and the slipperiness of this term and the provisos that often accompanied it spoke volumes about the relatively new category of person it tried to comprehend: laborers who moonlighted without having regular jobs, taking their wages in some combination of moonshine and money. When they did not want to or could not turn to family members or close friends for mutual aid, those townspeople who could afford to considered the possibility of "hiring a bum" (*nanimat' BOMZh*) or "collecting the bums" (*sobirat' BOMZhei*) to work in their households.

When I asked about these phrases, townspeople explained that there were no real bums in Sepych—the acronym BOMZh was Soviet-speak for people who did not have registration stamps in their internal passports (*Bez Opre-delennogo Mesta Zhitel'stva*).[18] Everyone in Sepych had a place to live, I was

18. The homology between the English "bum" and the Russian BOMZh is coincidental.

told, so technically no one was a BOMZh. Nevertheless, there was a stratum of unemployed and underemployed workers whom almost everyone thought of when the term *BOMZh* was mentioned. Many of these men also self-identified as bums, although only with self-mocking pride. If mutual aid could take place among friendly households of any social stratum or between households of different social strata (especially along the lines of extended family), then the moonlighting of the unemployed created lines of distinction between house-holds of different status that bought and sold labor power. Furthermore, it created these lines of distinction through the different materials of ethics trans-acted, for what precisely changed hands always figured in the calculations of both moonlighters and their employers.

The quality of work done by unemployed moonlighters was often suspect, depending in key part on whether the negotiated compensation settled primar-ily on money or moonshine. Several factors influenced the kind of agreement struck by the parties. A few households in town had enough monetary income not to worry about having to save it for those transactions for which money alone could serve as a medium of exchange. These households, with few con-cerns about maintaining a degree of cash liquidity, could afford to hire moon-lighters and pay them only in cash. In the mid-1990s, for instance, the owner of one of Sepych's new stores decided to build a new house for his family, and he employed a brigade of young men to do the work during the summer months. He paid them exclusively in rubles and, to cut off the commensality associ-ated with mutual-aid relationships, explicitly ordered members of his family and neighbors not to feed the workers or give them anything to drink. They were being paid money to work, he said, and he expected both the process and the end product to reflect that he had hired quality workers to build a quality house, paying them exclusively in money. From the moonlighters' perspective, work on a construction brigade for one of Sepych's wealthier residents was a good way to make a moderate income, and members of this brigade respected their employer a good deal. Although the monetary relationships certainly be-spoke a degree of social stratification and distance, many moonlighters also considered it beneficial to align themselves with a more powerful and wealthy employer, a way to earn promises of future jobs or favors.

Not many households in Sepych could afford—much less afford on a regular basis—to hire outside workers and pay them in money. One alternative was to hire bums and compensate them, on completion of their work, exclusively in bottles of moonshine to take with them rather than consume at table. This kind of moonlighting arrangement was in many ways the polar opposite of collecting helpers for mutual aid. The fact that the verb *sobirat'* (to collect) accompanied both kinds of labor transaction—collecting helpers and collect-ing bums—accentuated the extent to which one was an opposite of the other. This opposition hinged directly on the ambivalence of moonshine as an object of exchange, its ability to slip between centerpiece of hospitality and currency object. Unemployed moonlighters taking payment in moonshine "to go" at the end of a day's labor created social distance and stratification precisely because this form of exchange inverted the practice of mutual-aid labor arrangements, which were cemented by moonshine first during work and then at table after work. If moonshine in a mutual-aid relationship downplayed, as much as possible, the extent to which the work to be done might be calculated and revealed to be taking place among unequal households, then moonshine to go as compensation for the moonlighting of the unemployed served only to highlight the divide between those who gave and those who received labor power. In these cases, moonshine was still a relatively nondurable exchange object, but it was more socially transportable than that consumed in mutual aid. It outlasted the period of labor with which it was associated, to be consumed that night by the moonlighter with his friends, apart from the other party to the transaction— the employer.

In practice, the vast majority of cases of moonlighting by unemployed men involved some combination of money and moonshine, either in the same transaction or in the overall course of the exchange relationship, which usually included far more than a single episode of work. During recurrent interactions there was room for negotiation. At times, employers themselves preferred to compensate moonlighters in moonshine, diverting what cash liquidity they had for use in those market contexts in which it was necessary, passing on the lower costs and liquidities of moonshine to their workers. At other times, it was the unemployed moonlighters themselves who demanded bottles as payment, sometimes even on occasions when money was offered. Why would unemployed moonlighters accept moonshine rather than money in exchange for their labor? Consider the case of Fëdor and his moonlighters.

Fëdor was a middle-aged man in Sepych who was close to retirement and who often found himself in need of extra hands in his household. Both he and his wife were frequently ill, and although they managed their household well enough, they often could not complete strenuous household work by themselves. Fëdor sometimes relied on extended family, but because he was unable to reciprocate properly by offering his labor to family members in return, he often hired other townspeople. "Almost time to collect the bums," he would say when I passed him in the street and asked about his household plot. Fëdor usually preferred to pay his workers in cash, from his wife's pension and the couple's disability pay. I asked on one occasion why he did not pay in moonshine, saving money for store purchases. He did sometimes pay in moonshine, Fëdor said, usually when his workers demanded it instead of money. They would say to him, "We're not asking you for money this time, so sit down with us and drink this bottle." Somewhat reluctantly, he would.

As Fëdor was the first to point out, his workers could perfectly easily use whatever money he gave them to buy moonshine down the road, and they surely did so much of the time. Occasionally demanding moonshine at Fëdor's table afforded the unemployed moonlighters a chance to temporarily erase the lower status associated with selling their labor to Fëdor. Drawing attention to the differential characteristics of money and moonshine ("We're not asking you for money this time") allowed them a justification that Fëdor could not easily counter. To refuse to sit would have been to baldly affirm that he was so wealthy that the "moonshine discount" offered to him was insignificant. So, ambivalently, and unlike the store owner discussed above, he sat. Fëdor was not always pleased with this arrangement, wishing on many occasions that his workers would just take the money instead of getting roaring drunk in his kitchen. That is, he sometimes preferred the social distance and stratification of an exclusively monetary relationship, whereas the unemployed moonlighters sought to bring him down to their level by sitting and drinking with him, mutual-aid style, at his table. But sit he did. At other times, Fëdor praised the "humanity" of sitting and drinking with his workers and cited it as evidence that "there isn't really a market yet."

There was a second reason why many of Fëdor's moonlighters—and moonlighters in general—accepted and demanded moonshine from those to whom they sold their labor power. Payment in moonshine, whether to go or at table with the employer, aggravated moonlighters' wives no end. It meant that men were drunk and away from household work with no return at all, either in the form of money or reciprocal labor at a later date (as in mutual aid). It was thus an ideal way for husbands to resist their wives' attempts to control their inputs into the household. If moonlighters refused to bring home money, then their wives could not take it away from them; compensation for labor could be redirected into male drinking sociability, and men could avoid the double embarrassment of bringing home a pittance and having even that taken away. Indeed, when one of Fëdor's unemployed moonlighters whom I knew did accept cash for his work, he made sure that Fëdor did not mention to anyone exactly how much the payment had come to. This way, word would not leak back to his wife, and she would not miss the amount he skimmed off his payment on the way home for a bottle of moonshine to share with his friends. Here the vectors of social stratification in the creation of different kinds of subjects I have been describing overlap. For this moonlighter, choosing a currency that demanded immediate consumption was calculated in relation not only to the money that Fëdor or another employer might have paid but also to the household struggles over moonshine and money that were particularly acute in the homes of poorer, unemployed moonlighters.

Materials of Ethics and Global Convergences
after Socialism

Whether the transactions within and among households that I have been discussing took place in connection with haying, herding, or numerous other tasks, most were aimed toward a single goal: fattening and then selling livestock to supplement households' meager and unpredictable income from their primary employment. One woman, for instance, estimated that she and her husband had to sell a pig or calf each quarter to make ends meet (a slaughtered pig or calf could typically bring in the equivalent of several months' salary). From this calculation, the couple could work backward to determine how much hay, how much other feed, and how much extra labor power they would require at different points in the course of the year. Thus far, I have been exploring the intersecting axes of stratification and differently situated subjects that emerged in Sepych as nearly all households struggled, with varying amounts of ability and success, to execute the plans these calculations demanded.

Before the rubles gained from livestock sales were spent, however, they often went through two further transformations: into and then out of U.S. dollars. These crucial transactions further illustrate how different materialities and exchangeabilities produced unfamiliar kinds of inequalities in Sepych. Taking these ruble-dollar-ruble exchanges as a starting point, I situate Sepych's small-scale circuits of rubles, moonshine, and labor within the global-scale growth of foreign exchange currency markets over the last thirty years and the proliferation of hedge funds in the late 1980s and 1990s.[19] Tracing the links between these scales serves three purposes. First, it provides a fuller perspective on the levels of stratification in which townspeople found themselves implicated after the end of socialism—levels that most townspeople understood quite keenly. Second, it shows some of the ways in which townspeople encountered and sought to manage the risks that were so evident in the household sector, where blips in international currency markets could easily erase a season's worth of hard labor. Third, it shows that many of the dilemmas about materials of ethics that raged in post-Soviet Sepych were but one variation on a common theme in this age of finance capital and increasingly globalized markets. Indeed, future analysts of the global recession and financial crisis that began in 2008 would do well to look for antecedents in the first decade of postsocialist transformations in Eastern Europe and the former Soviet Union, for liquidity crises, systemic risks, and novel arrangements of capital accumulation and debt investment were proliferating in this part of the world long before they became the stuff of daily headlines everywhere. What this new, global configuration of circulation and exchange in this world meant for the ethical repertoire of townspeople in Sepych extended far beyond the new paths of moonshine, labor, rubles, and dollars—as subsequent chapters show.

Dollars were not particularly liquid assets in Sepych, with the nearest exchange point at least an hour away and even small denominations of dollars equal to far more than the price of most items for sale in Sepych's stores.

19. Alaina Lemon (1998) has shown how the entrance of the Russian ruble into the international foreign exchange system in the early 1990s led to new kinds of enchantment with the U.S. dollar and featured in the aesthetics and performances of post-Soviet social transformation.

Moreover, the purpose of dollars was the opposite of day-to-day exchange. Whether or not it had happened to them personally, everyone knew stories of accumulated rubles that had lost their value in unexpected bursts of inflation. Dollars, by contrast, indicated stability and risk avoidance. Townspeople saw them as a temporary shelter from inflation and ruble devaluation, to be held until such time as a large sum of rubles was required for durable goods, children's tuition, or other big-ticket items. Dollars were so closely associated with stability and large purchases that they were often less liquid than calves, pigs, or sheep, which might be slaughtered and sold more immediately and with less effort than it took to exchange dollars into rubles. The sharp difference between rubles and dollars, coupled with the common strategy of holding dollars, helped to ensure that it was, for the most part, townspeople's small salaries alone that served as the basis for women to manage their households' week-to-week level of ruble liquidity.[20]

In these ruble-dollar-ruble transactions, townspeople's immediate exchange partners were to be found not down the road in Sepych but wherever rubles, dollars, and the bonds issued by the Russian Central Bank changed hands on world markets. With the unraveling of the Bretton Woods system in 1971, world currencies were allowed to move freely against one another for the first time since the interwar period. The resulting foreign exchange markets enabled currency speculation, the practice of attempting to profit from bets on state currencies rising or falling in relation to one another. Currency speculation grew steadily through the late 1970s and 1980s and in the 1990s became a favorite activity of newly popular hedge funds. In this age of massive currency speculation, in which the world's central banks publicly defend state currencies against speculative attacks by (usually foreign) investors, with all parties waiting for the potential intervention of the International Monetary Fund (IMF), the universe of relationships involved in the "state of play between currencies" (Akin and Robbins 1999, 2) has widened exponentially. The place of townspeople in Sepych—and that of former socialist citizens more broadly—with respect to these global-scale patterns of exchange shifted drastically in the early 1990s. Much of this transformation can be conceptualized in terms of differential exchangeabilities, and a range of ensuing inequalities can be traced to the strategies, competencies, and risks involved in currency exchanges. Many of the visions of new kinds of moral communities I discuss in later chapters were dedicated precisely to mitigating these risks and inequalities.[21]

20. In all the cases of ruble-dollar and dollar-ruble exchange that I knew of, it was women who made the decisions, arranged the trips to the exchange point, and took charge of the subsequent purchases, often made on the same trip to the city. Women sometimes noted that their implication in circuits of exchange that included both rubles and dollars only further contributed to their husbands' feelings of provinciality and inadequacy.

21. On the significance of risk in other aspects of postsocialist transformation, see, especially, Verdery (2003), Dunn (2004), and Wolfe (2005).

For the second half of the twentieth century, the Soviet Union set ruble exchange rates more or less arbitrarily against other world currencies; only one Soviet bank (Vneshtorgbank) was legally permitted to execute currency trades. As a result, much of the economic exchange between socialist and capitalist blocs of the international system was conducted on the relatively slow and situational terms of barter (Humphrey and Hugh-Jones 1992, 5). This global-scale barter of decades past represents a quite different international organization of exchange from that of the post-Soviet era, when currency exchange points sprouted on nearly every corner in even medium-sized Russian cities. Suddenly everyone in Russia could legally buy and sell rubles and dollars, and traders around the world could wager on the rise or fall of the ruble and on the policies of the fledgling Russian Central Bank.

In other words, the postsocialist period in Russia brought into convergence the tentative currency-trading strategies of townspeople in Sepych and the profit-making activities of some of the world's most seasoned investors, currency speculators, and hedge fund managers. All these parties attempted to manage risk by correctly timing their purchases and sales of dollars and rubles. Although formally the same type of activity, in the case of wealthy currency speculators and their investors these exchanges were cast as a quest for profit, whereas in Sepych, as I have shown, they were understood as attempts not to lose money in the face of rapid inflation and general instability. These dynamics were especially evident in Russia's "August crisis" of 1998, which focused worldwide attention on nonmonetary payments, currency markets, and state monetary policy in Russia. The August crisis offers a propitious conjuncture at which to examine more concretely the place of Sepych in global-scale convergences: it demonstrates how the focus on different materials of ethics and their exchangeabilities I have adopted for understanding social stratification within Sepych also points to some of the larger inequalities that attend townspeople's new place in the global economy.

In the mid-1990s, one of the aspects of the so-called transition to capitalism in Russia that most worried Western reformers and officials at the World Bank and IMF was the continuing high level of nonmonetary transactions in Russia. The reformers were somewhat less worried about things like moonshine payments among households in rural villages than they were about the extensive cashless networks enabling firms like AOZT Sepych to minimize their ruble liquidity to avoid paying taxes. In 1998, these nonmonetary payments, coupled with domino effects from the Asian financial crises of 1997, helped provoke declining confidence in Russia's already very high-interest, short-term debt (GKOs) and a wave of speculation on the future of the ruble. Despite doubt about the progress of tax reform in Russia and rising pressure against the ruble, the conventional wisdom among foreign investors was that the United States and the IMF would never let Russia default and would instead put together a loan package sufficiently large to permit the Russian Central Bank to fend off speculators. When no sufficiently large rescue package was forthcoming, Russia both defaulted on its debt and devalued the ruble in mid-August 1998.

Many Russian banks folded overnight. In the short term, as money disappeared again, one effect was a further increase in nonmonetary payments throughout Russia. Although devaluation was more directly felt in cities, where a greater proportion of the Russian population held bank accounts that were wiped out (Anderson 2000b), the August crisis led to shifting prices, salary delays, and lack of confidence in the ruble in Sepych as much as anywhere else. M. Kozlov (2000, 89–90), for instance, notes the following principal effects of the financial crisis on agricultural commodity producers: "the deterioration of the social status of the rural population...a decline in the level of material and technical support for agriculture; a reduction in the size of state subsidies for enterprises in this sector; a decline in the amounts of favorable financing for agricultural producers; and an increase in the gap between prices for material and technical resources and agricultural products." To this one might add that, as of 2001, the August crisis remained one of the primary examples townspeople in Sepych relied on as evidence for the importance of maintaining minimum ruble liquidity and some portion of their assets in more-stable dollars. Their defensive posture and attempts to cling to the value brought in by their livestock sales stand in sharp contrast to the aggressive profit-making bets of currency speculators and hedge funds.

Like exchanges of rubles and dollars in Sepych, however, these bets were not risk free, as the crisis of August 1998 again shows. One of the many foreign players involved in Russian currency and bond markets in 1998 was Long-Term Capital Management (LTCM), at the time the crown jewel of hedge funds with nearly $4 billion in capital.[22] LTCM had bet massively and directionally (that is, without a fully hedged counterbet) against Russian default. The eventual default sent LTCM, already in trouble in the aftermath of the Asian crises, into a tailspin from which recovery proved impossible. At the time, its rapidly eroding capital base was leveraged to nearly $100 billion in a murky labyrinth of loans (not counting thousands of derivatives contracts) knitting together the world's investment banks. By the end of September 1998, the Federal Reserve Bank of New York stepped in to muscle private banks into orchestrating an unprecedented $3.5 billion bailout. Federal Reserve officers, the financial media, and the bankers themselves were beginning to wonder what would happen if the investment banks, in a global environment still reeling from the Asian and Russian crises, suddenly had to write off nearly $100 billion in

22. Hedge funds pool contributions—originally from wealthy individuals but increasingly from upper-middle-class investors and institutions—and leverage their capital with loans to make bets on the movement of all manner of financial markets, including currency markets. For other anthropological studies that include analysis of foreign exchange markets, see Hart (1986), Guyer (1995a), and Gregory (1997); see Miyazaki (2003) for an insightful ethnography of arbitrage, a favored practice of hedge funds.

bad loans to LTCM. It was not, however, simply LTCM's lack of cash liquidity that caused worry. The worries were systemic risk and a worldwide crisis of liquidity: on the horizon loomed global illiquidity in the sense of massive nonexchangeability, the never-before-encountered possibility that the world's financial markets might seize up.[23] What if the biggest banks underwriting the world's markets were all perceived (correctly or not) to be on the verge of bankruptcy at the same time? What if no one would sell the least risky assets (such as U.S. Treasury bonds) and no one would buy riskier assets at any price? What if trading—exchange—simply stopped? The bailout negotiations in New York were successful, and the immanent threat of full-blown global capitalist crisis receded for another decade.

Even in this abbreviated account of the August 1998 crisis, some of the global-scale inequalities and arrangements of risk in which townspeople in Sepych began to participate in the post-Soviet period start to come into focus. First, the size differential between the capital base of international currency traders and that of households in Sepych was enormous and expanding; this meant that LTCM and other investment firms could move (and threaten) world markets, whereas households in Sepych could only attempt to react to them. Second, and following logically, the currency exchanges executed by professional investors and neophyte townspeople were of quite different sorts: offensive bets to increase shareholders' value as compared with defensive bets to keep value from disappearing into global streams. Third, although none of these bets were risk free, it was the fund managers and their investors who were bailed out when their exchange strategies misfired. By contrast, one of the lessons that townspeople in Sepych learned over the course of the 1990s was that neither the state nor private banks were likely to notice risk or devaluation in their households or the Russian countryside more broadly, much less ride to the rescue. Hashing out the terms of LTCM's bailout in the conference room of the Federal Reserve Bank of New York, the CEOs of the world's biggest investment banks were wondering about the differential and relative exchangeabilities of transactables. Townspeople in Sepych wrestled with their own aspects of these very same dilemmas, although from a very different position in the global economy.

IN previous eras, including the Soviet period, all these shifting patterns of exchange and materials of ethics would likely have been cast as matters of this

23. The lack of state-enforced reporting requirements for hedge funds contributed to the problem. Because LTCM was not required to disclose its exposure and actively hid its positions to shield its trading secrets, no one knew just how big the problem might turn out to be. For accounts of the global crisis of liquidity associated with the collapse of LTCM, see Lowenstein (2000) and Dunbar (2000). Juliet Johnson (2000, 201–24) provides an analysis of the August 1998 crisis that situates the proximate role of international currency and bond trading within the institutional legacy of Soviet banking and the course of reform from 1987 to 1998.

world to be avoided by ascetic elders. Active Old Believers who were drawn too closely into them might, at a minimum, have received temporary excommunications and severe penances. Accusations of improperly mixing the worlds could even contribute to a schism, as they did in the decades after emancipation. The postsocialist period, however, was different. Unlike the rural socialism I discussed in part 2, the transformations of the early post-Soviet period on which I have focused thus far worked to undermine rather than incubate the brand of asceticism that had for so long organized ethical practice in and around Sepych. I show in later chapters, for instance, that many who sought baptism in the town's new church were looking for ritual protection in this world—rather than withdrawal from it—as one element in a broader portfolio of risk-management possibilities. Understanding this fundamental realignment of ascetic practices in Sepych requires attention not only to the emergent ethical subjects of the household sector but to new kinds of moral communities as well.

6 Which Khoziain? Whose Moral Community?

In the fall of 2001, I attended Sepych's annual public town meeting (*sel'skii skhod*), held in the auditorium of the House of Culture. The meeting was sparsely attended, with about sixty townspeople and a small delegation from the district administration present. Faina Timofeevna, the local "head of administration" and chief state official in Sepych, began with her annual report on her office's activities. She spoke for about ten minutes, covering the various details of the local administration's projects during the year and drawing particular attention to the fact that, with a considerable amount of effort, she had managed to keep all of Sepych's kindergartens running throughout the year (other administrations across the district were forced to close some of their kindergartens for months at a time because of lack of funds). During the comment period after her report, the criticisms began, with what I later learned was unexpected intensity. Many townspeople who spoke focused on infrastructure. The fall months had been particularly rainy and muddy and the lack of planks for sidewalks in even the muddiest sections of town was a repeated item of complaint. Others talked about how dark Sepych was at night—how could the administration not take better care of the streetlights?

Several speakers pointed to what they saw as the heart of the problem: in their view, Faina Timofeevna simply did not find ways to work around obstacles. She did not "get out there and talk to people" or "get people together," in the words of two speakers. Toward the end of the discussion period, his name having been invoked many times already, Andrei Petrovich, director of AOZT Sepych, took the floor. He agreed, he said, with criticisms about the roads, sidewalks, and streetlights, which, he pointedly reminded townspeople, had not been taken care of for years and were no longer the responsibility of the commercial farm. He went on to compare AOZT Sepych with the local state administration: "We take care of our own [in the privatized commercial farm]," he said, "and we can't take care of everyone else, too." These tasks were now the job of state institutions; he was just the director of the local business. Nevertheless, he continued, he would be glad to help—if Faina Timofeevna would invite him to meetings, which, he claimed, she had stopped doing. At the end of the meeting, the representative from the district administration, who until that point had remained nearly silent, stood. He noted that the level of dissatisfaction in the room was far higher than in any of the previous years he had been to Sepych's town meeting and promised that he would convey this to the head of district administration. He also underscored that the district administration did not believe there was any cause to remove Faina Timofeevna from her position. He exhorted her to work harder in the coming year.

Much of the discussion at the town meeting made use of concepts of khoziain and khoziaistvo. Recall that khoziain (master, owner, administrator, or boss) figures stood at the center of the wealth-in-people relationships of socialism. It was their task to transform constant shortage into improvised solutions, to cajole reluctant labor into the fields (often via the creative use of material'nye and moral'nye incentives), and to shunt resources from higher up in the party-state bureaucracy to their own domains. Doing this ineffectively, as was the case for the chairman of the collective farm Lenin's Path in Sepych in the early 1960s, led to negative exemplar status in the local newspaper and an outflow of rural inhabitants to the cities. Doing it well, as Andrei Petrovich did in the 1970s and 1980s, meant fame for State Farm Sepych and enormous wealth in people—both in and outside Sepych—for its director.

In the post-Soviet period, townspeople debated anew what it meant to be a khoziain. What qualities did a proper khoziain possess? What capabilities and actions were good evidence of one's status as a khoziain? What domains did various khoziaeva command, how, and to what effect? Were those attempting to consolidate power in the town, district, region, or country proper khoziaeva at all? At the town meeting in 2001, townspeople's criticisms that, her success with kindergartens notwithstanding, Faina Timofeevna did not work around difficult situations with sufficient alacrity and did not get people together (that is, accumulate wealth in people), generalized specific complaints about Sepych's infrastructure into the overall lack of proper leadership of a moral community. Faina Timofeevna, as several townspeople mentioned to me privately, was simply not sufficiently *khoziaistvennaia*. At the same time, Andrei Petrovich's comments at the meeting skillfully positioned him at once as the already unquestioned khoziain of the nonstate domain of AOZT Sepych and as ongoing potential khoziain to the new overlapping domain of the local state administration—if, that is, its representatives cared to place themselves further in his debt.

I suggest in this chapter that much of this debate about post-Soviet khoziaeva should be understood as part the remaking of moral communities—one element in broader struggles to shape an emergent ethical regime. As I outlined in the introduction, I use the term "moral community" to point to efforts to align ethical practices and subjectivities among collections of people. This process invariably involves power struggles and inequalities, as different parties compete to circumscribe what practices—and which practitioners—count in particular moral communities. Crucially, it also involves attending to aspirations and visions of unity, for part of what makes for a moral community is the expectation—however imperfectly realized in practice—that the ethical practices circulating within it are somehow different from those outside. After socialism, then, one important question became, Was the state, in its incarnation as a local administration and its associated population in and around Sepych, now also a moral community in the way that the local enterprise had long been? What was its relationship to the privatizing commercial farm and to households? If, as I suggest here, being a post-Soviet khoziain—and being in relationship to one—was a central element in the attempted construction of moral communities that would mitigate and diversify the new risks and inequalities so evident in the household sector, it was not at all clear which khoziain or whose moral community was best suited for this task. The Soviet-era rural institutions that helped to shape the familiar moral communities of rural socialism were changing quickly. Moreover, these institutions, like the moonshine and money of the household sector, were caught up in global transformations in the workings of capitalism.

The Moral Communities of Post-Soviet State Formation

The primary context for shifting khoziain relationships in post-Soviet Sepych was ongoing municipalization reforms, reforms designed to strip state functions from Soviet state farms and, at the same time, to empower new organs of local self-government as the main state presence in the countryside. Through the municipalization of state power, envisioned by the Yeltsin administration as proceeding hand in hand with rural privatization and decollectivization, the Soviet party-state was to be pruned back and replaced with a leaner and more effective set of state institutions.[1] The Soviet cultural sphere, including such components as Soviet Houses of Culture, was to be transferred to organs of local self-government, heirs to the Soviet-era rural soviets.[2] Responsibility for

1. For a policy-centered review of municipalization, see Healy et al. (1999) and the references therein.

2. Russian law makes an important distinction between "the state" (*gosudarstvo*), at federal and regional levels of governance, and organs of self-government (*organy mestnogo samoupravleniia*) supervised by local administrations (*mestnye administratsii*), at district and lower levels (see, for example, Alferova et al. 1998; World Bank 2003a). Although important in structural terms,

rural infrastructure, too, was to shift from the rapidly privatizing agricultural enterprises to local municipal authorities. Snowplowing, sidewalk construction, and streetlight maintenance, for instance, were all slated to become the domain of the local state administrations rather than state or collective farms. In step with privatization schemes the world over, the business of new rural enterprises like AOZT Sepych would become just that: business.

Over a decade after it began, however, municipalization was neither easy nor complete in the Russian countryside. In fact, it might well be argued that it had failed in many areas, at least judging by the standards of those international and Russian experts whose ideas of what proper state formation should look like charted the course of municipalization. Many local administrations had consolidated little power and enjoyed even less legitimacy. They often struggled mightily with the newly privatized farms, officially nonstate actors but endowed with resources, expectations, and personnel that were all heavily inflected with Soviet-era sensibilities about proper governance. The balance of power between Soviet rural institutions as they began the transition from socialism was but one of several factors inhibiting the planned pace of state formation in Sepych.[3] Throughout all these struggles and processes, however, Soviet-era sensibilities about governance and the creation of moral communities were a key resource that townspeople in Sepych drew on as they worked to resituate themselves with respect to emerging state and nonstate forms as potential moral communities.

Many theories of the state (postsocialist and otherwise) work from some variation of Weber's claim that the state can be defined as the unit holding monopolies—especially over legitimized force and currency transactions—in a given territory (see especially 1978, 54, 178). Although most famously deployed in accounts of early modern state formation in Western Europe, this family of theories has been quite useful in the study of the postsocialist world, where it has not been at all safe to assume that states have successfully consolidated monopolies over anything.[4] Vadim Volkov's (2002) study of the Russian mafia and associated "violence-managing agencies," for instance, charts the initial disappearance and, nearly a decade later, the slow reemergence of the Russian state's monopoly on legitimized force. David Woodruff (1999) makes

this was not a distinction that carried much weight in everyday discourse and practice in Sepych. See Kharkhordin (2005) for an exhaustive working through of the Russian concept of *gosudarstvo* in history and political theory and Gel'man (2002) and Evans and Gel'man (2004) for instructive analyses of local self-government. My analysis most closely fits the situation in Sepych before 2004, when a massive overhaul of local state institutions across Russia changed the dynamics described here.

3. Municipalization did not fail everywhere, a prime case of success being Moscow under Mayor Yurii Luzhkov. A broader consideration of post-Soviet municipalization might seek to explain why reforms attained their goals in some areas and not in others.

4. On the application of theories of early modern state formation to the postsocialist context, see especially Ganev (2005).

a similar claim for monetary consolidation, using detailed studies of barter and cashless networks in the energy sector to argue that the Russian state failed to exert sovereignty over currency exchange. Although I take some inspiration from the ways in which Volkov and Woodruff frame the issue of recent Russian state formation as a set of struggles between state and nonstate actors for substantial control (monopoly remains too strong a word) over different sets of transactions, my approach also differs in significant ways.

My focus here is not just on a particular item of exchange—such as violence or rubles—but on historically situated expectations about how one might go about fashioning a moral community by attempting to consolidate control over any one or several types of transactions that take place within it. Shifting concepts of what it means to be a khoziain were one important part of how different actors (state and nonstate) in post-Soviet Sepych have attempted to extend control over various domains of exchange and at multiple levels. Being a khoziain in post-Soviet Sepych, or failing to be one, was a constitutive element of governance and the exercise of power in the remaking of moral communities. It was linked, on the one hand, to the risks and inequalities of the household sector and, on the other hand—as later chapters show—to the shape of religious revival and ritual practice in post-Soviet Sepych. It was, in sum, a central front in the struggle to shape an emergent ethical regime.

Expectations of Khoziaeva Past: Households and AOZT Sepych

Throughout the 1990s and into the next decade, AOZT Sepych was what Humphrey has usefully termed a "suzerainty" (see esp. 2002, 5–20). As scholars across the former Soviet bloc have noted, the retreat of centralized authority resulted in a "parcellization of sovereignty" (Verdery 1996, 205–7) that allowed bosses at multiple levels to exert substantial control over their former domains and govern them with a high degree of autonomy (see also Garcelon 2005 on "feudalization"). In Volkov's and Woodruff's analyses of Russian state formation, discussed above, it was these bosses, not state agencies, who often enjoyed near monopolies on violence and currency transactions.

The residents of Sepych usually spoke of this process in terms of what they considered to be left of the nesting levels of Soviet moral communities that went by the label of khoziaistva. In the most commonly expressed view, the reforms beginning with Gorbachev's perestroika had eliminated the higher levels of khoziaistvo that most townspeople had grown up with: visible (if not always enthusiastic) participation in the Soviet agricultural sector and national "economic organization." What remained was the khoziaistvo of AOZT Sepych, which nearly everyone continued to refer to as the "state farm." Even when they did not use the term "state farm" (sovkhoz) to refer to AOZT Sepych, the phrase "in our economic organization" (*v nashem khoziaistve*) usually referred to whatever happened to be going on in the commercial farm at the time. Remaining, too, were all the townspeople's individual household economies, the lowest level of khoziaistvo. With the national, sectoral, and regional levels of moral community gone or at least rendered far less visible by the elimination of central planning, most townspeople worried that AOZT Sepych would be next to disappear, leaving only the household sector.

Their worries were not unfounded. Although the vast majority of collective and state farms across the Russian Federation had initially opted for conversion to one or another form of private shareholders' corporation, many of these privatized farms were unable to sustain their operations. Bankruptcy, failure to repay loans, and numerous other factors forced many privatized commercial farms to drastically scale back their operations and payrolls over the course of the postsocialist period. Often they disbanded entirely, dividing up what was left of the farm assets among creditors and shareholders. This was, in fact, the case in several of the farms near Sepych that I visited. In these towns and villages, I was often greeted with the comment that it was certainly better to live in Sepych, where "people were still organized." Where there was no more collective khoziaistvo, my interlocutors often used a collection of *ras/raz*-prefixed verbs (denoting dispersal) to describe both the farm infrastructure and the people in the associated towns and villages: pulled apart (*razobrali*), broken up (*razorvali*), split apart (*razkololi*), or even bombed out (*razbombili*).[5] The continued existence of a khoziaistvo above the level of individual households was the key indicator of what sort of moral community might be expected to exist there as well.

Townspeople in Sepych often worried that they, too, would "go to pieces" (*razvalivat'sia*), either by the time the next big bank loan came due (the pessimistic scenario) or when Andrei Petrovich stepped aside or died (the optimistic scenario). In my conversations about AOZT Sepych, Andrei Petrovich was often lionized as a strong khoziain, a linchpin holding the households of AOZT Sepych together into a moral community in the face of this lurking danger. In turning now to the specific exchanges on which his status as an effective khoziain rested, I focus on the shifting field in which Andrei Petrovich and households in Sepych created new kinds of post-Soviet relationships. My concern, in other words, is with the new relationships between two levels of khoziaistvo and the ways in which they were cemented through materials of ethics flowing between their respective khoziaeva: Andrei Petrovich (and often his brigade leaders) at the level of AOZT Sepych and heads of household at the next lower level. The questions I explore, then, reprise my analysis of monetary and nonmonetary transactions—and their ethical correlates—in the constitution of Sepych's pre-Soviet and Soviet moral communities.

---

5. See also Pesmen (2000, 67) and Paxson (2005, 103–7) on *ras/raz* verbs.

The most frequently discussed category of relationship between AOZT Sepych and individual households was the monthly payment of cash salaries to the farm's employees. During my visits to Sepych, everyone in town who worked received cash salaries, whether from the commercial farm or from other employers. The mid-1990s crises of demonetization, payment in kind, and lengthy delays in salaries were over, but they were a recent enough memory to keep townspeople slightly apprehensive about coming paydays. As important as these salaries were for households, the commercial farm also permitted—and even encouraged—its workers to elect *not* to take cash. The combination of cash salaries, credit, and possibilities for transfers among employees' salary accounts points to a significant reshaping of the moral community constituting Sepych's khoziaistvo. Whereas the Soviet-era State Farm Sepych employed a greater proportion of townspeople and served as the official center of gravity for nearly all the rest, the privatized AOZT Sepych was, in its official capacity, composed of a far more restrictive set of employees and households. Those no longer part of AOZT Sepych found themselves outside of significant—but not by any means the only—circuits of exchange marking membership in the khoziaistvo and official relationships with its khoziain.

Monetary salaries in the commercial farm were, by and large, lower than those in other organizations in town. Andrei Petrovich made up for this deficit by creating opportunities for the nearly six hundred townspeople who worked in AOZT Sepych to acquire a range of goods and services by purchasing them against their coming salaries—flexibility that was not possible in the strictly monitored budgets of the state organizations discussed below.[6] Moreover, in the case of services that could be provided by the commercial farm, such as plowing a household plot or mowing a meadow, AOZT Sepych provided steep discounts to employees and their immediate families. The accounting office simply subtracted the cost against employees' future salaries. The standard cost of commercial farm services for nonemployees was nearly twice as high as it was for employees. Unless they made special arrangements with Andrei Petrovich or some side deal with a brigade leader, non-farm workers had to pay for services in cash, full price, at the cashier's office.

In 2001, one of the most heralded accomplishments of AOZT Sepych was to open its own stores, at which workers could make everyday purchases against their current and future salaries. The commercial farm payroll, run out of the central accounting office, was in fact a mass of debits and credits, not only in accounts at the new commercial farm stores but among commercial farm workers themselves. Money could be transferred among workers to settle debts or collect money for a common purpose. If, for example, it was someone's

---

6. Although broadly similar opportunities existed at a much smaller scale elsewhere in Sepych—schoolteachers could buy bread in the school cafeteria against their salaries—this form of credit was a much-discussed benefit of working in the commercial farm.

birthday and the brigade or smaller group planned to celebrate at work, money for a group gift could be collected directly from everyone's payroll account. On one such birthday, the woman who was organizing the celebration commandeered an entire bus from the commercial farm, piling all her guests into it for a picnic in a faraway meadow. When I asked the driver what he was getting out of the deal, he replied that she would write off a bottle for him; that is, she would simply transfer twenty rubles for a bottle of moonshine to his salary account from hers. Some of the dynamics of moonshine, money, and labor that I traced in the household sector thus also obtained in relationships that passed through the commercial farm.

But the institutional context also allowed these materials of ethics to work differently than they did in the household sector. The various provisions for credit and cashless exchange associated with commercial farm salaries provided important opportunities for farm employees to even out some of the bumps and risks of economic transformation that came with unexpected bursts of inflation or demonetization. Here then was one set of ways in which Andrei Petrovich and the leadership of AOZT Sepych acted as khoziaeva to their employees, enabling a range of relationships that traced the borders of a new kind of moral community coterminous with those of the membership of AOZT Sepych. Their actions mitigated some inequalities in town (notably the lower salaries paid by the commercial farm and the stratification rampant in the household sector) by establishing others—through cut-rate services and credit offered exclusively to employees.

At the same time, these possibilities further isolated those newly unemployed townspeople—Humphrey's "dispossessed" (2002, 21–39)—who had no salaried employment anywhere and to whom the now-private AOZT Sepych had no obligation deriving from employment and the exchange of labor for rights in a moral community. Indeed, many nonfarm employees in town chafed at AOZT Sepych's provision of store credit and salary transfers, charging that these transactions were manifestly unfair because they were provided exclusively to commercial farm workers. From Andrei Petrovich's perspective, which he outlined to me on numerous occasions, he was "working for people" and "taking care of his people." In his eyes, those townspeople not working in the farm fell into several categories: those who should be working in the farm (his opinion of the unemployed); those who were employed elsewhere and were thus someone else's responsibility; and those who were making money through their own entrepreneurial activities. Each of these groups had to find routes other than official salaries and their various manipulations to access farm resources. By contrast, those townspeople who did remain in the commercial farm had not only a broad set of options for taking their salary but also a new set of obligations to the director, all of which served to further solidify his power as khoziain.

A second significant set of relationships between the two levels of khoziaistvo took place though nonsalary transfers of goods and services from the commercial farm to individual households. These reworkings of the pervasive patronage-style khoziain relationships of the socialist period became a source of abiding uncertainty in the post-Soviet period. Because they are more heavily tinged with the Soviet past than cash transactions, they are also a prime place to highlight the role of expectations and imaginations about khoziaeva in the field of post-Soviet governance. If cash salaries were regular and relatively de-personalized, patronage-style exchanges were irregular, highly personalized, and open to all manner of negotiation through competing claims. If salaries and their manifold permutations staked the borders of a new moral commu-nity around the officially private AOZT Sepych, patronage blurred them, for anyone in Sepych could request these sorts of unofficial transfers. Finally, if the dilemmas of how to be a khoziain had been largely settled with respect to salaries over the course of the 1990s (some residual grumbling aside), they re-mained quite unsettled when it came to patronage. Under what circumstances should Andrei Petrovich allot resources to townspeople who did not work in the farm? What should be done with those whose requests should technically be dealt with by fledgling state agencies or without any outside help at all? How could he keep the farm afloat as a business and at the same time continue to increase his wealth in people by instilling obligations in as many townspeo-ple as possible—obligations that reinforced his sterling reputation as khoziain both in and beyond Sepych? Such were the daily ethical dilemmas of the direc-tor's office, where the history and conceptual language of material'nye and moral'nye incentives—with all they implied for the accumulation of wealth in people and exchange of labor for money and goods passing through the direc-tor's office—met the harsh realities of the post-Soviet countryside.[7]

In contrast to the usually quiet halls of the local state administration build-ing, the offices of AOZT Sepych were almost without exception busy and cha-otic. When he was not there, Andrei Petrovich was assumed to be—and usually was—off working his contacts in the district and regional centers. When he was there, he dealt not only with the day-to-day problems that arose in the commercial farm but also with a seemingly never-ending parade of visitors to his office, nearly all of them bearing one request or another, from small loans to construction materials to discounted grain. I usually caught Andrei Petrovich in his office as well, where the general confusion meant that he was often dealing with multiple requests and questions at the same time.

On one occasion I found myself in the director's office with Anton, a young, unemployed, and frequently drunk man who was there on his second trip to see the director about his elderly father's damaged roof. Andrei Petrovich asked

---

7. To a lesser extent, they were also the dilemmas of lower-level officials in the commercial farm. Although they had no control over salaries, employees at lower tiers of the commercial farm might act as patrons, as a director would, doling out tractor time or other favors upon request (and often without the knowledge of their superiors).

whether Anton had counted how many tiles they would need to redo the entire roof. Anton replied that they had counted fifty-two sheets, and at 50 rubles apiece, that would come out to 2,600 rubles.[8] Andrei Petrovich wrote the number down on a piece of paper, stared at it, and said slowly, "That, of course, is awful." He looked up at Anton, "And this is for the barn?" "No, no," replied Anton, "for the house itself." Andrei Petrovich thought some more and reached for the phone to call in his chief accountant. When the accountant arrived from her office downstairs, Andrei Petrovich summarized the situation and said, "Let's try to get him the roofing material for, say, half price, for 1,300. It's for his father's work." The accountant replied that she didn't quite know how they would manage that, but they would figure something out. Andrei Petrovich turned to Anton and said that the next big order for roofing shingles would probably be placed in a couple of months. He would speak to the head of the construction brigade to make sure that they ordered enough to have fifty-two pieces left for Anton's father's house. Anton murmured his thanks and shuffled out, leaving Andrei Petrovich, the accountant, and me in the room. Anton himself didn't work, Andrei Petrovich said pointedly, and paused. He shook his head at the expense and said, "His father's very ill and practically blind now. He might not even live to see his new roof." He paused again and then went on, "But it's for his father's work. Even if he dies, his wife will still have to live there." When the accountant left, Andrei Petrovich groused that these requests were undermining his efforts to run a normal business, especially when he could no longer count on much in return. "Look at all that housing we built for people," he said by way of example, "and then [with privatization] they just waved their hands [goodbye] at us."

Anton's roofing project is but one example of the dilemmas that attended the patronage doled out by Andrei Petrovich in his role as post-Soviet khoziain and shaper of Sepych as a moral community. Against Anton's lack of employment and the prospect of little in return, the director weighed other rights and obligations in people. In his explanation of his decision to grant the 50 percent discount, the generational cycling of rights and obligations is especially noteworthy. Although I was unable to find out what Anton's father's position in State Farm Sepych had been, it is safe to assume that he had been, many years earlier, on the receiving end of Andrei Petrovich's moral'nye and material'nye incentives while in the socialist workforce. Like many others, Anton's father stayed in Sepych rather than leaving in the Brezhnev-era rush to the cities, and he labored in the state farm. When his labor was expended and he retired, Andrei Petrovich repaid that labor by providing a discount on roofing material ("it's for his father's work"). In so doing, he created, or at least hoped to create,

8. Just under $100 at the time, or three to four normal months' salary if Anton had been working at a low-skill job in AOZT Sepych.

a new set of obligations to AOZT Sepych in the next generation—represented, in this case, by Anton.

As a result of transactions like this, Andrei Petrovich's wealth in people continued to be enormous; the more Sepych appeared to insiders and outsiders as a healthy moral community, the more Andrei Petrovich was lauded as a stellar khoziain. Everyone owed him for something. His rare multigenerational wealth in people was, in fact, too enormous for some. The power that accrued to the director through his ability to use farm resources to aid all his workers and many others in town meant that, for many townspeople, patronage was something to be called upon sparingly. When, for example, the commercial farm was unable to pay its salaries in cash during the mid-1990s, the proportion of compensation to workers that took the form of noncash patronage increased exponentially. As a result of the scarcity of money in town and people's inability to obtain goods elsewhere without money, requests poured into the director's office for all sorts of aid. As one friend put it, annoyed at having had to beg all the time, "Andrei Petrovich was like a king (*karol'*) then." Khoziain relationships could go too far.

By 2000, circumstances had made it harder and harder to be a king, or even just a solid khoziain. Many townspeople complained that the farm and Andrei Petrovich no longer took care of them the way it they once had. One friend, when I mentioned an article in the district newspaper that spoke of Andrei Petrovich in typical glowing terms of "working for people," shook her head and said, "Maybe a few years ago, but not anymore." Even Anton later grumbled to me that if Andrei Petrovich had really been looking out for his people, those shingles would have been free. The ethics of being a khoziain were, then, a continual field of debate and claim making. Andrei Petrovich attempted to curtail the amount of patronage he gave out so as to tend to the farm and its members in difficult economic circumstances. At the same time, those same circumstances led to more patronage requests. What was the balance between the firm's attempt to stay solvent in rough economic waters and Andrei Petrovich's desire to keep accumulating wealth in people? Between new obligations and old obligations? Some of the reasons the director struck the balances he did will become clearer when I discuss local state agencies. First, however, I take up a final vector along which objects of significance moved from the khoziaistvo of AOZT Sepych to individual households all over town: theft.

By one friend's approximation, two-fifths of AOZT Sepych's grain disappeared into private hands over the cycle from fall harvest to spring sowing. His estimation is valuable not so much because its accuracy can be confirmed—it cannot—but because it conveys a sense of the scale this vector of transaction occupied in townspeople's imagination of how individual households in Sepych related to the commercial farm. By all accounts, theft from the local agricultural enterprise had increased substantially in the post-Soviet period. Back in the collective farm era (1929–65), I was told, many people found it difficult enough to smuggle home handfuls or shoefuls of grain. But with privatization, increasing domestic herd sizes, and the availability of private transport, some townspeople stole grain in cartloads to feed their domestic livestock and make at least some profit on their sale (see also Humphrey [1983] 1998, 463–64; Allina-Pisano 2008, 181–85).

Theft from other private households was extremely rare and universally condemned, but stealing from the commercial farm occupied a gray area in local expectations about propriety. Most townspeople I knew claimed that theft was, in general, not the proper way to go about obtaining inputs for their household. Under "normal" conditions, with reasonable salaries and a fair market, they would prefer to avoid having to steal to get by. But as it was, many cited the need to "survive" (*vyzhit'*) in their domestic economies by stealing a bit: if all the profits from selling a fattened calf were eaten up buying the grain to feed it, what was the point of raising livestock? Theft from AOZT Sepych came with a range of tentative explanations and justifications that point, once again, to the refiguring of the ethical field between levels of khoziaistvo. The old view that the fruits of collective labor were there for the collective taking—"everything around is the collective farm's, everything around is mine," as the ironic Soviet-era saying had it—no longer rang quite as true now that AOZT Sepych occupied a hazy middle ground between state enterprise and private business.

Like salaries and patronage, theft mitigated emerging inequalities, instabilities, and risks in the household sector through recourse to the next higher level of khoziaistvo—through participation in a moral community that diversified risks and inequalities by spreading them out through many actors engaging in similar practices at different times. But theft did this in different ways than salaries and patronage, with different implications for the kinds of ethical relationships and inequalities it imagined and quietly created. Unlike salaries, theft was an option for most households, not just employees of AOZT Sepych (although paying off a guard or other farm employee was often part of the deal). Unlike most patronage transactions, such as Anton's request for roofing materials, theft did not involve the director's office or any official commercial farm circuits. It was never, that is, a direct way for Andrei Petrovich to accumulate wealth in people.

His brigade leaders were, however, another story. Townspeople commonly assumed that higher-ups in the commercial farm made off with many more tons of grain than did rank-and-file workers. If a combine driver could manage to sneak a couple of tons for his household, then his supervisors were likely diverting several tons to their own households and those of their families. One combine driver confided in me that he had split two tons with a neighbor who drove the getaway truck, but his supervisor had asked him to set aside nearly ten tons for himself and his family. Being a *malen'kii khoziain* (small-time boss) at lower levels of the farm bureaucracy, then, often meant facilitating a good bit of theft along with more visible patronage.

But whatever moderate rights and obligations in people circulated under cover of darkness along with stolen grain, accumulated wealth in people at these levels never rivaled that of the director, in good part because it could never be made a matter of common knowledge. There were some signs that Andrei Petrovich was moving to bring theft—the only vector of exchange between the commercial farm and households that did not increase his wealth in people—under his purview as well. He talked on several occasions, including at the annual meeting of shareholders I attended, of shifting this form of risk and inequality reduction to the official accounts of the commercial farm. He set one of the long-term goals of the commercial farm as providing a set amount of grain to workers' households each year as a condition of employment "so that people don't have to look around for grain" each year. The extra "official" grain would mean that theft would be less necessary. Townspeople, in other words, would have to look to him for grain, as they did for so many other things.

In addition to playing a role in this sort of tug-of-war for wealth in people between bigger and smaller khoziaeva at different levels of the commercial farm, theft could figure in broader characterizations of the town of Sepych—and not just AOZT Sepych—as a moral community. A family who had lost a pig or calf to sickness, for instance, might—although not by any means easily—replace it with one purloined from a division of AOZT Sepych in the middle of the night. By turning to the commercial farm to deal with unexpected misfortune, they lessened the drain on the family members or friends they would have otherwise had to call on and avoided new obligations to the director.

Theft as a means of social insurance and marker of moral community came up in several conversations on this topic, often in comparisons with neighboring communities (and usually at my prompting, given people's general reticence to talk about it). For instance, on one of my periodic visits to neighboring towns where the former state farm had disbanded entirely into individual households, I spent the better part of two hours listening to the local head of state administration explain why things were far better in Sepych. He talked, in particular, about the benefit of salaries over attempting to make one's way exclusively on a household economy, about the importance of feeling part of an organization like AOZT Sepych that was bigger than oneself, and about Andrei Petrovich's great skill at diverting resources to Sepych. His town no longer had any of these possibilities. Near the conclusion of our conversation, I asked, "If there's no commercial farm here, from whom do people steal?" Although caught momentarily off guard by a question posed more directly than was perhaps advisable, he responded that this was, in fact, one dimension of a serious problem in town. It was much harder, as well as far more objectionable, to steal from private owners; in this town, there were only private owners. Unexpected events, whether from external economic causes such as inflation or simple misfortune like the death of a cow, had to be absorbed by an already-strapped household sector in which people were already becoming, in the head of administration's words, more and more "split apart" from one another.

Stolen goods, like the items that changed hands in salary and patronage transactions, are windows onto sensibilities about what kinds of exchanges were possible and proper in postsocialist times. But, I have suggested, they are also more than this. Situating the practices and discourses attending these transactions within a larger set of shifting expectations about what it means to be a khoziain and administer a khoziaistvo opens the analysis into the broader field of competition for post-Soviet governance. This is a field, as I have been arguing, that cannot be fully understood without attention to the dimensions of ethical practice in the struggle between state and nonstate actors. All the transactions I have discussed so far passed, in one way or another, through an officially nonstate entity, AOZT Sepych, and often through the person of Andrei Petrovich. Andrei Petrovich's efforts to tend to his khoziaistvo were significant—but not by any means the only—factors constraining attempts to municipalize the state in Sepych by empowering the new local state administration to lead its own kind of moral community.

Before I develop the state side of the comparison, though, it is useful to ask, What does one do with all that wealth in people? Why amass it? Many townspeople assumed that Andrei Petrovich used his golden reputation to cover the appropriation of some of AOZT Sepych's resources for himself and his family. I have no direct evidence for this, but it would be consistent with the practice of many others in his position. His high level of prestige and the number of obligations owed him meant that this kind of transaction was tolerated by most (see also Lampland 1995, 262–66). Indeed, it was expected that a proper khoziain would take care of himself at the same time that he took care of those in the domain he administered. However, to take care of oneself in this way without also attending to others in the khoziaistvo would no longer be characteristic of a virtuous khoziain but of someone who was *delovoi* (entrepreneurial, business-oriented)—an adjective suggesting a self-interested exit from a moral community rather than virtuous governance of it.[9]

There was also another reason for amassing wealth in people. What, one might reasonably ask, was Andrei Petrovich still doing way out in Sepych anyway? He had long been a member of the highest Soviet and post-Soviet committees in the regional center and spent much of his time on the roads back and forth to meetings about the future of agriculture in the Urals. Why had he not converted this extensive network of connections into a higher position? It was not, in fact, for lack of trying. In the mid-1990s, Andrei Petrovich had run for head of district administration, an elected office responsible for all state operations in the larger district of which Sepych was a part. He lost. In a close

9. I owe this point to Roz Galtz.

election, I was told, most people in Sepych voted against him in order to keep him from leaving his post as director of AOZT Sepych. I have no vote tallies to confirm this explanation, but its imaginative logic is precisely that of khozi-ain relationships transformed anew in the post-Soviet period. In this account, one common Soviet-era answer to the question of what to do with wealth in people—turn it into a higher position in the party-state bureaucracy—was thwarted by the votes of the accumulated people. Wealth in people did not get one *entirely* as far as it could in the Soviet period.

Is the State a Moral Community?
Households and the Local Administration

Thus far I have illustrated the ways in which Andrei Petrovich and the leader-ship of State Farm Sepych acted to create a new kind of postsocialist moral community that would allow at least some diversification of the risks and inequalities that beset townspeople. In later chapters I show that the com-mercial farm's community-formation and risk-reduction projects extended to relationships that included the other world as well—in the shape of Sepych's new church and its priests' baptismal rituals. But the moral community associ-ated with AOZT Sepych also existed in a wider ethical field; we cannot fully appreciate the commercial farm's role without an understanding of another vision of moral community with which it overlapped and, not infrequently, jousted. I therefore turn more specifically to the fate of post-Soviet municipal-ization reforms designed to reshape the lowest levels of the state apparatus. I compare—as people in Sepych often did—the privatized AOZT Sepych with the new local state administration, the two primary institutions in Sepych's local field of governance. In contrast to the leadership of the commercial farm, low-level state officials' everyday efforts to accumulate even moderate wealth in people and outline a new kind of moral community divorced from AOZT Sepych have been less than successful. The results have been largely failed state building, lack of legitimacy, and exceedingly weak state presence in domains that townspeople considered crucial to rural life. Although there are several reasons for this ongoing process, some of which were particular to Sepych and others of which likely obtained much more generally, my focus is on exploring those most closely connected with the dilemmas of how to be a khoziain in Sepych.

Of the three heads of administration in Sepych since 1991, I was best ac-quainted with Faina Timofeevna. Once an employee of State Farm Sepych, she was appointed head of administration in the late 1990s. Her portfolio included directly supervising some state functions, such as infrastructure main-tenance and Sepych's kindergartens, as well as coordinating activities among the local representatives of the Russia-wide ministries with a presence in town, including school (Education), hospital (Health), and club and library (Culture). Faina Timofeevna and the specialists she worked with thus had responsibilities both to their own state employees—from accountants to chauffeurs to town hall furnace workers—and to the residents of Sepych as a whole. They worked closely with other specialists at the district level, and most days saw either a visit to Sepych from district-level state functionaries or representatives from Sepych heading to the city for meetings and to deliver paperwork.

In discussions of the effectiveness of local state agencies, townspeople at large often began with gender. In the discussion of moonshine and money, above, I discussed expectations about the differential materials of ethics and competencies that attended the management of Sepych's households. Husbands were usually considered more adept at making connections and contacts that revolved around informal exchanges of labor, nonmonetary deals, and theft. Wives, on the other hand, more often controlled the household inputs and outlays of cash associated with salaries and purchasing in stores. While this division of labor often privileged women at the level of households, the reverse was often true when gender expectations were extrapolated to the local administration as household writ large (compare Burawoy et al. 2000). If, in other words, it had long been possible to think in terms of two khoziaistva at nested levels of local economic organization (whether Soviet state farm or privatized AOZT) and individual household, municipalization placed new questions before townspeople. Was the local civil administration now *also* a khoziaistvo? What *was* the status of the town as a moral community distinct from, if substantially overlapping with, AOZT Sepych? What characteristics were required to administer it properly? How did materials of ethics flow though its relationships and to what effects?

The lack of explicitly coordinated economic activity in the administrative domain of Sepych made it tricky to apply khoziaistvo in its standard usage to the local administration, and most did not. Nevertheless, townspeople were much more united in their opinion that, whatever Sepych as unit of civil administration was, it desperately needed a khoziain. As I walked through town with friends, they would often point to burned-out streetlights, missing sidewalks, or other dilapidated infrastructure now in the purview of the local administration and assert, "See, Sepych has no khoziain." In conversations about local politics, I often heard khoziain in its adjectival form: the biggest problem in Sepych was that Faina Timofeevna was "not *khoziaistvennaia.*" Andrei Petrovich, on the other hand, was lauded as "*shipko* [very] *khoziaistvennyi.*" "It's easier for a man to cut deals" (*muzhchine legche dogovorit'sia*), I heard time and time again. For many in Sepych, gender was a sufficient category of explanation for the relative weakness of the local administration. For them, the additional factors I discuss below were, however real, not especially pertinent: a truly skilled khoziain would be able to manage any adverse situation and transform it into the successful administration of the domain in question.

But the same townspeople also admitted that few men in town were suffi-ciently khoziaistvennyi for the job of head of administration. Moreover, Faina Timofeevna's predicaments were shared by her fellow bureaucrats—men and women—at multiple levels of the state administration. For all its local popular-ity, then, gender alone is not sufficient for my analytic purposes.

As they went about their duties, state officials in Sepych were often hampered not only by the weak heritage of rural civil administrations from the Soviet period that stacked the deck in Andrei Petrovich's favor from the get-go but also, in many cases, by the very post-Soviet municipalization reforms that were intended to reimagine and revitalize the state. Of particular concern to state officials after 2000 was the creeping audit culture arising from new regulations aimed at gaining control of the federal budget and combating "corruption" through strict new accounting procedures.[10] It is here that the financializa-tion and transparency aspects of recent capitalist transformations diverge in Sepych. I have already suggested that townspeople sought to diversify and, if possible, avoid exposure to the global risks of finance capital by relying on the networks and connections of AOZT Sepych. I now argue that new audit procedures, instead of achieving the general transparency they sought, undermined the legitimacy of the very state organs that utilized them. Instead of drawing more people in Sepych into more transparent exchanges in a new kind of moral community, these reforms further convinced townspeople that AOZT Sepych was the more legitimate and efficacious institution to approach for their needs.

The much-discussed audit regulations came about in the wake of battles over the federal budget throughout the 1990s. In 1998, for instance, an esti-mated 50 percent of state funds flowed outside the budget. Central authorities in Moscow often used the flexibility afforded by these off-budget accounts to negotiate with and attempt to buy the loyalty of leaders in Russia's power-ful regions (Solnick 1999). The sheer scale of the nonbudgetary transactions at all levels, and their significance in influencing political alliances, fostered widespread international critiques of "corruption" and lack of transparency in Russia. From the late 1990s on, partially in response to these critiques, and in close consultation with advisers from the IMF and World Bank, authori-ties in Moscow embarked on a wide-ranging plan to bring all state inputs and

10. My understandings of corruption in the following argument are influenced especially by Herzfeld (1992), Gupta (1995), and Dunn (2004), all of whom frame their discussions in terms of clashing systems of accountability and transparency. Krastev (2004) explores corruption as a form of protectionism and provides an important genealogy of the concept in neoliberal times, pointing out that it was not so long ago that corruption was considered evidence of emerging democracies, rather than something to be stamped out at all costs. On "audit cultures," see especially Strath-ern (2000); my argument here supports Kipnis's (2008) insistence that the anthropology of audit cultures be situated in local ethnography rather than assertions about a spreading, all-powerful, "neoliberal governmentality."

outputs into a single, auditable, and transparent budget and treasury system (*kaznacheistvo*).[11] The accounting reforms that contributed to ongoing headaches in Sepych should thus be seen as one corner of the much higher-level and broader attempts by the Russian state to end the 1990s-era parcellization of sovereignty and reassert state monopolies across many domains. These reforms were aimed precisely at the activities in which lower-level *khoziaeva* specialized: a fully functional, rational, transparent state bureaucracy would have no need for transformative and improvisational skills.

Conversions to treasury accounting were staggered across the Perm region and across units at each level of state administration. Sepych's own complete conversion to treasury accounting was not scheduled to take place until 2002, although rules and regulations for state budget expenditures were already tightening in 2000 and 2001. Several rules already in place stood out in my conversations with state employees: noncash expenditures were forbidden; all payments had to be processed through the state bank; there was no provision in the budget for gifts of any sort; no items that disappeared from inventory could be written off without evidence of where they had gone; and all transactions had to be recorded in log books that were frequently checked by higher-level treasury officials. At an informational meeting about the coming treasury reform, one of Sepych's local officials asked why such a system and the multiplying accountants and bureaucrats that came with it were necessary. The answer she received was quite direct: "So there will be more control over you." "Monitoring, monitoring," muttered another state official, when I asked about the new system.

These new regulations, I was often told, made it increasingly difficult for state officials to create the various rights and obligations in people that circled so effectively through the commercial farm and that townspeople, frustrated state employees included, viewed as key evidence of the existence of a proper khoziain and a healthy khoziaistvo. The evaluation of state exchanges involving salaries, patronage, and theft was often couched in negative terms—what was impossible, objectionable, or downright offensive—rather than in terms of what could be accomplished with a little effort. In the conceptual language I use here, auditing sought to freeze or closely channel the flow of precisely those materials of ethics that were, in local understandings, crucial to the formation of a moral community.

I should be clear on a point that is often misunderstood in discussions of so-called corruption: the examples below do not constitute an argument that the state officials I knew were annoyed that new regulations prohibited them from engaging in activities that benefited them or their friends. Even if such benefits might have been one outcome of being a khoziain, the state officials I knew were intensely critical of their fellow bureaucrats who profited excessively

---

11. Diamond (2002a; 2002b), World Bank (2003b, v–xii, 13), and Odling-Smee (2004) describe these efforts and the international consultations that shaped them.

from their state positions. As in the case of khoziaeva in AOZT Sepych, one could legitimately take care of oneself only along with, not by ignoring or at the expense of, those in one's domain. In the abstract, budget and treasury reforms were completely blind to these crucial distinctions of good and bad governance in smaller-scale administrative units. In practice, the picture was more complicated.

Theft is the easiest point at which to begin. Many of my conversations about inputs to households from various state and nonstate institutions took place during conversations in the school, the library, or the local administration offices. When I asked about the importance of theft in general, I was often reminded that people usually took things only from the commercial farm, not from state institutions. This situation owed as much to the kinds of items around the workplace as to regulation or anticorruption campaigns. As one woman who worked in the school put it, looking around her office, "What am I going to steal from here? This piece of paper?" Her husband's commercial farm job presented him with considerably more opportunities for creative inputs into their household. With the increasing demands of domestic economies, it was not the implements of state bureaucracy, culture, and education that were the most necessary and desirable.[12]

However, one set of concerns and dilemmas about theft from the state revolved directly around the strictures new auditing regulations placed on state employees. Many state employees resented the new demands for audit and the implication that if left to their own devices, they would simply walk off with everything in their workplaces. One of the kindergartens in an outlying village, under the jurisdiction of the local state administration, provides a case in point. The longtime director of the kindergarten (her official title was "manager of economic organization"—*zaveduiushchii khoziaistva*, or *zavkhoz* for short) was a vociferous critic of new auditing measures. On one occasion she used dishes as the primary example of her dissatisfaction. In the Soviet period, she told me, the kindergarten was a unit of State Farm Sepych. If she had an inventory of one hundred plates and in the course of the year, the children dropped twenty of them, she would have to go to the director of State Farm Sepych and ask him to sign a statement writing off the twenty broken plates. Now, with new auditing rules in place, if there were twenty broken plates, she would have to save the shards of every plate to show the auditor coming from the city at the end of the year. She took exception to this lack of trust and the implicit assumption that she and her

---

12. As long as AOZT Sepych continued to "hold together," land, an important item of potential conflict in other rural settings (e.g., Verdery 2003) was in fact not much of an issue in Sepych. The vast majority of the land around Sepych was leased to the commercial farm by its members as part of the terms of the incorporation of AOZT Sepych. If AOZT Sepych disbanded into constituent households, a member of the local administration said to me on one occasion, "then it would be war" (compare the similar language in Humphrey [1983] 1998, 473). As it was, there was sufficient and only mildly contested land for haying and small-scale grain growing.

colleagues were stealing plates out from under kindergarten children's lunches. On auditing days, rather than worrying about things that might be stolen by her employees, the kindergarten director's biggest concern was to remind her staff to make sure none of their personal cups or spoons, brought in from home to temporarily replace broken ones, were left lying around. If they were, they might be counted in the audit and claimed forever as state property.

Although strict auditing procedures already applied to her inventory, they did not yet apply to the payment of fees. She therefore often took payment from parents in potatoes or vegetables to feed the children in the kindergarten cafeteria. Fee payments in kind allowed families to keep more cash on hand and the cafeteria to regulate its food stores, but the director didn't know how long this off-the-books accounting possibility would last. In this case and in others, state officials and employees resented the implication that they would steal at every opportunity. That they might have was not the point: they bridled at the suggestion that they did not know exactly how much it was possible to steal without undercutting their ability to do their job effectively. Here, then, an important part of their ability act as khoziaeva—by judiciously responding to the situations at hand, making deals as necessary, and balancing rights and obligations in people—was being eroded.

As in the case of theft, patronage from state officials was not valued as highly as that from the commercial farm. The local administration had no tractors, no construction materials, no grain, and few of the other items essential to the survival of domestic economies.[13] State officials could perhaps give small favors to friends or family members when it came to allotting land for haying or building. They could help to speed paperwork through various higher levels of bureaucracy. Their frequent trips to the city on state matters were a source of rides and favors for their employees and others, but this, again, counted for comparatively little. Rarely did I hear any state officials, from the head of the Sepych local administration on down, referred to in anything close to the ways in which townspeople spoke of the advantages of a connection to Andrei Petrovich or other highly placed employees of the commercial farm. Anticorruption measures, of course, were aimed precisely at stanching the flow of these kinds of favors from state officials. Many of my acquaintances in state jobs thought that their higher-ups had gone just a little too far in this matter.

The regulation and auditing of gifts provide clear examples of attempts to curb anything remotely resembling patronage, as well as the social and political

---

13. In many local administrations where the local Soviet-era enterprise had disbanded entirely, local heads of administration had put together a "working group" (*khozgruppa*), which usually consisted of a tractor or two, perhaps a combine, an electrician, and some plumbers. Households could pay small fees to the local administration for the use of these specialists, and the administration itself would use them to care for local infrastructure. Given the influence of Andrei Petrovich, it is perhaps not surprising that no such group existed in Sepych and that most townspeople looked to AOZT Sepych for such services.

consequences of these regulations for those attempting to govern in accordance with their own and citizens' expectations about how moral communities work. The local state administration frequently came upon situations that required the presentation of gifts. There were gifts for the oldest townspeople on Elderly Persons' Day, token gifts at state functions such as the anniversary of the library, or gifts to the commercial farm on Agricultural Workers' Day. State employees and townspeople expected these gifts; they were the heirs to Soviet moral'nye incentives to labor marked by omnipresent certificates, lapel-pin medals, and ceremonies in Sepych's House of Culture. Officially recognizing achievements other than heroic socialist labor was one way to make a distinction between AOZT Sepych as a post-Soviet business and the town of Sepych as a separate, more encompassing, moral community. Faina Timofeevna, however, was consistently confronted with a serious dilemma: there was no money in her budget for gifts, and it was practically impossible to move money around for the purchase of gifts. Frustrated, she had long since decided to simply buy gifts with her own money when official functions called for them. The situation would be even worse with the advent of full-scale treasury accounting reforms, she said to me. Some state employees in nearby cities, who were already working under treasury accounting, testified that it would indeed be harder.

One urban culture worker I knew worried for weeks in advance of a House of Culture's anniversary party that she was not going to be able to present her career employees with flowers. Treasury system accounting meant that she was not allowed to purchase gifts from her state budget. There was a provision allowing state agencies that brought in their own money—such as library fees for photocopying—to use some of that money for gifts. But in those cases, there was still a tax on gifts, and taxes could not be paid with money from the federal budget. As a result, I was told, the person who received the gift was technically required to pay taxes on the gift and fill out all the appropriate paperwork. "Can you imagine that?" she said to me. It was hardly a gift, she went on, if you had to turn around and ask the recipient to pay some minuscule taxes on it. Another culture worker—this one employed in the regional center of Perm—told me, with similar barely disguised outrage, that his office was not permitted to buy flowers for actors and actresses on opening night, even when they were distinguished guests visiting from other cities.

In all these cases, auditing measures intended to eliminate the ability of state officials to give gifts—presumed to be evidence of corruption and influence peddling—severely hampered the ability of state representatives to enter into ethical relationships with their citizens, garner trust in their workers, or create the wealth in people style obligations that continued, even if in new ways, to characterize the proper consolidation of power within a given moral community. There were, to be sure, many types of manipulation available to circumvent the system. Faked receipts from trusted store employees abounded, and, particularly in small administrative units, agreements could be reached with treasury officials to look the other way for limited purposes that usually did not involve personal enrichment. There were, in the end, flowers for the House of Culture employees at their anniversary party, although all of the receipts were for different purchases. The state culture official in Perm told me that for the opening night of their play, they had bought flowers for all the visiting actors and counted them as set decorations (legal) rather than gifts (illegal). As one culture worker working under treasury accounting put it, "We're Russians. Of course we'll find a way around it."[14] But her comment was offered more in resignation and weariness than in delight at her own inventiveness. The space for manipulation was getting smaller and smaller, the stakes lower and lower, and the satisfaction at getting around the system harder and harder to enjoy. It was becoming a major victory to be able to present a bouquet of flowers to those who had worked in their state jobs all their lives. At least for these low-level state bureaucrats, the size of the obligations that resulted was approaching the point at which the obligations were no longer balanced by the rights that had to be expended in making the transaction work at all. Was it even worth it to try to be a khoziain anymore?

Faina Timofeevna sometimes wondered about this, especially when it came to Sepych's infrastructure. Caught in the sorts of predicaments I have described above, she was repeatedly put in positions that resulted in incomplete projects, dissatisfied workers, and angry townspeople. Even before the accounting reforms, there was little money in the local administration's budget for employees who could be assigned to install new streetlights or construct new sidewalks for Sepych's muddy roads. Forced to skimp, Faina Timofeevna frequently relied on family and friends or hired moonlighters known for their dubious work habits. The low-salaried pay for work in the furnace rooms that heated state buildings meant that these jobs were revolving doors; state officials were constantly beating the bushes for workers. More than once I saw Faina Timofeevna or a subordinate walking door-to-door late in the evening looking for a substitute stoker. Whenever it snowed, she relied on townspeople with access to their own tractors to plow many of Sepych's public streets of their own goodwill (the local administration was already in debt to the commercial farm for several tens of thousands of rubles' worth of snowplowing services). Some townspeople had simply begun changing the bulbs in the streetlights outside their houses on their own, shouldering the expense so that their children could see on the way to school. One of the biggest setbacks for the local administration one winter was that Faina Timofeevna's brother broke a rib at his job in the commercial farm, making him temporarily unavailable to do miscellaneous state jobs for free. His injury revealed just how much she had relied on him for work that did not need to be compensated from her budget.

14. See Herzfeld's instructive discussion of the ways in which bureaucratic practices become refracted through national stereotypes (1992, 72).

The scope of obligations and allegiances Faina Timofeevna was able to create was barely bigger than her family.

Faina Timofeevna's efforts were tireless and nothing less than heroic in the circumstances, but the results were often considered unsatisfactory—an injustice only some townspeople appreciated. When full-scale treasury accounting arrived in the coming years, Faina Timofeevna said, life would get even worse. She would no longer be able to transfer even limited sums among her accounts, as she still could to a degree, and all payouts would have to be signed for and take place through the state bank rather than her office. Circumstances would require even more flexibility, precisely the kind that would disappear with increased auditing and demands for transparency. The local administration would become more dependent on individuals and other institutions in Sepych. Already the situation meant that the much more flexible leadership of AOZT Sepych could ride to the rescue of struggling state-sector projects. No longer legally obliged to care for townspeople, Andrei Petrovich and his brigade leaders could cast their assistance to the local administration as pure generosity. Andrei Petrovich's increasing wealth in people and still-strong moral community was, in part, directly connected to Faina Timofeevna's decreasing ability to create obligations in townspeople.

The high level of dissatisfaction with the work of Sepych's head of administration at the town meeting with which I began this chapter was, then, heavily overdetermined. General contributing factors included the relative weakness of local state administrations from the outset, their continuing lack of sufficient resources from above, and, especially after 2000, budget and anticorruption reforms that undercut many attempts to work around these problems. Additional factors more specific to Sepych were Andrei Petrovich's massive store of multigenerational wealth in people located outside the state and a gender gap in expectations about the capacities of the heads of AOZT Sepych and the local administration. Over the course of the first post-Soviet decade, all these factors were debated in the vocabulary of who was an effective khoziain and who was able to more effectively collect people into a moral community.

I concluded my discussion of the moonshine and money circulating in the post-Soviet household sector with some examples of how these exchanges participated in recent shifts within capitalism writ large, especially the financialization of capital and the associated proliferation of currency speculation and global hedge funds. The increasing exchangeability of all manner of transactables under conditions of post-Fordist capitalism, I agreed with many other observers, has brought with it new kinds of risk, something that households in postsocialist Sepych worked hard to manage and, when possible, avoid. In this chapter, I have introduced and explored two additional facets of recent global capitalism as manifested in Sepych: privatization and a preoccupation with the audit, transparency, and visibility of all manner of exchanges. Privatization agendas lay behind the municipalization reforms, while auditing appeared most clearly in state and internationally sponsored anticorruption initiatives.

At the analytic level of global capitalism, the financialization of capital, privatization, and the increasing transparency created by audit and anticorruption reforms work in tandem: making more transactions visible and traceable makes them more exchangeable to more private parties without the interference of states. In economists' language, everything moves in the direction of a purer and purer market. At this level of abstraction—or perhaps asocial fantasy—capitalism's recent tendencies are, as James Ferguson has argued, "de-moralizing" (2006, 69–88). They are presented and discussed in a pure, incontrovertible economic logic with no consideration of any human values, practices, or consequences. One central task for anthropologists seeking to understand contemporary global transformations, then, is to ask how these large-scale projects and reforms are remoralized as they intersect and touch ground in specific places. I have therefore shown how financialization, privatization, and anticorruption reforms intersected in the broader field of struggles to shape an emergent ethical regime in Sepych with unexpected results—results that were heavily colored by the heritage of the socialist period.

In the broader ethical repertoire of the Upper Kama, however, the moonshine, money, labor, and khoziain relationships of both household exchanges and state formation had long been viewed as matters of this world to be marked off from Old Believer elders in search of Christian salvation. These bright lines of ritual and social distinction born in Sepych's early history, so paradoxically sustained in the Soviet period, began to shift and blur not long after the fall of socialism.

7 *Society, Culture, and the Churching of Sepych*

W hen I first visited Sepych on an archaeographical expedition in 1994, the frame of a modest wooden church was rising in the center of town. The church, I had learned even before our expedition left Moscow, was affiliated *not* with local Maksimovskie or Dëminskie elders but with the Belokrinitsy hierarchy of *priestly* Old Believers, whose influence in the Vereshchagino district had been confined to two parishes well to the east of Sepych until the 1990s. My archaeographer colleagues were astonished and puzzled at what seemed to be the rapid withering of priestless Old Belief in Sepych at precisely the moment it could finally emerge from the shadows; accounting for the sudden popularity of an ordained priest and his church was a primary task of our expedition. Our conclusions, based on dozens of conversations in which we asked elders why they had or had not joined the new church, was that decades of Soviet atheism had so eroded traditional culture and knowledge that many in the Upper Kama no even longer knew they were betraying the faith of their priestless ancestors by setting foot in a church.

By 2001, at the time of my longest stretch of fieldwork in Sepych, the church building had been completed and the first trickle of townspeople who appealed to the priests and their worldwide hierarchy for sacraments had become a flood. Living in Sepych for nearly a year also enabled me to ask a broader range of questions about the new church and to arrive at some different conclusions about its significance. For a time in the 1990s, I came to understand, everyone seeking to influence ethical practice in post-Soviet Sepych needed to position himself or herself in relationship to the new church; it was, in fact, a primary point of convergence—and often dispute—for nearly all emergent moral communities, materials of ethics, and moralizing discourses in post-Soviet Sepych. AOZT Sepych, the local state administration, former Communist Party

246

organizers, and a resurgent priestly Old Believer hierarchy based in Moscow all played significant roles in building the church and expanding its parish community. At the same time, archaeographers and ethnographers, traveling emissaries from priestless Old Believer concords, and even elements of the Russian Ministry of Culture tried to block the new church and counter its attempts to gain new members.[1] Each of these groups drew on particular languages of ethics as they worked to reposition themselves and to remake townspeople in Sepych for a new and still uncertain age. Each brought to this field of struggle divergent histories and differing capacities to influence the course of events in Sepych. Each, finally, sought to realize its agenda and ground its vision through the orchestration of now-familiar materials of ethics: money and labor for construction projects, food and drink on ritual or celebratory occasions, old manuscripts and other objects—and the new church building itself—as material evidence for the propriety of one or another moralizing vision.

I suggest in this chapter that Old Belief in post-Soviet Sepych was torn between post-Soviet moralizing discourses about "society" and "culture," with different alliances of townspeople and outsiders rallying around these terms and the moral communities and subjectivities they indexed.[2] Was reclaiming Old Belief in the post-Soviet period one way to rebuild society (*obshchestvo*) after earlier society-building initiatives associated with the Communist Party had been discredited? In this popular local view, embraced most enthusiastically by the leadership of AOZT Sepych and former party-state functionaries, a new church and a new priest might serve to create new ethical relationships that stood as a bulwark against the alienating, unfamiliar, and risk-filled relationships of global capitalism in which townspeople suddenly found themselves immersed. Or, on the other hand, could reclaiming Old Belief become an illustration of the tenacity of ancient Russian "traditional culture" (*traditsionnaia kul'tura*), steadfastly preserved by Old Believers in Sepych through even the most sustained attempts to eradicate it? In this view, actively promoted by archaeographers, ethnographers, and other scholars of Old Belief—even as they worried that traditional culture had suffered a mortal blow in the Soviet period—the new church, its priests, and the conversions they encouraged were the enemies of all that was unique about three centuries of priestless Old Belief in Sepych. As complementary as these moralizing visions of society and culture

1. Missing from this list, readers will no doubt note, is Western missionaries. In the landscape of post-Soviet religion, Sepych is somewhat atypical for being geographically isolated enough that it has not been directly visited by foreign missionaries, whose institutions and discourses play an important role in many other analyses of the remaking of Soviet subjects, communities, and moralities (e.g., Wanner 2007).

2. When using "society" and "culture" in this chapter I am thus referring exclusively to what anthropologists usually call "indigenous concepts"—those operative in the time and place under study. I do not employ either society or culture in any of the numerous analytic senses they have acquired in the West or in Russia.

might appear in the abstract, they were endorsed (and funded) by very different people and institutions in post-Soviet Sepych. Tracking the very different fates of these projects allows us to understand some of the precise mechanisms by which a new and specifically post-Soviet configuration of worldly powers helped recast the dilemmas and opportunities of those seeking Christian salvation in the Upper Kama.

Building a Church, Working for Society, Collecting People

"I told him, 'It's a society thing!' [eto obshchestvennoe delo]." So spoke Tat'iana Fëdorovna, a former Komsomol organizer, recalling how she successfully cajoled a young nonbeliever into donating some of his minuscule paycheck to the construction of Sepych's new church. Phrasing her request for a contribution in the language of "society" was not accidental; indeed, it likely conjured a particular set of associations for those who heard her appeal. Recall, for instance, that the Communist Party activist Liudmila Ivanovna, a chief architect of Sepych's moral'nye incentives to labor in the days of Sepych Weddings, conceived of her work as "society work" (obshchestvennaia rabota) and "work with people" (rabota s liud'mi).[3] In the 1990s, the possibility that the new church could serve as one foundation for rehabilitating a sense of belonging associated with society in the face of new risks and inequalities became attractive to many townspeople; indeed, nearly everyone working on the church discussed its benefits in terms of society. This was the case not only for small-scale solicitations like Tat'iana Fëdorovna's but especially for the work of more highly placed townspeople, who found in the church a way to distance themselves from the discredited aspects of their Communist Party backgrounds while, at the same time, casting themselves as new defenders and advocates of Sepych.

Society was, in other words, the centerpiece of a project in constructing a moral community, a community whose members' conceptions and practices of proper relationships—those directed both at this world and at the other world—should and could be substantially aligned with one another to the betterment of all. This vision of moral unity under the banner of society was, like so many of its predecessors in the Upper Kama, never fully realized and in fact was constantly subverted in all manner of ways. For the moment, however, my interest is in the politics and moralizing discourses that lay behind the

---

3. In tracing the church-building project in Sepych in part to new aspirations for society, I join an array of scholars who have noted the importance of obshche- concepts in post-Soviet discourse. See especially Pesmen (2000), Paxson (2005), Yurchak (2006, 148–51), Hemment (2008), and Zigon (2008) on obshchenie, as well as Volkov (1997) and David-Fox (2002) on obshchestvennost' and obshchestvennye organizatsii, respectively.

aspirations to form a moral community at the intersection of new priestly Old Belief and ideas of society. From this perspective, the vision behind the church appears both new and old: new because it reclaimed religion in an assertively public way after the end of socialism, old because the language of society in which much of this reclaiming took place, as well the actors and resources behind it, was quite familiar from the Soviet period.

The story of Sepych's new priestly Old Believer church begins shortly after the end of socialism. In July of 1994, an article appeared in the district newspaper announcing the construction of a new church in Sepych. It was entitled "Help Finish Building the Church" and signed by the Sepych Old Believer Community. It read in part:

> Not long ago, in the town of Sepych, the Sepych Old Believer Community was registered.... But the parishioners face a problem: where can they hold prayer services, be baptized, married, send relatives off on their final journey, or even simply to come at any time with one's troubles.... Our community now gathers in the homes of parishioners. And so the people of Sepych decided to build their own church.[4]

Without alluding to the fact that priestless services and rituals had been held in Sepych's private homes almost since the town's founding, the article went on to describe the current state of the new construction project: the walls and ceiling were done, but with that construction had stalled. The community appealed for further aid and listed the names of several people in Sepych and the surrounding towns who had already contributed.

The Sepych Old Believer Community was founded in 1992 with the organizational help of Tat'iana Fëdorovna—the fundraiser introduced above. Tat'iana Fëdorovna's family was affiliated with the Dëminskie concord of priestless Old Believers. Although she never joined the Communist Party, she was a member of the Komsomol and, in the late 1980s and early 1990s, one of Sepych's elected deputies to the district soviet (*raisovet*). She often spoke to me of her activities during the Soviet period in the language of socialist society work and working with people. "All my life I've led people; people are always coming to me," she told members of an archaeographical expedition in 1995.[5] In the early 1990s, people began coming to her about a new issue. They wanted to know what she could tell them about an Old Believer priest they had heard about in the nearby city.

After several such individual inquiries, Tat'iana Fëdorovna decided to put the issue to the Dëminskie old women as a group. An opportunity to do so presented itself on the first anniversary of her mother's death in 1991. She had

---

4. "Pomogite dostroit' tserkov'," *Zaria* (Vereshchagino), July 7, 1994, 4.
5. AAL MGU, Video Archive PV-95, 9.

summoned the elders to her house to offer prayers in memory of her mother, and, after the service and meal, she asked those gathered whether she should invite this priest to Sepych to see what he had to say. The consensus of the old women was affirmative, in light of the fact that the current spiritual mother was in bad health and the candidates for a replacement were hesitant. On her next trip to the city, Tat'iana Fëdorovna went to make the arrangements, standing through much of the long service at the Belokrinitsy church and approaching the priest afterward. A few weeks later, Father Vasilii came to Sepych for the first time and spoke to a standing-room-only crowd at the House of Culture. Tat'iana Fëdorovna recalled that Father Vasilii spoke "long and hard" about the history of Old Belief and about the differences between priestly and priestless Old Believers. He concluded by saying that he would be available if anyone was interested in beginning a new church community in Sepych.

After a quiet month or two had passed, several of the old women again asked Tat'iana Fëdorovna to bring Father Vasilii to Sepych. Again she invited him, and this time his impending visit stirred tremendous controversy among the old women of Sepych's Dëminskie and Maksimovskie councils of elders. In the days leading up to his arrival, arguments erupted among the elders about whether joining the new priest heralded the coming destruction or, perhaps, the long-awaited revitalization of their ancestors' faith. The nearly twenty old women who took the revitalization line met Father Vasilii at a private house. He had intended to begin baptizing converts from the Maksimovskie and Dëminskie concords, but it soon became apparent that he had forgotten the book with baptismal prayers and was forced to postpone the conversions. By the time a third visit was arranged, the group interested in forming a new priestly community had dwindled to twelve elderly women.

Priestly Old Belief's opening wedge into Sepych, then, was composed of a single medium-level former official in Soviet civil administration, acting on the wishes of a handful of uncertain old women. Although the new Sepych Old Believer Community did not begin as a project in redeployed socialist society work and visions of moral community, it rapidly became one. Starting with their own families, the elderly women talked more and more townspeople into baptisms on the occasions when the new priests visited town. They also began agitating for a church to be built. In their efforts, undertaken precisely in the years of widespread bankruptcy and demonetization, Father Vasilii and his growing flock relied heavily on allies inside and outside the town, allies without whose assistance there would have been no church. These allies were mostly former members of the Communist Party by background and personally ambivalent about Old Belief of any variety. They were, however, quite accustomed to building society and working for people, and the church appeared to them an ideal way to continue to do the work of building moral communities, although this time in a way that was distinctly non-Communist in content. Here, in other words, was a newly open domain in which to collect people, act as a khoziain, and perhaps increase the chances of one's own salvation along the way.

Sepych's local civil administration, in charge of titling property, allotted a central and very visible plot of land for the church. An abandoned merchant house and garden plot across the street were earmarked for the construction of a house for a permanent town priest when one became available for assignment. But the single most important and most visible patron of the church's building project in Sepych was the leadership of AOZT Sepych.[6] Although technically on the verge of bankruptcy during much of the period in question, AOZT Sepych nevertheless procured most of the material and labor needed for the construction of the church. As in all construction work in Sepych in the immediate postsocialist period, AOZT Sepych's near monopoly on the means of transportation meant that building materials could be transported only with commercial farm machinery and therefore at the personal behest of Andrei Petrovich.

When the head of the Vereshchagino district offered a million rubles (in inflated 1994 money) for the purchase of logs for the walls of the church structure, it was commercial farm employees and tractors that did the work. The logs were bought, already cut, from a private homebuilder, who had discovered that the new house he was building sat on unstable ground at the edge of Sepych. Commercial farm workers, partially on their own time and partially on commercial farm time (but always with commercial farm machinery) dismantled, transported, and reassembled the structure in the center of town. They extended two walls lengthwise by about a third to allow room for an altar area and completed the majority of the internal construction work, including finished woodworking, a floor, and a stove. Andrei Petrovich facilitated a deal whereby a neighboring commercial farm, in possession of its own wood-tooling shop, finished the wood used for the ceiling and walls inside the church for free. The only tasks left to the Old Believer community itself were the cupola and the iconostasis, both projects left for a religious specialist brought in from elsewhere in the Urals.

The efforts of Andrei Petrovich and others to build a church in Sepych came at least as much from the older model of socialist-style society work and associated coalition building as they did from interior stirrings of religious belief or affiliation with the Belokrinitsy church. In both cases, it was in large part irrelevant to former party members in Sepych whether or not they themselves believed in the vision, just as it had been largely irrelevant whether they believed in the lofty goals that lay behind the material'nye and moral'nye incentives to labor of the Soviet period. In both cases, they were interested in building society,

---

6. Humphrey ([1983] 1998, 488) also notes the instrumental role played by the agricultural collective in religious affairs in rural Buryatia.

8. Sepych's new church. Construction began in the early 1990s, and the church opened for services in 2000.

working for townspeople, and creating a moral community. In the process, they were also collecting obligations and burnishing their reputations.

"I built that church," Andrei Petrovich told me proudly one evening, explaining how he had organized the labor and construction process. "Why?" I asked. Because, he replied simply, there "should be" a church and a priest in Sepych, as there should be in every Russian town. Our conversation made it clear that although the church was the most recent public construction project undertaken by the farm, it fell into the same category as all the projects on which the local enterprise had embarked "for the people of Sepych" throughout the socialist and postsocialist periods. Publicly and privately, Andrei Petrovich spoke of the church in the same manner as these other projects, completed and planned: the concrete bridge over the river, the kindergarten in the middle of town featured in *Sepych Weddings*, and, he told me, a projected House of Culture to replace the current one. When I objected that in 2001 it was no longer the job of the now-privatized farm to build a House of Culture, since the socialist cultural sphere had been turned over to the local administration with broader municipalization reforms, he brushed aside my objection. "Everything is built through us," he countered, meaning the commercial farm and, more to the point, himself. Many others in Sepych took this view as well, openly placing the church alongside other acts of patronage, large and small, on Andrei Petrovich's part.

Father Vasilii himself was no exception. He once expressed his gratitude to the director for helping with the church project, comparing it in the next breath to the farm's recent acquisition of eight hundred hectares of fields—and consequent job creation—from a collapsed state farm nearby. "Andrei Petrovich helps everyone," Father Vasilii concluded. Indeed, although Father Vasilii and the Belokrinitsy had extensive fund-raising networks and made a substantial income from small businesses that produced icons, prayer ropes, and religious books, they always downplayed the role of money in their church building projects, in Sepych and elsewhere. When, for instance, Father Vasilii was interviewed about the new Old Believer church in Vereshchagino by archaeographers from Moscow in 1993, he responded as follows to a question about how he collected enough money to begin building a church in Vereshchagino:

> [Many people think that] money is necessary in order to begin some project. I would say that is entirely wrong. Why? Because when there is money, that is one type of exertion. That is, it's practically no exertion. I give you money, I pay you, we've done it, and that's it. It's not even interesting. But it's interesting when you have nothing at all, but you have the desire. When there is desire and you start to act...everything works out because there is exertion, exertion that is immediately passed on to [everyone]. We don't need any [monetary] sponsors. We don't need any easy money. We don't need them—it would be a great sin for us. [Here] everyone does what he can. One person starts to try to get something, works out a way, gets it. Another starts to get bricks, timber....Old Believers are capable people.[7]

I return in the next chapter to the significance of money—or its absence—in the building of the new church, as its role in the relationships and subjectivities enabled by the new church became a key topic of debate and dispute among members of Sepych's various religious communities. Here I want to emphasize the extent to which Father Vasilii cast himself and his community as the beneficiaries of connections and patronage ties—a common way of building churches of all denominations in the Soviet period as well—rather than direct monetary contributions.

Although most of the money collected from various sources, from Belokrinitsy publishing houses to pensions, went to compensate the commercial farm

7. AAL MGU, Video Archive 1993, 1.

for its work, it was generally agreed (and always emphasized) that much of the labor and many of the materials were provided gratis by Andrei Petrovich. Although district-level state officials did express a degree of interest, no state official in Sepych could possibly have called in enough favors or organized enough labor and transportation to build the church (nor could other state institutions, as I discuss shortly). In the building of Sepych's church of the Nativity of St. John the Forerunner, as in much else in postsocialist Sepych, the privatized farm continued to broker the important connections of the socialist era, in particular those that hinged on the personal connections and wealth in people of the director. As in relationships between households and the commercial farm, Andrei Petrovich's help for others, completed through transactions of money and labor facilitated by his vast web of connections, also increased his reputation and the townspeople's indebtedness to him.

The commercial farm's work and patronage was perhaps most in evidence and most discussed, but other highly placed townspeople in socialist-era Sepych also expended considerable effort to raise funds and labor power for the church. Tat'iana Fëdorovna explained her role in fund-raising and making contact with Father Vasilii as part of her personal attempt to make amends for the fact that she had once participated in what she considered, retrospectively, to be the desecration of a sacred building. In 1980, she had been one of the townspeople who helped remove and replace the old roof on Sepych's House of Culture—the prerevolutionary Russian Orthodox mission church. The two activities are of the same type—working with people and mobilizing them to do good for society—but, in her post-Soviet understanding, with opposite ethical valences. Building the church in the post-Soviet period could thus reverse what Tat'iana Fëdorovna now thought of as her sins in building the House of Culture, occasional home to atheist lectures and the party-sponsored rituals of State Farm Sepych.

Furthermore, although she was instrumental in bringing priestly Old Belief to Sepych and worried about her desecration of the old church, Tat'iana Fëdorovna herself (like many of those she lobbied) was ambivalent about the sort of religious practice envisioned by Father Vasilii. Like Andrei Petrovich, her goal in helping to build the church was more in the realm of working with people than in belief or practice. Tat'iana Fëdorovna did officially join the church community through baptism, but when asked if she went to church, she replied, with reference to her earlier part-time volunteer work in the library:

> I don't think I'm worthy. To go to church you have to truly [istinno] believe and...I don't know...I don't think I'm ripe yet....Maybe if I didn't work in cultur[al affairs]. We always had an atheists' corner, you know. It does pile up [over the years].[8]

8. AAL MGU, Video Archive PV-95, #9.

Tat'iana Fëdorovna did not, in other words, consider it problematic to encourage contributions to the church and to work hard herself to bring the priest to Sepych while at the same time being uncertain in her own beliefs. Indeed, her own thoughts about Old Belief more closely resembled older sets of locally significant distinctions among generations and expectations of ascetic withdrawal from the world in old age. In asserting, "I don't think I'm ripe yet," she enunciated a preference for deferred ritual practice of which her Dëminskie mother would probably have been more proud than Father Vasilii.

Ol'ga Vasil'evna, a well-respected schoolteacher and also a former member of the party-state bureaucracy, adopted a similar stance. If Tat'iana Fëdorovna rallied people to make small financial contributions to the church, Ol'ga Vasil'evna recruited the youngest workers from the school for carrying bricks, cleaning up, and other small tasks, just as she had marshaled Young Pioneers in the Soviet period. Despite this recruitment work and her own occasional attendance at the church, she was, throughout my time in Sepych, among the most insistent in reminding me that although it was certainly good for Sepych, the Belokrinitsy church was "not ours." As for herself, like her now-deceased mother and Tat'iana Fëdorovna, Ol'ga Vasil'evna told me that she might think about going more regularly after retirement, when it came time to "prepare her soul."

To Father Vasilii, this was nonsense. The church was open to anyone who was baptized, regardless of age or status in the world. The new priests—one or another of whom visited Sepych each month—inveighed against the generational distinctions and taboos on mixing the worlds that had long oriented life in the Upper Kama. Their pronouncements carried the force of a specialist, all-male, worldwide hierarchy and, as I discuss in more detail shortly, largely overwhelmed those remaining priestless elders who refused to join the church. In fact, this view of religious practice as open to everyone, rather than divided along generational lines, had something of an elective affinity with the agenda of Andrei Petrovich, Tat'iana Fëdorovna, and Ol'ga Vasil'evna. For these sponsors, building the church was a way to distance themselves from the less fondly remembered aspects of the Communist Party while at the same time seeking to shore up their leadership roles in ways quite similar to those that prevailed in the Soviet period. These were projects that could best be pursued for *all* the people of Sepych as an envisioned moral community. Why cast oneself as proud patron of a few elderly women when one could be the proud patron of a whole town?

Father Vasilii and the Belokrinitsy, then, skillfully plugged into a propitious configuration of local powers and moralizing discourses after socialism and thus created important conditions for the expansion of priestly Old Belief into Sepych. While I think it safe to say that they would not have gained traction in Sepych without these kinds of sponsorship, most of their local allies had somewhat different goals than did Father Vasilii. Whereas he was concerned to remind townspeople of their true nature as traditional priestly Old Believer Russians through the rites of baptism, the Soviet-era leaders of Sepych, still in influential positions, transformed his vision into a new way to work for the people of Sepych as a society and, in the process, to seek to define a new moral community. The framing of the church construction as society work and powerful actors' willingness to divert their resources and organizing capabilities to the project propelled the hesitant inquiries of a few old women into the baptism of nearly half the town. To be sure, townspeople's ethical sensibilities and encounters with Old Belief continued to diverge widely, as the cases of Tat'iana Fëdorovna and Ol'ga Vasil'evna begin to show. The range and direction of these encounters, however, was powerfully constrained by the broader politics of morality and community that emerged in Sepych's post-Soviet marriage of priestly Old Belief and notions of society.

ON a park bench in Perm one day, a Belokrinitsy Old Believer told me that the post-Soviet period was, as the verse from Ecclesiastes put it, "a time to gather." He used this phrase specifically to refer to the expansion of his concord of priestly Old Belief through the conversion of priestless Old Believers across the Perm region, including those in Sepych. I have shown so far that the gathering he had in mind was premised on another sort of gathering in which the Belokrinitsy were actively engaged: collecting powerful patrons and plugging into networks based on the accumulation of wealth in people. Indeed, all the church building projects that I knew the Belokrinitsy to have embarked on in the rural areas of the Urals in the 1990s were located in towns and villages where, as in Sepych, some form of privatized socialist enterprise continued to "hold together." Where state or collective farms had "gone to pieces," there were neither the labor and monetary resources nor the expectations of moral community from which the new church drew much of its strength in Sepych.

The Fate of the Maksimovskie and Dëminskie: An End to Schism?

Although the resources that the Belokrinitsy and their allies brought to bear in Sepych were powerful, they were by no means uncontested in the wide-open ethical field of the first post-Soviet decade. Maksimovskie and Dëminskie Old Believers in Sepych were descended from and, in the prerevolutionary period, often in communication with the Pomortsy Old Believer communities and groups of communities elsewhere in Russia. As discussed earlier, these connections played an important role in the early formation of the Upper Kama's ethical repertoire on matters ranging from decentralized religious authority to the possibility of marriage. Although the Soviet period had ruptured the prerevolutionary ties between Sepych and the Moscow- and Riga-based central councils of Pomortsy Old Belief, these centers rapidly became active again in the early 1990s. By the mid-1990s, the presence of the Belokrinitsy hierarchy in Sepych and the rate at which formerly priestless Old Believers were seeking baptisms in the new church attracted the attention of the Moscow-based Russian Council of the Ancient Orthodox Pomortsy Church. Ivan Vladimirovich, a representative of the council, was dispatched to the Upper Kama in 1998 to learn more about the situation and to provide aid and support to the priestless Old Believers in and around Sepych.

During his first visit to the region, I was told by elders in Sepych, Ivan Vladimirovich gave the remaining Maksimovskie and Dëminskie elders history lessons on the authenticity of priestless Old Belief and rehearsed his concord's standard arguments for the illegitimacy of the Belokrinitsy hierarchy. He prayed separately with both groups of old women and ascertained the extent to which Father Vasilii had been effective in winning new members. He also spoke at some length with Andrei Petrovich about the church building, which was nearly complete at the time (although services were still taking place in private houses). Before returning to Moscow, Ivan Vladimirovich attempted to convince the director of the important historical legacy of priestless Old Belief in Sepych and suggested the church building should be taken away from the Belokrinitsy community and given to a reunited Pomortsy community in Sepych as a house of prayer. Andrei Petrovich flatly refused.

Later that year, Ivan Vladimirovich contributed a short article entitled "Impressions from a Trip to the Upper Kama of the Perm Region" to an annual collection of documents published by his concord. The article described the state of priestless Old Belief in Sepych, in part, as follows: "[The Maksimovskie and the Dëminskie] had and now have their own lay leaders [*nastavnitsy*]. There are several, and all are old, semiliterate women who don't know the order of the service and know the history of Old Belief poorly."[9] As a result of the dismal condition of priestless Old Belief, the article went on, Father Vasilii had taken advantage of the situation and converted several hundred Pomortsy to the new Belokrinitsy church. The article described Ivan Vladimirovich's initial meetings with the membership of the Maksimovskie and Dëminskie and his efforts to convince them that the "unwritten rules" underlying their strict taboos for the separation of the worlds were unnecessary. There should be only one unified community of priestless Old Believers in Sepych, the article suggested, the better to compete with the Belokrinitsy priests.

Ivan Vladimirovich returned to Sepych the following year with the intent of following up on the previous year's meetings; this time he had marginally better luck with the remaining elders than he did with Andrei Petrovich. Members

9. "Putevye Zametki: Vpechatlenii ot Poezdki v Verkhokam'e Permskoi Oblasti," in *Izveshenie Rossiiskogo Soveta Drevlepravoslavnoi Pomorskoi Tservki* (Moscow, 1998), 31–32.

of both Maksimovskie and Dëminskie factions in Sepych agreed in principle to drop the polemics between them and form a single, united community. Ivan Vladimirovich suggested that a new pastor be chosen to head the unified council; Prokopii Daniilovich, near retirement age, was proposed at the gathering. His own background was Maksimovskie, but his wife's family was Dëminskie, and he was accepted by all factions as a compromise candidate. In the end, however, no reunification took place in Sepych. There were never any common services after the departure of Ivan Vladimirovich. Prokopii Daniilovich, the candidate for leadership of the unified group, did not immediately assume his duties, protesting in good local fashion (and to the dismay of Ivan Vladimirovich) that he needed to work for a couple more years before retiring from the world and devoting himself to the ascetic rituals of priestless Old Belief. He died before assuming his position. The remaining old women could not agree on a place to meet and, when I asked about the situation later, each group accused the other of bad faith in not inviting them for holiday services. The schism between Maksimovskie and Dëminskie, so fiery in the Upper Kama for a century and a half, was more likely to fade into irrelevance than to be healed from within, even with expert advice from the Pomortsy community in Moscow.

Many factors contributed to the failure of Ivan Vladimirovich's mission to the Upper Kama. First, he was too late. Second, he had only weak connections to Andrei Petrovich and thus could not plug into locally relevant power structures and networks. Third, Ivan Vladimirovich was not a hierarch: he had no authority other than the power of persuasion. Even his proposed reunification would have been effective only among the Maksimovskie and Dëminskie in Sepych itself; a council bringing together all the priestless communities of the Upper Kama would have been required to fully end the schism of 1866–88. The post-Soviet period was not an auspicious time to be promoting nonhierarchical religious authority, at least in the Upper Kama. Nor was it, as Ivan Vladimirovich himself told me, a good time to support women in nondomestic positions of authority. Fourth, unlike the supporters of the church, Ivan Vladimirovich articulated his position and his vision of moral community in a largely theological, doctrinal, and historical vocabulary, one that had far fewer resonances with people in Sepych than the language of society work used by Sepych's familiar Soviet-era molders of moral community. Finally, for all his authority as a representative of the center of Pomortsy Old Belief all the way from Moscow, he was not entirely in accord with the Maksimovskie and Dëminskie he spoke to. He agreed with Father Vasilii, in fact, that some of the central pillars of local ethical practice were completely unnecessary, including taboos on exchange between elders and the world and the deferral of ritual practice to the eldest generation. Although townspeople themselves had begun to reconsider and reimagine these practices, they remained too central to local sensibilities to be simply abandoned.

Old Belief as "Traditional Culture": Sepych's New Museum

Ivan Vladimirovich was not the only outsider to lend support to the Maksimovskie and Dëminskie communities in Sepych. Another source of aid came from the archaeographers and ethnographers who had first come to the Upper Kama in the late 1970s and whose personal relationships with elders, solidified by years of visits and exchanges, remained strong.[10] As a result of their ethnographic and folkloric expeditions in the 1990s, archaeographers and ethnographers were very concerned that the Belokrinitsy church had made inroads into Sepych, threatening what they had been arguing for decades was the more authentic priestless Old Believer practice of constructing austere moral communities apart from a fallen world. In addition to continuing to develop their personal connections with individual elders in the 1990s and publishing at a staggering rate (especially given the difficult financial circumstances of Russian higher education in those years), these scholars also sought to provide more generalized aid to the regeneration of priestless Old Belief in the Upper Kama. Several envisioned a museum of traditional culture in Sepych, one that would use materials collected during expeditions to educate townspeople about their true history as priestless Old Believers and their unique place in Russian national history. The museum was, in quite open and direct terms, the archaeographers' answer to the church rising in the center of town.[11]

As longtime critics of the Soviet regime, intellectuals, and urbanites, archaeographers and ethnographers did not have much time for Communist Party-inflected discourses of society work on state farms or the moral communities that rural work with people attempted to build. Their entry into Sepych's post-Soviet field of competing visions of moral community came, rather, through talk about culture and the institutions that specialized in it, particularly the Russian

---

10. The relationships between scholars and Old Believer hierarchies and central councils changed substantially in the post-Soviet period and ranged from new collaborations to new suspicions about the proper ownership of collected religious texts (see, e.g., Shcheglov 1990). Although I have no direct evidence of the connection, it seems to me almost certain that archaeographers alerted Ivan Vladimirovich to the situation in Sepych and encouraged his visits.

11. While museum workers in urban centers were retooling their expertise relatively quickly, these projects (like so many others) often lagged in the countryside, helping to generate the kinds of conflicts described here. See, for example, Dimukhametova (1999) on museums in the Perm region, and Bloch and Kendall (2004) for post-Soviet museums more broadly. The didactic elements of Sepych's new museum were most strongly supported by the veteran archaeographers and ethnographers who began their work in the 1960s and 1970s; some younger scholars I knew were working to construct more innovative, collaborative, and experimental museum spaces, although not in Sepych itself. In focusing on the museum and the efforts of an older generation of scholars, I set aside other developments in the post-Soviet relationships between younger scholars trained in archaeography and Old Believers in the Upper Kama, such as the centrality of films about the Upper Kama to the growth of Russian visual anthropology (see Aleksandrov 1998; Litvina 2001).

Ministry of Culture. Like society work and work with people, culture of various sorts carried significant resonances from the Soviet period. When they spoke of traditional culture, archaeographers and ethnographers had in mind an unbroken chain of rituals, beliefs, and social structures that extended essentially unchanged back through the centuries into prereform Russia.[12] Material objects such as books were the embodiment and best evidence for this continuity. By preserving these practices and items, priestless Old Believers in Sepych were, in this view, not only creating a special kind of Christian moral community among themselves; they were also preserving the true national identity of Russians in the process. In the Soviet period, archaeographers had sought to foster these traditions by collecting, preserving, and studying old manuscripts and by quietly supporting Old Believers when they could. They had to be careful, however, about propagating their understandings of long-term Russian traditional culture in order to avoid challenging official Marxist-Leninist historiography, which relegated such cultures to earlier phases of history.

Although official Marxist-Leninist historiography disappeared in the post-Soviet period, it was replaced by a different sort of obstacle to the archaeographers' understanding of traditional culture and their attempts to preserve and promote the moral communities of religion and nation they understood to be based on it. Townspeople in Sepych, including those in charge of the new museum, simply did not share the archaeographers' understanding of culture, with its assumptions about the authenticity of "the folk" and a chain of unbroken Russian national tradition. The concept of culture with which townspeople were most familiar bore the distinctive marks of the *Soviet* model of culture, usefully defined in Sonja Luehrmann's discussion of post-Soviet Houses of Culture as "anything that can be seen as an opposite of 'backwardness.'" (2005, 38). This brand of culture, and its allied concept of "cultural-enlightenment work" (*kul'turno-prosvetitel'naia rabota*), pointed not to traditions but to modernization, secularization, and the eradication of all that was a holdover from the past in the building of the moral communities of the socialist future. In the context of Soviet museum display, exhibiting culture meant celebrating the heroics of socialist collectives and preserving the memories of those who fought for revolution and defended the Soviet Union in World War II. These local expectations about what kinds of relationships culture embraced considerably transformed the archaeographers' plans for a museum of traditional culture in Sepych. In the end, this misconnection on the meaning and content of culture, coupled with the relatively weak post-Soviet institutions that supported the museum project, ensured that the museum of traditional culture proved an ineffective challenge to the powerful local institutions and

---

12. See the discussion in chapter 4 and see Kelly (2001), Patico (2005, 2008), Lemon (2000), and Adams (2008) for analyses of still other meanings and definitions of culture at play in Soviet and post-Soviet Russia.

discourses of society work that joined forces to build the Belokrinitsy church and reshape ethical practice in Sepych.

Sepych's museum of folk culture was one of many new or revitalized museums in Russia. As representatives from the Ministry of Culture tell the story, demand for new museums picked up in the late 1980s, but the early 1990s were years of confusion and lack of funds for culture. No one really knew what kinds of cultural events or projects were appropriate, and there was little money in any case. In the later 1990s, however, in the Perm region and elsewhere, the museum industry blossomed, with both high demand and increasing budgetary allowances for the specialist museologists called upon to design and build exhibits. The floor and exhibit plans for Sepych's new museum bear the date 1996. According to one scholarly review of the project, deeply invested in the model of culture as a domain of folk traditions, the goals of the museum should be "(1) to show in the museum the richness and distinctiveness of the folk culture created by the Russian Old Believer population over an extended period of time and (2) to promote the preservation and use of traditional agricultural, graphic, and oral forms of activity and the spiritual ethnoculture of the Russians as a whole." The second of these points, which explicitly talks about the museum as an effort to promote particular "forms of activity" and links those forms to "the [culture] of the Russians as a whole," underscores the museum as a project in encouraging the formation of linked and nested moral communities: priestless Old Belief in Sepych at the smallest level, Russian national culture at the largest level.

After the plans for the museum were developed in Perm in 1996, they were passed down to the district center, where they sat for several years as the Department of Culture searched for money and a place in Sepych to build the museum. It was 2001 by the time the project of educating townspeople in Sepych about their traditional culture finally gained some traction, funding, and a space to open a museum in Sepych. For several week-long sessions in the middle and late summer of 2001, experts from district and regional centers huddled with Sepych's museum workers to discuss which of the objects and photographs already in the collection would go into each of the display cases and what new items would need to be collected from the local population. At stake in these negotiations was the vision of Sepych as a moral community that would be represented in the town's new museum and what materials of ethics best served this purpose. In short, the gathered specialists asked one another, What aspects of Sepych's past and present serve as the best models for the relationships and communities of Sepych in the future? Significant compromises emerged as this question was debated and, later, as the materials were arranged into display cases and viewed.

First, as I have mentioned, the original plans and ideas designed at the highest level of the culture bureaucracy in Perm called entirely for a museum of priestless Old Believer traditional culture (the review mentioned above, for instance, made no reference at all to the post-1918 period). However, both the Department of Culture in the district center and the museum employees in Sepych wanted to reuse and reframe Soviet-era exhibits about the Sepych Uprising, the role of townspeople in World War II, and the successes of the local collective and state farms. This was a key element not of the archaeographers' traditional culture but of Soviet-style culture—providing young townspeople with models of the best socialist collectives in town in the aid of shaping socialist moral communities. By the time the plans had made it out of the district center, there were two separate rooms, with traditional culture in the larger one. Still later, by the time the final product was in process, budget cuts had shrunk two rooms to two halves of one room: the traditional culture of Old Belief on one side, the Soviet-style culture of revolution, war, and agriculture on the other side. In the official listing of the museum, expositions entitled "Social-Political Organization of the Town, 1917–1998" thus joined long-planned displays of "Spiritual Culture" and "Crafts" (see Dimukhametova et al., 2000, 74–75). This rearrangement was something of a victory for the local cultural representatives over the designers at the top—it embraced wider understanding of culture and Sepych's history than traditional culture permitted.

In the second relevant negotiation, the museum employees in Sepych were not as successful. While designing the religion display, the visiting specialists pointedly chose only photographs and material objects—such as the individual spoons and bowls that elders brought to services to keep their food segregated from laypeople's—that illustrated their points about priestless Old Believers. When Sepych's culture workers suggested adding at least one of several pictures of the church and some commentary about how high-ranking clerics had come to Sepych to bless it (clearly, they thought, an item worthy of note in their town museum), their suggestions were brushed aside. For at least this part of the museum, an unadulterated image of traditional culture as it was viewed by archaeographers and ethnographers prevailed.

As was the case with the link between priestly Old Belief and conceptions of society, the link between priestless Old Belief and culture in the museum was thus a hybrid of visions of Sepych as a moral community, one that was forged in a series of compromises about how to align townspeople's ethical sensibilities and practices in turbulent times. Like the church project, the visions of the museum were never fully realized and often subverted, a point aptly illustrated by the official opening of the museum in September of 2001. As it happened, the opening was scheduled for a day when Father Vasilii was to visit the church, a block away, on one of his monthly trips. On that day, in a useful illustration of the broader struggles to shape an emergent ethical regime, two carloads of outsiders concerned with Old Belief made their separate ways to Sepych. Their opinions of priestly or priestless Old Belief as the ideal moral community for townspeople rode on the different vectors of postsocialist power and discourse I have described—the local patrons of society work in

Sepych for the Belokrinitsy clergy, the Ministry of Culture's weaker and substantially diluted traditional culture for the museum specialists. The two delegations did not have any contact with each other, but the practical result was that the traditional culture supporters yielded. A key subset of townspeople was needed at both events: the elderly women of Sepych, who served as both primary attendees at the church service and a necessary element in opening any exhibit about the past. The museum opening waited for the end of the church service, and several of the old women left the church and went directly to the museum to talk about childhood memories at the invitation of one of Sepych's museum specialists.

The concerns that animated the archaeographers' project did not, in the end, transform the moral communities of post-Soviet Sepych in the ways in which they were designed. Not only was the museum on opening day considerably different from the one in the original plan, but the debates and doubts about the church that the museum's exhibits were intended to engender did not materialize, on that day or on any of the other days I visited the museum. Indeed, it was precisely the old women from the church—the very women at whom the Ministry of Culture's museum of traditional culture was targeted as a reminder—who strolled down the block to help inaugurate the museum. Ten years after the fall of socialism, the archaeographers got their museum, but they failed to stem the apparent tide away from the Maksimovskie and Dëminskie councils of elders to Sepych's new hierarchy of priestly Old Believers.

Judged against the church/society project, then, the museum/culture project had several disadvantages. As was the case for Ivan Vladimirovich, the first of these was timing. By the time the museum plans had been drawn up in 1996, the church was already well on the way to completion, and scores of townspeople had been baptized. For all their detailed knowledge about the history and practice of Old Belief in the Upper Kama, archaeographers were simply not able to respond fast enough as events unfolded in Sepych. Second, even when they did react, the fact that they needed to work through the underfunded and disorganized federal state cultural apparatus in the mid-1990s further slowed their counter to the church. The years in which these outsider scholars sought to stanch the flow of townspeople to priestly Old Belief were precisely those years in which central state power, such as that located in the Ministry of Culture, was at its ebb tide and that of local bosses like Andrei Petrovich was at its peak. Finally, the notion of traditional culture on which the museum project's vision of moral community rested was quite simply not shared by townspeople, who transformed the museum into a hybrid of traditional and Soviet cultural display. Neither of these forms of culture—one idealizing the past, one idealizing a failed vision of the future—proved very compelling to people in Sepych. In the uncertainties of the post-Soviet period, it took nearly all of the townspeople's energies to hold together some semblance of society in the present—an effort more in tune with the church than with the museum.

To summarize, I have thus far noted that multiple efforts to shape Old Belief in post-Soviet Sepych were successful to varying degrees, dependent in part on their advocates' abilities to hook their moralizing discourses into locally significant power structures. In the end, Father Vasilii was far more successful than Ivan Vladimirovich or the archaeographers, in large part because the ability of Andrei Petrovich and former party organizers to collect people and work for society trumped nearly all other vectors of power in the mid-1900s, even that of the federal state (through regional and national universities and the Ministry of Culture). This does not mean, however, that Father Vasilii was successful in fully transforming local moral communities any more than were outsiders of centuries past. Even the church's strongest proponents in town, as I have indicated, saw the church less in terms of belief or ritual than as an opportunity to shed some of the discredited aspects of their Communist Party past and, under the banner of society work, recast themselves as builders and defenders of a new kind of postsocialist moral community.

New Moral Communities, New Inequalities

Disputes about hierarchy had long characterized Old Belief in the Upper Kama. In the decades after emancipation in the 1860s, absence of religious hierarchy allowed for the rapid escalation of an apparently minor doctrinal dispute into a lasting schism between the Maksimovskie and Dëminskie. Later, in the Soviet period, this same decentralization enabled Old Believers in and around Sepych to evade many of the standard tactics of state-backed antireligious campaigns. In the post-Soviet period, the decentralized priestless communities in the Upper Kama have largely given way to the full-scale church hierarchy of the Belokrinitsy, one that centralizes decision-making processes and rests on a fundamental inequality between ordained clerics and ordinary laypeople—a kind of inequality that had been minimized in priestless Old Belief in Sepych for centuries.

As I have shown, this new brand of religious inequality in Sepych was closely associated with another kind of inequality: the redeployment of socialist patterns of patronage and networking in the post-Soviet period. After decades of marginalization and lack of funding, religious groups all over the postsocialist world needed some combination of sponsors and resources. The former Soviet officials who were most often in a position to offer these things were accustomed to—indeed, especially good at—dealing with hierarchical bureaucracies and the connections to friends in high places they could bring. In 1998, Metropolitan Alimpii, head of the Moscow-based Russian Orthodox Old Believer Church (the official name for the Belokrinitsy hierarchy) came with great fanfare to Sepych to bless and open the Church of the Nativity of St. John the Forerunner. He and his successors have since returned several times on their trips through the ever-growing number of parishes in the Urals Diocese. Andrei Petrovich has been their proud host in Sepych on most of these occasions. A connection to Father Vasilii was, in other words, also a connection to his boss, one that Andrei Petrovich did not hesitate to boast about in the same way he spoke of his other high-level contacts.

The waning of priestless Old Belief in Sepych was thus multiply caught up in new kinds of hierarchies. First, the decentralized priestless councils were being replaced by a hierarchy of clerics based far from town, and the arcane religious knowledge that was formerly the province of local elders was being subordinated to experts whose authority derived from ordination into a priesthood.[13] Second, this process was closely tied to attempts by elements of the former Communist Party leadership in Sepych to bring religion under its umbrella of patronage and society work and thereby to launder their reputations; even the Belokrinitsy found themselves subordinate to powerful patrons in Sepych and elsewhere. The priestless Old Believers of Sepych, however, were largely excluded from this new possibility of attaching themselves to powerful and effective patrons. With no hierarchy to attract those adept at negotiating bureaucracies, the remaining priestless Old Believers of the Upper Kama found themselves on the subordinate end of yet another axis of inequality. Even if not by explicit design, then, the attempts to form a new kind of moral community through an amalgamation of priestly Old Belief and society work helped to create new kinds of rankings and inequalities that shaped the ways in which Old Belief could be reclaimed, by whom, and how.

Intersecting with these hierarchical inequalities were new forms of gendered inequalities and exclusions. Indeed, when I asked about the differences between the church and the priestless councils of elders, townspeople's first line of comparison was often gender—as it was in their comparisons between AOZT Sepych and the local state administration. Believing and unbelieving townspeople alike drew a distinction between the advanced specialist knowledge of

---

13. Movements to "recover" priesthood have been common among priestless Old Believer communities around the world (e.g., Robson n.d.). Debates and disputes about recovering priests and affiliating or cooperating with Old Believer or Russian Orthodox communities with clerical hierarchies rocked the central councils of priestless Old Belief in the former Soviet world during the 1990s. For some of these disputes, which grew largely from initiatives taken by priestless communities in the Baltics to explore communion with hierarchies, see Sergei Puchugin, "Ispytanie Vremenem," 3–9; Synod of Bishops of the Russian Orthodox Church Outside of Russia, "Obrashchenie Russkoi Pravoslavnoi Zarubezhnoi Tserkvi k Staroobriadtsam," 83–84; and Sergei Puchugin, "Tserkov' i Obshchestvo: Starovery v Amerike," 108–11—all in *Staroobriadcheskii Pomorskii Tserkovnyi Kalendar' na 2001 God* (Riga: Tsentral'nyi Sovet Drevlepravoslavnoi Pomorskoi Tservki Latvii, 2001). For the response from Moscow's Council of Pomortsy communities, see "Zaiavlenie Soveta Drevlepravoslavnoi Pomorskoi Tserkvi," in *Kalendar' Drevlepravoslavnoi Tserkvi na 2001 God* (Moscow: Rossiiskii Sovet Drevlepravoslavnoi Pomorskoi Tserkvi 2001), 3–4. Although elders in Sepych were not, so far as I know, aware of these disputes or of other attempts to reclaim priesthood, Ivan Vladimirovich and Father Vasilii certainly saw themselves as part of these broader dynamics.

the male priests and a lack of any such knowledge on the part of the priestless old women. The priest was associated with order (*poriadok*) and important connections inside and outside Sepych, while the priestless old women suffered a reputation for lacking sufficient knowledge of the services and provincial irrelevance by comparison with leaders of the new church. Father Vasilii's visits always presented a through-and-through masculine face, and he usually arrived with between two and five heavily bearded assistants or visitors. Their deep voices echoed through the small church, and the old women in attendance frequently cited them as one of the reasons their prayers were better when Father Vasilii was in town.

Tat'iana Fëdorovna, the cultural affairs worker who originally brought Father Vasilii to Sepych, reflected on the priest's second visit.

> What struck me was that [Father Vasilii] arrived and with him three young men came in, all with beards—they were about thirty to forty years old. They came in and crossed themselves. And, you know, I remember before, when I was little, that people came into houses and prayed like that and I saw here, well, this was just like it used to be.... They were from Perm.[14]

The much rarer but more impressive visits of high-level clerics from Moscow were even greater displays of masculinity, as they trailed a full—entirely male—delegation from Moscow, Perm, and Vereshchagino. One schoolteacher told me, with a smile of admiration and satisfaction at her personal acquaintance with the metropolitan, that when they sang before their meal in the school cafeteria, the men nearly lifted the roof off with their deep and resonant voices. Many of the townspeople who joined the Belokrinitsy church made similar observations, linking their childhood memories of the times where male voices were still heard singing during domestic services with the recent monthly visits of clergy from the city. For those who joined him, the coming of the priest and his church had begun to transform the key distinctions of gender and generation by placing different sorts of subjects in newly hierarchical relationships to one another. They did this, in part, by replacing an older set of expectations about how to form a moral community in search of salvation—the taboos of Maksimovskie and Dëminskie elders—with a new kind of distinction that was no longer centrally about moral communities walled off from a fallen world at all.

Despite the desired presence of the male clerics, the lack of men at their own services on a regular basis was a frequent topic of lament among the women of the new Belokrinitsy parish. Many waited anxiously for the day when a young Old Believer priest would be permanently assigned to Sepych. In the absence of a priest, the day-to-day operation of the church was handled by one of the old women (although Father Vasilii remained officially in charge).

14. AAL MGU, Video Archive 1995, 9.

At a rare meeting of the full church community that I attended, Father Vasilii sought to convince one of the women to take charge of day-to-day operations at the church. Although she ultimately refused the job on the grounds of poor health, the long conversation provided Father Vasilii with a chance to elaborate his criteria for someone to head the church community: chiefly someone who was "authoritative" (*avtoritetnaia*). When I recounted the substance of this meeting to a member of the Dëminskie concord, her response was that this candidate was not authoritative but domineering (*vlastnaia*); this was one old woman, she said, the Dëminskie group was happy to see go, since the leader of a religious community should be humble and understanding, and not put herself above others.

Nevertheless, even those who defended nonhierarchical priestlessness and refused to join the church longed for men in leadership positions, particularly now that part of the job description included at least tacit competition with the priest. When I mentioned to the Dëminskie spiritual mother that there were two men who sometimes attended the services of the Maksimovskie group, she was impressed: "They're rich if they have two men. We have none." It was certainly the opinion of Ivan Vladimirovich that the priestless Old Believers in Sepych suffered not only because they were divided between Maksimovskie and Dëminskie but because women led both groups. The choice of Prokopii Daniilovich—who died before being able to assume his leadership of the combined community—was not coincidental. In both his writings and conversations with me, Ivan Vladimirovich expressed his desire that a man lead the group in its opposition to the Belokrinitsy. This criterion was even more important than being well versed in the services, it seems, for the priestless old women, whatever their state of knowledge, were certainly more familiar with the order of the service than was Prokopii Daniilovich. For only a small minority of townspeople did adherence to the priestless Old Belief of their ancestors trump the attractive trinity of masculinity, hierarchy, and connections to society work that prevailed in the most powerful and successful vision of Sepych as post-Soviet moral community. In this respect, then, Old Belief in Sepych tracks well with other observations about gender relations after the Soviet Union: while women's roles were amplified in the household sector and subsistence economy (certainly the case in Sepych), public positions increasingly sidelined women (see esp. Burawoy et al. 2000).

OLD Belief in post-Soviet Sepych was caught up in numerous ways with struggles about how to best build new moral communities amid the uncertainty and rapid transformations of the Russian countryside. These struggles, I have shown, drew on old vocabularies refashioned for new circumstances and on old capacities for action still operative in the changing present. They extended far beyond the borders of Sepych, fractured along the lines of locally relevant discourses and power structures, and, in their successes and failures, aided in the creation of some new and significant lines of inclusion and exclusion. Although these struggles over moral communities did not fully determine how particular townspeople might encounter Old Belief in their own lives, they powerfully shaped the ways in which it was possible to do so. The ethical worlds and moral communities of townspeople in post-Soviet Sepych were, in sum, substantially constrained by visions they only sometimes shared and forces they only partially controlled. In this there was nothing new about the post-Soviet period.

But the opening of the Belokrinitsy church in Sepych also reveals more than this. Sepych's new church was the post-Soviet nexus for emergent realignments and reconfigurations in the larger ethical repertoire I have been tracing from the earliest settlements of the Upper Kama. The multifaceted struggles associated with the new church reopened some very old questions and debates about what kinds of moral communities and materials of ethics properly facilitated Christian salvation. Dilemmas abounded. Younger townspeople I knew began to wonder why they were not permitted to pray in priestless councils of elders if they wished. Some elders were concerned with other matters. Was it a case of mixing the worlds for an enterprise such as AOZT Sepych to contribute money and labor to the construction of a church—as when the pastor Maksim Zhdanov amassed capital in this world and simultaneously attended to spiritual affairs in the decades after emancipation? What should the consequences be? Were the polemics between the Maksimovskie and Dëminskie about the proper renunciation of the world still justifiable and sustainable in light of new challenges from the priestly church? With another massive shift in the movements of money, food, and labor in and beyond the household, were elders' taboos on eating with laypeople or others of the world really necessary anymore?

What, in short, would come of the local practices of Christian asceticism—with all the expectations and sensibilities, techniques of self-fashioning, and communities of ethical practice—that had grown up around them for centuries?

8 *Separating Post-Soviet Worlds?*

Priestly Baptisms and Priestless Funerals

As we were sitting on the bench outside her home one evening, I asked a friend who had not joined the new church whether she was planning to summon the Dëminskie old women to pray on the upcoming anniversary of a family member's death. She replied that she was, and I asked which old women she intended to invite. We both began laughing by about the third name on her list: not one of the women was over fifty, all of them still worked, and each would have resented mightily being called an old woman. The common phrase "to summon the old women" had, in this case, outlasted many of the priestless old women themselves, so many of whom had died or joined the new church. On a separate occasion, an acquaintance commented on the omnipresence of one of these same under-fifty women on Sepych's social scene: "She drinks and swears...and she prays!" The pause and pointed chuckle with which he delivered this line highlighted the extent to which the participation of some middle-generation townspeople at priestless services transgressed earlier expectations about the importance of holding the drinking and swearing of worldly relationships apart from the ascetic rituals and prayers of elders in search of salvation.

As these humorous incongruities suggest, there were several new attendees at the Dëminskie and Maksimovskie services beginning in the 1990s: middle-aged women—and one or two men—who had been baptized in their childhoods but who had not begun to show a serious interest in matters otherworldly until the close of the Soviet period. With the decreasing number of elders and their increasingly poor health, priestless services relied more and more on the assistance of these middle-generation laypeople. Indeed, many of these new participants at the Maksimovskie and Dëminskie services found themselves in the awkward position of having quickly learned the prayers and rituals better than their now-infirm elders; townspeople sometimes called upon them to perform funeral services in place of spiritual mothers.

The assistance of a few younger, working-age townspeople at Maksimovskie and Dëminskie services was but one of many ways in which long-familiar lines between the worlds of work and prayer began to blur and, in some cases, fade altogether in the 1990s. This chapter follows these shifting ascetic boundaries in order to ask of the post-Soviet period what previous chapters asked of the postemancipation and Soviet periods: How did new patterns of accumulation and shifting circuits of exchange help to create unfamiliar dilemmas for those concerned with living a Christian life in the Old Believer Upper Kama? With what results? I have explored some of this ethical terrain in recounting the construction of the new Belokrinitsy church in Sepych. But still closer examination allows us to see that the groups of outsiders working for and against the new church in Sepych made a crucial error in assuming that townspeople's expectations about moral community and ethical subjectivity would line up along easily discernible and stable denominational lines. For all their indisputable importance in setting conditions for the new shape of Old Belief in post-Soviet Sepych, these outsiders' moralizing pronouncements and projects were—like those of the Stroganovs and Soviets before them—at best incomplete measures of townspeople's ethical dilemmas, debates, and aspirations.

Asceticism after Socialism?

The distinctive trappings of Christian asceticism in Sepych emerged in the century and a half between the arrival of Brother Grigorii in 1730 or 1731 and the local schism between Maksimovskie and Dëminskie in 1866–88. Despite all its secularizing projects, the Soviet period later sustained the possibility of making sharp distinctions between the affairs of this world and those of the other world (although elders also reformulated the precise means of extracting themselves from worldly material relations). From the 1990s on, the new circuits traced by postsocialist materials of ethics, coupled with the multifaceted conflicts between different visions of Sepych as a moral community, opened the question of asceticism anew—and perhaps more widely than at any time since the schism of the late nineteenth century. Although the ascetic practices of elders had always been heavily caught up in the shifting materialities of this world despite their best efforts to escape it, most townspeople I knew, elders among them, began to question the logic and necessity of pouring so much energy into holding the worlds apart at all.

SUPERFLUOUS TABOOS AND BROKEN FRIENDSHIPS

The idea that Christian salvation is best achieved through the all-encompassing withdrawal from the material relationships of this world was under assault from nearly all quarters in the post-Soviet Upper Kama. Not only did Father Vasilii and the traveling Pomortsy emissary Ivan Vladimirovich repeatedly dismiss the importance of the many restrictions and taboos associated with priestless elders, but even many local practitioners began to criticize the taboos intended to separate the practices of the council of elders from those of the world. Those old women who left the Maksimovskie and Dëminskie councils for the new priestly church, for instance, often followed Father Vasilii in observing that the strict taboos of the priestless councils were "superfluous" (*lishnye*) and nowhere to be found in the Scriptures. At least some of those elders who remained loyal to the Maksimovskie and Dëminskie relaxed their own restrictions as well, allowing themselves to take medicine, visit the hospital, or attend weddings. Stiff penances, once the hallmark of Maksimovskie and Dëminskie councils of elders in the Soviet period, were, by all accounts, no longer meted out with anything near the frequency or severity of earlier years.

But such explicit statements about the decline of taboos are not a complete guide to the ways in which Old Believer asceticism was discussed and debated in post-Soviet Sepych. In fact, there remained a generalized expectation that those active in religious practice of any sort should be somehow separate from worldly social relationships, especially those of food and drink. Even as they decried the old taboos as superfluous, for instance, many of the old women who had joined the new Belokrinitsy church continued their own attempts to separate themselves from other townspeople. Some even claimed to be better at this mode of constructing ethical relationships than those remaining in the Maksimovskie and Dëminskie councils. Indeed, many an old friendship among Sepych's elderly women fractured along the lines of whether or not taboos were superfluous on the road to Christian salvation and who was more effectively upholding them.

In my discussion of priestless communities in the Soviet period, I introduced two of the women who joined the Dëminskie council after years of work in socialist agriculture: Evdokia Aleksandrovna, former chair of the Sepych rural soviet, who was upbraided in reports to the Council on Religious Affairs; and Anastasia Ivanovna, whose party-member husband ferried the old women on his horse cart to pray. Revisiting these two elderly women in the post-Soviet period helps to illustrate the ways in which the new church sowed discord among former friends—discord that, even though situated in the shifting context of the post-Soviet present, took place in the language of very old accusations and debates about asceticism. On the morning of May 8, I attended Sepych's Victory Day celebration in the House of Culture, joining the town's remaining veterans, others who had lived through the Great Patriotic War years, and assorted town dignitaries for a film, short speeches, and recollections. At the subsequent meal, vodka flowed freely, and many of the veterans became quickly tipsy. Anticipating this development, I suspect, many of the older residents who were active in Sepych's three religious communities had chosen not to attend in the first place. I was surprised, however, to see Anastasia Ivanovna, who had refused to join the church and stayed with the priestless old women. She sat next to an old friend who had nominally joined the church community, although I knew she attended services very infrequently. I didn't see whether they drank with the others, but they sang war and folk songs with everyone else long after I had left. They hadn't seen each other in several years, I later learned, and each told me separately that they had thoroughly enjoyed the chance to sit, reminisce, and sing old songs.

Anastasia Ivanovna, clearly upset, also told me something else. On her way to the House of Culture, she had run into Evdokia Aleksandrovna, who was now very active in the church community and one of Father Vasilii's closest contacts in town. Evdokia Aleksandrovna had, in the middle of the road, thoroughly castigated her old acquaintance for attending a public, worldly event at which she would sit at table and drink. When I later asked her about this encounter, Evdokia Aleksandrovna repeated to me her opinion that Anastasia Ivanovna had violated her duties as a member of the Dëminskie community and an elder in Sepych. Evdokia Aleksandrovna, an avowed member of the noticeably more worldly church, was accusing one of those elders who had refused to join the church of being even more worldly than she herself had become by dropping restrictive taboos altogether.

For my purposes here, it does not matter which of these elderly women was in fact more worldly. More significant are the kinds of accusations that could convincingly be leveled against someone in a competing religious group. When Evdokia Aleksandrovna looked for a charge on which to indict Anastasia Ivanovna, it was the same accusation that had echoed around the Upper Kama over a century earlier, at the time of the schism between Maksimovskie and Dëminskie: of participating too closely in affairs of this world while occupying a position notionally focused on the other world. The effect that this accusation had on Anastasia Ivanovna demonstrates the extent to which the categories of a very old ethical repertoire remained relevant even as they were reworked for a new set of material transformations and conflicts. As much as taboos themselves might have faded for nearly all elders, talk about them was still a powerful and significant shaper of local expectations and relationships.

GENDER AND GENERATION AT THE TABLE

A second example of the ways in which new struggles over an emergent ethical regime played out in terms of very old debates also comes from eating and drinking practices. I have already discussed food and drink as materials of ethics in the context of worldly household exchanges of labor and moonshine after socialism; here I return to them in the ritually and spiritually charged contexts of elders' eating taboos. In the post-Soviet period, the ascetic practice of eating separately from laypeople after services continued among Sepych's few remaining Maksimovskie and Dëminskie elders. However, the old women who joined the church ate neither together nor separately from those who did not attend the church.[1] Nevertheless, even without the superfluous taboos, food and eating remained a significant index of power relations and increasingly hierarchical relationships for the members of the church. Indeed, the food rituals associated with religious services provide a useful example of emergent gender inequalities in and among Sepych's religious groups.

Each month, when Father Vasilii and his entourage came to Sepych, they stayed overnight between the Saturday evening prayers and baptisms and the Sunday morning liturgy. I usually attended both of these church services, standing at the back of the church with the old women. After the evening services, I was usually invited along to the house in which the visitors stayed overnight. Efrosia Viktorovna, in her mid-sixties and never married, lived alone, and her home provided an ideal place to stay with minimal disruption. After the service, the rest of the old women dispersed to their homes, while the men— Father Vasilii, his deacons and guests, and I—would go to Efrosia Viktorovna's house for dinner and conversation. We would sit at table and talk while Efrosia Viktorovna brought us course after course of food, which she would leave the church early to prepare. The food came from the church garden, from Efrosia Viktorovna's own kitchen, and from the kitchens or stores of some of the other old women associated with the church. On one occasion, Elena Pavlovna, the designated head of the church community, joined us to eat and discuss several issues that had arisen since Father Vasilii's last visit.

On these evenings, my little notebooks would fill with Father Vasilii's observations about everything from international terrorism to the theological delusions of the Russian Orthodox Church. I would in turn field questions about the United States and insist—to a skeptical audience—that I had grown accustomed to living in Sepych. Efrosia Viktorovna ate by herself, afterward sometimes sitting off to the side of the table, listening to the conversation and contributing when the topic turned to specific people or situations in Sepych. In other words, she served, sat, and talked in the same way that lay priestless Old Believers might have in deference to their elders at the table after services. After the closing prayers, around ten o'clock, Efrosia Viktorovna often excused herself to sleep at a friend's house, and I would leave the other men and go home between eleven and twelve. Another meal at Efrosia Viktorovna's house usually followed the Sunday liturgy, and the clergy would return to Vereshchagino in the early afternoon.

These eating arrangements point to a significant shift in the types of inequality and hierarchy created by the practice of Old Belief in Sepych. The serving of an all-male clergy by a single old woman had, in the new, public, and

---

1. An exception was funeral and memorial services, discussed below.

masculine-identified church, replaced the serving of the priestless elders by the younger generation in the home. In other words, for those who joined him, the coming of the priest and his church had begun to transform key distinctions of gender and generation by placing different sorts of subjects and objects in newly hierarchical relationships to one another. They did this, in part, by re-placing one set of restrictions about how to hold apart the worlds—the ascetic taboos of Maksimovskie and Dëminskie elders—with a new kind of distinction that was no longer about separating the relationships of this world from those of the other world. The very masculine, more worldly, and well-connected priests appeared in between women and the other world, at least in services held at the church.

From the perspective of the members of the new church community, as I have noted, this masculine presence was, generally, all to the good; it was one of the chief ways in which the members claimed that services in their group were more authoritative and more likely to lead to salvation than the services in the remaining priestless councils. But there also lurked a danger in this mas-culinization, for men could easily be drawn into moonshine relationships that were, even according to those who pronounced older taboos superfluous, still far too worldly for comfort. This problem occasionally arose in quite specific and practical ways for the elderly women who had joined the church. On the majority of weekends and holidays, when Father Vasilii or other clergy from out of town were not present, the old women prayed by themselves, occasion-ally joined by a young male reader (*ustavshchik*) who had recently moved to Sepych with his family and had taken a job in AOZT Sepych. The old women's conviction that their prayers were more effective on those days when this young man joined them was balanced by an equally strong distaste for his frequent drunkenness, for which they periodically drove him from church and reported him to Father Vasilii.

For the elderly women of the church, one result was an almost never-ending worry about the state of their prayers, far better with male participation, far worse when delivered with a hangover caused by too much participation in this world. Although I did not have occasion to speak to him about it directly, we can easily see the bind in which this young man was caught. On the one hand, drinking with other men was an integral part of running a household, especially when a family had recently moved to Sepych and did not have the kinship or workplace relationships of more established families. On the other hand, precisely these necessary connections undercut his standing in the new church community in which he was expected to play an important role. In other words, for all that the new church began to realign some gendered and generational configurations in Sepych, expectations about the material separa-tion of work from prayer and the dangers that arose from their inappropriate mixing remained powerful.

9. Gender and generation: priestless Old Believer elders sit at a table following a service.

MILOSTYNIA AND MONEY

I was first alerted to the shifting significance of monetary and nonmonetary transactions in Sepych's three religious communities by Leonid, a young friend who, knowing that I occasionally visited the new church, was quizzing me one evening. One of his first questions was whether those who attended the church contributed money. To my affirmative reply, he pointed out that a neighbor of his, who was at the time serving as spiritual mother for the Dëminskie council of old women, usually received only apples, eggs, or other small foodstuffs as *milostynia,* or alms, in exchange for her prayers for the deceased. In comparison with money, he pointed out to me, eggs were relatively useless. He continued: those priests probably ride around in cars and have lots of women (*baby*) as well, right? I confirmed that they did arrive for services each month in cars but confessed to having no inside information on the issue of *baby.* Leonid expressed his approval of the power of money compared with that of apples and eggs; we both knew how much easier his family's life would be if he earned enough cash in his commercial farm job to purchase a car or small tractor.

He also told me of his own recent contribution to Sepych's new church. Oleg, who lived on the other side of town, had made it known that he was accumulating scrap metal, eventually to be cast into a bell for the new church. Leonid and a few other young men had just that day given him some metal left over from the commercial farm construction brigade. In doing so, Leonid explained, they also gave over some of their many sins (*sdali grekhi*). Just as significant was what they did not do with the construction materials: turn them in for money or moonshine on the scrap-metal market. Indeed, in explaining his bell project to me later, Oleg drew an explicit contrast between those young men who brought him metal and those who chose to transform it into moonshine, at whom he shook his head in disdain. For Leonid, the priest's money meant purchasing power, mobility, and the tantalizing possibility of freedom from marital and family obligations. His neighbor's eggs and his own scrap-metal donation spoke of relationships closer to home, relations that effectively commemorated the dead and, despite the fact that he had never set foot in the church, cleansed some of his sins.

The circulation of money and its implications for the creation of certain kinds of subjects and communities was a prime topic when conversations turned to differences between—and the legitimacy of—the new Belokrinitsy church and the remaining Maksimovskie and Dëminskie councils. This was not as binary an issue as Leonid's proposed dichotomy between money and eggs seemed to suggest, for money moved in all the religious communities involved. What is significant is how this particular material of ethics was talked about, handled, and manipulated so as to downplay its relationship to worldly circuits of exchange—like those of the household sector—extending well beyond Sepych.

I begin with the Dëminskie council of elders in Sepych. Although Leonid drew specific attention to offerings of small foodstuffs to the spiritual mother and other members of the Dëminskie council in making his contrast to the church, money did, in fact, circulate among priestless Old Believers in Sepych, although in limited ways. It was often a matter of some discussion whether and how money could facilitate or inhibit the attainment of salvation for specific elders and councils of elders. During a break in one holiday service I attended, Faina Romanovna, an elderly acquaintance, explained to me the difference between two kinds of money exchanged during the service, both of which fall under the general term *milostynia*. On the table in the front of the room was a small plate with coins in it, to which everyone was expected to contribute a token amount of money. Faina Romanovna emphasized that this money goes "to God" (*k Bogu*). This money was *sobornye*, or belonging to the council of elders as a whole. It was in the control of the spiritual mother, who would use it for the purchase of candles, incense, and other necessary items, including each year's church calendar, published in Moscow or, these days, bought at cost from members of university archaeographical expeditions. In the past, this money might have been used to purchase communal service books, which would also then have belonged to the council and rotated with the office of spiritual mother or father.

Faina Romanovna contrasted this money with a second kind of money, also called milostynia, that was given to others while asking for prayers in memory of the dead or other petitions. At most gatherings of the priestless Old Believers, a mixture of money and food served as petition milostynia; some old women preferred to give only money, others only foodstuffs, still others a combination. As an attendee at the Easter service, I received around ten rubles in installments of two or three rubles, two apples, and two eggs (my standard protests that I was not "theirs" were heeded by some, ignored by others). Faina Romanovna told me that I should take the two rubles she had given me and go the next day to buy something small, candy or bread perhaps, and say prayers for the person whose name had been given to me along with the money.

Recall that a disagreement about the exchange of money for prayers and rituals played a role in the debate between an elder in Sepych and the Russian Orthodox mission priest Lukanin in the 1850s. The Old Believer argued against monetary compensation for those who performed baptisms on the grounds that souls should not be for sale, while Lukanin argued that the exchange of money did not necessarily mean that Christian souls themselves were being corrupted by the things of this world. Beginning in the 1990s, versions of these discussions were now taking place among the priestless elders themselves. Although it did not concern Faina Romanovna that she had just given me money in exchange for prayers, it greatly concerned others in the council, who on occasion argued that it was forbidden to give money as petition alms and criticized those who did. "My parents never gave money as alms," one old woman publicly asserted at a *godina*, the yearly anniversary of a death. "They don't do it over in Krivchana," observed another, referring to the Dëminskie council in one of the neighboring towns, usually regarded by the old women in Sepych as more knowledgeable about the order of the services. On another occasion, a family I knew was preparing to visit a relative's grave the next day and was listing the things they should bring. One woman commented that they had to bring alms, but it couldn't be money. Bread or fruit can serve as alms, she was adamant, but not money.

The opening of discussions—most of them congenial—about money as alms among the priestless Old Believer communities of the Upper Kama is yet another way in which understandings of how to properly separate the worlds were shifting in the post-Soviet period. As was the case in debates about money in previous centuries, however, these debates and discussions were not isolated from broader transformations in and outside town. Despite sometimes disagreeing among themselves about the proper uses of money, for example, the Dëminskie and Maksimovskie communities of Sepych were unified in their vocal opinion that the new church and its clerics were leading townspeople down the wrong path precisely because they were too closely implicated in the money economy. Those townspeople who remained faithful to priestless Old Belief often criticized the Belokrinitsy community by alleging that in the church money *did* serve as capital, reproducing itself and circulating widely and unpredictably beyond the community. One lay member of the Dëminskie group asked a group of elders and laypeople why the church needed a potato plot since the members didn't eat together after their services. Her sister, sitting next to her, commented that the church harvested the potatoes and sold them on the market, making money to finance its operations and expansion. "They're involved in business," (*oni zanimaiutsia biznesom*) she alleged pejoratively, using one of the terms people in Sepych (and in Russia more broadly) used for exploitative capitalism of the sort that destroyed rather than defended or enhanced moral communities. Both of these women were well aware of the limited ways in which money circulated in the Dëminskie group, but they drew the line at selling potatoes to make a profit rather than harvesting them to support commensality after the service, as in the priestless councils. They were accusing the new church of being too implicated in worldly circuits of exchange and accumulation to truly facilitate salvation.

These accusations aside, the circulation of money in the Belokrinitsy church was no less complex than in the priestless councils. Those potatoes from the church garden did travel far and wide, but they were never sold. The women locally in charge of the church group had hired a private tractor driver in Sepych to plow the potato field and, through a schoolteacher-patron, had recruited schoolchildren to help with the planting and harvesting. The potatoes fed the Old Believer clergy in Vereshchagino and Perm. Carloads of them were dispatched to Moscow, nearly a thousand kilometers away, where they helped enable urban church centers to keep their money for things other than provisions. On a day-to-day basis in the church community, money circulated slightly differently than in the priestless councils. Most people bought their own candles for two or three rubles at the small stand in the back of the church, lighting them and placing them in front of the icons of their choice at the front of the church. The church made a small profit each month from the sale of candles and a smaller profit from the sale of books and Old Believer newsletters, most of which were printed in typefaces far too small for their potential readership in Sepych. Collection plates did not circulate in Sepych, as they did in urban and larger Belokrinitsy communities, but there was a small box at the back of the church at which monetary contributions were accepted. The old women in charge of the community were reminded of the church's participation in larger circuits of exchange by their monthly trips to the tax office in Vereshchagino, where they paid eleven separate state taxes on the tiny amounts of money their community brought in.

While Belokrinitsy Old Believers mostly avoided public representations that they were involved in any "business," or indeed, in transactions involving money at all, they, like Leonid and the two priestless sisters in Sepych mentioned above, did not shy away from accusing others of doing so. One day I was attending a Belokrinitsy service in Sepych and noticed that the old women at the counter were selling Old Believer wall calendars for the 2002 year. Just the day before, I had bought one myself in the Sepych school cafeteria for six rubles (about fifteen cents at the time). I had noticed that the calendar was printed and distributed by the Russian Council of the Ancient Orthodox Pomortsy Church, the umbrella organization for priestless Old Believers in Russia, and it puzzled me that it was being sold in Sepych's new priestly church. When one of the visiting clergy came over to the stand, he noticed the calendar, and I waited for him to embark on a tirade against selling the calendar of the group that he was so actively engaged in converting. There was indeed a tirade, but it had nothing to do with the confessional histories that usually fired Father Vasilii. "This is for six rubles?" he exclaimed. He went on to say that he knew who distributed these calendars, and did we know how much of a profit she made on them? "She's involved in business!" he alleged. Buy them if you want, he continued, but you should have waited for the calendars from our own printing press, because we don't mark up the price, and you could have them for two or three rubles. Here, as in the accusations leveled by the priestless elders against the church, the superiority of one's own community was claimed by alleging that competitors were involved in profit making in the religious sphere. Father Vasilii took this line of argument one step further, construing the market activities of his group as service to the community—a kind of society work. In both cases, to level the accusation that someone or some community was engaged in business was analogous to suggesting that someone working in the leadership of AOZT Sepych or the local state administration was *delovoi* (entrepreneurial) rather than khoziaistvennyi. It is no surprise, then, that Father Vasilii and his parishioners played up their links to Andrei Petrovich and his nonmonetary patronage of the church whenever possible.

One of the challenges faced by religious groups after the Soviet Union was to walk a tightrope between a market reality in which they must participate if they were to survive or expand and a widespread opinion—not by any means limited to Sepych—holding that links to the other world comprised a domain of subject formation where capital should not circulate. The free circulation and reproduction of money in and beyond the moral community were often seen, in the examples I have given here, to corrupt that moral community and interfere with the possibilities for Christian salvation pursued within it. The result was that townspeople of many different social locations and religious proclivities, from Leonid to the women of the church community to the Maksimovskie and Dëminskie elders, worried about the possibilities of salvation with particular intensity when it came to money as a material of ethics.

Natasha and Misha

Thus far, I have cataloged some of the pervasive uncertainties and incongruities characteristic of Old Belief in the Upper Kama after socialism: jokes about blurring boundaries between the worlds or work and prayer; fully employed working-age women praying with councils of elders; attendants at the new church declaring the old taboos superfluous but nevertheless claiming to live a more ascetic life than Dëminskie elders; and an array of accusations and worries about money and moonshine as they crossed, perhaps threateningly, into the religious sphere. These examples begin to flesh out the ways in which the competing moralizing discourses that surrounded the arrival of the Belokrinitsy in Sepych were received into townspeople's long-running expectations about how to properly form moral communities and ethical subjects. The net result of these challenges to local ascetic practices was not a new schism—as it seems to have been in the postemancipation period of marketization and intensified worldly production—but nor was it simply mass confusion and discord. In fact, townspeople were largely in agreement with one another on a crucial distinction that went unrecognized and unappreciated by all the outsiders who vied for their loyalties: the priests of the new church were most effective for baptisms, while old women were best summoned to sing the funeral canons.

The vast majority of townspeople I knew in post-Soviet Sepych attended baptisms and funerals far more commonly than they did weekend or holiday services. Aside from society work, such as making contributions to the new church, it was in these family-centered rituals that townspeople most often encountered and made judgments about Old Belief in the post-Soviet period. To understand the place of these rituals in townspeople's new efforts to piece together ethical lives, I follow one family in town and discuss the ways in which they have navigated the dilemmas of arranging baptisms and funerals after 1991. I take the experiences of this family not as strictly representative in and of themselves but as one very common crystallization of possibilities and as a platform upon which to make a set of broader observations that link up with other elements of my analysis of the post-Soviet period. The events and decisions I discuss below illuminate the formation of different kinds of ethical subjects and moral communities at their smallest scales: in snap decisions and compromises not altogether satisfying; in worries about the right things to do and say; and, more rarely, in carefully calculated choices.

Natasha and Misha were a middle-aged couple in Sepych when I first met them in 2000. Both were originally from outlying villages in the Sepych rural administration and both had large and complex extended families. They had five children, two of whom were married, and two grandchildren. As a child, Natasha had been baptized into the Dëminskie concord by a spiritual mother in her native village; Misha had never been baptized. They did not consider themselves especially inclined toward matters otherworldly. In our conversations, Natasha wavered on the matter, volunteering on one occasion that "I'm really not much of a believer" and on another, "I suppose, in my soul, I do believe." When one of the representatives of the new church encouraged her to begin attending services, her response, as so often in Sepych, rested not on a rejection of religion but on deferred practice: "I'm not ready yet."

Misha, quite typically for men in late Soviet and post-Soviet Sepych, and in light of the gendered distinctions I have discussed, was even less inclined to concern himself with relationships with the other world than was Natasha. During preparations for the funeral I discuss in some detail below, for instance, the Dëminskie old women asked Misha to put up an icon shelf in the living room of the house. The spiritual mother told him it was too high—she couldn't reach it to place the icons or light the candles. "You'll have to teach me the order of the service [ustav]," Misha replied while lowering it, "I don't know anything." She responded, "Your mother should have taught you," to which Misha answered matter-of-factly, with neither regret nor pride, "I was born at the wrong time." Despite their own skepticism with respect to religious belief and practice and the antireligious times in which they were born, Natasha and Misha have, since 1991, nevertheless been confronted with questions of proper baptism for themselves, their children, and their grandchildren. They have also arranged funerals for deceased relatives.

Baptisms: Between Social Reproduction and Risk Reduction

As former officials in State Farm Sepych—Misha even made a cameo appearance in the film *Sepych Weddings*—it would have been somewhat tricky, although certainly possible, for Natasha and Misha to have had their children baptized in the late Soviet period. If they considered the option at all, they decided against baptism. Since 1991, however, Natasha has twice decided to bring members of her family to one of the new priests of the Belokrinitsy hierarchy: in the mid-1990s to baptize all five children and again in the summer of 2002 to baptize a grandchild. The reasons and negotiations behind her decisions about these baptisms do not line up well with what Father Vasilii might have hoped, but they do speak to the expectations about ethical practice and social reproduction that Natasha and Misha valued most. They also provide a window onto some of the most recent reorganizations within townspeople's ethical repertoire.

BAPTISM AND SOCIAL REPRODUCTION

Although some individual baptisms into the new church community took place during the monthly visits of the Belokrinitsy clergy, most were scheduled for July, when it was warm enough to permit immersions outside, in a small tributary of the river Sepych. The elderly women of the church community announced these mass summer baptisms well in advance, both by word of mouth and by hanging small handwritten notices in Sepych's public spaces. On some of these occasions, twenty or twenty-five people of all ages would present themselves for baptism. Along with family and friends there to watch, the crowd around the small baptismal pool on the outskirts of town could easily grow to a hundred people.[2]

Whatever the time of year and the circumstances, townspeople in Sepych officially joined the new Belokrinitsy church by one of three slightly different ritual routes: by baptism (*kreshchenie*—if they had never been baptized a Christian), by rebaptism (*perekreshchenie*—if they had been baptized into the Russian Orthodox Church or another Christian denomination), or by having their baptisms "finished" (*dokreshchenie*—if they had been baptized as a priestless Old Believer). Father Vasilii or one of his designees decided which of these three rituals variations—explained in more detail below—was appropriate during the service itself, as they ascertained the backgrounds of each of those presenting themselves for baptism, their parents, and the proposed godparents. One result of this procedure was that the baptism of one person into the Belokrinitsy church often turned into the baptism of many more by the conclusion of the service.

One Saturday afternoon, I went to the church to observe a baptism that had been hastily arranged for a young child. With the child were both of his parents and also a male friend of the father's to act as godparent. Father Vasilii began the service by asking who would answer for the child, since the child could not answer the baptismal questions for himself. The mother replied that she would. He then asked whether she had been baptized; when she replied that she had been, he interrogated her as to when and by whom. After some discussion, it became apparent that, although she had been born in Sepych, she had been baptized in the 1970s in a church in Uzbekistan, where her family lived at the time. Father Vasilii told her that it could not have been an Old Believer church (since there were none in Uzbekistan at that time) and that she must therefore be Russian Orthodox. She did not object to his conclusion. Father Vasilii then informed her that she could not properly answer the baptismal questions on behalf of her son while she herself was a member of a different religious denomination. She would therefore have to be rebaptized. She readily agreed, and the service continued until the point at which the godfather was asked to participate. The priest asked him whether he had been baptized, and he replied that he was originally from Sepych and a Dëminskie spiritual mother had baptized him in the river. Father Vasilii said that he could not be the godfather and instruct the child to grow up according to the teachings of the church without having his priestless baptism finished and joining the Belokrinitsy church. He agreed as well, and the service again resumed, with Father Vasilii performing the appropriate rituals for each of the three new members of his church. One new member of the Belokrinitsy church had become three in less

---

2. On baptisms among Old Believers in the Urals more broadly, see Listova (1992).

than fifteen minutes. On occasions when more than one baptism had originally been planned, the number sometimes increased dramatically during the course of the service.

Baptism was not, then, always a matter of careful, calculated choice about affiliation or the ritual formulation of relationships; as often as not, it was a matter of unanticipated choices and hasty decisions made under pressure and in the midst of the service. This was certainly the case for Natasha when she decided to bring her own children to the church for baptism in the mid-1990s. She recalled that Father Vasilii reached the part of the service where he usually ascertained that those who had brought the candidates for baptism were also part of the Belokrinitsy community. He asked Natasha whether she had been baptized by a priestless spiritual mother. It was apparent from the questioning of others in line for baptism that day that if she replied honestly in the affirmative, she would be required to have that baptism finished or else her children would not be baptized. Weighing her options on the fly, Natasha opted for deception and said that she had already been baptized into the Belokrinitsy church. With the large crowd in attendance, the priest did not press her on the issue, and the service continued. Her children were baptized without further delay.

Before analyzing in more detail Natasha's decision to lie to the priest, it is useful to consider her thinking on a subsequent baptismal conundrum presented by the addition of a grandson to her family several years later. With her son already baptized into the Belokrinitsy church, Natasha wanted very much for his family to be all of the same faith, so she lobbied for both her daughter-in-law (who had never been baptized) and her new grandson to sign up for baptisms in the church. The child's other grandparents had moved to Sepych in the 1980s and had long ago been baptized into the Russian Orthodox Church, although they were no more inclined to think about matters of salvation than were Natasha and Misha. The other grandmother hoped, although rather more quietly than Natasha, that when her daughter and grandson did get baptized, it would be into the Russian Orthodox Church. Periodic discussions between the grandmothers postponed the baptisms for several months, but in the end Natasha prevailed, largely on the grounds that her son had already been baptized into the Belokrinitsy church and that there was simply no Russian Orthodox Church in Sepych. Eventually, with both families in attendance at the outdoor location for the Belokrinitsy priests' summer baptisms, both Natasha's daughter-in-law and her young grandson were baptized.

Natasha's navigation of the complicated field of baptism in post-Soviet Sepych demonstrates several points about the formation of different kinds of ethical relationships and subjects in the field of Old Belief. To begin with, it is notable that these decisions were largely made by Natasha herself rather than in consultation with Misha (who himself remained unbaptized). Despite the more general remasculinization of religion in Sepych, then, judgments about this key vector of social reproduction have remained, as in the Soviet period,

10. A crowd gathers for an outdoor priestly baptism.

largely in women's domain. Indeed, it is significant that Natasha understood her decisions about baptisms in the post-Soviet period as matters of family connection and social reproduction. She was not especially concerned with theological or doctrinal distinctions among the various specialists. This is a far cry from the postemancipation period, when Maksimovskie and Dëminskie elders marked their final split by declaring each other's rituals of baptism invalid. In those days, baptismal affiliation with one or another group mattered a great deal more for a range of social and community-level interactions among the newly emancipated peasants of the Upper Kama. In the post-Soviet period, by contrast, Natasha could make her decisions about baptism without worrying about any consequences for her other relationships in town. In fact, as I discuss in the next section, the priestless old women of the Dëminskie council were more than happy to pray at a funeral Natasha and Misha arranged.

Baptism, it is evident, appeared for Natasha above all as a matter of social reproduction that sustains and creates connections among generations within a family. She explained her deception of the priest by telling me that even though she did not know precisely who had baptized her in the 1950s, that spiritual mother had "taken on a responsibility for my soul," one that she "did not have the right" to abrogate by joining the Belokrinitsy church. Similarly, she wanted her son's family to be baptized into the same religious community. Even though her son's mother-in-law hoped that the whole family would be baptized into the Russian Orthodox Church, the two grandmothers agreed on the underlying principle that families should, to the extent possible, be united in their baptisms. Natasha's clever deception even allowed her to bridge the gaps between her Dëminskie heritage and her son's new affiliation with the priests. On the one hand, she refused the option of having her baptism finished and thus did not break the links she felt with the spiritual mother who had baptized her. On the other hand, she was permitted to participate fully in the church rituals for her children under the guise of already being a member of the Belokrinitsy church, thus establishing a similar link with the next generation. To the extent that there was a difference between the older baptismal practices and the new church baptisms in Sepych, Natasha worked hard to emphasize the maintenance of intergenerational family connections rather than their rupture or difference across generations. Through decisions like Natasha's, intergenerational social reproduction through the rites of baptism continued in the Upper Kama, even if it was now partially routed through a fundamentally new religious community and even if it no longer carried the same significance for social relationships.

CONVERSION?

The ritual of dokreshchenie, which Natasha faced and ducked, deserves special attention, for around it swirled many of the disputes about shifting denominational loyalties in the context of family—and Sepych's—history. From a procedural standpoint, this ritual involved the same steps as the standard baptism or rebaptism ritual, except it did not require triple immersion in the river or, at other times in the year, in the large basin that served as baptismal font in the church. Dokreshchenie was explained to me by the Belokrinitsy clergy as follows: a priestless Old Believer pastor can baptize children in the river, but she does not know all the right prayers and does not anoint the baptized with oil. This kind of baptism must be finished or concluded (*zaversheno*) by a Belokrinitsy priest in order for the person to become a true Christian. Dokreshchenie was, in other words, something of a compromise ritual, exclusively for priestless Old Believers who were less distant from the true Christian faith than were members of the Russian Orthodox Church or other Christian denominations. Although townspeople I knew paid little attention to the precise symbolism of the various rituals involved, the terminological distinction between different kinds of baptism enabled Father Vasilii and his supporters to assert that they were not *re*baptizing or *converting* the priestless Old Believers who came to them. They were simply completing baptisms already begun, often decades earlier, but not properly concluded.[3]

3. The theological reasoning behind dokreshchenie—never explained to me or, so far as I know, to townspeople—has to do with the classification of different kinds and levels of schism and

The option of dokreshchenie was directed precisely at Natasha's dilemma about whether or not to remain faithful to the childhood relationships and obligations into which she had been baptized. Although she deceived the priest because she believed that concluding her baptism would violate those bonds, it was the judgment of many others—most notably the twelve respected old women who were the original members of the Belokrinitsy church in Sepych—that it would not. Dokreshchenie allowed those who chose it to argue that they had not been rebaptized or converted at all and that therefore their own strongly felt connections to parents, ancestors, or original baptism had *not* been broken. In one of my early interviews about the arrival of Father Vasilii, for instance, I attempted to get a better understanding about the differences between the new church and the councils of priestless elders by asking a series of comparative questions. My interlocutor—one of the first women to join the church—reduced me to puzzled silence by repeatedly insisting that there were no differences whatsoever between the priestless faith of her ancestors and the new church in the center of town. In the many years of persecution extending back into the pre-Soviet past, she said, it was simply not possible to have a proper priest or church. That situation could now be reversed, baptisms concluded, churches built, and a truer path to salvation followed.

Those townspeople who remained in the priestless councils of elders countered that of course dokreshchenie really *was* rebaptism, and that, in the words of one elder, "everyone knows" it is a great sin to be rebaptized. From this point of view, the priest's habitual midservice additions to the roster of baptisms for the day were deceptive and predatory. More than one friend told me to be on my guard when talking to him lest I suddenly find myself agreeing to baptism. I heard these sentiments with a good deal of frequency from those critical of the church, even from those townspeople who were otherwise not very articulate or discerning in matters of properly orchestrating this-worldly and otherworldly relationships. One afternoon, for instance, I ran into an almost perpetually drunk acquaintance in the middle of the street near the church. With no invitation from me, he launched into a meandering story about how he had learned that the priest had tricked him into getting baptized into the church along with his young children. He had later found out from his father what he himself had suspected all along: that if you didn't know precisely who had baptized you and when, this didn't make your baptism invalid (as, according to him, the priest said it did). One Dëminskie woman, privately accusing the priest of deception and those who went over to him of ignorance, singled out Efrosia Viktorovna to me and said, "She should know better [than

---

heresy within Eastern Orthodox Christianity. That is, priestless Old Believers were considered theologically and doctrinally close enough to the Belokrinitsy church not to warrant full baptisms. Dokreshchenie was not a post-Soviet invention; it was offered to priestless Old Believers in Russia in earlier centuries as well (see Smirnov 1909, 214–15).

to be rebaptized], her mother was a true [*istinnaia*] Old Believer." The ritual of dokreshchenie, however, allowed Efrosia Viktorovna to claim that she had remained entirely faithful to her mother, her grandmother, and earlier generations. The frequent use of dokreshchenie is, then, a measure of the strength of Sepych's intergenerational kinship and baptismal bonds of social reproduction. For all the significant powers arrayed behind the church, it would not have had the success it did in recruiting the priestless Old Believers of Sepych unless its initiation rituals had provided a way in which those who felt the tug of existing ancestral ties could plausibly claim that joining the church was not conversion after all.[4] As in earlier periods in the Eastern Christian Upper Kama, conversion poorly captures the processes of religious transformation at both the community and personal levels.

BAPTISM AS INSURANCE

I have established that Natasha thought of baptism primarily in terms of intergenerational family connections concretized in rituals and only secondarily as a matter of securing salvation or of denominational loyalty. Why, then, bring her children to the Belokrinitsy priests and not to the Dëminskie spiritual mother, where there would have been no question whatsoever of continuity of baptism across the generations? Natasha was no exception to others in town in answering this question by talking about rituals of baptism as a way of receiving a guardian angel and thus becoming "protected." I was told over and over again, by Natasha and many others, that "a baptized person is a protected person" (*kreshchenyi chelovek—zashchityi chelovek*). "Protected from what?" I often asked. Disease, other physical ailments, lightning, and early death were some of the answers I received from people of all ages, both those who brought their children to the priest and those fewer and fewer who chose one or another spiritual mother. A grandmother who was bringing her grandchild to the Dëminskie spiritual mother for baptism told me that she had chosen the spiritual mother only because she was afraid the child was sick and wanted him baptized as soon as possible, before the priest came to town.[5] Although the visiting specialists of the Belokrinitsy church preferred to see baptism first in terms of religious affiliation and then in terms of the protection afforded by a guardian angel, townspeople often prioritized these relationships differently.

For Natasha and others in Sepych, part of effective protection lay in the sense that the rituals of baptism had been performed correctly, completely,

---

4. Pelkmans (2006, 149) also describes a post-Soviet context in which talk of conversion was downplayed in order to emphasize continuity with the past.

5. These comments track well with observations about the importance of acquiring some sort of spiritual or magical protection elsewhere in Russia (Lindquist 2006; Margaret Paxson, personal communication).

and expertly. Indeed, efficacy was often the context in which people decided to approach the priest rather than a spiritual mother for baptism. Even those townspeople who strongly defended the priestless groups in other situations were doubtful about the effectiveness of their rituals of baptism, performed as they were by elderly and often ailing women who constantly discussed and debated the order of the service among themselves. I heard one day from Irina, a sometime lay attendee at the Dëminskie services, that the spiritual mother of the Dëminskie concord had just returned from one of Sepych's outlying villages, where she had baptized fourteen people. I registered some surprise and said that I thought most people were choosing to go to the church for baptism these days. No, she told me, not everyone went to the priest, but more and more certainly would if priestless baptisms continued to play out the way this one had. She recounted that the spiritual mother had not explained any of the taboos associated with priestless baptism and had quite likely not said all the prayers correctly, and that mass confusion reigned by the side of the river. Those who had summoned the spiritual mother were, Irina reported to me, worried that the baptisms were not going to be as effective as they should have been. Most in Sepych, including Natasha, had already decided that the priests, with their self-assured deliveries and practiced orchestration of the baptismal rituals, provided more effective baptisms when it came to the crucial element of protection.

Choices about baptism, then, were caught up in the broader remasculinization of Old Belief and the Belokrinitsy priests' efforts to portray the Maksimovskie and Dëminskie spiritual mothers as incompetent. More than this, though, all the talk of baptism as protection and the new church as the best place to acquire protection was yet another way in which townspeople sought to place themselves under the aegis of Andrei Petrovich in their fervent pursuit of this-worldly risk reduction. As I discussed in detail in previous chapters, townspeople repeatedly looked to AOZT Sepych for forms of insurance—from loans to payroll deductions to occasional theft—against the turbulence and soaring risks of the growing household sector. Andrei Petrovich, likewise, repeatedly cast himself as chief guardian of AOZT Sepych and on occasion of the whole area surrounding Sepych as a moral community. He had contributed commercial farm labor time and resources to the construction of the church in the first place precisely in order to facilitate the emergence of this new moral community.

To put all of this another way: How is stealing from the commercial farm like getting your child baptized by a priest? The answer is that both were forms of this-worldly risk reduction made possible by the circulation of rights, obligations, and materials of ethics through AOZT Sepych. Both were thus harder to accomplish in neighboring towns where the former socialist enterprises had disbanded entirely. In those areas, at least in the Vereshchagino district, there was neither a communal place from which to steal nor a church where one might go to seek the protection afforded by the rites of baptism. There was, moreover, precedent for the intervention of the local agricultural enterprise in life-cycle rituals: the signature markers of the famous worldly moral communities of the late socialist period were, after all, the wedding festivals of State Farm Sepych. Although Andrei Petrovich did not, of course, preside at baptisms in the way he had at Sepych's once-plentiful folk-socialist weddings, the new church was still closely associated with his patronage, especially in its early years.

Edward LiPuma and Benjamin Lee conclude their study of the recent globalization of risk by observing that those who live outside the Euro-American metropole have yet to find a way to hedge effectively against the all-encompassing power of global finance capital (2004, 189). On the basis of their experiences in the turbulent 1990s and early part of the next decade in rural Russia, where taking on risk led to ruin far more often than to reward, the townspeople of Sepych might well have agreed with LiPuma and Lee's bleak assessment. Yet this portrayal is only true in a strictly economic sense. There remained a range of social, communal, and ritual ways in which townspeople could seek to defend against and reduce the pervasive and global-scale risks of the postsocialist period. Nearly all these strategies relied in one way or another on the local commercial farm as guarantor of the relationships that made for a community of ethical practice and the subjects constituting it. Baptism was, in other words, one part of the balanced risk portfolio offered with the aid of AOZT Sepych.

In previous eras, such close proximity of Old Believer ritual and worldly affairs would likely have been understood as an inappropriate mixing of the worlds, a conflation of what must be held separate at the risk of imperiling salvation. This was no longer the case in post-Soviet Sepych, where the close links between the quite worldly AOZT Sepych and the new church were precisely what fed the widespread perception that church baptisms were more efficacious in providing much-needed protection. For most in Sepych, to be adequately and correctly protected in this world was much more important than to have chosen the correct religious group for baptism. In the risk-filled environment of the postsocialist period, most townspeople judged the new priests, with their more powerful worldly connections and association with the moral community of AOZT Sepych, to be more effective at providing baptismal protections than the remaining priestless women. To the extent that aspirations for sharp lines of separation between different worlds remained in post-Soviet Sepych at all, they were to be found at the uncertain and besieged borders of AOZT Sepych as a moral community. They aimed to separate the defensive and risk-reducing strategies—now both worldly *and* otherworldly—of those within from the unfamiliar forces of global circulation and devaluation swirling outside. There was, however, one telling exception to this rearrangement of the ascetic sensibilities of earlier eras. If the new priests and their more effective rituals had come to dominate baptisms, Sepych's old women, and along with them an older set of expectations about the separation of the worlds, held unambiguous sway at funerals and rites of commemoration. Natasha and Misha again serve as guides.

Funerals: Separating the Worlds

It was in the late and already chilly fall that Aleksandr, an elderly relation of Misha's, died. On the scale of deaths in Sepych, Aleksandr's was not particularly notable and not excessively grieved; he had no remaining immediate family of his own and had been ill for some time. In his last months, Natasha and Misha had taken him into their home in the center of town, since they were somewhat better able to afford it than were other family members. He died there in his small bedroom. No invitations to the funeral were necessary, as word of his death, like that of all deaths in Sepych, spread rapidly through town. Family members, others who knew Aleksandr, and Natasha and Misha's close friends knew enough to come to their house early Thursday afternoon, on the third day after Aleksandr's death. Natasha and Misha spent most of the time between Tuesday and Thursday preparing for the funeral and the various categories of visitors for whom they would be providing hospitality. In making the arrangements, their primary concern, Natasha told me, was to do things "the right way" so that Aleksandr would not be insulted and would be properly sent off to the other world (compare Paxson 2005, 191–211).[6]

Between Tuesday evening and Thursday morning, both Natasha and Misha spent a good deal of time consulting with friends about what kinds of preparations and service would be most appropriate. This was not a process that unfolded smoothly or intuitively for either of them; at one point, just before the funeral service finally began on Thursday, Natasha whispered to me nervously that this was the first time they had arranged a funeral and they did not quite know what to do. The stakes, however, were high, for questions of otherworldly salvation pressed most obviously upon the living in the days immediately after a death.

In preparing for the funeral, the first set of tasks fell to Misha, as they involved making arrangements with men outside the household. On Tuesday afternoon, he had summoned a carpenter to measure the body; by early evening he had arrived home with a simple wooden coffin and a cross. Several female relatives who had begun to gather washed Aleksandr's body, dressed him in white, and set him in the coffin. Until the funeral service, the coffin would rest,

---

6. On funerals and death rituals in the Old Believer Upper Kama, see also Kremlëva (1992), Kulikova (2001), and Makarov (2001). On death and its management in postsocialist times more broadly, see also Verdery (1999).

closed, across two stools in the room where Aleksandr died. Misha and his brother removed Aleksandr's bedding and clothes from his room and burned them outside. While Misha attended to the coffin and the body, Natasha began considering what sort of funeral would be appropriate. Her first thought was simply to host a lay funeral, attended only by family and friends, since Aleksandr had had nothing to do with any of Sepych's religious groups. Indeed, since there was considerable doubt about whether he had been baptized in the first place, Natasha thought at first that there was really no need to summon the old women or do things the way one did for the elders (*po-starikovskii*). Eventually, however, she changed her mind. By Tuesday evening she had decided to summon the Dëminskie old women to pray the funeral canons at their house on Thursday. In the evening, while Misha went to recruit gravediggers, Natasha set out to invite the Dëminskie old women.

The range of death rituals in Sepych included the funeral services themselves, held on the third day after death, as well as nine- and forty-day commemorations (a nine-day mourning period is common in many Christian contexts; in Eastern Christianity, the soul is believed to depart for the other world on the fortieth day). Thereafter, families might commemorate the anniversary of a death (*godina*) each year, often with trips to the cemetery; most families also visited the cemetery on Trinity Sunday in May.[7] The extent to which families participated in these rituals varied a good deal, as did the participation of Sepych's three religious groups. At one end of the spectrum, at least one death while I was in Sepych brought no representatives of any religious community at all. The family sat and drank for the three days between death and burial. Other families asked a member or two of one of the Old Believer groups to come and recite prayers, dispensing with the full rituals of the council of old women. At the other end of the spectrum, the death of an elderly and respected member of one of the priestless communities brought old women from the councils of several neighboring villages and towns. Similarly, some families might ask for the old women's prayers on the nine- and forty-day commemorations and on the yearly commemoration for several years following a death. Others went to the cemetery only on Trinity Sunday.

In the postsocialist period, it was almost universally Sepych's old women, in the priestless *as well as* priestly communities of Old Believers, who handled matters of death and transition to another world. In these cases, by contrast with the rituals of baptism, the spiritual mothers of the priestless groups were summoned no less frequently than old women of the Belokrinitsy community. There were several reasons for this, the most elementary being that funerals cannot be timed in the same way that baptisms can and the priest was not always available. To rest analysis at this point would, however, be a

---

7. In older times, I was told, there were often twenty-day and half-year commemorations as well.

very reductive explanation of the field of subject-forming relationships related to baptisms and funerals in Sepych. Only those who had officially joined the church community were entitled to Belokrinitsy funerals; in matters of doubt (like Aleksandr's) or lack of baptism, the spiritual mothers could be reliably summoned. Moreover, all funeral services, whether Belokrinitsy, Maksimovskie, or Dëminskie, took place in private homes. Although the officially published guidelines of the Belokrinitsy church envision funeral services without a priest only in the extreme circumstances when a priest cannot be called, as of 2004 there had yet to be a funeral led by a priest in Sepych, either at home or in the church. Indeed, priestless Old Belief in the Upper Kama had long been more concerned with death rituals than had priestly Old Belief, to the extent that preparing the clothes in which one would be buried was a condition of entrance into the council of elders.

In talking to families who arranged funerals, it became clear to me that it was at least as important that old women be summoned for a funeral as that any particular women be summoned. Although families did in general attempt to match the group of old women they invited with the deceased's baptismal affiliation, no one ever questioned the expertise of the old women in sending off the dead in the way that was so common in discussions of baptism. On the contrary, they were the ritual practitioners of choice for sending off people to hoped-for salvation in the other world. Even the elderly women of the new church community functioned almost as another priestless council when it came to funerals. All these groups of old women were—or at least were usually thought to be—practitioners of taboos and restrictions that kept them apart from the relationships of worldly exchange that the Belokrinitsy priests were so skilled at manipulating. This withdrawal made them ideal conduits for accomplishing effectively what townspeople understood to be the purpose of funeral services: sending the dead off to the other world. In the realm of funerals, when questions of salvation were closest at hand, older ascetic ideals about the separation of the worlds remained operative. To show how this was the case and with what consequences, I first describe the course of events on the day of Aleksandr's funeral and then analyze the sets of relations and distinctions about different kinds of subjects that emerged from them.

I was at Natasha and Misha's house early on Thursday morning, helping to prepare for the funeral. The evening before, Misha had burned Aleksandr's name and dates of birth and death into the small square of wood above the central bar on the eight-pointed Orthodox cross he had commissioned. He had also, after consulting with a friend, removed and repositioned one of the three crossbars, which they had determined (by comparing it with icons) to be tilting in the wrong direction. When I arrived in the morning, the cross rested against the wall outside the house, waiting for the trip to the cemetery. Two of Natasha's friends were already there. They were beginning to prepare food and appropriate items of alms for three groups: the gravediggers, the Dëminskie elders, and the family and friends who would arrive in the afternoon. There was a good deal of debate in the family about what to give the old women who had come for the service. They consulted on this matter with one of their friends, whose parents had been active priestless Old Believers and who knew how to arrange a funeral. The answer they arrived at collectively was to give the women a small amount of money but to hide it in newly purchased head scarves (socks were used on other occasions, and handkerchiefs were substituted for head scarves on the rare occasion that men were present). "They take money?" I asked in surprise as I helped stash ten-ruble notes in newly purchased scarves. "Yes," was the reply, "only like this, so it can't been seen."[8]

The six gravediggers recruited by Misha arrived by eight in the morning. None of them were agnatic kin, who were prohibited from touching the coffin or any of the instruments of burial. The gravediggers gathered gruffly around the table downstairs, in the kitchen. Natasha served them soup, meat, and moonshine; they pointedly refused separate shot glasses for their drink, preferring to pass a single glass in a circle among them. When they had finished eating, we carried Aleksandr's coffin—still covered at this point—from his bedroom to the main living room, where we placed it across a pair of stools to await the old women's instructions. Natasha packed more meat and moonshine for the gravediggers to take with them, and Misha drove them to the cemetery on his tractor, to a spot near family members that he and his brother had chosen the day before.

Misha returned shortly, and we began to prepare for the arrival of the Dëminskie old women. We moved a table to the living room for their service books, Misha set to work building an icon shelf in the corner of the room, and one of Natasha and Misha's daughters covered all the mirrors and the television with spare sheets. Cooked on the small electric stove only—the more capacious wood-burning stove had not been heated for two days for the pragmatic reason that there was a dead body in the house—two separate caches of food grew steadily in the kitchen, one for the old women and a much wider variety for the remainder of the guests and family. When she had invited the Dëminskie spiritual mother on Tuesday evening, Natasha had explicitly asked about the food preparation and was told (to her great relief) that she could use the same stove and the same pots and pans to cook the two sets of food, as long as the old women's portions were kept separate from everyone else's after preparation. ("It's not as though you're all pagans!" the Dëminskie spiritual mother had teasingly reassured her.)

Misha had sent a car for the three old women and they arrived on time at ten o'clock, accompanied by a couple of younger lay Dëminskie adherents who were friends of Natasha's. The women readied themselves for the funeral

---

8. See also Pesmen's discussion of similar hidings of money (2000, 131) and Lemon (1998).

service in the living room upstairs, while food preparation and conversation continued downstairs. One of Natasha and Misha's daughters and I shuttled back and forth between the two groups, ferrying requests from the women to those downstairs and questions about the propriety of the menu to the women upstairs. Eventually, the spiritual mother asked us to remove the lid from the coffin, affixed candles to its four sides, placed a small metal icon on Aleksandr's chest, and uncovered his face. She got out her service books and began the lengthy discussion of which prayers and canons the elders would sing. Most of the upstairs preparation, as indeed the entire service, went unnoticed by those in the kitchen. Some of the family and friends arriving to help with the food made quick detours upstairs to bid farewell to Aleksandr, bowing three times at the corner of his coffin. But when the old women prayed, they prayed alone, assisted at times by one of their younger lay attendees.

The Dëminskie elders prayed for just over two hours, singing and reading the funeral canons, while the rest of us talked quietly and cooked in the kitchen below them. When the service ended, the old women closed the coffin, fished from their bags the dishes and spoons each had brought separately, and sat at table to be served by their hosts. We brought their plates of food upstairs from the kitchen to the living room, leaving them on a small table next to the larger one at which they sat. Natasha was suddenly shy and uncertain, and it was one of her friends who officially invited the old women to eat. She began filling their bowls one by one from the plates at the side table. They ate heartily, and one of the younger laywomen who prayed with them endured the usual light-hearted teasing about whether or not she qualified as an old woman. As the old women finished eating, Natasha distributed the new head-scarves, ten-ruble notes invisible inside. The old women gathered their things and were driven home. They did not accompany the coffin to the cemetery with the rest of us.

By one o'clock, the third group of guests—more distant family and friends—began to arrive in force at Natasha and Misha's. We rearranged chairs and extended the living-room table to accommodate the twenty or so new arrivals, who sat and ate across from the coffin while everyone filtered in. It was not long before a tractor with a large cart in tow, for which Misha had arranged through a friend, arrived to bring all of us and the coffin to the cemetery. Misha deputized me and several other nonrelatives to carry Aleksandr's coffin outside and place it in the center of the cart. The guests crowded into seats on improvised benches around the sides. We stood the large wooden cross bearing Aleksandr's name in the front of the cart and lashed it in place, facing inward, thereby marking the tractor and the car that followed it as a funeral cortege for the trip along Sepych's rutted roads and fields to the cemetery.

In the copse of pine that served as one of Sepych's cemeteries, the grave-diggers had finished their work and were waiting around a small fire. They took the coffin from the cart and rested it on logs set across the open grave. Family members filed clockwise around the grave to bid their last farewell to

Aleksandr, crossing themselves and bowing to their knees three times, their hands at the coffin's corner, their foreheads dipping to touch their hands. After the coffin was lowered into the ground on long sheets of white fabric, the family again filed past, each throwing a handful of dirt into the grave. The grave-diggers filled in the remainder of the dirt with their shovels, while the rest of us chatted quietly by the fire or wandered around the cemetery to look in on relatives' graves. We were back at the house by three o'clock. Most of the guests remained to sit and drink at table for another hour or so, helping themselves to plates of food passed around the table. Natasha presented the gravedig-gers with their alms, new towels with hundred-ruble notes wrapped inside. Her daughter handed alms to the remaining guests as they departed—small handkerchiefs with no money. By four-thirty or five o'clock, all but the closest relatives had left.

In this account of Aleksandr's funeral day, I have not dwelled on the extent to which Natasha and Misha, the old women, or anyone else followed or did not follow some version of the correct or traditional procedures for an Old Believer funeral. Nor do I maintain that every family, in the shifting religious landscape of post-Soviet Sepych, carried out these precise procedures and ritu-als at every funeral.[9] Instead, I have sought to preserve some of the uncertainty of the moment, drawing attention to the ways in which Natasha and Misha, in constant consultation with friends and not without some worry, pieced to-gether an appropriate funeral day for Aleksandr. Their goal was to set them-selves and their family in good and proper relationship with his spirit, to do what they could to ensure his salvation. Whatever their self-ascribed status as "believers," this was one instance of Christian ethics at the smallest of scales in post-Soviet Sepych.

Natasha and Misha's efforts involved carefully orchestrating several sets of contrasting yet complementary relationships—with gravediggers and elders, with men and women, with relatives and nonrelatives—all of them mediated by food, offerings of gifts and money, and different arrangements of time and space. This orchestration relied on expectations about—and helped to create in practice—both certain kinds of ethical subjects and a variety of moral com-munities standing behind them. Across all these relationships and materials of ethics, it should already be clear, Natasha and Misha relied on a much greater degree of separation of the worlds of work and prayer than they, along with nearly everyone else in town, had come to consider most effective in the rites of baptism.

---

9. I do want to insist, however, that funeral and commemoration services conducted by the Belokrinitsy old women were not, as a group, fundamentally distinguishable from those of the Dëminskie and Maksimovskie. Especially from the perspective of the middle-generation towns-people like Natasha and Misha who most often arranged the funerals, there was certainly no awareness of differences in the prayers and order of the service.

The arrangements for Aleksandr's funeral day starkly opposed two groups of nonrelatives who, in fact, never saw each other during the course of the funeral day: the younger male gravediggers and the Dëminskie elders. Natasha and her female friends and relatives served both groups specific types of food that had been prepared and stored separately. In the downstairs kitchen were meat and moonshine for the gravediggers as compensation before and during their labor. These worldly tasks and foods were counterposed to those prepared for the old women upstairs, specialists in relationships with the other world. The gravediggers, recruited from Misha's labor-and-moonshine exchange network, insisted on drinking their moonshine from a common shot glass, suggesting social connectedness; the old women ate from dishes that each had maintained and brought separately, indicating their withdrawal from the social world of food and drink. It was just this withdrawal, this association with preparations for death, that enabled the old women to most effectively mediate Aleksandr's transition to the other world. The eating rituals after the service (unlike those for the priest during his visits, described above) subordinated the younger generations to the older generation through the serving of food. In contrast to the two marked categories of male gravediggers and old women, the extended family and friends who made up the bulk of the funeral guests ate and drank together, without any segregation by gender or generation, without dietary restrictions, and without being directly served by the host family.

Each of these groups also received different kinds of alms from Natasha and Misha: handkerchiefs without money for simple guests like me, head scarves and towels (with ethically ambiguous money folded carefully out of sight) for the old women and gravediggers. These two groups had provided Natasha and Misha with their complementary yet contrasting services of prayer and work. The materials of ethics to be used as alms, as I discussed earlier in this chapter, were most worried over, debated, and disguised in those cases where offering them might be seen as inappropriately mixing the worlds—such as in the process of prayers offered for dead relatives.

For Natasha and Misha, the measure of Aleksandr's funeral day was not to be found in celebrating or recalling Aleksandr's life, in judging the correctness of the old women's prayers, or in counting the number or sorts of guests who had attended. Although each of these elements played a part in their plans and thinking, it was, in the end, the successful orchestration of these sets of relations that set their family in proper relationship to Aleksandr's spirit. This orchestration was accomplished by *separating the worlds* and, with the help of many others in their various roles, guiding Aleksandr appropriately from one to the other. The ascetic distinctions that had animated local Old Belief in earlier centuries may have been deemed superfluous or irrelevant as overall guides for lives in this world—most dramatically at the point of baptism—but they remained crucially important to efforts to access the other world after death, or, in other words, when it came to some of the final opportunities to set the conditions for salvation.

By the end of the day, Natasha and Misha were already moving on from Aleksandr's funeral service, taking advantage of relatives visiting from the city to help spread manure around their garden plot before the first snows. When they finished, Misha flagged down a passing tractor from the commercial farm, hired the driver to plow, and joined him in the cab. I sat on a bench with Natasha, her son Ivan, and some other relatives, watching the tractor plow neat rows and reflecting on the long day. Aleksandr should go to heaven, Ivan volunteered. What sins could he have? He had never offended anyone. Natasha agreed. She added that she was satisfied, that despite the fretting and the demanding preparation, they had done things the right way in the end. Aleksandr should not be offended at them.

Thirty-seven days later, Natasha stopped by the house of the Dëminskie spiritual mother on the way home from work to drop off some alms—a few apples and eggs—and request her prayers. When I saw her later that evening, Natasha mentioned that Aleksandr had left (*ushël*) and that she had removed the bread and salt that had sat on the table in his small room for forty days.

Conclusions

Natasha and Misha's selection of the Belokrinitsy priest for baptisms and the old women for funerals was quite common in town—it constituted the chief axis of what might appear as syncretism to some observers or the gradual death of priestless Old Believer tradition to others. However, from the perspective of those making the choices, the criteria for proper judgments were not the strict lines of denominational affiliation emphasized by occasionally visiting clergy (the blurring of which yields syncretism); nor were they the abstracted yardsticks of Old Believer tradition advocated by some scholars (the measurement by which yields death of tradition).[10] Natasha and Misha's decisions were, rather, windows onto some of the new ways in which townspeople had drawn on and refashioned very old conversations to inform their ethical practice in dialogue with an array of postsocialist worldly processes.

Priestly and priestless Old Belief became, in the post-Soviet period, not so much confessions with which to affiliate or among which one could convert but varieties of ethical practice appropriate to different stages of life. In other

10. My argument here differs from Mikhail Epstein's much-cited contention that the atheism of the Soviet period eliminated any sense of denominational differences, leaving the primary post-Soviet experience one of "faith pure and simple" or "minimal religion" (1999). Differences and specific confessional identities continued to matter a great deal in post-Soviet Sepych, as they did in Soviet Sepych; the boundaries between and among them were simply not those that most outsiders were primed to see.

words, the people of Sepych again actively reworked many of the expectations foisted upon them by powerful outsiders, just as their serf ancestors on the Stroganov estates temporarily switched religious affiliation to skirt the campaigns of landlord, tsar, and church, and just as Soviet-era generations of elders refashioned their ascetic practices as a way to withdraw from the world in its specific socialist incarnations. Post-Soviet worries over salvation—like those of earlier centuries—developed in mutually constituting relationship to the shifting materialities of this world. The specific workings of Sepych's moonshine and money economies, as well as the wealth-in-people connections facilitated by Andrei Petrovich and the worldly connections of the new Belokrinitsy priests, mattered a great deal for the most recent reinvention of Old Belief in the Upper Kama.

The choices of Natasha, Misha, and their fellow townspeople about baptisms and funerals were, then, some of the precipitate of the convergence between the town's historically deep ethical repertoire and wide-ranging struggles to shape an emergent ethical regime in the post-Soviet period. It is too soon to say, I think, whether the division between "priestedness" and "priestlessness" at baptisms and funerals is here to stay—whether it is, in fact, a stable part of a new ethical regime in Sepych or whether the Belokrinitsy priests will eventually extend their influence over the rituals of death as well. There is, perhaps, good reason to think that some version of the ascetic desire to separate the worlds at the point of death will continue for some time yet. My claim throughout this book has been that ethical practices continue or do not continue over time for specific, identifiable reasons, not out of simple historical inertia, tradition, or some essential attribute of a peasantry. If this is so, then the circumstances of the postsocialist period might well combine to favor the continued relevance of ascetic withdrawal from this world at the point of death. In light of the often diminished options and hardships that aspects of today's global capitalism have brought to post-Soviet Sepych, holding this world at bay when questions of eternal salvation are most urgent would seem an eminently ethical thing to do.

ONE of the axioms of historical anthropology is that pasts are always multiple and recombinant yet often muffled by the shifting currents of the present. This is the spirit in which I began this book at the (approximately) ninetieth anniversary celebration of Sepych's town library, an occasion on which different understandings of Sepych's long history—and different ways of knowing that history—came into unexpectedly sharp relief. I aligned my own approach to Sepych's history neither with Father Vasilii's fact-filled sermon on history and identity nor with the quiet, dialogic, and embodied historical consciousness evident in the librarian's brief skit about a soldier returning to his native village after a quarter century of service. Rather, by tacking between these two historical epistemologies, I have sought to trace the ways in which a lengthy series of transformations, including power-laden moralizing discourses like Father Vasilii's, has been received into the protean set of expectations and sensibilities that constitutes Sepych's ethical repertoire. The library's anniversary celebration, as should now be clear, was but one episode in a much wider set of struggles to shape an emergent ethical regime in the aftermath of socialism. By way of conclusion, I highlight three interrelated analytic benefits that derive from viewing these struggles in light of three centuries' worth of ethical transformation.

First, longer histories enrich our understandings of the postsocialist period by adding new dimensions along which continuities and discontinuities might be discerned and accounted for. Many studies have wrestled with the question of whether present-day phenomena are best understood as holdovers or legacies of the socialist past or responses to new circumstances (see, for example, Burawoy and Verdery 1999). In Sepych, we can see both processes at work simultaneously and, through the analytical lens of an ethical repertoire, understand them as part of a still longer and more intricate set of continuities and discontinuities in the Upper Kama. State Farm Sepych's support of the new Belokrinitsy church and its priests, for instance, was a modified redeployment of Soviet-era society work and work with people in response to specifically post-Soviet uncertainties and changes. At the same time, it was part of the most recent reworking of elements in an ethical repertoire that had its genesis among peasant Old Believers on the Stroganov family estates.

Central to this old ethical repertoire was an ascetic distinction between fields of ethical practice oriented toward this world and those applicable to the other world—a distinction that was beginning to blur in the post-Soviet period. But this blurring was far from the only point of my story, for fault lines separating fields of ethical practice continued to exist in the turmoil of the 1990s and beyond. The most notable of these surrounded the many activities of AOZT Sepych. Within the commercial farm's purview—imagined, discussed, and materially traced—circulated the familiar ethical relationships of collective labor, mutual obligation, risk reduction (now including priestly baptism), and inequalities based on differential wealth in people. Outside AOZT Sepych, by contrast, swirled the unfamiliar, threatening, yet often tempting relationships associated with global circuits of capital, new forms of accumulation, and massive gulfs of inequality. Townspeople, as I have shown, had as much difficulty separating relationships inside AOZT Sepych from those outside as priestless elders had long had separating the worlds of work and prayer. Indeed, these difficulties were intimately related. The central thread of part 3 has been the claim that the ethical strivings of the postsocialist era bore the distinctive marks of much older discussions and dilemmas: in frequent jokes about middle-age elders, in instincts to defer ritual practice, in debates about the corrupting nature of money and wealth, in a new round of accusations and worries about mixing the worlds, and in a sharp divide between baptismal and funeral practices. I have suggested, in sum, that we gain important insight into the strategies, tactics, hopes, and aspirations of the postsocialist period by analyzing them not just against the backdrop of the Soviet past but in light of three centuries' worth of specific efforts to draw boundaries around the material practices that make for an ethical life.

A second benefit of historical ethnography that looks back from the postsocialist era is that it can shed new light on the distinctiveness of earlier times. Soviet Sepych, for instance, was bracketed by two periods of rapid change associated with the coming of markets, monetization, and the accumulation of wealth in capital. Viewed from this perspective, the officially godless Soviet era was, on the whole, less transformative of local practices and expectations about Old Belief than were the surrounding periods of marketization and the crises about mixing the worlds that they provoked. The first of these, in the postemancipation period, created conditions of inequality and intensified worldly exchange—both factors that contributed powerfully to the schism between Maksimovskie and Dëminskie; the second, beginning in the early 1990s, helped to push that schism into near irrelevancy in the face of the post-Soviet alliance between AOZT Sepych and the Belokrinitsy priests. By contrast, the intervening decades of socialism—years of comparatively shriveled circuits of exchange and elevated importance of accumulating wealth in people over wealth in capital—fostered the continuation, and even the entrenchment, of ascetic practices intended to divide work from prayer and thereby enable Christian salvation. This was true for both Maksimovskie and Dëminskie factions of local Old Believers as they continued and deepened their rivalry. As part 2 demonstrated, this story has everything to do with the ways in which Sepych's particularities intersected with the wider ethical regime of socialism. Sepych is thus not generalizable any more than is any other place; the point is merely that long-term historical ethnography—still among the most underdeveloped genres in the study of Russian and Soviet history—can offer significant insights into the past in part because of the foothold it maintains in the present.

Third, a long view of Sepych's history demonstrates just how all-encompassing the transformations since the 1990s have been, both in Sepych and on a global scale. Such periods of transformation are not, of course, without precedent in Russia or elsewhere. An earlier such age, in fact, produced the modern social science of morality and ethics. Émile Durkheim's first major scholarly effort, *The Division of Labor in Society* ([1890] 1997), sought to bring the emerging positive sciences to bear on the "moral crisis" that followed the fall of the Second French Empire and, more generally, the dislocations of rapidly expanding industrial capitalism in the late nineteenth century. The proliferating studies of morality and ethics in early-twenty-first-century anthropology and social and cultural theory reflect struggles to come to grips with crises and reorganizations within global capitalism no less pervasive than those of

Durkheim's time. It is from this growing, multifaceted conversation about ethics that I have drawn inspiration and to its advancement that I hope, in concert with the people who appear in this historical ethnography, to have contributed. However much Durkheim's specific analytic formulations may now feel inadequate, we should still heed his call for a humanistic social science of ethics that is critical of both the moralists, who reason through abstracted philosophy alone, and the economists and utilitarians, whose imaginations and projects do so little justice to so many ways of being human.

Epilogue

I am often asked whether anyone will be left in Sepych in a decade or two, whether the three-century story I have told here will end with the forest's reclaiming yet another corner of the Russian countryside. Predictions about the depopulation of Sepych are nothing new. They have been made many times in the town's past, from the destruction of the original religious dissenters' monastic cells in the mid-1720s to the large-scale movement to cities in the Brezhnev era. Will they come true this time? Although anthropologists prefer to leave forecasting to more model-driven corners of the social sciences, the question is not so easily ducked. Indeed, my friends and acquaintances in Sepych often discussed the future of their town; their predictions clustered along the lines of familiar ethical distinctions and debates, projected into an uncertain future.

For younger and middle-generation townspeople—those with careers in State Farm Sepych and the institutions and moral communities of rural socialism—the future was often discussed in terms of youth and labor. How many young families were staying in Sepych? Were there jobs and specialized training to be had? Would private investors arrive and pump cash into the farm's aging infrastructure? Could the farm attract a new wave of young specialists to town, the kind that had the education and connections to navigate the increasingly complicated maze of bank and state loans necessary to large-scale agriculture? Were there government programs to support the building of new houses in Sepych and more computers in its school? Who, in the end, would replace the khoziain Andrei Petrovich, who in 2008 was in his incredible thirty-sixth year as director of Sepych's agricultural enterprise? In this strain of thinking about the future of Sepych, the death of Andrei Petrovich could potentially lead to the wholesale collapse of enterprise-based farming, a moral community-demolishing grab for what was left of the farm, and, in short order, a mass exodus. Pensioners, to be sure, would be around for some time to come, but much of the vibrancy and complexity of life in town—not to mention salaries—would fade quickly.

Perhaps, it was often pointed out to me, the exodus had already begun. A smaller and smaller percentage of school graduates were staying to labor in Sepych. The urban technical schools and vocational colleges in which young people enrolled did not usually produce the kinds of specialists that were likely to be employable in Sepych in the future. Indeed, many aspired to enter more urban and, they said, more promising careers. This was not true just of younger townspeople. By 2008, at the height of Russia's oil boom, many middle-aged men I knew had decided that their salary income could be substantially increased by migration to Perm and its rapidly expanding suburbs to do short-term labor. Men with whom I had spent hours in the fields had begun to quit their jobs in AOZT Sepych and spend only alternate weeks in town. While in Sepych, they attended to household affairs and drank moonshine with friends; while in Perm, they bunked with family or friends and built the homes and cottages of the city's new oil-and-gas elite by day (or guarded them by night).

On the other hand, Sepych was once again becoming the administrative and institutional center it had been at several points in its history. A brand-new, two-story school with room for six hundred students opened to great fanfare in 2006; the school enabled the centralization of education in Sepych and the closing of smaller schools in the surrounding area. A new round of reforms of local self-government in 2004–5 combined three local administrations into a single rural population zone (*poselenie*) with its center in Sepych and a territory as large as State Farm Sepych at its most massive. Of those young townspeople who left immediately after school, some came back, drawn to family in Sepych or, I was told, worn down by city life. It seems likely that falling oil prices will return many Perm commuters to full-time life in Sepych. Moreover, even as Sepych's own youth left for the cities, they were replaced by families moving in from poorer, outlying villages. On my visits to town in 2006 and 2008, there was a brisk market for rooms in town—most of these new renters were farm workers and other employees of AOZT Sepych looking for housing nearer to their jobs at the commercial farm's new dairy barns. For these families, the long-running ethical sensibilities of the Upper Kama continued to resonate. Indeed, their movements were a new round of the generationally patterned resettlements so characteristic of the Soviet period, with younger laborers moving to Sepych and Old Believer elders remaining in outlying villages.

For those outsiders concerned with Old Belief in the Upper Kama, predictions about the future of Sepych took different shapes. Archaeographers scaled back their interest in Sepych in the late 1990s, dismayed by the apparent success of Father Vasilii and the death of most of the elders they had first met in the 1970s and 1980s. They devoted the bulk of their time and resources to searching for traditional culture elsewhere and dedicated new attention to manuscripts and books already in Russian archives and libraries. Expeditions continued, however, to "measure the pulse of Sepych," as one colleague put it, just in case a new revival of traditional Old Belief was in the offing in the place it had once been so strong. The appointment of a recently retired and well-respected man as spiritual father of the Maksimovskie in Sepych piqued the archaeographers' interest, as did priestless stirrings in several areas of the Upper Kama farther from the influence of Sepych's new church. Sepych's museum of traditional culture still stood, but its expositions had drifted still further from the moralizing discourses in which it was conceived and, most recently, toward memorializing Sepych's war casualties, spanning from the Great Patriotic War to Afghanistan and Chechnya. Father Vasilii, too, had moved on, to higher offices in the Belokrinitsy hierarchy, where his administrative skill and missionary zeal resounded still more widely. His replacements for periodic services in Sepych, though admired and thoroughly competent, did not usually stir the aspirations and mobilize the moral visions that Father Vasilii's periodic visits to town did. In 2008, there was talk that the Russian Orthodox Church would soon be filing a claim for the return of Sepych's House of Culture—the town's original Russian Orthodox mission church. Some intimated that yet another conflict in the town's long-running battles of ritual, hierarchy, and moral community seemed to be on the horizon.

Old Believer elders in Sepych had their own views of the future, proffered to me from an ethical vantage point different from that of both younger generations and outsiders. Once every two weeks or so, I used to visit Evdokia Aleksandrovna, onetime representative of the rural soviet, former Dëminskie elder, and, most recently, stalwart member of the new church community, at her small house on the edge of town. Sometimes cantankerous, she relished her role as one of the oldest and, by common agreement, wisest residents of Sepych. From the bench outside her house, she dispensed bits of medical advice, local history, gardening know-how, and guidance from the Scriptures and Holy Fathers to all who dropped by. On one of my last visits before her death, she called me back as I was leaving to add something. "You know what I wanted to tell you?" she said pointedly. "My father told me that this place was once a *pustynia,* and that it will be once again." *Pustynia* here meant not the "desert" of modern Russian but rather a "wilderness," a Christian refuge from the sinful world that could be found most often these days in rounds of spiritual verse (such as the epigraph to part 1) sung when the elders gathered. Pustynia recalled the wilderness of Jesus' forty-day sojourn of fasting and prayer. It linked the hermitic cells of the Desert Fathers of Egypt and the Vyg Fathers of the Russian north to the first—and future—inhabitants of Sepych. Despite her participation in the new Belokrinitsy church and its comparatively closer links to the world, Evdokia Aleksandrovna's vision of the coming times in Sepych was thoroughly ascetic. For her, the depopulation of the town augured the arrival of the truest form of Christianity, of elders and councils of elders in harmony with one another, apart from the world, and on the path to salvation.

The vicissitudes of the Russian and global political economy make it impossible to predict Sepych's fate in the early decades of the twenty-first century. Yet we can safely surmise that many who remain in Sepych will have judged that an ethical life, perhaps one in pursuit of Christian salvation, is best sought amid a familiar, if mutable, repertoire of landscapes and labors, people and objects, and rituals and prayers. Equally, we can be sure that those who leave Sepych will take this mutable repertoire with them, drawing upon it as they participate in other moral communities and navigate other currents of power and inequality. For nearly three centuries, such have been the promises and consolations of Sepych's ethical repertoire.

Bibliography

Manuscripts

All manuscripts are held at the Division of Rare Books and Manuscripts, Scientific Library of Moscow State University, Perm-Verkhokam'e Collection (ORKiR NB MGU, PV). Reference numbers, manuscript titles, and dates correspond to those in Ageeva et al. (1994); page number citations are given as folio and recto/verso.

641   Sbornik uchitel'nyi s dukhovnymi stikhami i chinami. Early nineteenth century.

803   Sbornik pomorskikh gramot, pomorskogo i verkhokamsokogo "Rodoslovii," vypisok iz otsov tserkvi i issledovanii po istorii vostochnoi i russkoi tserkvei s zhitiem Korniliia Vygovskogo. Early twentieth century.

1118   Sbornik slov, pouchenii, pritch i vypiskok iz raznykh knig so Strastiami Khristovymi, Shestodnevom, pomorskimi gramotami i "Podlinnikom o razdele." Late nineteenth century.

1127   Sbornik pomorskikh gramot s zhitiem Korniliia Vygovskogo. 1870s–90s and early twentieth century.

1419[1]   Sinodik-pomiannik. 1960s.

1423   Sinodik-pomiannik Dëminskogo sobora: "Pominal'nik." Twentieth century.

1425   Sbornik dukhovnykh stikhov na kriukovykh notakh. Early nineteenth century.

1548   Dokumenty i pis'ma Krivchanovskogo sobora Dëmintsev (iz arkhiva Sil'vestra Petrovicha Solov'eva). 1950s–60s.

1574   Rodoslovie verkhokamskikh staroobriadtsev pomorskogo tolka. Twentieth century.

1577   Sbornik Dëminskii, polemicheskii. 1920s–1960s.

1578   Deianiia i ulozheniia sobora po dogmaticheskim i kanonicheskim voprosam. December 29, 7431 (1922).

1579   Melekhin Grigorii Nikolaevich. Edinenie s Maksimovtsami. c. 1925.

1685[5]   Sobornoe reshenie Maksimovtsev o sovmestnom vladenii i pol'zovanii knigami. Late nineteenth century.

1983   Sbornik verkhokamskikh gramot. Mid-nineteenth century.

1996   O razdele. Maksimovskaia versia. Late nineteenth century.

2005   Sinodik-pomiannik sela Putino (Vereshchaginskii raion Permskoi oblasti) s dukhovnymi stikhami. Late nineteenth century and twentieth century.

2049   Sinodik-pomiannik Sepychëvskago sobora Dëminskogo soglasiia. 1960s–82.

2050   Sbornik apokrifov i dukhovnykh stikhov. Mid- to late twentieth century.

2285   Pis'mo-obrashchenie staroobriadcheskogo sobora k "brat'iam po vere" po povodu istinnosti Maksimovskogo kreshcheniia. June 23, 1947 and 1948.

Archives

The following abbreviations are used throughout. Except in the case of AAL MGU, references are to *fond, delo, opis', list.*

AAL MGU	Arkhiv Arkheograficheskogo Laboratorii Moskovskogo Gosudarstvennogo Universiteta
	Video Archive (year, cassette number)
	Letter Archive (file, date)
	Expedition Reports (region code, year)
	Perm-Verkhokam'e Field Diaries (number, page)
AOAVR	Arkhivnyi Otdel Administratsii Vereshchaginskogo Raiona
GAPO	Gosudarstvennyi Arkhiv Permskoi Oblasti
GARF	Gosudarstvennyi Arkhiv Rossiskoi Federatsii
GOPAPO	Gosudarstvennyi Obshchestvennyi-Politicheskii Arkhiv Permskoi Oblasti
POKM	Permskii Oblastnoi Kraevedcheskii Muzei
RGADA	Rossiskii Gosudarstvennyi Arkhiv Drevnikh Aktov
VRKM	Vereshchaginskii Raionii Kraevedcheskii Muzei

Published Sources

Adams, Laura. 2008. "Globalization, Universalism, and Cultural Form." *Comparative Studies in Society and History* 50 (3): 614–40.

Agafonov, P. N. 2003. "Permskaia Eparkhiia v 20-e Gody XX Veka." In *Vekhi Khristianskoi Istorii Prikam'ia: Materialy Chtenii, Posviashchennykh 540-Letiiu Kreshchenniia Permi Velikoi,* edited by P. N. Agafonov, 69–83. Perm: Izdatel'stvo Bogatyreva.

Ageeva, E. A., N. A. Kobiak, T. A. Kruglova, and E. B. Smilianskaia, eds. 1994. *Rukopisi Verkhokam'ia XV–XX vv: Iz Sobraniia Nauchnoi Biblioteki Moskovskogo Universiteta Imeni M. V. Lomonosova.* Moscow: Tsimeliia.

Ageeva, E. A., I. V. Pozdeeva, and E. B. Smilianskaia. 1992. "Sobranie, Izuchenie, Vozvrashchenie: K 25-Letiu Polevykh Arkheograficheskykh Issledovanii MGU." In *Mir Staroobriadchestva,* vol. 1, *Lichnost', Kniga, Traditsiia,* edited by I. V. Pozdeeva and E. B. Smilianskaia, 5–10. Moscow: Khronograf.

Ageeva, E. A., R. R. Robson, and E. B. Smilianskaia. 1997. "Staroobriadtsy Spasovtsy: Puti Narodnogo Bogosloviia i Formy Samosokhraneniia Traditsionnykh Obshchestv v Rossii XX Stoletia." *Revue des études slaves* 69 (1–2): 101–17.

Akin, David, and Joel Robbins, eds. 1999. *Money and Modernity: State and Local Currencies in Melanesia*. Pittsburgh: University of Pittsburgh Press.

Aleksandrov, E. A. 1998. "Sozdanie Videogalerei Staroobriadchestva: Printsipy, Rezultaty, i Problemy." In *Mir Staroobriadchestva*, vol. 4, *Zhivye Traditsii: Rezul'taty i Perspektivy Kompleksnykh Issledovanii Russkogo Staroobriadchestva*, edited by I. V. Pozdeeva, 123–31. Moscow: Rosspen.

Aleksandrov, Vadim Aleksandrovich. 1989. *Na Putiakh iz Zemli Permskoi v Sibir'. Ocherki Etnografii Severnoural'skogo Krest'ianstva XVII–XX vv*. Moscow: Nauka.

———. 1990. "Land Re-allotment in the Peasant Communes of Late-Feudal Russia." In *Land Commune and Peasant Community in Russia: Communal Forms in Imperial and Early Soviet Society*, edited by Roger Bartlett, 36–44. New York: St. Martin's.

Alferova, E. V., V. A. Lapin, I. A. Umnova, and V. I. Fadeeva, eds. 1998. *Gosudarstvennaia Vlast' i Mestnoe Samoupravlenie v Rossii*. Moscow: INION RAN.

Allina-Pisano, Jessica. 2008. *The Post-Soviet Potemkin Village: Politics and Property Rights in the Black Earth*. Cambridge: Cambridge University Press.

Anagnost, Ann. 1997. *National Past-Times: Narrative, Representation, and Power in Modern China*. Durham, NC: Duke University Press.

Anderson, David. 2000a. "Fieldwork and the 'Doctoring' of National Identities in Arctic Siberia." In *Fieldwork Dilemmas: Anthropologists in Postsocialist States*, edited by Hermine G. DeSoto and Nora Dudwick, 130–48. Madison: University of Wisconsin Press.

———. 2000b. "Surrogate Currencies and the 'Wild Market' in Central Siberia." In *The Vanishing Rouble: Barter Networks and Non-monetary Transactions in Post-Soviet Societies*, edited by Paul Seabright, 318–44. Cambridge: Cambridge University Press.

Anderson, John. 1991. "The Council for Religious Affairs and the Shaping of Soviet Religious Policy." *Soviet Studies* 43 (4): 689–710.

Appadurai, Arjun. 1988. *The Social Life of Things: Commodities in Cultural Perspective*. Cambridge: Cambridge University Press.

———. 2006. *Fear of Small Numbers: An Essay on the Geography of Anger*. Durham, NC: Duke University Press.

Aristotle. 1976. *Nichomachean Ethics*. Translated by J. A. K. Thompson. London: Penguin.

Arrighi, Giovanni. 1994. *The Long Twentieth Century: Money, Power, and the Origins of Our Times*. London: Verso.

Asad, Talal. 2003. *Formations of the Secular: Christianity, Islam, Modernity*. Stanford: Stanford University Press.

Balzer, Marjorie Mandelstam. 1999. *The Tenacity of Ethnicity: A Siberian Saga in Global Perspective*. Princeton: Princeton University Press.

Bezgodov, A. A. 2005a. "Istoriia Sepychëvskogo Vosstaniia 1918 goda po Novym Istochnikam." In *Mir Staroobriadchestva*, vol. 6, *Traditsionnaia Kul'tura Permskoi Zemli*, edited by I. V. Pozdeeva, 271–90. Yaroslavl: Izdatel'stvo Remder.

———. 2005b. "Sud'ba Verkhokamskoi Derevni v XX veke na Primere Koniatskogo Sel'skogo Obshchestva Sivinskogo Raiona (po Vospominaniiam Zhitelei, Pokhoziaistvennym Knigam i Periodike)." In *Mir Staroobriadchestva*, vol. 6, *Traditsionnaia Kul'tura Permskoi Zemli*, edited by I. V. Pozdeeva, 291–300. Yaroslavl: Izdatel'stvo Remder.

Binns, Christopher. 1979. "The Changing Face of Power: Revolution and Accommodation in the Soviet Ceremonial System, I." *Man*, n.s., 14 (4): 170–87.

———. 1980. "The Changing Face of Power: Revolution and Accommodation in the Soviet Ceremonial System, II." *Man*, n.s., 15 (1): 585–606.

Bloch, Alexia, and Laurel Kendall. 2004. *The Museum at the End of the World: Encounters in the Russian Far East*. Philadelphia: University of Pennsylvania Press.

Borneman, John. 1997. *Settling Accounts: Violence, Justice, and Accountability in Postsocialist Europe.* Princeton: Princeton University Press.

Bourdieu, Pierre. 1977. *Outline of a Theory of Practice.* Cambridge: Cambridge University Press.

——. 1980. *The Logic of Practice.* Stanford: Stanford University Press.

——. 1993. *The Field of Cultural Production: Essays on Art and Literature.* New York: Columbia University Press.

Bowman, Linda. 2003. "Seeking Salvation: Moral Economies and Management at the Morozov Mills, 1885–1905." *Social History* 28 (3): 322–45.

Bridger, Sue. 2003. "The Heirs of Pasha: The Rise and Fall of the Soviet Woman Tractor Driver." In *Gender in Russian History and Culture,* edited by Linda Edmondson, 194–211. London: Palgrave.

Bringa, Tone. 1995. *Being Muslim the Bosnian Way: Identity and Community in a Central Bosnian Village.* Princeton: Princeton University Press.

Brooks, Jeffrey. 1985. *When Russia Learned to Read: Literacy and Popular Literature, 1861–1917.* Princeton: Princeton University Press.

Burawoy, Michael, Pavel Krotov, and Tatyana Lytkina. 2000. "Involution and Destitution in Capitalist Russia." *Ethnography* 1 (1): 43–65.

Burawoy, Michael, and Katherine Verdery. 1999. Introduction to *Uncertain Transition: Ethnographies of Change in the Postsocialist World,* edited by Michael Burawoy and Katherine Verdery, 1–17. Lanham, MD: Rowman and Littlefield.

Burbank, Jane. 2004. *Russian Peasants Go to Court: Legal Culture in the Countryside, 1905–1917.* Bloomington: Indiana University Press.

Burds, Jeffrey. 1998. *Peasant Dreams and Market Politics: Labor Migration and the Russian Village, 1861–1905.* Pittsburgh: University of Pittsburgh Press.

Caldwell, Melissa. 2004. *Not by Bread Alone: Social Support in the New Russia.* Berkeley: University of California Press.

Cannell, Fenella, ed. 2006. *The Anthropology of Christianity.* Durham, NC: Duke University Press.

Carrithers, Michael, Steven Collins, and Steven Lukes, eds. 1985. *The Category of the Person: Anthropology, Philosophy, History.* Cambridge: Cambridge University Press.

Cartwright, A. L. 2001. *The Return of the Peasant: Land Reform in Post-Communist Romania.* Aldershot, UK: Ashgate Dartmouth.

Castañeda, Quetzil. 2006. "Ethnography in the Forest: An Analysis of Ethics in the Morals of Anthropology." *Cultural Anthropology* 21 (1): 121–45.

Cellarius, Barbara A. 2000. "'You Can Buy Almost Anything with Potatoes': An Examination of Barter during Economic Crisis in Bulgaria." *Ethnology* 39 (1): 73–92.

Chagin, G. N. 1992. "Traditsionnye Sviazi Dukhovnoi Kul'tury Sem'i i Obshchinoi Russkogo Staroobriadcheskogo Naseleniia Verkhokam'ia." In *Traditsionnaia Dukhovnaia i Material'naia Kul'tura Russkikh Staroobriadcheskikh Poselenii v Stranakh Evropy, Azii i Ameriki: Sbornik Nauchnikh Trudov,* edited by N. N. Pokrovskii, 162–66. Novosibirsk: Nauka.

——. 1998a. "Rol' Druzhki v Svadebnom Obriade Staroobriadtsev Verkhokam'ia (1920–1980-e gg.)." In *Mir Staroobriadchestva,* vol. 4, *Zhivye Traditsii: Rezul'taty i Perspektivy Kompleksnykh Issledovanii Russkogo Staroobriadchestva,* edited by I. V. Pozdeeva, 283–90. Moscow: Rosspen.

——. 1998b. "Zaselenie i khoziastvennoe osvoenie Verkhokam'ia v kontse XVIII-pervoi treti XX veka." In *Mir Staroobriadchestvo,* vol. 4, *Zhivye Traditsii: Rezul'taty i Perspektivy Kompleksnykh Issledovanii Russkogo Staroobriadchestva,* edited by I. V. Pozdeeva, 265–74. Moscow: Rosspen.

——. 1999. *Istoriia v Pamiati Russkikh Krest'ian Srednego Urala v Seredine XIX-Nachale XX Veka.* Perm: Perm State University Press.

——. 2001. "Krest'ianskaia Sem'ia Verkhokam'e v Kontse XVIII—Nachala XX v." In *Staroobriadcheskii Mir Volgo-Kam'ia: Problemy Kompleksnogo Izucheniia,* edited by G. N. Chagin, 31–40. Perm: Perm State University Press.

———. 2005. "Khleb i Pitanii v Obriadakh Russkikh Krest'ian Verkhokam'ia." In *Mir Staroobriadchestva*, vol. 6, *Traditsionnaia Kul'tura Permskoi Zemli*, edited by I. V. Pozdeeva, 94–97. Yaroslavl: Izdatel'stvo Remder.

Chaianov, A. V. 1986. *A. V. Chaianov on the Theory of Peasant Economy*. Edited by Daniel Thorner, Basile Kerblay, and R. E. F. Smith. Madison: University of Wisconsin Press.

Cherniavsksy, Michael. 1966. "The Old Believers and the New Religion." *Slavic Review* 25 (1): 1–39.

Chernysheva, M. B. 1982. "Muzykal'naia Kul'tura Russkogo Naseleniia Verkhokam'ia." In *Russkie Pismennye i Ustnye Traditsii i Dukhovnaia Kul'tura*, edited by I. D. Koval'chenko, 127–50. Moscow: Moscow State University Press.

Chulos, Chris J. 1995. "Peasant Perspectives of Clerical Debauchery in Post-Emancipation Russia." *Studia Slavica Finlandensia* 12 (8): 33–53.

———. 2003. *Converging Worlds: Religion and Community in Peasant Russia, 1861–1917*. De Kalb: Northern Illinois University Press.

Clarke, Roger A. 1968. "Soviet Agricultural Reforms since Khrushchev." *Soviet Studies* 20 (2): 159–78.

Clay, Eugene. 2004. "The Antichrist as the Eschatological Enemy among Priestless Old Believers of Perm' Province." Paper presented at the 36th National Convention of the American Association for the Advancement of Slavic Studies, Boston, December 6.

Coleman, Heather J. 2005. *Russian Baptists and Spiritual Revolution, 1905–1929*. Bloomington: Indiana University Press.

Collier, Stephen J., and Andrew Lakoff. 2005. "On Regimes of Living," In *Global Assemblages: Technology, Politics, and Ethics as Anthropological Problems*, edited by Aihwa Ong and Stephen J. Collier, 22–39. London: Blackwell.

Comaroff, Jean, and John L. Comaroff. 1991. *Of Revelation and Revolution: Christianity, Colonialism, and Consciousness in South Africa*. Chicago: University of Chicago Press.

Corrigan, Phillip and Derek Sayer. 1985. *The Great Arch: English State Formation as Cultural Revolution*. Oxford: Basil Blackwell.

Crate, Susan A. 2006. *Cows, Kin, and Globalization: An Ethnography of Sustainability*. Lanham, MD: AltaMira.

Creed, Gerald W. 1995. "The Politics of Agriculture: Identity and Socialist Senitment in Bulgaria." *Slavic Review* 54 (4): 843–68.

———. 1998. *Domesticating Revolution: From Socialist Reform to Ambivalent Transition in a Bulgarian Village*. University Park: Pennsylvania State University Press.

———. 2002. "(Consumer) Paradise Lost: Capitalist Dynamics and Disenchantment in Rural Bulgaria." *Anthropology of East Europe Review* 20 (2): 119–25.

———, ed. 2006. *Seductions of Community: Emancipations, Oppressions, Quandaries*. Santa Fe: School of American Research Press.

Crummey, Robert O. 1970. *The Old Believers and the World of Antichrist: The Vyg Community and the Russian State, 1694–1855*. Madison: University of Wisconsin Press.

———. 1993a. "Interpreting the Fate of Old Believer Communities in the Eighteenth and Nineteenth Centuries." In *Seeking God: The Recovery of Religious Identity in Orthodox Russia, Ukraine, and Georgia*, edited by Stephen K. Batalden, 144–59. De Kalb: Northern Illinois University Press.

———. 1993b. "Old Belief as Popular Religion: New Approaches." *Slavic Review* 52 (4): 700–712.

———. 1994. "Origins of the Old Believers' Cultural Systems: The Works of Avraamii." *Forschungen zur Osteuropäischen Geschicte* 50:121–38.

Czap, Peter, Jr. 1978. "Marriage and the Peasant Joint Family in the Era of Serfdom." In *The Family in Imperial Russia: New Lines of Historical Research*, edited by David L. Ransel, 103–23. Urbana: University of Illinois Press.

———. 1983. "'A Large Family: The Peasant's Greatest Wealth': Serf Households in Mishino, Russia, 1814–1858." In *Family Forms in Historic Europe*, edited by Richard Wall, Jean Robin, and Peter Laslett, 105–51. New York: Cambridge University Press.

Czarnikow Russian Market Weekly Report. 2000. January 14–21.

Darrow, David. 2001. "From Commune to Household: Statistics and the Social Construction of Chaianov's Theory of Peasant Economy." *Comparative Studies in Society and History* 43 (4): 788–818.

Das, Veena. 2006. *Life and Words: Violence and the Descent into the Ordinary.* Berkeley: University of California Press.

David-Fox, Michael. 2002. Review of *Obshchestvennye Organizatsiiya Rossii v 1920-e gody,* by I. N. Ilina. *Kritika: Explorations in Russian and Eurasian History* 3 (1): 173–81.

DeGeorge, Richard T. 1969. *Soviet Ethics and Morality.* Ann Arbor: University of Michigan Press.

Diamond, Jack. 2002a. "Budget System Reform in Transitional Economies: The Experience of Russia." IMF Working Paper WP/02/22.

——. 2002b. "The New Russian Budget System: A Critical Assessment and Future Reform Agenda." IMF Working Paper WP/02/21.

Dimukhametova, S. A., O. L. Kut'ev, E. G. Litvinova, E. N. Merkusheva, V. V. Mukhin, eds. 1999. *Muzei XXI veka: Vzgliad v proshloe i budushchee: Materialy mezhdunarodnoi nauchno-prakticheskoi konferentsii.* Perm: Permskii Oblastnoi Kraevedcheskii Muzei.

Dimukhametova, S. A, O. L. Kut'ev, and A. V. Shilov, eds. 2000. *Muzei Permskoi Oblasti: Informatsionnyi Spravochnik.* Perm: Permskii Oblastnoi Kraevedcheskii Muzei.

Dinello, Natalia. 1998. "Russian Religious Rejections of Money and *Homo Economicus*: The Self-Identifications of the 'Pioneers of a Money Economy' in Post-Soviet Russia." *Sociology of Religion* 59 (1): 45–64.

Dmitriev, Aleksandr. 1889–92. *Permskaia Starina: Sbornik" Istoricheskikh" Statei i Materialov" o Permskom" Krae.* 4 vols. Perm: Tipografiia P. F. Kamenskago.

Douglas, Mary. 1966. *Purity and Danger: An Analysis of the Concepts of Pollution and Taboo.* London: Routledge.

Dragadze, Tamara. 1993. "The Domestication of Religion under Soviet Communism." In *Socialism: Ideals, Ideologies, and Local Practice,* edited by C. M. Hann, 149–56. London: Routledge.

Druzhinin, N. M. 1949. *Krest'ianskoe Dvizhenie v 1861 godu posle Otmeny Krepostnogo Prava.* Moscow: Akademiia Nauk SSSR. Institut Istorii.

——, ed. 1963. *Krest'ianskoe Dvizhenie v Rossii v XIX—nachale XX veka.* Moscow: Izdatel'stvo Sotsial'no-Ekonomicheskoi Literatury.

Dudley, Kathryn Marie. 2000. *Debt and Dispossession: Farm Loss in America's Heartland.* Chicago: University of Chicago Press.

Dunbar, Nicholas. 2000. *Inventing Money: The Story of Long-Term Capital Management and the Legends Behind It.* Chichester, UK: Wiley.

Dunn, Elizabeth. 2003. "Audit, Corruption, and the Problem of Personhood: Scenes from Postsocialist Poland." In *Entangled Histories and Negotiated Universals: Centers and Peripheries in a Changing World,* edited by Wolf Lepenies, 127–45. Berlin: Campus.

——. 2004. *Privatizing Poland: Baby Food, Big Business, and the Remaking of Labor.* Ithaca: Cornell University Press.

Durgin, Frank A. 1964. "Monetization and Policy in Soviet Agriculture." *Soviet Studies* 15 (4): 375–407.

Durkheim, Émile. [1890] 1997. *The Division of Labor in Society.* New York: Free Press.

——. 1973. *Émile Durkheim on Morality and Society.* Edited by Robert Bellah. Chicago: University of Chicago Press.

Edelman, Marc. 2005. "Bringing the Moral Economy Back In...to the Study of 21st Century Transnational Peasant Movements." *American Anthropologist* 107 (3): 331–45.

Eley, Geoff. 2005. *A Crooked Line: From Cultural History to the History of Society.* Ann Arbor: University of Michigan Press.

Engel, Barbara Alpern. 1990. "Peasant Morality and Pre-Marital Relations in Late 19th Century Russia." *Journal of Social History* 23 (4): 695–714.

———. 1994. *Between the Fields and the City: Women, Work, and Family in Russia, 1861–1914.* Cambridge: Cambridge University Press.

Engelke, Matthew. 2007. *A Problem of Presence: Beyond Scripture in an African Church.* Berkeley: University of California Press.

Engelstein, Laura. 1999. *Castration and the Heavenly Kingdom: A Russian Folktale.* Ithaca: Cornell University Press.

———. 2003. "Old and New, High and Low: Straw Horsemen of Russian Orthodoxy." In *Orthodox Russia: Belief and Practice under the Tsars,* edited by Valerie Kivelson and Robert H. Greene, 23–32. University Park: Pennsylvania State University Press.

Engelstein, Laura, and Stephanie Sandler, eds. 2000. *Self and Story in Russian History.* Ithaca: Cornell University Press.

Epstein, Mikhail. 1999. "Post-Atheism: From Apophatic Theology to 'Minimal Religion.'" In *Russian Postmodernism: New Perspectives on Post-Soviet Culture,* edited by Mikhail Epstein, Aleksandr Genis, and Slobodanka Vladiv-Glover, 345–93. New York: Berghahn.

Ershova, O. P. 1999. *Staroobriadchestvo i Vlast'.* Moscow: Unikum Tsentr.

Etkind, Alexandr. 2003. "Whirling with the Other: Russian Populism and Religious Sects." *Russian Review* 62 (4): 565–88.

Evans, Alfred B., and Vladimir Gel'man, eds. 2004. *The Politics of Local Government in Russia.* Lanham, MD.: Rowman and Littlefield.

Farmer, Paul. 2004. "An Anthropology of Structural Violence." *Current Anthropology* 45 (2): 305–25.

Farnsworth, Beatrice. 1986. "The Litigious Daughter-in-Law: Family Relations in Rural Russia in the Second Half of the Nineteenth Century." *Slavic Review* 45 (1): 49–64.

Faubion, James D. 2001a. *The Shadows and Lights of Waco: Millennialism Today.* Princeton: Princeton University Press.

———. 2001b. "Toward an Anthropology of the Ethics of Kinship." In *The Ethics of Kinship: Ethnographic Inquiries,* edited by James D. Faubion, 1–28. Lanham, MD: Rowman and Littlefield.

Fëderov. V. A. 1979. "Semeinye Razdely v Russkoi Poreformennoi Derevne." In *Sel'skoe Khoziaistvo i Krest'ianstvo Serevo-Zapada RSFSR v Dorevoliutsionnom Periode,* edited by A. A. Kondrashchenkov, 29–46. Smolensk: Tipografiia im. Smirnova.

Fehér, Ferenc, Ágnes Heller, and György Márkus. 1983. *Dictatorship over Needs.* New York: St. Martin's.

Ferguson, James. 2006. *Global Shadows: Africa in the Neoliberal World Order.* Durham, NC: Duke University Press.

Field, Deborah A. 1998. "Irreconcilable Differences: Divorce and Conceptions of Private Life in the Khrushchev Era." *Russian Review* 57 (4): 599–613.

Figes, Orlando. 1989. *Peasant Russia, Civil War: The Volga Countryside in Revolution (1917–1921).* London: Phoenix.

———. 1990. "The Red Army and Mass Mobilization during the Russian Civil War, 1918–1920." *Past and Present* 129:168–211.

Filipov, Ivan. 1862. *Istoriia Vygovskoi Staroobriadcheskoi Pustyni.* Saint Petersburg: Obshchestvennaia Pol'za.

Fischer, Michael M. J. 2003. *Emergent Forms of Life and the Anthropological Voice.* Durham, NC: Duke University Press.

Fitzpatrick, Sheila. 1978. "Cultural Revolution as Class War." In *Cultural Revolution in Russia, 1928–1931,* edited by Shelia Fitzpatrick, 8–40. Bloomington: Indiana University Press.

———. 1994. *Stalin's Peasants: Resistance and Survival in the Russian Village after Collectivization.* Oxford: Oxford University Press.

Fortes, Meyer. 1971. *On the Concept of Person among the Tallensi.* Paris: Centre de la Recherche Scientifique.

Foucault, Michel. 1976. *The History of Sexuality.* Vol. 1, *An Introduction.* Translated by Robert Hurley. London: Penguin Books.

———. 1985. *The History of Sexuality.* Vol. 2, *The Use of Pleasure.* Translated by Robert Hurley. New York: Random House.

———. 1994. *Ethics: Subjectivity and Truth.* Edited by Paul Rabinow. New York: New Press.

Frank, Stephen P. 1999. *Crime, Cultural Conflict, and Justice in Rural Russia, 1856–1914.* Berkeley: University of California Press.

Freeze, Gregory L. 1976. "The Disintegration of Traditional Communities: The Parish in Eighteenth-Century Russia." *Journal of Modern History* 48 (1): 32–50.

———. 1989. "The Orthodox Church and Serfdom in Prereform Russia." *Slavic Review* 48 (3): 361–87.

———. 1990. "Bringing Order to the Russian Family: Marriage and Divorce in Late Imperial Russia, 1760–1860." *Journal of Modern History* 62 (4): 709–46.

———. 1993. "The Wages of Sin: The Decline of Public Penance in Imperial Russia." In *Seeking God: The Recovery of Religious Identity in Orthodox Russia, Ukraine, and Georgia,* edited by Stephen K. Batalden. De Kalb: Northern Illinois University Press.

———. 2001. "Recent Scholarship on Russian Orthodoxy: A Critique." *Kritika* 2 (2): 269–78.

Frierson, Cathy. 1987. "Razdel: The Peasant Family Divided." *Russian Review* 46 (1): 35–51.

———. 1990. "Peasant Family Divisions and the Commune." In *Land Commune and Peasant Community in Russia: Communal Forms in Imperial and Early Soviet Society,* edited by Roger Bartlett, 303–20. New York: St. Martin's.

———. 1993. *Peasant Icons: Representations of Rural People in Late 19th Century Russia.* Oxford: Oxford University Press.

Gaddis, John Lewis. 2005. *The Cold War: A New History.* New York: Penguin.

Gaddy, Clifford, and Barry W. Ickes. 2002. *Russia's Virtual Economy.* Washington, DC: Brookings Institution Press.

Gal, Susan, and Gail Kligman. 2000. *The Politics of Gender after Socialism.* Princeton: Princeton University Press.

Ganev, Venelin I. 2005. "Postcommunism as an Episode of State-Building: A Reversed Tillyan Perspective." *Communist and Post-Communist Studies* 38 (4): 425–45.

Garcelon, Marc. 2005. *Revolutionary Passage: From Soviet to Post-Soviet Russia, 1985–2000.* Philadelphia: Temple University Press.

Gel'man, Vladimir. 2002. "The Politics of Local Government in Russia: The Neglected Side of the Story." *Perspectives on European Politics and Society* 3 (3): 495–508.

Gerschenkron, Alexander. 1966. *Economic Backwardness in Historical Perspective.* Cambridge: Harvard University Press.

Glickman, Rose L. 1984. *Russian Factory Women: Workplace and Society.* Berkeley: University of California Press.

———. 1990. "Women and the Peasant Commune." In *Land Commune and Peasant Community in Russia: Communal Forms in Imperial and Early Soviet Society,* edited by Roger Bartlett, 321–38. New York: St. Martin's.

———. 1996. "'Unusual Circumstances' in the Peasant Village." *Russian History* 23 (1–4): 215–29.

Gorovoi, F. S. 1951. *Volneniia Krest'ian Permskogo Predural'ia v 60-x godakh XIX veka.* Molotov: Molotovskoe Oblastnoe Gosudarstvennoe Izdatel'stvo.

———. 1954. *Otmena Krepostnogo Prava i Rabochie Volneniia na Urale (v Permskoi Gubernii).* Molotov: Molotovskoe Knizhnoe Izdatel'stvo.

Gorsuch, Anne E. 2000. *Youth in Revolutionary Russia: Enthusiasts, Bohemians, Delinquents.* Bloomington: Indiana University Press.

Grant, Bruce. 1995. *In the Soviet House of Culture: A Century of Perestroikas.* Princeton: Princeton University Press.

Grant, Steven A. 1976. "Obshchina and Mir." *Slavic Review* 35 (4): 636–51.

Gregory, Christopher A. 1997. *Savage Money: The Anthropology and Politics of Commodity Exchange.* Amsterdam: Harwood Academic Publishers.

Gupta, Akhil. 1995. "Blurred Boundaries: The Discourse of Corruption, the Culture of Politics, and the Imagined State." *American Ethnologist* 22 (2): 375–402.

Gus'kov, V. V. 2000. *Skazanie o Moskovskom Preobrazhenskom Monastyre. Iz Istorii Monastyria v Svidetel'stvakh i Dokumentakh XVII–XX vv. Chast' II.* Moscow: Moskovskaia Preobrazhenskaia Staroobriadcheskaia Obshchina.

Guyer, Jane. 1995a. "Introduction: The Currency Interface and Its Dynamics." In *Money Matters: Instability, Values and Social Payments in the Modern History of West African Communities,* edited by Jane Guyer, 1–35. Portsmouth, NH: Heinemann.

——. 1995b. "Wealth in People, Wealth in Things—Introduction." *Journal of African History* 36 (1): 83–90.

——. 2004. *Marginal Gains: Monetary Transactions in Atlantic Africa.* Chicago: University of Chicago Press.

Hachten, Charles. 2005. "Property Relations and the Economic Organization of Soviet Russia, 1941–1948." PhD diss., University of Chicago.

Halfin, Igal. 2003. *Terror in My Soul: Communist Autobiographies on Trial.* Cambridge, MA: Harvard University Press.

Halfin, Igal, and Jochen Hellbeck. 1996. "Rethinking the Stalinist Subject: Stephen Kotkin's 'Magnetic Mountain' and the State of Soviet Historical Studies." *Jahrbücher für Geschichte Osteuropas* 44:456–63.

Hann, C. M. 1998. "Introduction: The Embeddedness of Property." In *Property Relations: Renewing the Anthropological Tradition,* edited by C. M. Hann, 1–47. Cambridge: Cambridge University Press.

——. 2007. "The Anthropology of Christianity *Per Se.*" *European Journal of Sociology* 48: 383–410.

Hann, C. M., and Hermann Goltz, eds. In press. *Eastern Orthodox Christianities in Anthropological Perspective.* Berkeley: University of California Press.

Harpham, Geoffrey Galt. 1995. "Ethics." In *Critical Terms for Literary Study,* 2d ed., edited by Frank Lentricchia and Thomas McLaughlin, 387–405. Chicago: University of Chicago Press.

Harris, James R. 1999. *The Great Urals: Regionalism and the Evolution of the Soviet System.* Ithaca: Cornell University Press.

——. 2002. "Resisting the Plan in the Urals, 1928–1956 Or, Why Regional Officials Needed 'Wreckers' and 'Saboteurs.'" In *Contending with Stalinism: Soviet Power and Repression in the 1930s,* edited by Lynn Viola, 201–27. Ithaca: Cornell University Press.

Hart, Keith. 1986. "Heads or Tails? Two Sides of the Coin." *Man,* n.s., 21 (4): 637–56.

Harvey, David. 1989. *The Condition of Postmodernity: An Enquiry into the Origins of Culture Change.* Oxford: Basil Blackwell.

Hayden, Robert M. 2007a. "Moralizing about Scholarship about Yugoslavia." *East European Politics and Societies* 21 (1): 182–93.

——. 2007b. "Moral Vision and Impaired Insight: The Imagining of Other People's Communities in Bosnia." *Current Anthropology* 48 (1):105–31.

Healy, Nigel M., Vladimir Leksin, and Aleksandr Svetsov. 1999. "The Municipalization of Enterprise-Owned 'Social Assets' in Russia." *Post-Soviet Affairs* 15 (3): 262–80.

Hellbeck, Jochen. 2006. *Revolution on My Mind: Writing a Diary Under Stalin.* Cambridge, MA: Harvard University Press.

Hemment, Julie. 2008. *Empowering Women in Russia: Activism, Aid, and NGOs.* Bloomington: Indiana University Press.

Hernandez, Richard L. 2001. "The Confessions of Semen Kanatchikov: A Bolshevik Memoir as Spiritual Autobiography." *Russian Review* 60 (1): 13–35.

Herzfeld, Michael. 1990. "Icons and Identity: Religious Orthodoxy and Social Practice in Rural Crete." *Anthropological Quarterly* 63 (3):109–21.

——. 1992. *The Social Production of Indifference: Exploring the Symbolic Roots of Western Bureaucracy.* Chicago: Chicago University Press.

——. 2004. *The Body Impolitic: Artisans and Artifice in the Global Hierarchy of Value.* Chicago: University of Chicago Press.

Hirsch, Francine. 2005. *Empire of Nations: Ethnographic Knowledge and the Making of the Soviet Union.* Ithaca: Cornell University Press.

Hirschkind, Charles. 2006. *The Ethical Soundscape: Cassette Sermons and Islamic Counterpublics.* New York: Columbia University Press.

Hivon, Myriam. 1994. "Vodka: The 'Spirit' of Exchange." *Cambridge Anthropology* 17 (3): 1–18.

Hobsbawm, Eric, and Terrence Ranger, eds. 1983. *The Invention of Tradition.* Cambridge: Cambridge University Press.

Hoch, Steven L. 1986. *Serfdom and Social Control in Russia: Petrovskoe, a Village in Tambov.* Chicago: University of Chicago Press.

Hoffmann, David L. 2003. *Stalinist Values: The Cultural Norms of Soviet Modernity, 1917–1941.* Ithaca: Cornell University Press.

Holquist, Peter. 2002. *Making War, Forging Revolution: Russia's Continuum of Crisis, 1914–1921.* Cambridge, MA: Harvard University Press.

Howell, Signe, ed. 1997. *The Ethnography of Moralities.* London: Routledge.

Hudson, Hugh D. 2002. "Religious Persecution and Industrial Policy in the Reign of Anna I: V. N. Tatishchev and the Old Believers Reconsidered." *Jahrbücher für Geschichte Osteuropas* 50 (1): 22–36.

Hughes, James. 1994. "Capturing the Russian Peasantry: Stalinist Grain Procurement Policy and the 'Ural-Siberian Method.'" *Slavic Review* 53 (1): 76–103.

Humphrey, Caroline. [1983] 1998. *Marx Went Away but Karl Stayed Behind. Updated Edition of Karl Marx Collective: Economy, Society, and Religion in a Siberian Collective Farm.* Ann Arbor: University of Michigan Press.

——. 2002. *The Unmaking of Soviet Life: Everyday Economies after Socialism.* Ithaca: Cornell University Press.

Humphrey, Caroline, and Stephen Hugh-Jones. 1992. "Introduction: Barter, Exchange and Value." In *Barter, Exchange, and Value: An Anthropological Approach,* edited by Caroline Humphrey and Stephen Hugh-Jones, 1–20. Cambridge: Cambridge University Press.

Humphrey, Caroline, and Ruth Mandel, eds. 2002. *Markets and Moralities: Ethnographies of Postsocialism.* Oxford: Berg.

Husband, William B. 2000. *"Godless Communists": Atheism and Society in Soviet Russia, 1917–1932.* De Kalb: Northern Illinois University Press.

Iakuba, E. A. 1970. *Pravo i Nravstvennost' kak Reguliatory Obshchestvennykh Otnoshenii pri Sotsializme.* Kharkov: Izdatel'stvo Khar'kovskogo Universiteta.

Iserov, A. A. 2004. *Filippovskoe Rodoslovie: Istoricheskie Sochenenie Staroobriadtsev-Filippovtsev Povolzh'ia i Iuzhnoi Viatki.* Moscow: Arkheodoksiia.

Iukhimenko, E. M. 1999. "Sokhranenie Vygovskimi Staroobriadtsami Drevnerusskoi Modeli Monastyria Kak Dukhovnogo i Kul'turnogo Tsentra." In *Monastyrskaia Kul'tura: Vostok i Zapad,* edited by E. G. Vodolazkin, 177–83. Saint Petersburg: Rossiiskaia Akademiia Nauk, Institut Russkoi Literatury.

Jacob, Marie-Andreé, and Annelise Riles. 2007. "The New Bureaucracies of Virtue: An Introduction." *PoLAR: Political and Legal Anthropology Review* 30 (2): 181–91.

James, Wendy. 1988. *The Listening Ebony: Moral Knowledge, Religion, and Power among the Uduk of Sudan.* Oxford: Clarendon Press.

Johnson, Juliet. 2000. *A Fistful of Rubles: The Rise and Fall of the Russian Banking System.* Ithaca: Cornell University Press.

Jowitt, Ken. 1992. *New World Disorder: The Leninist Extinction.* Berkeley: University of California Press.

Kaiser, Daniel H. 2003. "'Whose Wife Will She Be at the Resurrection?' Marriage and Remarriage in Early Modern Russia." *Slavic Review* 62 (2): 302–23.

——. 2006. "Church Control over Marriage in Seventeenth Century Russia." *Russian Review* 65 (4): 567–85.

Karinskii, S. S. 1966. *Material'nye i Moral'nye Stimuly k Povysheniu Proizvoditel'nosti Truda*. Moscow: Iuridicheskaia Literatura.

Karlström, Mikael. 2004. "Modernity and Its Aspirants: Moral Community and Developmental Eutopianism in Buganda." *Current Anthropology* 45 (5): 595–619.

Keane, Webb. 2006. "Anxious Transcendence." In *The Anthropology of Christianity*, edited by Fenella Cannell, 308–24. Durham, NC: Duke University Press.

———. 2007. *Christian Moderns: Freedom and Fetish in the Mission Encounter*. Berkeley: University of California Press.

Kelly, Catriona. 2001. *Refining Russia: Advice Literature, Polite Culture, and Gender from Catherine to Yeltsin*. Oxford: Oxford University Press.

Kharkhordin, Oleg. 1999. *The Collective and the Individual in Russia: A Study of Practices*. Berkeley: University of California Press.

———. 2005. *Main Concepts of Russian Politics*. Lanham, MD: University Press of America.

Kideckel, David. 1993. *The Solitude of Collectivism: Romanian Villagers to the Revolution and Beyond*. Ithaca: Cornell University Press.

———. 2008. *Getting By in Postsocialist Romania: Labor, the Body, and Working-Class Culture*. Bloomington: Indiana University Press.

Kipnis, Andrew. 2008. "Audit Cultures: Neoliberal Governmentality, Socialist Legacy, or Technologies of Governing." *American Ethnologist* 35 (2): 275–89.

Kivelson, Valerie A., and Robert H. Greene, eds. 2003. *Orthodox Russia: Belief and Practice under the Tsars*. University Park: Pennsylvania State University Press.

Kleinman, Arthur. 1995. *Writing at the Margin: Discourse between Anthropology and Medicine*. Berkeley: University of California Press.

———. 1998. "Experience and Its Moral Modes: Culture, Human Conditions, and Disorder." Paper presented at the Tanner Lectures on Human Values, Stanford University, April 13–16.

———. 2006. *What Really Matters: Living a Moral Life amidst Uncertainty and Danger*. Oxford: Oxford University Press.

Kleinman, Arthur, Veena Das, and Margaret Lock, eds. 1997. *Social Suffering*. Berkeley: University of California Press.

Kligman, Gail. 1988. *The Wedding of the Dead: Ritual, Poetics, and Popular Culture in Transylvania*. Berkeley: University of California Press.

Klimov, E. F. 2003. *Tragediia: Istoriia Sudeb Liudei i Dereven' Staroverov: Sokolovskii Krai (Region) v Sostave Trekh Sel'sovetov: Sokolovskii, Sergeevskii, Nifoniatskii. Period 1918–1998 gg. 80 Let*. Sokolovo: Pechatnik.

Kobiak, N. A. 1992. "Tsitaty i Tsitatsiia v Staroobriadcheskikh Rukopisnykh Sbornikakh Verkhokamskogo Sobraniia MGU." In *Traditsionnaia Dukhovnaia i Material'naia Kul'tura Russkikh Staroobriadcheskikh Poselenii v Stranakh Evropy, Azii i Ameriki: Sbornik Nauchnikh Trudov*, edited by N. N. Pokrovskii and R. Morris, 173–79. Novosibirsk: Nauka.

Koenker, Diane P. 2001. "Fathers against Sons/Sons against Fathers: The Problem of Generations in the Early Soviet Workplace." *Journal of Modern History* 73 (4): 781–810.

Koester, David. 2003. "Interethnic Ramifications of Russian Drinking Practices: A Case Study from Kamchatka." Paper presented at SOYUZ Annual Symposium, Amherst, MA, February 7.

Konrád, George, and Iván Szelényi. 1979. *The Intellectuals on the Road to Class Power*. Translated by Andrew Arato and Richard E. Allen. New York: Harcourt Brace Jovanovich.

Konstantinov, Yulian. 1997. "Memory of Lenin, Ltd.: Reindeer-herding Collectives on the Kola Peninsula." *Anthropology Today* 13 (3): 14–19.

Kornai, Janos. 1980. *Economics of Shortage*. Amsterdam: North-Holland Publishers.

Kotkin, Steven. 1995. *Magnetic Mountain: Stalinism as a Civilization*. Berkeley: University of California Press.

Kotsonis, Yanni. 1999. *Making Peasants Backward: Agricultural Cooperatives and the Agrarian Question in Russia, 1861–1914*. New York: St. Martin's.

Kotsonis, Yanni. 2004. "'No Place to Go': Taxation and State Transformation in Late Imperial and Early Soviet Russia." *Journal of Modern History* 76 (3): 531–77.

Koval'chenko, I. D., ed. 1982. *Russkie Pismennye i Ustnye Traditsii i Dukhovnaia Kul'tura.* Moscow: Moscow State University Press.

Kozlov, M. 2000. "The Financial Crisis and the State of Agricultural Commodity Producers." *Problems of Economic Transition* 43 (2): 85–95.

Krasnoperov, E. I. 1896. *Podvornoe Izsledovanie Ekonomicheskogo Polozheniia Sel'skogo Naseleniia Okhanskogo Uezda Permskoi Gubernii, Proizvedennoe v 1890–1891 gg.* Perm.

Krastev, Ivan. 2004. *Shifting Obsessions: Three Essays on the Politics of Anticorruption.* Budapest: Central European University Press.

Kremlëva, I. A. 1992. Pokhoronno-pominal'naia Obriadnost' u Staroobriadtsev Severnogo Priural'ia. In *Traditsionnaia Dukhovnaia i Material'naia Kul'tura Russkikh Staroobriadcheskikh Poselenii v Stranakh Evropy, Azii i Ameriki,* edited by N. N. Pokrovskii and R. Morris, 202–6, Novosibirsk: Nauka.

Kulikova, I. S. 2001. "Pamiat' Smerti. Razmyshlenie Staroverov-bespopovtsev Verkhokam'ia (fragmenty vstrech 1995–2001 gg.)." In *Staroobriadcheskii Mir Volgo-Kam'ia: Problemy Kompleksnogo Izucheniia,* edited by G. N. Chagin, 46–53. Perm: Perm State University Press.

Kut'ev, O. L. 1998 "Edinoverie v Permskikh Votchinakh Stroganovykh." In *Mir Staroobriadchestva,* vol. 4, *Zhivye Traditsii: Rezul'taty i Perspektivy Kompleksnykh Issledovanii Russkogo Staroobriadchestva,* edited by I. V. Pozdeeva, 275–82. Moscow: Rosspen.

———, ed. 2004. *Il'inskii: Stranitsy Istorii.* Perm: Pushka.

Laidlaw, James. 2002. "For an Anthropology of Ethics and Freedom." *Journal of the Royal Anthropological Institute* 8 (2): 311–45.

Lakoff, Andrew, and Stephen J. Collier. 2004. "Ethics and the Anthropology of Modern Reason." *Anthropological Theory* 4 (4): 419–34.

Lambek, Michael. 2000. "The Anthropology of Religion and the Quarrel between Poetry and Philosophy." *Current Anthropology* 41 (3): 309–20.

———. 2008. "Value and Virtue." *Anthropological Theory* 8 (2): 133–58.

Lampland, Martha. 1995. *The Object of Labor: Commodification in Socialist Hungary.* Chicago: University of Chicago Press.

———. 2002. "The Advantages of Being Collectivized: Cooperative Farm Managers in the Postsocialist Economy." In *Postsocialism: Ideals, Ideologies, and Practices in Eurasia,* edited by C. M. Hann, 31–56. London: Routledge.

Lane, Christel. 1981. *The Rites of Rulers: Ritual in Industrial Society—The Soviet Case.* Cambridge: Cambridge University Press.

Laptin, M. N. 1962. *V. I. Lenin o Material'nykh i Moral'nykh Stimulakh k Trudu.* Moscow: Izdatel'stvo Ekonomicheskoi Literatury.

Lass, Andrew. 1988. "Romantic Documents and Political Monuments: The Meaning-Fulfillment of History in 19th-Century Czech Nationalism." *American Ethnologist* 15 (3): 456–71.

Ledeneva, Alena. 1998. *Russia's Economy of Favours: Blat, Networking, and Informal Exchange.* Cambridge: Cambridge University Press.

———. 2006. *How Russia Really Works: The Informal Practices That Shaped Post-Soviet Politics and Business.* Ithaca: Cornell University Press.

Leibovich, O. L., M. A. Ivanova, L. A. Obukhov, M. G. Nechaev, A. B. Suslov, T. B. Bezdenezhnykh, and G. F. Stankovskaia, eds. 2004. *Politicheskie Repressii v Prikam'e 1918–1980 gg. Sbornik Dokumentov i Materialov.* Perm: Izdatel'stvo Pushka.

Lemon, Alaina. 1998. "'Your Eyes Are Green like Dollars': Counterfeit Cash, National Substance, and Currency Apartheid in 1990s Russia." *Cultural Anthropology* 13 (1): 22–55.

———. 2000. *Between Two Fires: Gypsy Performance and Romani Memory from Pushkin to Postsocialism.* Durham, NC: Duke University Press.

Leonard, Pamela, and Deema Kaneff. 2002. *Post-Socialist Peasant? Rural and Urban Constructions of Identity in Eastern Europe, East Asia, and the Former Soviet Union.* New York: Palgrave.

Levin, Eve. 1989. *Sex and Society in the World of Orthodox Slavs, 900–1700.* Ithaca: Cornell University Press.

Levi-Strauss, Claude. 1966. *The Savage Mind.* London: Weidenfeld and Nicholson.

Lewin, Moshe. 1990. "The Obshchina and the Village." In *Land Commune and Peasant Community in Russia: Communal Forms in Imperial and Early Soviet Society,* edited by Roger Bartlett, 20–35. London: Macmillan.

Lindquist, Galina. 2006. *Conjuring Hope: Magic and Healing in Contemporary Russia.* New York: Berghahn.

LiPuma, Edward, and Benjamin Lee. 2004. *Financial Derivatives and the Globalization of Risk.* Durham, NC: Duke University Press.

Listova, T. A. 1992. "Tainstvo kreshchenie u staroobriadtsev Severnogo Priural'ia." In *Traditsionnaia Dukhovnaia i Material'naia Kul'tura Russkikh Staroobriadcheskikh Poselenii v Stranakh Evropy, Azii i Ameriki: Sbornik Nauchnikh Trudov,* edited by N. N. Pokrovskii, 207–12. Novosibirsk: Nauka.

Litvina, N. V. 2001. "Sostav, Soderzhanie, i Znachenie Videonarrativnykh Istochnikov o E. A. Chadovoi." In *Staroobriadcheskii Mir Volgo-Kam'ia: Problemy Kompleksnogo Izucheniia,* edited by G. N. Chagin, 54–60. Perm: Perm State University Press.

Lowe, Brian. 2006. *Emerging Moral Vocabularies: The Creation and Establishment of New Forms of Moral and Ethical Meanings.* Lanham, MD: Lexington.

Lowenstein, Roger. 2000. *When Genius Failed: The Rise and Fall of Long-Term Capital Management.* New York: Random House.

Luehrmann, Sonja. 2005. "Recycling Cultural Construction: Desecularization in Post-Soviet Mari-El." *Religion, State, and Society* 35:33–56.

Lukanin, A. 1868. "Bespopovtsy Pomorskogo Tolka v Okhanskom Uezde Permskoi Gubernii." *Permskie Eparkhial'nye Vedomosti* 14:223–28; 16:256–61; 17:277–83; 21:343–51; 24:410–19; 25:434–46; 28:485–94; 31:535–40; 34:573–84; 41:641–46; 47:759–67; 48:769–73; 50:797–806; 52:817–835.

MacIntyre, Alasdair. 1981. *After Virtue: A Study in Moral Theory.* Notre Dame: University of Notre Dame Press.

Mahmood, Saba. 2005. *Politics of Piety: The Islamic Revival and the Feminist Subject.* Princeton: Princeton University Press.

Makarov, L. Iu. 2001. "Pogrebal'nyi Obriad Staroobriadtsev Verkhokam'ia (po Arkheologicheskim Materialam i Etnograficheskim Paralleliam)." In *Staroobriadcheskii Mir Volgo-Kam'ia: Problemy Kompleksnogo Izucheniia,* edited by G. N. Chagin, 41–45. Perm: Perm State University Press.

Makarovskaia, M. V. 2005. "Izustnoe Bytovaniie Bogosluzhebnogo Peniia Staroobriadtsev-Bespopovtsev Verkhokam'ia." In *Mir Staroobriadchestva,* vol. 6, *Traditsionnaia Kul'tura Permskoi Zemli,* edited by I. V. Pozdeeva, 198–26. Yaroslavl: Izdatel'stvo Remder.

Makashina, T. C. 1992. "O Brake i Svadebnom Obriade Staroobriadtsev Severnogo Priural'ia v Kontse XIX—Nachale XX v." In *Traditsionnaia Dukhovnaia i Material'naia Kul'tura Russkikh Staroobriadcheskikh Poselenii v Stranakh Evropy, Azii i Ameriki: Sbornik Nauchnikh Trudov,* edited by N. N. Pokrovskii, 223–29. Novosibirsk: Nauka.

Malyshev, V. I. 1951. "Otchë ob arkheograficheskoi komandirovke v 1950 g." *Trudy Otdela Drevnerusskoi Literaturoi Akademiia Nauk SSSR* 8:362–78.

Maurer, Bill. 2006. "The Anthropology of Money." *Annual Review of Anthropology* 35:15–36.

Mauss, Marcel. 1985. "A Category of the Human Mind: The Notion of Person; the Notion of Self." Translated by W. D. Halls. In *The Category of the Person: Anthropology, Philosophy, History,* edited by Michael Carrithers, Steven Collins, and Steven Lukes, 1–26. Cambridge: Cambridge University Press.

McDowell, Jennifer. 1974. "Soviet Civil Ceremonies." *Journal for the Scientific Study of Religion* 13 (3): 265–79.

Meehan-Waters, Brenda. 1992. "To Save Oneself: Russian Peasant Women and the Development of Women's Religious Communities in Prerevolutionary Russia." In *Russian Peasant Women,* edited by Beatrice Farnsworth and Lynne Viola, 121–33. New York: Oxford University Press.

Mel'chakov, V. G. 1993. *Vereshchagino—Zapadnye Vorota Urala.* Perm: Mashinostroitel'.

———. 1994. *Vereshchagino: Istoriia Goroda i Raiona.* Perm: Litera.

———. 1996. *Vereshchagino: V Trude i v Boio.* Borodulino: Pechatnik.

———. 1998. *Vereshchagino: Prodolzhenie Istorii.* Borodulino: Pechatnik.

Mel'chakova, O. A. 2003. "Zakrytie Tserkvei v Permskoi Eparkhii v 20–30-e gody XX veka." In *Vekhi Khristianskoi Istorii Prikam'ia: Materialy Chtenii, Posviashchennykh 540-Letiiu Kreshchenniia Permi Velikoi,* edited by P. N. Agafonov, 84–92. Perm: Izdatel'stvo Bogatyrev P. G.

Melton, Edgar. 1990. "Enlightened Seigniorialism and Its Dilemmas in Serf Russia, 1750–1830." *Journal of Modern History* 62 (4): 675–708.

Metzo, Katherine R. 2001. "Adapting Capitalism: Household Plots, Forest Resources, and Moonlighting in Post-Soviet Siberia." *GeoJournal* 54:549–56.

———. 2005. "Articulating a Baikal Environmental Ethic." *Anthropology and Humanism* 30 (1): 39–54.

Mialo, Kseniia. 1988. "Oborvannaia Nit': Krest'ianskaia Kul'tura i Kul'turnaia Revoliutsiia." *Novyi Mir* 8:245–57.

Michels, Georg. 1993. "The First Old Believers in Tradition and Historical Reality." *Jahrbücher für Geschichte Osteuropas* 41:481–508.

———. 1999. *At War with the Church: Religious Dissent in Seventeenth-Century Russia.* Stanford: Stanford University Press.

———. 2001. "Rescuing the Orthodox: The Church Policies of Archbishop Afanasii of Kholmogory, 1682–1702." In *Of Religion and Empire: Missions, Conversion, and Tolerance in Tsarist Russia,* edited by Robert P. Geraci and Michael Khodarkovsky, 19–37. Ithaca: Cornell University Press.

Miller, Daniel, ed. 2005. *Materiality.* Durham, NC: Duke University Press.

Milogolova, I. N. 1987. "Semeinye Razdely v Russkoi Poreformennoi Derevne (na Materialakh Tsentral'nykh Gubernii)." *Vestnik Mosovskogo Universiteta. Seriia 8 Istoriia* 6:37–46.

Miyazaki, Hirokazu. 2003. "The Temporalities of the Market." *American Anthropologist* 105 (2): 255–65.

Montoya, Rosario. 2007. "Socialist Scenarios, Power, and State Formation in Sandinista Nicaragua." *American Ethnologist* 34 (1): 71–90.

Moore, Sally Falk. 1993. *Moralizing States and the Ethnography of the Present.* Arlington, VA: American Anthropological Association.

Morozov, V. A. 1965. *Trudoden', Den'gi, i Torgovlia na Sele.* Moscow: Izdatel'stvo Ekonomika.

Mosheva, Aleksandra Valer'evicha. 2004. "Vosstanie v Sele Sepych Okhanskogo Uezda v Avguste 1918 goda." Term paper, Sepych Middle School.

Mueggler, Erik. 2001. *The Age of Wild Ghosts: Memory, Violence, and Place in Southwest China.* Berkeley: University of California Press.

Myers, Fred, ed. 2001. *Empire of Things: Regimes of Value and Material Culture.* Santa Fe: School of American Research Press.

Nagengast, Carole. 1991. *Reluctant Socialists, Rural Entrepreneurs: Class, Culture, and the Polish State.* Boulder, CO: Westview.

———. 1994. "Violence, Terror, and the Crisis of the State." *Annual Review of Anthropology* 23:109–36.

Nechaev, M. G. 2003. "Permskaia Eparkhiia v Sinodal'nyi Period." In *Vekhi Khristianskoi Istorii Prikam'ia: Materialy Chtenii, Posviashchennykh 540-Letiiu Kreshchenniia Permi Velikoi,* edited by P. N. Agafonov, 36–55. Perm: Izdatel'stvo Bogatyrev P. G.

——. 2004. *Tserkov' na Urale v Period Velikikh Potriasenii: 1917–1922*. Perm: Redakt-sionno-Izdatel'skii Otdel Permsogo Gosudarstvennogo Pedagogicheskogo Universiteta.

Nechaev, S. D. [1826] 1894. *Iz arkhiva S. D. Nechaeva: Izsledovaniia o Permskom Raskole v Nachale Tsarstvovaniia Imperatora Nikolaiia*. Reprinted from *Bratskoe Slovo*. Moscow, 1893 and 1894.

Needham, Rodney. 1973. *Belief, Language, and Experience*. Chicago: University of Chicago Press.

Nietzsche. 1999. *On the Genealogy of Morals*. New York: Oxford.

Nikitina, S.E. 1982. "Ustnaia Traditsiia v Narodnoi Kul'ture Russkogo Naseleniia Verkhokam'ia." In *Russkie Pismennye i Ustnye Traditsii i Dukhovnaia Kul'tura*, edited by I. D. Koval'chenko, 91–126. Moscow: Moscow State University Press.

Northrup, Douglas. 2004. *Veiled Empire: Gender and Power in Soviet Central Asia*. Ithaca: Cornell University Press.

Odling-Smee, John. 2004. "The IMF and Russia in the 1990s." IMF Working Paper WP/04/155.

Ong, Aihwa. 2006. *Neoliberalism as Exception: Mutations in Citizenship and Sovereignty*. Durham, NC: Duke University Press.

Ortner, Sherry. 1984. "Theory in Anthropology since the Sixties." *Comparative Studies in Society and History* 126 (1): 126–66.

Paert, Irina. 2001a. "Gender and Salvation: Representations of Difference in Old Believer Writing from the Late Seventeenth Century to the 1820s." In *Gender in Russian History and Culture*, edited by Linda Edmonson, 29–51. New York: Palgrave.

——. 2001b. "Popular Religion and Local Identity during the Stalin Revolution: Old Be-lievers in the Urals, 1928–41." In *Provincial Landscapes: Local Dimensions of Soviet Power, 1917–1953*, edited by Donald J. Raleigh, 171–93. Pittsburgh: University of Pennsylvania Press.

——. 2003. *Old Believers, Religious Dissent, and Gender in Russia, 1760–1850*. Man-chester, UK: Manchester University Press.

——. 2004a. "Memory and Survival in Stalin's Russia: Old Believers in the Urals during the 1930s–50s." In *On Living Through Soviet Russia*, edited by Daniel Bertaux, Paul Thomp-son, and Anna Rotkirch, 195–213. London: Routledge.

——. 2004b. "Penance and the Priestless Old Believers in Modern Russia." *Studies in Church History* 40:278–90.

——. 2004c. "Regulating Old Believer Marriage: Ritual, Legality and Conversion in Nicho-las I's Russia." *Slavic Review* 63 (3): 555–76.

——. 2005. "Preparing God's Harvest: Maksim Zalesskii, Millenarianism, and the Wander-ers in Soviet Russia." *Russian Review* 64 (1): 44–61.

Pallot, Judith. 1979. "Rural Settlement Planning in the USSR." *Soviet Studies* 31 (2): 214–30.

Pandian, Anand. 2008. "Devoted to Development: Moral Progress, Ethical Work, and Di-vine Favor in South India." *Anthropological Theory* 8 (2): 159–80.

Papkov, S., and K. Teraiama, eds. 2002. *Ural i Sibir' v Stalinskoi Politike*. Novosibirsk: Si-birskii Khronograf.

Parry, Jonathan. 1986. "*The Gift*, the Gift, and the Indian Gift." *Man*, n.s., 21:453–73.

Parry, Jonathan, and Maurice Bloch, eds. 1989. *Money and the Morality of Exchange*. Cam-bridge: Cambridge University Press.

Patico, Jennifer. 2002. "Chocolate and Cognac: Gifts and the Recognition of Social Worlds in Post-Soviet Russia." *Ethnos* 67 (3): 345–68.

——. 2005. "To Be Happy in a Mercedes: Tropes of Value and Ambivalent Visions of Mar-ketization." *American Ethnologist* 32 (4): 479–96.

——. 2008. *Consumption and Social Change in a Post-Soviet Middle Class*. Washington, DC: Woodrow Wilson Center Press and Stanford University Press.

Paxson, Heather. 2004. *Making Modern Mothers: Ethics and Family Planning in Urban Greece*. Berkeley: University of California Press.

Paxson, Margaret. 2005. *Solovyovo: The Story of Memory in a Russian Village.* Blooming-
ton: Indiana University Press and Woodrow Wilson Center Press.
Pelikan, Jaroslav. 1977. *The Christian Tradition: A History of the Development of Doctrine.*
Vol. 2, *The Spirit of Eastern Christendom (600–1700).* Chicago: University of Chicago Press.
Pelkmans, Mathijs. 2006. *Defending the Border: Identity, Religion, and Modernity in the
Republic of Georgia.* Ithaca: Cornell University Press.
Pera, Pia. 1986. "Theoretical and Practical Aspects of the Debate on Marriage among the
Priestless Old Believers from the End of the Seventeenth to the Mid-nineteenth Century."
PhD diss., University of London.
——. 1990. "The Secret Committee on the Old Believers: Moving away from Catherine
II's Policy of Religious Toleration." In *Russia in the Age of the Enlightenment,* edited by
Roger Bartlett and Janet Hartley, 222–41. New York: St. Martin's.
Peris, Daniel. 1998. *Storming the Heavens: The Soviet League of the Militant Godless.*
Ithaca: Cornell University Press.
Pervukhina, V. I., A. E. Bedel', and T. I. Slavko, eds. 1994. *Sud'ba Raskulachennykh Spets-
pereselentsev na Urale (1930–1936 gg).* Vol. 1. Ekaterinburg: Izdatel'stvo Ural'skogo
Universiteta.
Pesmen, Dale. 2000. *Russia and Soul: An Exploration.* Ithaca: Cornell University Press.
Petrone, Karen. 2000. *Life Has Become More Joyous, Comrades: Celebrations in the Time
of Stalin.* Bloomington: Indiana University Press.
Petryna, Adriana. 2005. "Ethical Variability: Drug Development and Globalizing Clinical
Trials." *American Ethnologist* 32 (2): 183–97.
Piankov, Palladii (Archimandrite). 1863. *Obozrenie Permskogo Raskola, Tak Nazyvaemogo
"Staroobriadchestva."* Saint Petersburg.
Pilkington, Hilary. 1994. *Russia's Youth and its Culture: A Nation's Constructors and Con-
structed.* London: Routledge.
Pine, Frances. 1996. "Redefining Women's Work in Rural Poland." In *After Socialism: Land
Reform and Social Change in Eastern Europe,* edited by Ray Abrahams, 133–56. Oxford:
Berghahn.
——. 2002. "Retreat to the Household? Gendered Domains in Postsocialist Poland." In
Postsocialism: Ideals, Ideologies, and Practices in Eurasia, edited by C. M. Hann, 95–113.
London: Routledge.
Pochinskaia, I. V., ed. 2000. *Ocherki Istorii Staroobriadchestva Urala i Sopredel'nykh Ter-
ritorii.* Ekaterinburg: Izdatel'stvo Ural'skogo Gosudarstvennogo Universiteta.
Pocock, D. F. 1986. "The Ethnography of Morals." *International Journal of Moral and
Social Studies* 1 (1): 3–20.
——. 1988. "Persons, Texts, and Morality." *International Journal of Moral and Social Stud-
ies* 3 (3): 203–16.
Pokrovskii, N. N. 1974. *Antifeodal'nyi Protest Uralo-Sibirskikh Krest'ian-Staroobriadtsev v
XVIII v.* Novosibirsk: Nauka.
——. 1984. *Puteshestvie za Redkimi Knigami.* Moscow: Kniga.
——. 1991. "Za stranitsei 'Arkhipelaga GULAG.'" *Novyi mir* (9):77–90.
——. 1994. "Trends in Studying the History of Old Belief by Russian Scholars." Paper delivered at "Russia's Dissident Old Believers," St. Olaf College, Northfield, MN.
Ponosov, A. M. 2003. "Staroobriadcheskaia Sem'ia Verkhokam'ia v XVIII–XX vv." Master's thesis, Perm State University.
Pozdeeva, I. V. 1982. "Vereshchaginskoe Territorial'noe Knizhnoe Sobranie i Problemy Istorii Dukhovnoi Kul'tury Russkogo Naseleniia Verkhov'ev Kamy." In *Russkie Pismennye
i Ustnye Traditsii i Dukhovnaia Kul'tura,* edited by I. D. Koval'chenko, 11–39. Moscow:
Izdatel'stvo Moskovskogo Universiteta.
——. 1992. "Traditsionnaia Knizhnost' Sovremennogo Staroobriadchestva." In *Mir Staroobriadchestva,* vol. 1, edited by I. V. Pozdeeva and E. B. Smilianskaia, 11–27. Moscow:
Khronograf.

——. 1995. "30 Let Polevoi Arkheografii Moskovskogo Universiteta (1966–1995)." *Arkheograficheskii Ezhegodnik za 1995* 37:48–59.

——. 1996. "Prodolzhenie Traditsii: Knizhnaia Kul'tura Staroobriadcheskogo Verkhokam'ia." In *Mir Staroobriadchestva*, vol. 3, *Kniga, Traditsiia, Kul'tura*, edited by I. V. Pozdeeva, 6–45. Moscow: Pechatnik.

——. 1998. "Kompleksnye Issledovaniia Sovremennoi Traditsionnoi Kul'turoi Russkogo Staroobriadchestva. Rezul'taty i Perspektivy." In *Mir Staroobriadchestva*, vol. 4, *Zhivye Traditsii: Rezul'taty i Perspektivy Kompleksnykh Issledovanii Russkogo Staroobriadchestva*, edited by I. V. Pozdeeva, 12–20. Moscow: Rosspen.

——. 2001. "Kniga-Lichnost'-Obshchina: Instrumenty Vosproizvodstva Traditsionnoi Kul'tury (30 Let Izucheniia Staroobriadcheskikh Obshchin Verkhokam'ia)." In *Staroobriadcheskii Mir Volgo-Kam'ia: Problemy Kompleksnogo Izucheniia*, edited by G. N. Chagin, 7–30. Perm: Perm State University Press.

——. 2003. *Kirillicheskie Izdaniia XVI–XVII vv. v Khranilishchakh Permskoi Oblasti*. Perm: Permskoe Khizhnoe Izdatel'stvo.

——. 2005. "Knizhnost' Staroobriadcheskogo Verkhokam'ia: Istoki, Chitateli, Sud'by." In *Mir Staroobriadchestva*, vol. 6, *Traditsionnaia Kul'tura Permskoi Zemli*, edited by I. V. Pozdeeva, 120–40. Yaroslavl: Izdatel'stvo Remder.

Pozdeeva, I. V., and M. V. Makarovskaia, eds. 2008. *Komu Povem Pechal' Moiu: Dukhovnye Stikhi Verkokam'ia*. Moscow: Danilovskii Blagovestnik.

Pushkov, V. P. 1999a. "Krest'ianskoe Khoziaistvo Staroobriadcheskogo i Pravoslavnogo Naseleniia Verkhokam'e v Kontse XIX v." In *Rossiia v Srednye Veka i Novoe Vremia: Sbornik Statei k 70-letiiu chl-korr RAN L.V. Milova*, edited by V. A. Kuchkin, 302–32. Moscow: Rosspen.

——. 1999b. "Revizskaia Skazka 1795 g. po Sel'tsu Sepych kak Istochnik po Istorii Staroobriadtsev Verkhokam'ia." In *Mir Staroobriadchestva*, vol. 5, *Istoriia i Sovremmennost'*, edited by I. V. Pozdeeva, 41–74. Moscow: Moscow State University Press.

——. 2005a. "Grafskie Novatsii i Krest'ianskie Traditsii." In *Mir Staroobriadchestva*, vol. 6, *Traditsionnaia Kul'tura Permskoi Zemli*, edited by I. V. Pozdeeva, 239–70. Yaroslavl: Izdatel'stvo Remder.

——. 2005b. "Zemlia i Liudi Verkhokam'ia vo Vtoroi Polovine XVII–Nachala XVIII v." In *Mir Staroobriadchestva*, vol. 6, *Traditsionnaia Kul'tura Permskoi Zemli*, edited by I. V. Pozdeeva, 33–63. Yaroslavl: Izdatel'stvo Remder.

Radcliffe-Brown, A. R. 1952. *Structure and Function in Primitive Society*. London: Cohen and West.

Raleigh, Donald J. 2002. *Experiencing Russia's Civil War: Politics, Society, and Revolutionary Culture in Saratov, 1917–1922*. Princeton: Princeton University Press.

Ransel, David. 2000. *Village Mothers: Three Generations of Change in Russia and Tataria*. Bloomington: Indiana University Press.

Rausing, Sigrid. 2004. *History, Memory, and Identity in Post-Soviet Estonia: The End of a Collective Farm*. Oxford: Oxford University Press.

Reid, Susan E. 2002. "Cold War in the Kitchen: Gender and De-Stalinization of Consumer Taste in the Soviet Union under Khrushchev." *Slavic Review* 61 (2): 211–52.

Rekovskaia, I. F. 1987. *Material'nye i Moral'nye Faktory Trudovogo Vospitaniia Molodezhi v Sotsialisticheskom Obshchestve*. Moscow: Akademii Nauk.

Rethmann, Petra. 2000. "Skins of Desire: Poetry and Identity in Koriak Women's Gift Exchange." *American Ethnologist* 27 (1): 52–71.

Ries, Nancy. 1997. *Russian Talk: Culture and Conversation During Perestroika*. Ithaca: Cornell University Press.

——. 2002. "'Honest Bandits' and 'Warped People': Russian Narratives about Money, Corruption, and Moral Decay." In *Ethnography in Unstable Places: Everyday Lives in Contexts of Dramatic Political Change*, edited by Carol J. Greenhouse, Elizabeth Mertz, and Kay B. Warren. Durham, NC: Duke University Press.

Rivkin-Fish, Michele. 2005. *Women's Health in Post-Soviet Russia: The Politics of Interven-tion*. Bloomington: Indiana University Press.

Robbins, Joel. 2004. *Becoming Sinners: Christianity and Moral Torment in Papua New Guinea*. Berkeley: University of California Press.

———. 2007. "Continuity Thinking and the Problem of Christian Culture." *Current Anthro-pology* 48 (1): 5–38.

Robson, Roy R. 1995. *Old Believers in Modern Russia*. De Kalb: Northern Illinois Univer-sity Press.

———. 2004. "Spiritual Fathers in Conflict: Riga's Old Believer Nastavniki after WWII." Paper presented at the 36th National Convention of the American Association for the Advancement of Slavic Studies, Boston, December 6.

———. n. d. "Recovering Priesthood and the Émigré Experience among Contemporary Ameri-can Bespopovtsy Old Believers." Unpublished manuscript.

Rofel, Lisa. 1999. *Other Modernities: Gendered Yearnings in China after Socialism*. Berke-ley: University of California Press.

Rogers, Douglas. 2004. "An Ethics of Transformation: Work, Prayer, and Moral Practice in the Russian Urals, 1861–2001." PhD diss., University of Michigan.

———. 2005. "Moonshine, Money, and the Politics of Liquidity in Rural Russia." *American Ethnologist* 32 (1): 63–81.

———. 2006a. "Historical Anthropology Meets Soviet History." *Kritika* 7 (3): 633–49.

———. 2006b. "How to Be a *Khoziain* in a Transforming State: State Formation and the Eth-ics of Governance in Post-Soviet Russia." *Comparative Studies in Society and History* 48 (4): 915–45.

———. 2008. "Old Belief Between 'Society' and 'Culture': Remaking Moral Communities and Inequalities on a Former State Farm." In *Religion, Morality, and Community in Post-Soviet Societies*, edited by Mark Steinberg and Catherine Wanner, 115–48. Bloomington: Indiana University Press.

———. 2009. "Iz Eticheskoi Istorii Verkhokam'ia: Tri Siuzheta." In *Staroobriadcheskaia Verkhokam'ia, Perezhitoe i Nastoiashee*, edited by N. V. Litvina, Moscow.

———. In press. "*Ex Oriente Lux,* Once Again" Epilogue to *Eastern Christianities in Anthro-pological Perspective,* edited by C. M. Hann and Hermann Goltz. Berkeley: University of California Press.

Rosenberg, William G., ed. 1990. *Bolshevik Visions: First Phase of the Cultural Revolution in Soviet Russia, Part 1.* 2d ed. Ann Arbor: University of Michigan Press.

Rovinskoi, I. L. 1999. "Opisanie Sobornogo Zavedeniia Knig i Ikon i Prochikh Prinosnykh i Pozhertvovanykh Veshei." In *Mir Staroobriadchestva,* vol. 5, *Istoriia i Sovremennost',* edited by I. V. Pozdeeva, 377–94. Moscow: Moscow State University Press.

Scheffel, David. 1991. *In the Shadow of Antichrist: The Old Believers of Alberta.* Peterbor-ough, Ontario: Broadview.

Scheper-Hughes, Nancy. 1995. "The Primacy of the Ethical: Propositions for a Militant An-thropology." *Current Anthropology* 36 (3): 409–40.

Scott, James C. 1976. *The Moral Economy of the Peasant: Rebellion and Subsistence in Southeast Asia.* New Haven: Yale University Press.

Seabright, Paul, ed. 2000. *The Vanishing Rouble: Barter Networks and Non-Monetary Transactions in Post-Soviet Societies.* Cambridge: Cambridge University Press.

Semibratov, V. K. 2001. "Podvizhnik Viatskikh Staroobriadtsev L. A. Grebnev v Kontek-ste Rossiiskoi Istorii i Kul'tury Kontsa XIX—Pervoi Treti XX v." In *Staroobriadcheskii Mir Volgo-Kam'ia: Problemy Kompleksnogo Izucheniia,* edited by G. N. Chagin, 164–69. Perm: Perm State University Press.

———. 2005. "L. A. Grebnev—Prosvetitel', Tipograf, Knizhnik." In *Mir Staroobriadchestva,* vol. 6, *Traditsionnaia Kul'tura Permskoi Zemli,* edited by I. V. Pozdeeva, 353–65. Yaro-slavl: Izdatel'stvo Remder.

Shcheglov, A. 1990. "Obirat' ili prosveshat' (problemy polevoi arkheografii)." *Zlatostrui: Starovercheskii zhurnal* 1 (1): 48–50.

Shcherbak, F. N. 1973. *Moral'nye Stimuly v Trude*. Leningrad: Lenizdat.

Shevchenko, Olga. 2008. *Crisis and the Everyday in Postsocialist Moscow*. Bloomington: Indiana University Press.

Shilov, A. V. 2001. "Otchëty o Sostoianii Raskola v Permskoi Eparkhii Kak Istochnik po Istorii Staroobriadchestva." In *Staroobriadcheskii Mir Volgo-Kam'ia: Problemy Kompleksnogo Izucheniia*, edited by G. N. Chagin, 79–86. Perm: Perm State University Press.

Shreeves, Rosamund. 2002. "Broadening the Concept of Privatization: Gender and Development in Rural Kazakhstan." In *Markets and Moralities: Ethnographies of Postsocialism*, edited by Ruth Mandel and Caroline Humphrey, 211–36. Oxford: Berg.

Siegelbaum, Lewis H. 1988. *Stakhanovism and the Politics of Productivity in the USSR, 1935–1941*. Cambridge: Cambridge University Press.

———. 1998. "'Dear Comrade, You Ask What We Need': Socialist Paternalism and Soviet Rural 'Notables' in the Mid-1930s." *Slavic Review* 57 (1): 107–32.

Siu, Helen. 1989. *Agents and Victims in South China: Accomplices in Rural Revolution*. New Haven: Yale University Press.

Sivaramakrishnan, K. 2005. "Introduction to 'Moral Economies, State Spaces, and Categorical Violence.'" *American Anthropologist* 107 (3): 321–30.

Slatter, John. 1990. "Communes with Communists: The *Sel'sovety* in the 1920s." In *Land Commune and Peasant Community in Russia*, edited by Roger Barlett, 272–86. New York: St. Martin's.

Slezkine, Yuri. 1994. "The USSR as Communal Apartment, or How a Socialist State Promoted Ethnic Particularism." *Slavic Review* 53 (2): 414–52.

Smilianskaia, E. B. 1995. "'Iskra Istinnago Blagochestiia': Religioznye Vozzreniia Staroobriadtsev Verkhokam'ia." *Rodina* 2:10–13.

———. 1997. "O Nekotorykh Osobennostiakh Krestian-Staroobriadtsev Verkhokam'ia." In *Traditsionnaia Narodnaia Kul'tura Naseleniia Urala: Materialy Mezhdunarodnoi Nauchno-Prakticheskoi Konferentsii*, edited by S. A. Dimukhametova, O. L. Kut'ev, and G. N. Chagin, 119–124. Perm: Perm Regional Studies Museum.

Smilianskaia, E. B., and N. A. Kobiak. 1994. "Predislovie." In *Rukopisi Verkhokam'e, XV–XX vv*, edited by E. A. Ageeva, N. A. Kobiak, T. A. Kruglova, and E. B. Smilianskaia, 5–16. Moscow: Tsmeliia.

Smirnov, P. S. 1909. *Spory i Razdeleniia v Russkom Raskole v Pervoi Chetverti XVII Veka*. Saint Petersburg: M. Merkushev.

Smollett, Eleanor Wenkart. 1989. "The Economy of Jars: Kindred Relationships in Bulgaria—An Exploration." *Ethnologia Europaea* 49 (2): 125–40.

Smorgunova, E. M. 1982. "Permskaia Rukopis' XIX v. 'O Razdele.'" In *Russkie Pismennye i Ustnye Traditsii i Dukhovnaia Kul'tura*, edited by I. D. Koval'chenko, 247–65. Moscow: Moscow State University Press.

———. 1992. "Iz Rukopisei Verkhokam'ia: Osoby Vid Vzaimodeistviia Ustnoi i Pis'mennoi Traditsii." In *Mir Staroobriadchestva*, vol. 1, edited by I. V. Pozdeeva and E. B. Smilianskaia, 46–57. Moscow: Khronograf.

Solnick, Steven. 1999. "Federalism and State-Building: Post-Communist and Post-Colonial Perspectives." Paper presented at "Constitutional Design 2000" Conference, University of Notre Dame. Available online: http://www.nd.edu/~kellogg/events/pdfs/Solnick.pdf.

Ssorin-Chaikov, Nikolai. 2000. "Bear Skins and Macaroni: The Social Life of Things at the Margins of a Siberian State Collective." In *The Vanishing Rouble: Barter Networks and Non-monetary Transactions in Post-Soviet Societies*, edited by Paul Seabright, 345–61. Cambridge: Cambridge University Press.

———. 2003. *The Social Life of the State in Subarctic Siberia*. Stanford: Stanford University Press.

———. 2006. "On Heterochrony: Birthday Gifts to Stalin, 1949." *Journal of the Royal Anthropological Institute* 12 (2): 355–75.

State Farm Sepych. 1976. Plan Organizatsionno-khoziastvennogo Ustroistva Sovkhoza Sepychëvskii Vereshchaginskogo Raiona Permskoi Oblasti. (AOZT Sepych, photocopy).

Steinberg, Mark D. 1992. *Moral Communities: The Culture of Class Relations in the Russian Printing Industry 1867–1907*. Berkeley: University of California Press.

——. 1994. "Workers on the Cross: Religious Imagination in the Writings of Russian Workers, 1910–1924." *Russian Review* 53(2):213–239.

Steinberg, Mark, and Catherine Wanner, eds. 2008. *Religion, Morality, and Community in Post-Soviet Societies*. Bloomington: Indiana University Press.

Stites, Richard. 1989. *Revolutionary Dreams: Utopian Vision and Experimental Life in the Russian Revolution*. New York: Oxford University Press.

——. 1991. "Bolshevik Ritual Building in the 1920s." In *Russia in the Era of NEP*, edited by Shelia Fitzpatrick, Alexander Rabinowitch, and Richard Stites, 295–309. Bloomington: Indiana University Press.

Stock, Brian. 1983. *The Implications of Literacy: Written Language and Models of Interpretation in the Eleventh and Twelfth Centuries*. Princeton: Princeton University Press.

Strathern, Marilyn, ed. 2000. *Audit Cultures: Anthropological Studies in Accountability, Ethics, and the Academy*. London: Routledge.

Suny, Ronald Grigor, and Michael D. Kennedy, eds. 2001. *Intellectuals and the Articulation of Nation*. Ann Arbor: University of Michigan Press.

Thompson, E. P. 1971. "The Moral Economy of the English Crowd of the Eighteenth Century." *Past and Present* 50 (1): 76–136.

——. 1993. *Customs in Common*. New York: New Press.

Tian-Shanskaia, Olga Semyonova. 1993. *Village Life in Late Tsarist Russia*. Edited and translated by David L. Ransel with Michael Levine. Bloomington: Indiana University Press.

Tikhomirov, M. 1948. "Pis'mo v Redaktsiiu." *Voprosy Istorii* 3:159.

Tirado, Isabel A. 1988. *Young Guard! The Communist Youth League, Petrograd 1917–1920*. New York: Greenwood.

——. 1993. "The Komsomol and Young Peasants: The Dilemma of Rural Expansion, 1921–1925." *Slavic Review* 52 (3): 460–76.

——. 2001. "Peasants into Soviets: Reconstructing Komsomol Identity in the Russian Countryside of the 1920s." *Acta Slavica Japonica* 18:42–63.

Todorov, Tzvetan. 2003. *Hope and Memory: Lessons from the Twentieth Century*. Translated by David Bellos. Princeton: Princeton University Press.

Uehling, Greta Lynn. 2004. *Beyond Memory: The Crimean Tatars' Deportation and Return*. New York: Palgrave Macmillan.

Valeri, Valerio. 1999. *The Forest of Taboos: Morality, Hunting, and Identity Among the Huaulu of the Moluccas*. Madison: University of Wisconsin Press.

Van der Veer, Peter, ed. 1996. *Conversion to Modernities: The Globalization of Christianity*. New York and London: Routledge.

Vargin", V. H. 1899. "Iz" Poezdki po Okhanskomu Uezdu." Perm.

Verdery, Katherine. 1991. *National Ideology under Socialism: Identity and Cultural Politics in Ceauşescu's Romania*. Berkeley: University of California Press.

——. 1996. *What Was Socialism and What Comes Next?* Princeton: Princeton University Press.

——. 1999. *The Political Lives of Dead Bodies: Reburial and Postsocialist Change*. New York: Columbia University Press.

——. 2003. *The Vanishing Hectare: Property and Value in Postsocialist Transylvania*. Ithaca: Cornell University Press.

Viatka Diocese. 1912. *Viatskaia Eparkhiia: Istoriko-Geograficheskoe i Statisticheskoe Opisanie*. Viatka: Tipo-lit Shkliaevoi.

Viatkin, V. V. 2003. "Permskaia Eparkhiia v Gody Khrushchëvskikh Gonenii na Tserkov' (1958–1964)." In *Vekhi Khristianskoi Istorii Prikam'ia: Materialy Chtenii, Posviashchennykh 540-Letiiu Kreshchenniia Permi Velikoi*, edited by P. N. Agafonov, 93–102. Perm: Izdatel'stvo Bogatyrev P. G.

Viola, Lynne. 1987. *The Best Sons of the Fatherland: Workers in the Vanguard of Soviet Collectivization*. New York: Oxford University Press.

——. 1996. *Peasant Rebels under Stalin: Collectivization and the Culture of Peasant Resistance.* New York: Oxford University Press.

Volkov, Vadim. 1997. "Obshchestvennost': Zabitaia Praktika Grazhdanskogo Obshchestva." *Pro et Contra* 2 (4): 77–91.

——. 2002. *Violent Entrepreneurs: The Use of Force in the Making of Russian Capitalism.* Ithaca: Cornell University Press.

Vologdin, I. 1895. "Zhizn' Kreposnykh" liudei gr. Stroganovyk v' Okhanskom uezde Permskoi gubernii." In *Permskii Krai: Sbornik Svedenii o Permskoi Gubernii,* vol. 3, edited by A. A. Dimitrieva, 200–217. Perm.

Wagner, William G. 1994. *Marriage, Property, and Law in Late Imperial Russia.* Oxford: Clarendon Press.

Wanner, Catherine. 2003. "Advocating New Moralities: Conversion to Evangelicalism in Ukraine." *Religion, State, and Society* 31 (4): 273–87.

——. 2005. "Money, Morality, and New Forms of Exchange in Postsocialist Ukraine." *Ethnos* 71 (4): 515–37.

——. 2007. *Communities of the Converted: Ukrainians and Global Evangelism.* Ithaca: Cornell University Press.

Warhula, James. 1992. "Central vs. Local Authority in Soviet Religious Affairs, 1964–89." *Journal of Church and State* 34:15–37.

Wegren, Stephen K. 1998. *Agriculture and the State in Soviet and Post-Soviet Russia.* Pittsburgh: University of Pittsburgh Press.

Weber, Max. 1978. *Economy and Society.* Vol. 1. Berkeley: University of California Press.

West, James, and Iurii A. Petrov, eds. 1998. *Merchant Moscow: Images of Russia's Vanished Bourgeois.* Princeton: Princeton University Press.

Widlock, Thomas. 2004. "Sharing by Default? Outline of an Anthropology of Virtue." *Anthropological Theory* 4 (1): 53–70.

Wolfe, Thomas C. 2005. *Governing Soviet Journalism: The Press and the Socialist Person after Stalin.* Bloomington: Indiana University Press.

Woodruff, David. 1999. *Money Unmade: Barter and the Fate of Russian Capitalism.* Ithaca: Cornell University Press.

World Bank. 2003a. *Local Self-Government and Civic Engagement in Rural Russia.* Moscow: Astro-Plus Plublishers.

——. 2003b. "Russian Federation Country Financial Accountability Assessment." Working Paper. September 16.

Worobec, Christine. 1990. "Temptress or Virgin? The Precarious Sexual Position of Women in Postemancipation Ukrainian Peasant Society." *Slavic Review* 49 (2): 227–38.

——. 1991. "Victims or Actors? Russian Peasant Women and Patriarchy." In *Peasant Economy, Culture, and Politics of European Russia, 1800–1921,* edited by Esther Kingston-Mann and Timothy Mixter, 177–206. Princeton: Princeton University Press.

——. 1995. *Peasant Russia: Family and Community in the Post-Emancipation Period.* De Kalb: Northern Illinois University Press.

Wortman, Richard. 1995. *Scenarios of Power: Myth and Ceremony in Russian Monarchy.* Princeton: Princeton University Press.

——. 1998. "The Russian Imperial Family as a Symbol." In *Imperial Russia: New Histories for the Empire,* edited by Jane Burbank and David L. Ransel, 60–86. Bloomington: Indiana University Press.

Young, Glennys. 1997. *Power and the Sacred in Revolutionary Russia: Religious Activists in the Village.* University Park: Pennsylvania State University Press.

Yurchak, Alexei. 2006. *Everything Was Forever, Until It Was No More: The Last Soviet Generation.* Princeton: Princeton University Press.

Zbierski-Salameh, Slawomira. 1999. "Polish Peasants in the 'Valley of Transition': Responses to Postsocialist Reforms." In *Uncertain Transition: Ethnographies of Change in the Postsocialist World,* edited by Michael Burawoy and Katherine Verdery, 189–222. Lanham, MD: Rowman and Littlefield.

Zhuk, Sergei. 2004. *Russia's Lost Reformation: Peasants, Millennialism, and Radical Sects in Southern Russia and Ukraine, 1830–1917*. Washington, DC: Woodrow Wilson Center Press.

Zigon, Jarrett. 2007. "Moral Breakdown and the Ethical Demand: A Theoretical Framework for an Anthropology of Moralities." *Anthropological Forum* 7 (2): 131–50.

———. 2008. "Aleksandra Vladimirovna: Moral Narratives of a Russian Orthodox Woman." In *Religion, Morality, and Community in Post-Soviet Societies*, edited by Mark Steinberg and Catherine Wanner, 85–114. Bloomington: Indiana University Press.

Zinochkin, A. 1960. *Ot Trudodnia k Denezhnoi Oplate*. Riazan: Riazanskoe Knizhnoe Izdatel'stvo.

Index

abandoned villages, continuing spatial significance of, 120–21
Ageevo, 150
agriculture. *See* rural economy
alcohol, home-brewed. *See* moonshine
Aleksandr (relative of Natasha and Misha), 290–97
Aleksandr II (tsar), 64n49, 72, 86
Aleksei Mikhailovich (tsar), 35
alms *(milostynia)*, 275–79, 293, 296, 297
Anastasia Ivanovna, 44–46, 93, 123, 174–76, 271–72
Andrei Petrovich: AOZT Sepych, as director of, 196, 211, 227–36, 302; churching of Sepych, role in, 251–55, 257, 258, 263–65, 279, 289; elder status of father of, 172; as post-Soviet khoziain, 222–23, 227–38, 241, 244, 288–89, 298; State Farm Sepych, as director of, 136, 138, 140, 141n40, 142, 172, 185; wealth in people, 232–36, 244
anthropology. *See* ethnography; Soviet and Russian ethnography and ethnographers
antireligion efforts in Soviet-era Sepych, 149–58
Anton, 230–33
AOZT Sepych: author's decision not to work for, 25; church in Sepych, construction of, 246, 247, 251, 254, 265, 268, 299; future of, 302–3; insurance provided by, 288–89; khoziain, post-Soviet concept of, 222–23, 226–36; local state administration, compared to, 222–23, 238, 244; monetary and nonmonetary exchanges, 196–97, 200, 218, 228–30, 232; physical description of

town, 21; separation of ethical relationships inside and outside, 299; SPK Sepych, change of name to, 196n3; State Farm Sepych, post-Soviet transition from, 196–97; theft from, 232–35
archaeography and archaeographers: churching of Sepych, response to, 246–47, 259–60; ethnography and, 27–32, 77; Old Believers, scholarly attention to, 159, 165–73, 259–60, 303–4
Aristotelian ethics, 11n9, 14
ascetic practice of Old Believers: generational deferral of, 7, 45–50, 154–58, 179–86; post-Soviet changes in, 246, 270–79
audit regulations, 238–42
August crisis (1998), 218–20

baptism: as conversion, 282–83, 285–87; as insurance or protection, 287–90; of laypeople, 46–49; Maksimovskie/Dëminskie *razdel* and, 284; in priestless Old Belief, 54, 282, 283, 285–88; priestly, post-Soviet preference for, 280–90, 284; as social reproduction, 281–85
Batalovy, 122
Belokrinitsy hierarchy: baptism and rebaptism in, 281–88; conversion efforts of, 256, 285–87; in Ochër, 39; in Sepych (*See* churching of Sepych; Vasilii, Father)
book culture. *See* textual community, Old Believers as
Borodulino, 22
Bourdieu, Pierre, 11n8–9, 14
Brezhnev era, 119n17, 136, 211, 231, 302
"bums" *(BOMZhi)*, 212–13